P9-CKK-110

IE

DISCARD

MANAGEMENT OF THE PHYSICALLY AND EMOTIONALLY ABUSED

MANAGEMENT OF THE PHYSICALLY AND EMOTIONALLY ABUSED

Emergency Assessment, Intervention, and Counseling

Edited by

CARMEN GERMAINE WARNER, R.N., M.S.N., F.A.A.N.

Associate Professor, California State University System;
Consultant, Community Health Systems and Emergency Medical Care,
San Diego, California

G. RICHARD BRAEN, M.D.

Associate Professor, Emergency Medicine and Internal Medicine;
Director, Department of Emergency Medicine, University of Kentucky,
Lexington, Kentucky

With 24 Illustrations

A Capistrano Publication

APPLETON-CENTURY-CROFTS / Norwalk, Connecticut

Copyright © 1982 by Capistrano Press, Ltd.

All rights reserved. No part of this book may be reproduced in any manner without written permission from the publisher.

Capistrano Press, Ltd.
P.O. Box 3450, Long Beach, California 90803

82 83 84 85 / 10 9 8 7 6 5 4 3 2 1

Library of Congress Cataloging in Publication Data

Warner, Carmen Germaine
  Management of the physically and emotionally abused.

  "A Capistrano publication."
  Bibliography: p.
  Includes index.
    1. Victims of crimes—Services for—United States.
2. Family violence—United States. 3. Abused wives—
Services for—United States. 4. Rape victims—Services
for—United States. 5. Child abuse—Services—United
States. I. Warner, Carmen Germaine, 1941-
II. Braen, G. Richard, [DNLM: 1. Counseling.
2. Emergency medical services. 3. Violence. WX 215
M2667]
HV6250.3.U5M33   1982   362.8'8   82-11674
ISBN 0-8385-6120-9

Publisher, B. Wallace Hood, Jr.
Production Editor, Barbara L. Halliburton
Cover Design and Art, John W. Brown
Book Design, Alice Harmon

Printed in the United States of America

Contributors

LUCY BERLINER, M.S.W.

Sexual Assault Center, Harborview Medical Center,
Seattle, Washington

JANET L. BLENNER, R.N., PH.D.

Associate Professor, Program Director,
Graduate Program in Advanced Psychiatric
Nursing, University of San Diego, Alcala
Park,
San Diego, California

G. RICHARD BRAEN, M.D.

Associate Professor, Emergency Medicine
and Internal Medicine; Director,
Department of Emergency Medicine,
University of Kentucky,
Lexington, Kentucky

RENÉE L. TANKENOFF BRANT, M.D.

Assistant in Psychiatry, Children's Hospital
Medical Center and Judge Baker Guidance
Center; Clinical Instructor, Psychiatry,
Harvard Medical School,
Boston, Massachusetts

BARBARA A. CARSON, M.A.

Predoctoral Fellow, Family Violence
Research Center, and the Department of
Sociology, University of New Hampshire,
Durham, New Hampshire

RICHARD L. DOUGLASS, M.P.H., PH.D.

Research Scientist, Institute of Gerontology,
Institute for Social Research, Highway
Safety Research Institute, University of
Michigan,
Ann Arbor, Michigan

NORMAN S. ELLERSTEIN, M.D.

Associate Professor, State University of New
York at Buffalo, School of Medicine,
Department of Pediatrics, Children's
Hospital of Buffalo,
Buffalo, New York

THEODORE N. FERDINAND, PH.D.

Director, Graduate Program, College of
Criminal Justice, Northeastern University,
Boston, Massachusetts

DAVID FINKELHOR, PH.D.
Family Violence Research Program,
University of New Hampshire,
Durham, New Hampshire

GILBERT GEIS, PH.D.
Professor, Program in Social Ecology,
University of California at Irvine,
Irvine, California

WENDY G. GOLDBERG, R.N., M.S.N.
Clinical Specialist, Psychiatric-Mental
Health Nursing, Henry Ford Hospital,
Detroit, Michigan

**KIMBERLY KATHRYN GREEN, B.A.,
M.S., J.D.**
Attorney at Law, Wyatt, Tarrant, &
Combs,
Louisville, Kentucky

ADELE HALE, B.A., M.S.W.
Director, Social Services, Joseph J. Peters
Institute,
Philadelphia, Pennsylvania

GLENN M. LARKIN, M.D.
Staff Pathologist, Allegheny County
Coroner's Office,
Pittsburgh, Pennsylvania

PATRICIA SPEZESKI MULDARY, M.A.
Alcoholism Information and Referral
Center, Emma L. Bixby Hospital,
Adrian, Michigan

THOMAS W. MULDARY, PH.D.
Psychologist in Private Practice, Ann
Arbor, Michigan; Lecturer, Psychology,
Eastern Michigan University, Ypsilanti,
Michigan; National University,
San Diego, California

JOHN H. ROBBINS, B.S., M.S.W.
Chief, Planning and Evaluation,
Department of Social Services, County of
San Diego,
San Diego, California

PATRICIA RUBY-DOUGLASS, M.S.W.
Social Worker, Michigan Department of
Social Services,
Ann Arbor, Michigan

SUZANNE M. SGROI, M.D.
Codirector, Saint Joseph College Institute
for the Treatment and Control of Child
Sexual Abuse,
West Hartford, Connecticut

ASHLEY WALKER-HOOPER, B.A.
Director, YWCA/Battered Women's
Services,
San Diego, California

**CARMEN GERMAINE WARNER, R.N.,
M.S.N., F.A.A.N.**
Associate Professor, California State
University System; Consultant, Community
Health Systems and Emergency Medical
Care,
San Diego, California

JILL WATERMAN, PH.D.
Adjunct Associate Professor of Psychology,
University of California at Los Angeles,
Los Angeles, California

CYRIL H. WECHT, M.D., J.D.
Director, Pittsburgh Institute of Legal
Medicine; Clinical Associate Professor of
Pathology, University of Pittsburgh Schools
of Medicine and Dental Health; Adjunct
Professor of Pathology, Duquesne
University School of Pharmacy,
Pittsburgh, Pennsylvania

LINDA MEYER WILLIAMS, PH.D.
Research Criminologist, Lecturer in
Sociology, Bermuda College,
Pembroke, Bermuda

LANA K. WILLINGHAM, M.S.W.
Chief, Special Projects, Department of
Social Services, County of San Diego,
San Diego, California

JANET YOUNG, M.D.
Consulting Developmental Pediatrician,
San Francisco, California

Dedication

To John, my husband and friend
and
To Susan and Sarah

Foreword

Violence in American society may be called the preeminent illness of the late twentieth century. It affects millions of us and has a significant impact upon the social and economic well-being of our society. It is no respecter of age, class, or economic standing. It is so pervasive that violence to persons has become a political problem to be considered by legislatures at the federal, state, and local levels. The current federal administration is marshalling resources to combat what has been referred to as an epidemic outbreak of violence against persons. Police departments have special units to handle "crimes against people." These units emphasize a burgeoning criminal activity and the need for special training of law enforcement officers.

The scope of crimes against spouses, children, the elderly, and people in general is far more common than most of us would like to believe. Carmen Germaine Warner and G. Richard Braen have assembled an impressive group of experts to address this topic. Their comments bring together in one volume much of the salient available information. The information not only presents facts valuable to the health professional but also suggests modalities of recognition and care to a host of other professionals. In the case of child abuse, this material is particularly valuable. The research is poignantly clear that child abusers were likely to have been abused themselves in their younger years. Prevention of the trauma of abuse is a keystone of the contemporary practitioner's armamentarium.

As the recent victim of a mugging when I was jogging about a well-lighted city park in the early evening, I am witness for all of us who unsuspectingly think, "It can't happen—or if it does, not to me." The crisis of violence is a daily concern for everyone, but particularly so for those intimately involved in the delivery of emergency medical care—both before and after the victim arrives at the hospital.

This volume serves well as a missing link in the literature currently available. And it does so in an excellent manner. The reader will benefit in multifold ways from its contents.

Richard L. Judd, Ph.D., R.E.M.T.A.

Master Instructor, Emergency Medical Services, State of Connecticut; Executive Dean and Professor, Emergency Medical Sciences, Central Connecticut State College, New Britain, Connecticut

Preface

An increasing number of women, children, and even men are being treated by emergency care personnel and social service professionals after incidents of interhuman violence. As a result, the education and the definition of roles of these professionals are ever more important.

The complexities of the medical, social service, and legal procedures required in assessment, intervention, and documentation have led to the need for and the design of numerous treatment protocols. These protocols have consistently dealt with each entity of interhuman violence—for example, child abuse, domestic violence, and rape—as a separate, unrelated incident. The editors of this book believe that there are commonalities not only in the dynamics and impact of these types of abuse situations but also in the proper techniques of communication, intervention, and follow-up for these victims.

For this reason, we have chosen to design and develop a single text that would address all these problems and offer related treatment considerations for each facet of interhuman violence. This method will permit professionals to visualize similar precipitating factors and to inaugurate initial treatment, client teaching, and follow-up counseling for the entire family unit. This approach offers a more comprehensive and preventive form of short-term and long-term intervention.

We hope that this systematized approach to interhuman violence will generate a deeper understanding and perception by professionals and encourage the evolution of a more appropriate system for serving these patients.

Writing about an issue as sensitive as human violence requires considerable commitment, a conscious effort, and dedication. The professionals who have contributed to this book possess a special type of devotion that enables them to cope with the emotional stressors and pressures associated with human violence. To these individuals, I am sincerely grateful.

G. Richard Braen, my coeditor, for whom I have the greatest respect, continues to be a reliable, supportive colleague and a real inspiration. His commitment to achieving the ultimate level of quality care for survivors of human violence is indefatigable. It is a privilege to work with this man.

Pat Summers, my longtime friend and amanuensis, continues to make the process of designing and organizing books a real pleasure. Her reliability and high standards make my job much easier and indeed more organized.

The artistic talents of John Brown and the quality editing of Barbara Halliburton have given this book the professional quality that makes it so special.

To all these people and to the thousands of individuals who, because of their commitment to the survivors of human violence, will read this book, I salute you and offer my praise and admiration.

Carmen Germaine Warner, R.N., M.S.N., F.A.A.N.

Contents

III. Adult Abuse

IV. Sexual Violence and Adults

VI. Evaluation and Planning

MANAGEMENT OF THE PHYSICALLY AND EMOTIONALLY ABUSED

Unit I

Violence in American Society

1

THE SCOPE OF CONTEMPORARY SOCIAL AND DOMESTIC VIOLENCE

Barbara A. Carson, M.A.
David Finkelhor, Ph.D.

The fear of becoming a victim of violence is one of major proportions. In a national survey, nearly two-thirds of all Americans believed that the danger of being attacked had increased; only five percent thought it had decreased.[1] Crime is a pressing topic in political campaigns and receives extensive coverage in the media. This growing concern parallels the increasing amount of violence that appears in police blotters and on court dockets.[2]

Yet, a serious misconception exists about the real source of danger. The typical American describes the most probable situation for a physical or sexual assault as an encounter with a maniacal stranger in a deserted park or on a ghetto street. It comes as a shock then to most to realize that people are more likely to become victims at the hands of someone they know. In fact, violence very often occurs between people who not only know one another, but also claim to love one another: members of the same family.

Lest this claim seem farfetched, consider some of the statistics. In 1977, 60 percent of all murders known to the police were committed by someone the victim knew, and 30 percent were committed by immediate relatives.[2] Surveys of the general population estimate that 73 percent of all American children will be victims, at some time in their childhood, of a violent act committed by a parent or guardian.[3] Studies of sexual assault show that rape by husbands and boyfriends is much more common than rape by strangers. These statistics of brutality and carnage within the home suggest that the family is the most violent institution in American society; the only exception is the military in time of war.[4]

Covering Up Family Violence

Why is it so surprising to find out that families are violent? There are several reasons why people contradict even their own experience so that they might believe that the home is a safe and peaceful environment. One is that everyone has a stake in preserving the image of the family as a cradle of love and harmony. Typically, much of life is spent with other family members, and people want to believe that the home is a safe place. Even social scientists (who ought to know better) have, for a long time, sustained the myth that the family is a tranquil and harmonious island in a world of strife.

Another reason for the misconception is the reluctance of victims of family abuse to reveal their plight. Society has tended to show more contempt than sympathy towards victims of family abuse, so many victims concealed their situation. Other family members who witnessed the violence did not report it because they wanted to protect the entire family from public embarrassment. When people did draw attention to abuse in their families, they were not always believed and were not always assisted. In the traditional value system, the family is a private group, and outsiders, even today, feel awkward about "butting into" family affairs.

What Is Abuse?

Although the subject of violence in the family has received some attention, there has been no consensus on how to define domestic abuse. One of the two predominant approaches defines abuse as any intentional act that causes physical injury to another person. In the strictest view, this definition includes only situations that require medical attention. The problem is that serious violence does not always result in injury, especially medically treatable injury. For example, what does one call the situation if a husband fires a gun at his wife and misses? In this case there is no injury, yet the potential for harm is a severe and alarming possibility.

This type of situation has prompted an alternative way to characterize abuse: to look at the perpetrator's intentions regardless of the resulting injury. Then, if a husband attempts to hurt his wife, it is considered abuse whether or not he actually causes injury. This definition generally leads to larger estimates of the amount of abuse than the one that limits itself to instances of actual harm. Yet, it is also a more difficult definition to use in research since it requires a judgment about intentionality. "Yes, I threw the frying pan, but I really wasn't trying to hit her," says the offender. This judgment can be difficult to make. This chapter cites studies that use each definition of abuse and tries to make it clear which definition of abuse is being used.

SOURCES OF INFORMATION ON FAMILY ABUSE

Information about domestic abuse comes primarily from three sources. The following brief review points out the strengths and weaknesses of each one. Occasionally the different methods yield conflicting conclusions.

First, there are the official or legal reports of abuse recorded by police or social workers (depending upon the laws in the area). For instance, the most common source of reported data on child abuse is the American Humane Association (AHA) which uses standardized forms to collect all the official reports on child abuse from states across the country.[5]

An obvious weakness of this type of data is that it includes only reported cases. Research that uses official reports only may result in conclusions that are misleading, not only about the scope of the problem but also about where it is most likely to occur, what is most likely to happen, and why. Research on deviant behavior has shown that the characteristics of those who are caught may be quite different from the characteristics of those who are not. For example, lower-class people are more likely to be detected when they violate social rules. This information could lead to a mistaken conclusion that the problem is primarily lower-class in origin. On the other hand, a major benefit of official reports is that they provide in-depth descriptions about the types of abuse and demographic characteristics of some abusive families.

A second source of information is clinical data. Generally, these are studies of people receiving some type of counseling or services.[6,7] These people may or may not be included in the official reports of abuse. Information gained from clinical studies suffers from many of the same kinds of problems as data obtained from official reports. Abusers or victims of abuse who are in treatment are not necessarily representative of abusers or victims in general. However, because clinicians may know their clients very well, clinically based research can be very valuable for suggesting hypotheses about the nature and causes of abuse. (The sections in this chapter on abuse of adolescents and the elderly demonstrate the usefulness of clinical data).

The third, and usually most reliable, source of information is surveys of the general population. In surveys people are asked to report any abuse or violence in their families, whether it has been officially reported or not and whether or not they are receiving counseling. Since the respondents are usually randomly selected, the results are more likely to apply to the population at large. However, surveys have their weaknessess, too. Since contact between researcher and subject is relatively brief, information from surveys is more superficial than information from in-depth interviews in clinical practice.

Another weakness of surveys is that people may be inaccurate about the extent of violence in their family. People forget about violent episodes, they tend to deny the presence of violence, and many may not define the situation as abusive. Thus, information gained from surveys (as well as from the other two methods) usually underestimates the real rates of domestic violence. However, even though the figures are far from accurate, they drive home the indisputable reality that violence exists in alarming proportions in American families.

CHILD ABUSE

The definitions used in research on child abuse are similar to the various types discussed before. Some authorities define child abuse as a physical injury requiring medical attention;[8,9] others define it as acts that have the intention of harming.[3] In some studies the perpetrators must be the caretakers of the child. Other researchers are very general and define abuse as any act that violates community or professional standards for the well-being of children.[10,11]

Child abuse is usually distinguished from child neglect (the latter involving acts of omission rather than commission), but in reality it is very difficult to separate the two, and the labels may have little to do with the facts of the case. For example, some child protection services prefer to label a case "neglect" because it is an easier charge to confirm. Other agencies prefer to charge a family with abuse because their states require immediate action in cases of abuse.

Neglectful acts are difficult to define and measure because of the extreme, individual variation on what constitutes neglect. In addition, there has been little research on the nature and scope of neglect.[12] The main focus of this discussion will be child abuse.

Scope of Child Abuse

A study by Straus et al. offers sound estimates on the extent of violence towards children.[3] In a national survey they randomly selected intact families representative of the entire United States. One adult member of each family was interviewed about the extent of domestic violence in the member's home. In this study, the researchers defined abuse as "an act which has the high potential for injuring the person being hit." This very broad definition of violence includes acts that are potentially harmful but do not cause any actual harm.

The data indicate that 1.0 to 1.9 million children were kicked, bitten, or punched by their parents or caretakers in 1975, and 275,000 to 750,000 children were beaten up. All told, three percent of the respondents with children 3 to 17 years old reported using some serious violence against their children in 1975. The researchers estimate that 3.1 to 4.0 million children in the United States are kicked, bitten, or punched sometime in their lifetime.

Children who were exposed to any act of violence were likely to be exposed to it more than once. In this study, children who were kicked, bitten, or punched at all experienced violence an average of 8.9 times during the preceding 12 months, and those children who were beaten were beaten an average of 5.9 times per year. It is apparent that information about a single incident of abuse is like the tip of the iceberg. A single incident is rare, and it should be considered as only a part of an extensive pattern of domestic conflict.

In an earlier study, Gil asked a national random sample of respondents if they personally knew families involved in incidents of child abuse that had caused physical injury in the preceding 12 months.[9] From the results he estimated that 2.5 to 4.0 million families abused their children. However, a re-analysis of these data by Light, based on more plausible assumptions about the sample, suggested that the figure was closer to 124,000 to 500,000 families.[13]

The least speculative statistics on the scope of child abuse come from the AHA.[5] Their records, collected from almost all states, indicate that there were 614,000 cases of child abuse and neglect in 1978, up almost 50 percent from the 412,000 in 1976. If neglect and unsubstantiated reports are excluded, the number of child abuse cases is reduced to around 100,000 for 1978. Even without acknowledging that only a small percentage of incidents of real abuse reach the status of a "report," these figures chronicle a heavy toll of suffering among American children.

Why such different figures on the extent of abuse? Part of the reason has to do with definitions of abuse and part with the methods of study. Official reports represent only those families in which abuse was detected; one would expect these rates to be smaller. The differences between the Straus and Gil surveys[3,9] probably reflect the different types of questions asked and the different definitions of abuse used in each. The study by Straus et al.[3] questioned respondents about specific violent acts that had the potential to cause injury, while Gil's work[9] asked respondents to report only incidents that had resulted in injury. Also, Gil's subjects were asked to report incidents of abuse in other families, not their own as in Straus et al. People are more likely to be aware of violence in their own families, and this fact helps account for the higher rates discovered by Straus et al.

Nature of Child Abuse

The most frequent type of child abuse is hitting children with a hand or a blunt instrument.[3,5] Sources also agree that children under six years of age are at the highest risk.[9,14,15] This is partly because younger children are physically more fragile and more susceptible to injury. But surveys of the use of force (without injury) also show that younger children are more often the recipients of violence.[3] They are more often hit and more often injured.

Why is more violence directed at younger children? (1) They may require more attention than older children and, therefore, are more likely to incur a parent's ire. (2) They are less susceptible to control through reason and suggestion, and so parents may be more tempted to use force. (3) They are less powerful and agile themselves; they cannot run away or fight back. (4) They can not appeal easily to another parent or authority for protection.

There are somewhat different patterns for violence against boys and girls. Among younger children, boys are the more frequent victims; among adolescents, girls are the preponderant victims.[3] The more active and aggressive behavior of little boys may explain their higher rate of victimization. However, parental control of adolescents is stricter for girls than for boys; hence, girls of that age suffer more violence.

Data from the AHA indicate that approximately 30 percent of all reported cases involve teenagers as victims.[5] This rate is undoubtedly an underestimate of adolescent abuse because several states do not count the maltreatment of 15 to 17-year-olds as child abuse. Clinical data also suggest that many adolescents are not labeled as victims of abuse but called "incorrigible" or "delinquent" instead because they respond to their parents' violence with rebellion.[7] Research about abuse of adolescents is sparse, but it prompts people to expect it more often than they did before.

Most sources agree that parents are usually the perpetrators of child abuse,[16] younger parents more often than older ones.[17,18] In pure numerical terms, mothers are the actual offenders slightly more often than fathers. However, since mothers generally spend much more time with children than fathers do, mothers are actually less violent per hour of contact time with children.

The relationship between economic status and child abuse has been a much debated topic. It appears that families below the poverty level are more likely than other families to abuse their children. Official reports of abuse show a disproportionate number of low-income families (the median income of all reported families in 1976 was below the poverty level for that year), but this number also reflects the fact that poor people who abuse their children are more likely to be detected. Random surveys, which do not suffer from this bias, also suggest that economic class is related to abuse. Straus et al. found that families earning less than $6,000 per year were twice as violent as families earning more than $20,000.[3] This observation does not mean that wealthier families do not abuse their children but that the phenomenon is more common among the poor.

Other disadvantages also appear to be related to abuse. For example, abusive fami-

lies tend to have lower accumulated levels of education,[3] they usually live in substandard housing units,[19,20] and the parents are frequently unemployed.[20-22] Larger families also tend to be more abusive,[9,13] but this tendency may be related to their particular financial burdens.

A final characteristic of abusing families is social isolation from outside contacts. Smith found that abusing mothers, as compared to their nonabusing peers, rarely had contact with parents, relatives, neighbors, or friends.[18] It was also found that abusing mothers, as well as abusing fathers, engaged in fewer social activities. Young added to this picture with findings that these families also refused to let their children engage in normal educational and recreational activities.[23]

Reporting Child Abuse

Friends, neighbors, and relatives account for 40 percent of all reports of child abuse. School officials, law enforcement officials, and medical personnel each report approximately 10 percent of all cases.[5] School personnel, especially school nurses, are most likely to report instances that involve older children, and medical professionals are most likely to report cases that involve younger children.[5]

In conclusion, child abuse appears to be a widespread problem. Children tend to be repeated victims: if it has happened once, it is apt to happen again, not just twice, but several times. Young children are at particularly high risk, but adolescent females also tend to be targets of abuse. The families of these children generally have inadequate incomes and the related problems of irregular employment or unemployment.

SEXUAL ABUSE OF CHILDREN

The sexual abuse of children, like physical abuse, is much more common than was once thought. In 1970 reports of sexual abuse were unusual in clinical practice; by 1980 it was the fastest-growing form of reported child abuse.[24] Research indicates that sexual abuse may touch one girl out of every four or five at some time in her life.

Sexual abuse is generally defined as sexual activity between an adult or much older person and a child. Tabulations usually include adolescent victims, especially if the offender is a family member or someone in authority over them.

Moreover, sexual activity between minors is considered to be sexual abuse if there is a large enough difference in the ages of the two children. Researchers and drafters of state statutes on sexual abuse commonly set this difference at five years. There are many cases of adolescents exploiting younger children as in the case of abusing baby-sitters.

Many people presume that the word "abuse" in the phrase "sexual abuse" refers to some kind of physical force or threat. In reality, much of what is considered sexual abuse takes place without the use of force or threat and rarely results in actual physical trauma to the child. One hospital-based treatment program found that only 24 percent of the cases of sexual abuse showed any physical manifestations, let alone trauma.[25]

In many cases, children comply or passively cooperate with the offenders. When children are promised rewards in exchange for sexual activity, such cooperation is understandable. The offender may be a person the child trusts, even loves, and habitually obeys. In other cases, since children are small and intimidated by the power of adults, they may simply be too afraid to resist.

In other words, the abuse of sexual abuse is not force or injury to the victim. The abuse is an abuse of power: the older person takes advantage of the child's naivete, dependency, or gullibility to involve the child in socially taboo sexual activity.

Researchers are discovering that the problem of sexual abuse is dramatically different from the "child molester" stereotype of yesteryear. Most sexual abusers are well known to the child; many are among the child's closest relatives. Studies regularly show that 75 percent of reported abuse occurs at the hands of acquaintances, friends, and relatives.[26,27] Probably one-half of all abuse occurs within the family; fathers and brothers are often the offenders.

Moreover, much sexual abuse does not involve intercourse or attempts at intercourse. Sexual abusers more commonly try to touch and fondle the child's genitals or ask the child to touch and fondle theirs. Intercourse is more common in relationships that exist for a long time, especially those that extend into adolescence. Evidence suggests, however, that sexual activities short of intercourse can be just as disturbing and have just as lasting an effect on a child.[27] As a result, few researchers or treatment programs make strong distinctions between sexual abuse that involves intercourse and that which does not.

Prevalence

Although the rate of reporting has increased dramatically, only a modest number of cases of sexual abuse are officially reported nationally (about 38,000 in 1978). However, reports by adults, both in general surveys and in clinical settings, suggest that sexual abuse is much more widespread than the reported figures might imply.

A survey by Russell in San Francisco in 1978 collected histories of sexual assault and abuse from 930 randomly selected women.[28] Twenty-six percent of this sample reported an episode of sexual abuse by a family member. Six percent had an unwanted sexual experience with a father or stepfather, and about one-half of these involved genital contact.

Finkelhor also reported sexual abuse on this scale in a survey of 796 New England college students.[27] Nineteen percent of the women reported a childhood sexual experience with an adult or a person at least five years older. About 20 percent of these were encounters with exhibitionists, but nearly one-half were with family members. Unwanted sexual experiences with older persons and family members seem to be a common feature of childhood for many women.

Clinical data and surveys indicate that boys are victims of sexual abuse, too. Treatment programs find that as many as one-quarter to one-third of their reports come from boys.[29] The Finkelhor study reported that nine percent of the men in the sample reported experiences similar to those recorded by the women.[27] The main difference was that the offenders who abused boys were usually not family members.

Why has abuse of such magnitude been publicly unrecognized for so long? Most researchers and clinicians agree that the vast majority of sexual abuse is never reported. Finkelhor found that 75 percent of the boys and 66 percent of the girls told no one about their experiences, not even parents. Moreover, even when parents know about such events, they tend to keep them secret to avoid public embarrassment or shame and often to protect the offender and the family.

Professionals, too, have ignored the problem, partly because of the emotional overtones and partly because they did not know how to handle such reports. Increased knowledge and vigilance on the part of professionals and increased candor and outrage on the part of victims and their families have caused an upsurge in reporting. In addition, increased family instability and the widespread disappearance of sexual prohibitions may have contributed to a rise in the true incidence of sexual abuse itself, not just in the reporting rate.

High-risk Children

Research on sexual abuse is sparse, but certain stereotypes about child victims are no longer believed. The problem is by no means limited to disorganized, lower-class families or to isolated rural people. Sexual abuse may be more frequent in these settings, but it also occurs in many affluent, stable, and highly respected families. Children who have ever — lived apart from their mothers or who have poor relationships to their mothers seem to be at higher risk, as do girls who live with stepfathers.[27] Child abuse may occur more often — in families with histories of alcohol abuse and in families with substantially submissive mothers. Sexual abuse by a father often appears to start after an emotional or career setback for him, when he may have substantial time alone with his daughters. Hence, a father's unemployment may place a girl at risk.

SPOUSE ABUSE

Another extremely frequent type of domestic violence is spouse abuse. Boston City Hospital reports that approximately 70 percent of all assault victims who come to its emergency department are women who have been attacked in their homes, usually by a husband or lover. Stark et al. found that close to one out of every four women who visited the emergency department at a major urban hospital had histories that suggested abuse.[30] The hospital judged that over 30 percent of the injuries it saw could be the result of spouse abuse. In 1971, 33 percent of all aggravated assaults in Kansas City were the result of domestic disturbances, and 40 percent of all homicides in that city were cases of spouse killing spouse. In nearly 50 percent of the same cases, police had been summoned five or more times within a two-year period before the murder occurred. In California almost 33 percent of all female victims of homicide were murdered by their husbands.[31] In 1973 the Federal Bureau of Investigation reported that 25 percent of all murders occurred within the family and 50 percent of these were husband-wife killings.[31]

Survey data also indicate a high frequency of spouse abuse. Straus et al., who used a broad definition of violence, found that at least one act of violence by a spouse against another was committed in 16 percent of all American families in 1975.[3] Some 28 percent of all couples in the United States had such an episode in the course of their marriage, and 3.8 percent of these partners experienced severe abuse.

A random survey in the state of Delaware found that during a marriage, physical force was used by at least one spouse against the other in 60 percent of all families with at least two children.[33] Another study in Kentucky found 1 out of 10 women was abused by her spouse every year and that 21 percent of the women in that state were abused at least once during a marriage.[32]

One surprising, and not often believed, fact is that rates of violence by wives against husbands are nearly equal to rates of violence by husbands against wives.[3,33] This finding has led some to claim that women are no more vulnerable to abuse than men are.

Although violence by women against men is a frequent occurrence, and no family violence is trivial, there are many reasons to consider violence against wives a more serious social problem. For one thing, wives are at greater risk of injury from violence than husbands. On the average, women weigh 28 pounds less than men and are less skilled in the use of their limbs for delivering blows. Secondly, much of the violence committed by women occurs in self-defense in exchanges initiated by men. Thirdly, because of their greater economic and social dependence, more women are "trapped" in violent situations and unable to leave. Although little is known about the differences between the victimization of husbands and that of wives, these reasons argue that battered women pose a more pressing current social problem than battered men.

One particular time when women are at high risk is during pregnancy.[33-35] In fact, a study of patients in an emergency department found that battered women were three times more likely to be pregnant than nonbattered women.[30]

Battered Women in Emergency Settings

Stark et al. evaluated the sociomedical profiles of 481 women who sought aid for injuries in a major urban emergency department.[30] The women were categorized as having either been abused or not abused. Several trends were revealed. The battered women were 13 times more likely to have had injuries on their faces, breasts, chests, and abdomens than the nonabused women, and they were likely to have been abused at least three times before. This study reported only prior instances of abuse that were serious enough to warrant medical treatment and thus entry in the medical records. It did not include potentially harmful situations that did not result in injury.

The medical records showed some interesting and common patterns. One out of four abused women had attempted suicide at least once, one out of seven abused alcohol, and 1 out of 10 abused drugs. These problems, as well as others—psychotic disorders, self-abuse, and increased personal stress—quickly followed the first recorded incident that was suggestive of abuse.

The same study found that physicians recorded only 1 out of 35 women as "abused," but the medical histories indicated that the real number was probably closer to one out of four. A possible explanation for this disparity is that physicians in an emergency department tend to use a strictly medical approach. Since a medical approach implies treatment only, an injury from a "fall" is not significantly different from an injury from a "punch." The cause of an injury is frequently neither pursued nor questioned. As a result, many women return to their homes, to the same place where they were initially injured.

The physicians did recognize the existence of personal problems in these abused women because at least one out of four received prescriptions for tranquilizers—more than among the nonbattered women, a difference that could not be explained by differences in the nature of the physical injury. Stark et al. believe the effect of such treatment is to push the battered woman back into the home setting and to make her less effective for dealing with abusive situations in the future.[30] They conclude that this medical practice reflects stereotypes about the role of wives and tends to promote further abuse.

Social Factors and Spouse Abuse

Surveys have discovered several social factors associated with spouse abuse. These associations are important because they demonstrate that domestic abuse cannot be explained merely by psychopathology. For example, both the Kentucky study[32] and Straus et al.[31] found the highest prevalence of spouse abuse among young, nonwhite, urban couples. The Kentucky study found no significant differences among various occupational and income levels. Straus et al. found slight differences in the level of education of the couples (couples with a high school degree or some high school education were most abusive, and those with no high school education or some college education were least abusive) and stronger differences among income and occupational levels. Couples whose annual income was below the poverty level (less than $6,000) used five times more violence than families making more than $20,000 per year, and blue-collar workers were twice as likely as white-collar workers to be involved in spouse abuse. Unemployment or part-time employment was also a significant factor.

In summary, spouse abuse is an extensive problem in the United States. Both men and

women commit violent acts against their spouses, but women are more likely to receive the more severe injuries. There is a high probability that a battered woman will be pregnant and that her injuries will be on the face, breasts, chest, and abdomen. The consequences of abuse can be long-range and include drug and alcohol abuse and psychiatric problems. Inadequate income, unemployment, urban residence, youth, and minority-group status are social factors commonly associated with spouse abuse.

SEXUAL ABUSE OF WIVES

Awareness has grown that many women who are beaten by their husbands are also raped. Three different surveys questioned victims who were staying at shelters for battered women. All three reported virtually the same findings: about one-third of these women had been sexually assaulted at some time by their husbands.[36-38]

Marital rape is even more heavily shrouded in secrecy than battering because it is such an intimate kind of humiliation. The popular belief, also embodied in legal tradition, that there is no such thing as rape in marriage contributes to this secrecy. Sex is often considered a right of husbands and a duty of wives. Until the late 1970s almost no state recognized a husband's rape of his wife as a crime. Not surprisingly, victims of such violence tended to keep silent and blame themselves.

Evidence suggests that forced sex in marriage occurs much more frequently than ever previously imagined. Russell surveyed 930 San Francisco women who had been sexually assaulted and found that more women reported rape by their husbands than by any other person.[28] Twelve percent of the married women (eight percent of the sample) reported a sexual assault by their husband that would qualify under the legal definition of rape, while four percent of the whole sample said they had been raped by a stranger. In a study of intimate violence, eight percent of married women who responded to a newspaper survey said their husbands had used force to have sex with them.[39] Even in a *Cosmopolitan* magazine survey of 106,000 women, three percent of the respondents were willing to use the stigmatizing word "rape" to describe something their husbands had done to them.

Some, but not all, of these victims are also "battered women." Many women who have never or rarely been struck by their husbands report an experience of forced sex. Instances of forced sex often occur in situations of long-standing disagreements over the frequency and timing of sexual activity or when the husband wants his wife to perform some sexual activity she wishes not to. Finkelhor and Yllo report that many episodes of forced sex involve attempted or completed anal intercourse.[40]

There is very little recognition of this problem, even among professionals who have regular contact with battered women; the subject is still too sensitive to discuss. Antiquated state laws still exempt spouses from prosecution for rape and, in effect, give a husband license to demand sex from his wife whenever and wherever he chooses. As of August 1980 only seven states had legal reforms that clearly acknowledged the possibility of marital rape.[32]

SIBLING ABUSE AND PARENT ABUSE

The prevalence of sibling conflict in our society makes it difficult for people to picture it as abuse. Yet its frequency and occasional severity make it relevant. According to Straus et al., in 1976 there was a violent attack by one child upon another in four out of five families that had siblings between 3 and 17 years old.[3] In 53 percent of the families, the attack was severe, and in 3 out of 1000 cases

the attack involved a knife or a gun. Clearly, sibling abuse can be as dangerous as spouse or child abuse.

Steinmetz did an in-depth study of 88 pairs of siblings, aged 3 to 17 years.[33] She found that the sources of conflict were influenced by the age of the children. Conflicts among younger children revolved around possessions; among early adolescents, around personal space. For older teens, conflict stemmed from responsibilities, obligations, and social awareness. Of these three groups, the younger children were the most likely to use violent force. In general, pairs of male siblings threw things and hit or punched each other more often than female pairs. However, the highest rate of violence was between sibs of the opposite sex.

Another little-known type of domestic violence is abuse of parents by their children. Straus et al. predict that one out of every three children between 3 and 17 years old will hit a parent every year.[3] Many instances of "parent abuse" may be acts of retaliation; that is, the parent actually hits first and the child hits back. In other cases, the children may be modeling their behavior after that of the parents. Whatever the reason, this type of domestic abuse does exist and should be considered when dealing with injured victims.

In both sibling abuse and parent abuse, the perpetrators of violence are children. One must remember that children are also part of abusive families. While they may not be ultimately responsible for their own use of physical force, children, even very young ones, can cause extreme injury to other family members.

ABUSE OF THE ELDERLY

Information on abuse of the elderly is scarce, but estimates by Block and Sinnot suggest that four percent of the nation's elderly are victims of abuse or neglect.[41] This type of abuse may be more difficult to recognize than spouse abuse or child abuse because older people tend to be less visible to the public and more socially isolated than most women or children. Moreover, many elderly victims try to hide the abuse since disclosure may mean institutionalization.

Recognition of this type of abuse is minimal. In April 1980 only 12 states had enacted comprehensive adult protection laws that authorized social service agencies to investigate reports of elderly abuse and to provide services.[42] These laws usually define abuse in broad terms that include failure to support as well as physical injury. This type of definition may help bring instances of abuse to light.

Clinical studies describe family conditions that may lead to abuse of the elderly. Green found three predominant situations.[43] In the first, the family was initially loving and quite happy to make a home for a bereaved parent, but increasing disability soured the relationship. In the second, the old person was taken in reluctantly because of a stroke or inability to provide self-care. In the third, the family was already in stress, and violence was likely to break out whether or not the old person was there.

In conclusion, abuse of the elderly may be a more serious problem than people realize. Little research is available, but the extremely high frequencies of the other types of domestic abuse and the history of their discovery make it highly probable that abuse of the elderly occurs more frequently than one suspects.

IMPLICATIONS

Describing each type of abuse separately may have created the impression that the various types of domestic abuse occur independently of each other. This is not true. Similarities in the family characteristics make it apparent that those families who engage in one type of domestic violence are likely to engage in others.[4,44]

It must be emphasized that an abusive incident within the family should not be considered an isolated case. If it happens once, it is extremely likely to happen again. This behavior is extremely common in American families. The conclusion is that all injuries should suggest domestic abuse as a possible cause. Remember that Stark et al.[30] found that one out of four women seen in the emergency department were abused, and other research has documented the high frequency of all types of abuse.

Medical personnel are in a strategic position to learn about abuse. They are the professionals most likely to see the victims of violence who have injuries severe enough to require medical attention. This initial contact could be an opportune time to ask the family about the cause of the injury. At that time, the perpetrator or the victim may not admit that the injury is the result of abuse, but the family, and especially the victim, may become aware that someone suspects a problem and that someone cares. A few simple questions may give a person enough courage to bring up the problem later and to ask for help.

REFERENCES

1. Garafalo J: *Public Opinion About Crime.* US Dept of Justice, Law Enforcement Administration Association, 1977.

2. *Source Book of Criminal Justice Statistics.* US Dept of Justice, Law Enforcement Administration Association, 1979.

3. Straus MA, et al: *Behind Closed Doors.* New York, Anchor Press, Doubleday & Co Inc, 1979.

4. Steinmetz S, Straus M: *Violence in the Family.* New York, Harper & Row Publishers Inc, 1974.

5. *National Analysis of Official Child Neglect and Abuse Reporting.* Denver, American Humane Association, 1978.

6. Fontana J: *Somewhere a Child is Crying: Maltreatment Causes and Prevention.* New York, Macmillan Publishing Co Inc, 1977.

7. Lourie IS: The phenomenon of the abused adolescent: a clinical study. *Victimology* **2**: 268–276, 1977.

8. Kempe CH: *The Battered Child.* Chicago, University of Chicago Press, 1962.

9. Gil DG: *Violence Against Children: Physical Child Abuse in the United States.* Cambridge, Mass, Harvard University Press, 1970.

10. Parke R, Collmer C: Child abuse: An interdisciplinary analysis, in Hetherington, EM (ed): *Review of Child Development Research.* Chicago, University of Chicago Press, 1975, vol 5.

11. Garbarino J, Gilliam G: *Understanding Abusive Families.* Lexington, Mass, Lexington Books, 1980.

12. Giovannoni JM, Becerra RM: *Defining Child Abuse.* New York, The Free Press, 1979.

13. Light RJ: Abused and neglected children in America: a study of alternative policies. *Harvard Ed Rev* **43**:551–598, 1973.

14. Ferguson DM, et al: Epidemiology and family characteristics of severely abused children. *Br J Prev Soc Med* **29**:205–221, 1972.

15. Johnson CL: *Child Abuse in the Southeast: An Analysis of 1172 Reported Cases.* Athens, Ga, Georgia University, Athens, Welfare Research, 1974.

16. Maden MF: *Toward a Theory of Child Abuse: A Review of the Literature.* Ann Arbor, Mich, Masters Abstracts, 1975.

17. Lauer, B: Battered child syndrome: review of 130 patients with controls. *Pediatrics* **54**:67–70, 1974.

18. Smith SM: *The Battered-Child Syndrome.* London, Butterworth, 1975.

19. Holler HC, Friedman JE: Principles of management in child abuse cases. *Am J Orthopsychiatry* **38**:127–136, 1968.

20. Johnson B, Morse H: *The Battered Child: A Study of Children with Inflicted Injuries.* Denver, Denver Dept of Welfare, 1968.

21. Baldwin JA, Oliver JE: Epidemiology and family characteristics of severely abused children. *Br J Prev Soc Med* **29**:205–211, 1975.

22. Steel B, Pollock C: A Psychiatric Study of Parents Who Abuse Infants and Small Children, in Helfer R, Kempe CH (eds): *The Battered Child,* ed 2. Chicago, University of Chicago Press, 1974.

23. Young L: *Wednesday's Child: A Study in Child Neglect and Abuse.* New York, McGraw Hill Inc, 1964.

24. McFarlane K: Child sexual abuse. Talk presented to Citizens Advisory Commission in National Council for Prevention and Control of Rape, Washington, DC, 1980.

25. Rogers C: Findings from a hospital-based sexual abuse treatment program. Presented at Children's Hospital Medical Center Conference, Washington, DC, 1979.

26. DeFrancis V: *Protecting the Child Victim of Sex Crimes Committed by Adults.* Denver, American Humane Association, 1969.

27. Finkelhor D: *Sexually Victimized Children.* New York, The Free Press, 1979.

28. Russell D: The prevalence and impact of marital rape in San Francisco. Presented at American Sociological Association, New York, 1980.

29. Swift C: Sexual victimization of children. *Victimology* **2**:322–327, 1977.

30. Stark E, et al: Medicine and patriarchal violence: the social construction of a private event. *Int J Health Serv* **9**:461–493, 1979.

31. Martin D: *Battered Wives.* San Francisco, Glide Publications, 1976.

32. Schulman M: *A Survey of Spousal Violence Against Women in Kentucky.* New York, Louis Harris Associates, 1979.

33. Steinmetz S: Wife beating, husband beating: A comparison of the use of physical violence be-

tween spouses to resolve marital fights, in Roy M (ed): *Battered Women.* New York, Van Nostrand Reinhold Co, 1977, pp 205–211.

34. Gelles R: Violence and pregnancy: a note on the extent of the problem and needed services. *Fam Coordinator* **24**:81–86, 1975.

35. Flitcraft A: *Battered Women: An Emergency Room Epidemiology with Description of a Clinical Syndrome,* doctoral thesis. Yale University School of Medicine, New Haven, Conn, 1977.

36. Pagelow MD: Does the law help battered wives? some research notes. Paper presented for Annual Meeting of the Law and Society Association, Madison, Wis, 1980.

37. Amir M: *Patterns in Forcible Rape.* Chicago, University of Chicago Press, 1978.

38. Bart P: Rape doesn't end with a kiss, *Viva,* June 1975, pp 40–107.

39. Doron J: Conflict and violence in intimate relationships: focus on marital rape. Presented to American Sociological Association, New York, 1980.

40. Finkelhor D, Yllo K: *License to Rape.* New York, Holt, Rinehart & Winston, 1982.

41. Bloch MB, Sinnot JD (eds): *The Battered Elderly Syndrome.* College Park, Md, University of Maryland Center on Aging, 1979.

42. Mancini M: Adult abuse laws. *Am J Nurs,* **80**: 739–740, 1980.

43. Green D: Cited in Renvoize J: *Web of Violence.* London, Routledge & Kegan Paul Ltd, 1978.

44. Steinmetz S: *The Cycle of Violence: Assertive, Aggressive and Abusive Family Interaction.* New York, Praeger Publishers Inc, 1977.

2

CONTEMPORARY ATTITUDES TOWARDS VIOLENCE

Thomas W. Muldary, Ph.D.

Despite a wealth of accumulated findings, the relationship between attitudes and behavior is not completely understood. Some theorists postulate that attitudes are predispositions to behavior,[1] some maintain that attitudes follow behavior,[2] and others have their own respective notions.[3] All theorists, however, do agree on some points. In particular, there is little disagreement that attitudes are learned and that they are always directed toward some object—work, Christmas, science, self, and so on.

This chapter examines the relationship between attitudes and violence: What are people's attitudes toward violence? How are those attitudes learned? What connection exists between attitudes and violent behavior? If attitudes toward violence are amenable to change, how can this change be accomplished?

Four positions serve as bases for discussion: (1) attitudes toward violence in America are variable and situation-specific; they depend upon individual values and moral standards for justification; (2) attitudes toward violence are learned the same way other attitudes are learned and are especially sensitive to the influences of modeling agents during the socialization process; (3) the reciprocal relationship between attitudes and aggressive behavior can be interpreted according to the theory of cognitive dissonance,[3] attribution theory,[4-7] and equity theory;[8,9] (4) a change in attitude is a function of new learning; this change is influenced by other people and must be viewed against contemporary standards of morality.

THE JUSTIFICATION OF VIOLENCE

As a society that professes the value of humanitarianism, Americans have a curiously flexible tolerance for violence. This acceptance of violent behavior in specific situations reflects a sense of moral relativity. Consider the responses to some of this country's most tragic events. After Lee Harvey Oswald was murdered by Jack Ruby in 1963, many Americans voiced their approval.[10] After Lieutenant William Calley was court-martialed for the Mai Lai massacre in the

Vietnam war, numerous people regarded him as a folk hero.[11] When four students at Kent State University were killed by the Ohio National Guard in 1970, some people expressed their satisfaction over the deaths of the young students.[12,13]

These are only three instances of profound violence that attracted worldwide attention, but they illustrate a range of attitudinal phenomena with direct bearing on the problem of human violence. Specifically, people who observe violent acts committed by others tend to base their reactions on existing preconceptions about the justifiability of the act.[9,11-14] In the examples cited, Oswald's murder could be justified because he was an "assassin"; Calley only "followed orders" when he killed the "gooks"; and the Kent State students were "dirty, hippie radicals." Somehow, many observers could adopt the attitude that these individuals got what they deserved. Although this apparent belief in a just world is a dramatic phenomenon, it has received convincing supportive evidence.[14]

Instances of domestic violence are much less notorious, but similar responses occur among those who can somehow justify rape ("She teased him and led him on"), spouse assault ("She pushed him too far with her nagging"), or even child abuse ("The kid needed to learn a lesson"). All such responses are sustained by some moral base for justification. The eventual consequence of justifying violence is a reinforced tolerance for it and an increased tendency to engage in it on one's own terms whenever the violence can be justified. Of course, as Feshbach suggested, an individual's reaction to perceived violence depends on previous learning, particularly the learning of moral values.[13]

The attitudes individuals hold toward violence and, more importantly, the processes they use to justify violent acts are complex phenomena of special social significance. The theory of cognitive dissonance[3] and attribu-

tion theory[4-7] are useful frameworks for interpreting the processes involved in justifying violence. The basic theory of cognitive dissonance assumes that the simultaneous holding of incompatible beliefs and attitudes results in psychological conflict, and this state of distress motivates the individual to reduce the incompatibility. The methods for resolving the conflict need not be rational. The basic assumption of attribution theory is that people have a need to explain experiences by means of a cause-and-effect relationship. The attribution of causation is influenced by numerous factors. One of these is a pervasive belief that the world is basically a just place.

The two theories are not incompatible since no single theory can be expected to explain multidimensional phenomena. Interpretations based on these views may help in understanding factors that influence justification, the derogation of perpetrators or victims of violence, and the maintenance of attitudes toward violence.

Blaming Perpetrators and Victims

Certainly, everyone has experienced the distress of being unable to account for senseless acts of violence. According to the theory of cognitive dissonance, the awareness of a senseless act of violence is an upsetting experience which typically throws people off balance, shakes their view of the world as an orderly and predictable place, and brings them painfully close to the recognition of their own vulnerabilities. People relieve this distress by explaining the violence in a way that restores a sense of perspective. According to attribution theory, one way to achieve this result is to blame someone for the act: either the perpetrator or the victim.

As a dramatic example, consider the Jonestown massacre in which hundreds of people were murdered in Guyana, South America.

The predominant reactions to this ultraviolent tragedy were utter disbelief, shock, and undeniable revulsion. It was difficult to comprehend any reason for such an unthinkable destruction of human lives.

Consequently, many people gained some perspective and understood the Guyana tragedy only by finding that the cause was the "insanity" of the perpetrator Jim Jones. By labeling Jones "insane," they could make "sense" of a senseless mass murder. In the same way, without apparently justifying similar acts of violence, many people made "sense" of the senseless acts of individuals such as Charles Manson, Sirhan Sirhan, and Richard Speck only by identifying the "cause" as the perpetrator's obvious "insanity."

Indeed, Jones and other perpetrators of profound violence may have been disturbed personalities, but the drawback of this tendency to call a perpetrator "insane" is that the label is purely descriptive. It offers no explanation for the violence and little understanding of pertinent etiological factors. However, the label does serve a purpose for observers. It defines perpetrators as deviant, sets them apart from decent folk, and makes them solely responsible for the violent acts. Thus, observers can effectively distance themselves from the problems surrounding violence, restore predictability to their worlds, discount their own vulnerabilities, maintain their beliefs that insanity is the cause, and avoid the idea that some conditions in society might actually be precursors of violence.

Likewise, when observers cannot justify domestic violence, they may explain it by labeling the perpetrators "insane." And, if blaming the perpetrators is impossible, they may resort to blaming the victims.[15,16] Historically, victims of rape have been blamed and degraded in the courts and by law enforcement agencies.[17,18] Judges and attorneys have argued that a woman would not have been raped if she had not provoked it. A prominent San Diego attorney stated that his client's rape victims were "semiwilling," that any girl who was bothered by the fact that somebody had a knife held her honor very cheap.[19]

This tendency to hold the victim responsible is consistent with attribution theory and the theory of cognitive dissonance. People may blame the victim in an attempt to convince themselves that such misfortune would not befall them because they would behave differently under similar circumstances.[9] The reduction of distress by attributing blame to the victim allows the observer to maintain an attitude of equity in the world and reinforces the belief that, in a just world, people get what they deserve.

Apparently, it is much easier for individuals to attribute blame to a perpetrator or a victim than it is to consider the upsetting possibility that society, of which they are a member, may be partly responsible. The ability of individuals to justify any form of violence reflects the social system which provides the moral standards for making such judgments. In American society, with its sanctions against violence, any justification of violent acts is a paradox. The process of labeling perpetrators results in a simpleminded approach to the resolution of social problems.[12] When the rapist is labeled "depraved," when the wife batterer is labeled "sadistic," when the child abuser is labeled "sick," people are responding to concepts of "depravity," "sadism," and "sickness," concepts that do not really explain the violence.

Likewise, labeling victims "willing" or "deserving" does not promote an understanding of violence. Labeling the victim reinforces the tendency of individuals to justify violent acts, and this justification can make it extremely difficult for anyone to internalize different attitudes toward violence.

It seems that a person who has internalized a stable system of moral values would find it very hard to justify violence. However, according to the theory of cognitive dissonance, the justification of violence need not be a rational process, so long as the individual can eliminate the distress brought on by the awareness of violence. And, as attribution theorists have pointed out, the attribution of blame depends much more on the personal values of the observer than on the objective facts.[11]

It seems clear that problems of domestic violence must be examined in the context of the social system and its standards of morality. Any attempt to alter attitudes toward violence is misguided if it ignores the moral bases that permit the justification of violence and the maintenance of existing attitudes or fails to secure the backing of society's most influential institutions.

ATTITUDES, LEARNING, AND AGGRESSIVE BEHAVIOR

It appears that attitudes are acquired through classical and operant conditioning, as well as observational learning, but the underlying mechanisms of the learning processes and the effect of environmental variables are still unclear. Thus, accounting for the development of attitudes toward violence is a difficult task. Nevertheless, there are certain general descriptions which highlight the significance of the socialization process in the learning of such attitudes.

The learning of attitudes toward aggression is influenced most strongly in the context of the family. Here behavior and attitudes are acquired directly through experience with rewards and punishments and vicariously through observation of adult and television models. Most people know that direct experience with rewards and punishments affects subsequent behavior, but they are typically less cognizant of the effects of modeling on behavior and attitude formation among children. The following section discusses the important influences of modeling on the development of attitudes within the family context and highlights the reciprocal relationship between attitudes and violent behavior.

Modeling in the Family Context

"Society" transmits its values, attitudes, and standards during the socialization process, but "individuals" are the true agents of transmission. The agents principally responsible for passing on culture to children are, of course, parents and other family members. Thus, the family becomes the main context for the introduction of attitudes, including the universal prohibition against interpersonal aggression.

Considerable research on the processes by which people learn aggressive behavior and attitudes has focused on the effects of modeling. Investigators have attempted to determine the relationships among observed aggression, its consequences, and subsequent aggressive predispositions of observers.

An early study by Bandura and Huston which suggested that aggressive behavior could be socially learned[20] was confirmed by research which reported the imitation of aggressive models by nursery school children.[21,22] These and other investigations have indicated rather conclusively that aggression can be learned through observation of aggressive models. In addition, modeling appears to instill attitudes,[23] including attitudes toward aggression.

Within any social context, including the family, modeling influences have various effects. Children can learn aggressive behavior merely by being exposed to it in the home.[24] Seeing parents behave aggressively is sufficient to cause the learning of aggressive behavior among children. Similarly, hearing parents verbalize hostile attitudes can influence an identification with and internalization of those hostile attitudes in children.

Whether or not a child subsequently acts on this new learning depends on various factors.

The consequences of a model's aggression may have inhibitory or disinhibitory effects. If a child has seen others punished for acting aggressively, the aversive consequences tend to inhibit the child's own aggressive inclinations. This effect may occur, for example, when a young boy witnesses his brother's punishment for hitting a playmate. There is, of course, no guarantee that the boy will avoid subsequent aggression simply because his brother was punished. He has learned aggression by observing his brother and is thus potentially capable of behaving aggressively when nonpunitive consequences are expected.

Conversely, a disinhibitory effect occurs when the perceived aggression is followed by a successful or rewarding outcome.[25] For example, by watching their father and mother fight, children may learn that one way to resolve interpersonal conflicts is to strike the other person. And a more subtle learning occurs when children are taught that there is some noble purpose behind the severe spanking they have received from their mother (physical aggression as a means of controlling others).

Another example of the disinhibitory effect is the finding that children who are physically abused tend to become parents who abuse their own children.[14] The theory of social learning suggests that such people learned through observation of their parents' behavior that physical abuse of children is somehow appropriate discipline.

Predispositions toward aggression and violence may precede any overt act of aggressiveness, or as the self-perception theory of Bem[2] suggests, seeing oneself behave in an aggressive manner may result in a predisposition to act aggressively. However such predispositions develop, they represent attitudes toward aggression, and in observational learning the basic modeling process is the same regardless of the form through which it occurs.[23]

Television Violence

From 1960 to 1980 no other aspect of human aggression has been investigated more than the relationship between violence and the mass media.[14] This emphasis is not surprising, since public concern over television programing has been correspondingly strong over the same period. Media critics argue that there is excessive violence on television and that this violence has an adverse effect upon viewers, expecially children. Media spokespersons, on the other hand, deny that television has such an influence and say that they are only giving the public what it wants.[11]

There are three issues in this heated debate: (1) whether there is, in fact, excessive violence on television, (2) whether people are attracted to television violence, and (3) whether television violence has adverse effects on viewers. It might be logical to argue that if television advertising can influence attitudes toward commercial products, then television programing can influence attitudes toward violence; but what does the research indicate?

Findings published by the Surgeon General of the United States in 1972 pointed toward the conclusion that violence portrayed on television has no uniformly adverse effect on most children.[11,26,27] However, many of the studies included in the Surgeon General's report have been criticized on methodological grounds.[28,29] Other criticisms have pointed out the biased manner of selecting committee members to study the problem. According to Johnson, the Surgeon General allowed television executives to veto the selection of committee members.[11] As a result, several of the most prominent authorities on the subject were excluded, including Albert Bandura, Leonard Berkowitz, and several others.[30]

Some of the findings of Bandura[e.g.,21,22] and Berkowitz[e.g.,31-33] stand in direct contrast to those presented by the Surgeon General, and, on the whole, data on the effects of television violence indicate that viewing violence may lead to an increase in aggressive behavior.[14]

Viewing violence may involve a process that mediates a disinhibition of aggressive tendencies; this disinhibition is influenced by an expectancy of nonpunitive consequences. In addition, a disinhibitory effect may influence an alteration of attitudinal predispositions toward aggression. Television violence may influence not only aggressive behavior but also an individual's views of aggression and the world in general.[14] A child who is continually exposed to violence on television may develop an attitude that aggressive behavior is a common and, therefore, appropriate way of handling problems.[31]

Longitudinal studies by Eron and his associates examined the potential for the development of such attitudes in children.[34-38] In summary, there appears to be a critical developmental period, from age 8 years to age 19 years. During this time the viewing of television violence leads to the building of aggressive habits, and continued watching may have a cumulative effect. According to Eron, the violence of the television programs preferred by an eight-year-old boy were the single best predictor of how aggressive he would be when he was 19 years old.[34] By the time an individual is 19 years old, television violence no longer has the same direct influence. These studies suggest that television violence has a direct impact on the subsequent behavior of males and illustrate the influence of socialization practices—particularly sex-role learning, since viewing violence on television did not have the same effect on females. The findings reviewed here must be treated prudently, lest people come to see television as the scapegoat for social ills. Not all children learn to become aggressive by watching television. Most of them do not act on the learning they acquire through the observation of violence on television. The reasons for such variance are probably the family context itself since socialization experiences within the family system have the major impact upon personality development. Future research should help determine what television programs influence which individuals under what circumstances.

Perpetrators' Attitudes Toward Doing Harm

Another significant aspect of attitude formation is associated with the reciprocal relationship between attitudes and behavior and with the phenomena of justification. Whenever an aggressive act injures another person, the perpetrator often experiences some degree of distress. Aronson suggested that this distress occurs because most people do not see themselves as malevolent persons.[12] Harming another typically violates the self-concept that one is a decent person. The reality of the injury is often unambiguous and undeniable. Consequently, perpetrators are motivated to restore their self-esteem by justifying their acts. One way is to derogate the victim, to rationalize that the victim deserved to suffer. This tendency is particularly strong when the perpetrator perceives that there was some freedom "not" to cause the injury and when the harmful results cannot be denied.[39] This inclination to denigrate the victim is stronger among perpetrators with higher self-esteem.[12,40]

Aggressors may follow another course, predicted by equity theory, and compensate their victims for the suffering incurred.[41] Choosing this alternative seems to depend on two situational factors: the adequacy of available compensation and the cost, to the perpetrator, of providing compensation.

"Adequate" compensation is compensation that the perpetrator perceives to be commensurate with the harm done. Too little compensation does not help the perpetrator reduce the distress. Excessive compensation is also unsatisfactory; it eliminates the victim's suffering, but causes inequity for the perpetrator.[9] A perpetrator will also avoid "adequate compensation" if "adequate justification" is possible. If justification is sufficient to remove the perpetrator's distress, compensation will not be attempted. Likewise, compensation will not be provided if the cost, psychologically or otherwise, is too great.

Another factor that seems to influence the perpetrator's response is the capacity of the victim to retaliate.[12] A perpetrator who is aware that the victim may retaliate in the future anticipates that equity will be restored and, consequently, has no need to justify the aggression by denigrating the victim.

When equity cannot be restored through compensation, the perpetrator tends to restore it through justification. This process typically involves denigrating the victim and makes the victim more disliked by the perpetrator. The consequent attitude toward the victim, and toward doing harm, may predispose the perpetrator to doing harm in the future.

The main point is that many acts of violence lead to justification, a process that leads to more violence. As Aronson pointed out, the rationalization involved in justifying aggression against others not only makes it possible to aggress against another person but also guarantees that the aggression will continue.[12]

Aronson further contended that the derogation of victims, which reduces prohibitions against harming others, would be very difficult if people were more empathic. According to Feshbach and Feshbach, the more empathy a person has, the less likely that person is to aggress against others.[42]

TOWARD THE REDUCTION OF AGGRESSION AND VIOLENCE

While the search for ways to alter attitudes toward aggression is necessary, it is important to recognize the tremendous complexity of attitudes in general. They are not necessarily reliable predictors of behavior. A person's tolerance of aggression is by no means an indication that the same person will behave aggressively. Conversely, one may deplore violence, yet engage in it. Therefore, the focus must be on "behavior" and the means available for influencing it.

Socialization Practices

The family context seems to be an excellent environment for altering aggressive predispositions. Eron, for example, found that the effects of television viewing were different for boys than for girls.[34] One plausible explanation for the findings is the different socialization experiences of boys and girls.

Eron suggested that efforts be directed toward a resolution of what it means to be "masculine" in our society.[34] He contended that society must discourage boys from aggression very early in life and reward them for alternative behaviors. He observed that the goals of the women's liberation movement should not insist that little girls should be treated like little boys. Instead boys should be socialized the way girls traditionally have been socialized. They should be encouraged to develop socially positive qualities such as tenderness, sensitivity to feelings, nurturance, cooperativeness, and aesthetic appreciation. Eron argued that aggression can be reduced if male adolescents and adults, as a result of socialization, function according to the same standards of behavior traditionally advocated for women. This proposal appears tenable, since nonaggressive societies such as the Arapesh of New Guinea and Lepchas of Sikkim in the Himalayas make no distinctions between male and female roles and no attempts to inculcate aggressive masculinity in males.[43]

Data on the effects of modeling suggest that parents can have a positive impact as models of prosocial behavior. If children can learn aggressive behavior by observing parent models, they can learn prosocial behavior from the same models. Thus, training parents to become more effective models of adaptive behavior would be beneficial, and there are educational means available to teach them skills in parenting, communication, and conflict resolution. This approach has been suggested often, and its legitimacy and reasonableness are clearly evident.

Another aspect of modeling prosocial behaviors is the modeling of empathic skills. Research indicates that observers who feel some empathic involvement with victims of violence do not devalue those persons.[42,44] It is very difficult to justify the suffering of another person with whom one can identify. Encouraging empathy in children might lead to the decrease of many forms of violence. One means for developing empathic skills in children is the modeling of empathy by parents, particularly parental empathy toward the children themselves.

Humanistic writers tell of the growth-producing benefits associated with the utilization of empathic skills. One benefit is often the formation of satisfying and meaningful relationships. In these relationships individuals are less likely to express hostility through violence. When hostility does surface, it can be handled adaptively without resorting to aggressive measures. Another benefit is the development of more positive and stable self-concepts. At home the promotion of positive self-concepts is extremely important; a favorable self-concept is less likely to promote aggression than an unfavorable self-concept. When persons with positive self-concepts behave aggressively, they often experience enough distress to prevent further transgressions that would violate their self-image.

Similarly, the theory of cognitive dissonance predicts that individuals who help another person must justify their altruism by convincing themselves that their beneficiary was worth the effort. There is some evidence that benefactors do come to like their beneficiaries.[9,12] If so, it seems that aggression against a beneficiary would be difficult. The implication, of course, is that the socialization process should encourage helping behaviors among children. When adult models behave in charitable ways, children receive training in morality. Such modeling experiences may increase a child's level of moral judgment.

The Importance of Empathy

According to Clark, the highest and most difficult level of empathy attainable is that which embraces all humanity.[45] Religion has marginal success in reinforcing this level of empathy because it is difficult for individuals to express it consistently and functionally. Education often neglects it by advocating moral relativity at the expense of moral sensitivity. This high level of empathy is directly related to the issues of attitudes and violence, since a person who has attained it cannot justify the naked use of power, tyranny, flagrant or subtle injustices, cruelties, sustained terrorism, killings, wars, and eventual extinction.[45]

Most individuals are capable of empathy. The ability to identify with, understand, and respond to the experience of others is a prerequisite to the development of moral sensitivity and attitudes of nonviolence. As this chapter repeatedly emphasizes, individuals who empathize with the suffering of others find it extremely difficult to justify violence.

It may be desirable to find ways, in addition to modeling by parents, of developing empathy within the home environment. When empathy is fostered, it can become a prosocial motive for altruistic behavior; the reinforcements associated with performing altruistic actions may increase the likelihood of similar actions occurring more frequently.

Values, Morals, and Responsibilities

Lifton posited the concept of psychohistorical dislocation to describe his perceived disassociation of society and the important symbols of cultural tradition (family, religion, education, government).[46] More recently,

Harmon pointed out various indications of a transformation of values.[47] They included an increased public acceptance of hedonism, an increased sense of alienation, and increased rates of violent crime and social destruction. As cultural changes continue, the role of parents in mediating them becomes even more important. Many writers, including Bronfenbrenner,[48] have emphasized the need for greater involvement of parents and other adults in the lives of children. Bronfenbrenner also advocated using the positive potential of the peer group to promote prosocial behavior.

As Bem argued, the greatest influence on people is people.[2] Years ago, Katz hypothesized a "two-step flow of communication" in which family members, friends, and peers serve as middlemen in the flow of ideas from the media to individuals.[49] These persons are "opinion leaders" who do more than transmit filtered information; they help establish and maintain social norms, and they function as models for appropriate behavior and acceptable attitudes.[2] It seems important that parents and community leaders become aware of their potential as models and "opinion leaders" and use their influence to shape socially appropriate attitudes among children.

Education is a principal agent of socialization; it transmits society's most valued and vital social standards. Unfortunately, the various disciplines, especially the social sciences, have often substituted the inculcation of moral relativism for moral sensitivity.[45] Furthermore, although educational processes are inseparable from value issues, education often ignores any consideration of values. As Lerner maintained, one task may be to transform education into a values dialogue which uses life itself as the substance for shaping and internalizing values.[50]

The educational system must be an integral component of efforts to reduce violence. Besides offering formal coursework in specific areas such as parenting, communica-

tion, and conflict resolution, education must recognize its obligation to promote moral sensitivity among youth and adults. These steps can have a positive impact on the problem of aggression in society.

Finally, in the important issues of morality and values and their relationships to violence, moral differences may depend on divergent opinions about matters of assumed fact. Such differences of opinion are crucial; they pose necessary challenges to one's thinking. In addition, science may play a significant role in moral and value issues. Science aids in the unification of empirical knowledge, and both, science and empirical knowledge, favor a unification of many opinions.

FINAL NOTE

The 1970s witnessed a shift in society toward increased self-absorption, personal concern, and autonomy. Many writers have observed a commensurate shift in the individual's sense of responsibility to others and to the social system. Various popular movements, including some factions within psychology itself, have promoted autonomy and independent functioning as the ideal mode of living. At the same time, these movements have neglected responsibility as an integral and inseparable component of personal freedom. The result has been described as the "me-first" generation.

Some connection must be made between autonomy and responsibility. Kanfer stated that a critical problem for survival is the proper mix of social and personal control that will yield a code of conduct compatible with both human nature and the requirements for group survival.[51] He also suggested that one critical bridge between theories of individual behavior and socially relevant action is a better understanding of motivational bases for prosocial behavior.

The "me-first" philosophy offers little toward managing aggression. Consequently, many researchers have become increasingly interested in studying prosocial behavior. Perhaps this is a trend that will continue. For, as Rotter concluded, the consequences of modeling and encouraging trust within smaller circles of influence can be beneficial; the risks do not seem to be too great, and a younger generation may be a little more ready for a better world—just in case there is one coming.[52]

REFERENCES

1. Rokeach M: *Beliefs, Attitudes and Values.* San Francisco, Jossey-Bass Inc Publishers, 1968.

2. Bem D: *Beliefs, Attitudes and Human Affairs.* Belmont, Calif, Brooks/Cole Publishing Co, 1970.

3. Festinger L: *A Theory of Cognitive Dissonance.* Stanford, Stanford University Press, 1957.

4. Heider F: *The Psychology of Interpersonal Relations.* New York, John Wiley & Sons Inc, 1958.

5. Jones EE, Davis KE: From acts to dispositions: The attribution process in person perspective, in Berkowitz L (ed): *Advances in Experimental Social Psychology.* New York, Academic Press Inc, 1965, vol 2.

6. Kelley HH: Attribution theory in social psychology, in Levine D (ed): *Nebraska Symposium on Motivation.* Lincoln, Neb, University of Nebraska Press, 1967, vol 15.

7. Kelley HH: The process of causal attribution. *Am Psychol* **28**:107-128, 1973.

8. Walster E, et al: *Equity: Theory and Research.* Boston, Allyn & Bacon Inc, 1978.

9. Berscheid E, Walster E: *Interpersonal Attraction,* ed 2. Reading, Mass, Addison-Wesley Publishing Co Inc, 1978.

10. Feshbach N, Feshbach S: Personality and political values: A study of reactions to two accused assassins, in Greenberg BS, Parker EB (eds): *The Kennedy Assassination and the American Public.* Stanford, Stanford University Press, 1965.

11. Johnson RN: *Aggression in Man and Animals.* Philadelphia, WB Saunders Co, 1972.

12. Aronson E: *The Social Animal,* ed 2. San Francisco, WH Freeman & Co, 1976.

13. Feshbach S: Aggression, in Mussen PH (ed): *Carmichael's Manual of Child Psychology.* New York, John Wiley & Sons Inc, 1970, vol II.

14. Goldstein JH: *Social Psychology.* New York, Academic Press Inc, 1980.

15. Godfrey BW, Lowe CA: Devaluation of innocent victims: an attribution analysis within the just world paradigm. *J Pers Soc Psychol* **31**:944-951, 1975.

16. Walster E: The assignment of responsibility for an accident. *J Pers Soc Psychol* **3**:73-79, 1966.

17. Kahn A, et al: Attribution of fault to a rape victim as a function of respectability of the victim: a failure to replicate or extend. *Represent Res Soc Psychol* **8**:291-305, 1977.

18. Krulewitz JE, Payne EJ: Attributions about rape: effects of rapist force, observer sex and sex-role attitudes. *J Appl Soc Psychol* **8**:291-305, 1978.

19. *Los Angeles Times,* July 1, 1978, part II, p 1.

20. Bandura A, Huston AC: Identification as a process of incidental learning. *J Abnorm Soc Psychol* **63**:311-318, 1961.

21. Bandura A, et al: Transmission of aggression through imitation of aggressive models. *J Abnorm Soc Psychol* **63**:575-582, 1961.

22. Bandura A, et al: Imitation of film-mediated aggressive models. *J Abnorm Soc Psychol* **66**:3-11, 1963.

23. Bandura A: Social learning theory, in Spence JT, et al (eds): *Behavioral Approaches to Therapy.* Morristown, NJ, General Learning Press, 1976.

24. Bandura A: *Aggression: A Social Learning Analysis.* Englewood Cliffs, NJ, Prentice-Hall Inc, 1973.

25. Bandura A, et al: Disinhibition of aggression through diffusion of responsibility and dehumanization. *J Res Pers* **9**:253-269, 1975.

26. *Television and Growing Up.* The Surgeon General's Advisory Committee on Television and Social Behavior, 1972.

27. Liebert RM: Television and social learning: Some relationships between viewing violence and behaving aggressively, in Murray JP, et al (eds): *Television and Social Behavior.* Washington, DC, US Govt Printing Office, 1972.

28. Singer JL: The influence of violence portrayed in television or motion pictures upon overt aggressive behavior, in Singer JL (ed): *The Control of Aggression and Violence.* New York, Academic Press Inc, 1971.

29. Weiss W: Effects of the mass media on communication, in Lindzey GA, Aronson E (eds): *Handbook of Social Psychology,* ed 2. Reading, Mass, Addison-Wesley Publishing Co Inc, 1969, vol 5.

30. Gould J: U.S. aide accused on TV violence. *New York Times,* January 12, 1972.

31. Berkowitz L: Some aspects of aggression. *J Pers Soc Psychol* **2**:359-369, 1965.

32. Berkowitz L: The contagion of violence: an S-R mediational analysis of some effects of observed aggression, in Arnold WJ, Page MM, (eds): *Nebraska Symposium on Motivation.* Lincoln, Neb, University of Nebraska Press, 1970.

33. Berkowitz L, Geen RC: Film violence and the cue properties of available targets. *J Pers Soc Psychol* **3**:525-530, 1966.

34. Eron LD: Prescription for reduction of aggression. *Am Psychol* **35**:244-252, 1980.

35. Eron LD, et al: *Learning of Aggression in Children.* Boston, Little, Brown & Co, 1971.

36. Eron LD, et al: Does television violence cause aggression? *Am Psychol* **27**:253-263, 1972.

37. Huesmann LR, et al: Television violence and aggression: the causal effect remains. *Am Psychol* **28**:617-620, 1973.

38. Lefkowitz MM, et al: *Growing Up to be Violent.* New York, Pergamon Press Inc, 1977.

39. Davis KE, Jones EE: Changes in interpersonal perception as a means of reducing cognitive dissonance. *J Abnorm Soc Psychol* **61**:402-410, 1960.

40. Glass DC: Changes in liking as a means for reducing cognitive discrepancies between self-esteem and aggression. *J Pers* **32**:520-549, 1964.

41. Walster E, et al: *Equity: Theory and Research.* Boston, Allyn & Bacon Inc, 1978.

42. Feshbach N, Feshback S: The relationship between empathy and aggression in two age groups. *Dev Psychol* **1**:102-107, 1969.

43. Wrightsman L: *Social Psychology in the Seventies.* Monterey, Calif, Brooks/Cole Publishing Co, 1972.

44. Aderman D, et al: Empathic observation of an innocent victim: the just world revisited. *J Pers Soc Psychol* **29**:342-347, 1974.

45. Clark K: Empathy: a neglected topic in psychological research. *Am Psychol* **35**:187-190, 1980.

46. Lifton RJ: Self-process in protean man, in *The Acquisition and Development of Values: Perspectives on Research.* Bethesda, Md, National Institute of Child Health and Human Development, 1968.

47. Harmon WW: The coming transformation. *Futurist* **9**:5-12, 106-112, 1977.

48. Bronfenbrenner U: *Two Worlds of Childhood: U.S. and U.S.S.R.* New York, Russell Sage Foundation, 1970.

49. Katz E: The two-step flow of communication: an up-to-date report on a hypothesis, *Public Opin Q* **21**:61-78, 1957.

50. Lerner M: *Values in Education.* Bloomington, Ind, Phi Delta Kappa Educational Foundation, 1976.

51. Kanfer FH: Personal control, social control and altruism: can society survive the age of individualism? *Am Psychol* **34**:231-239, 1979.

52. Rotter JB: Interpersonal trust, trustworthiness and gullibility. *Am Psychol* **35**:1-7, 1980.

Unit II

The Family and Violence

3

FAMILY VIOLENCE IN CONCEPT AND ACTION

Theodore N. Ferdinand, Ph.D.

Understanding family violence in modern society is a difficult task, and the goal of this chapter is to clarify some of the problems involved. First, what is family violence, and how does it differ from normal, controlled coercion among family members? Second, what is the history of family violence? Has it diminished since the nineteenth century, along with violent crime and capital punishment, or has it increased as the family has changed? Third, what are the explanations of family violence, and how persuasive are they? And fourth, what are the legal avenues open for control of family violence?

WHAT IS FAMILY VIOLENCE?

Defining the nature of family violence sets the bounds of subsequent explanation and remedy. Much care must be taken to include only the essential facts. Superficially, family violence refers to violence inflicted by one family member on another, but the key to this definition is the meaning of violence. As used here, violence refers to physical force

that is *not* permitted by normative or legal rules. Thus, family violence is physical force, inflicted by one family member on another, that exceeds normative or legal bounds. In exceeding these bounds, family violence becomes liable to sanctions and often comes to the attention of nonfamily observers, including the police and the courts. Family violence then becomes a public issue and forces public officials to formulate policy about it.

According to this definition, family violence in different social settings reflects not only variations in actual violence but also different standards of evaluation. Cross-cultural or historical comparisons must consider variations in normative standards (as well as variations in the incidence of violence) when interpreting differences that may appear. A higher incidence of wife beating among Mediterranean families, for example, probably reflects not only a greater tendency to violence among Mediterranean husbands but also a broader normative acceptance of violence among Mediterranean cultures.[1] Similarly, a higher incidence of child abuse in

31

lower-class families may reflect a greater tolerance of violence there as well.[2,3] Thus, if legally or scientifically trained observers use the standards of the middle class, they may find more violence among the lower class than even the family members themselves are willing to acknowledge. Professionals must keep the standards of evaluation distinct from the standards of the actors themselves. If the actor's standards are more permissive than the evaluator's standards, actions that the evaluator considers family violence may be normal family interaction to the actor. Emergency personnel should be fully aware of the standards being used in discussing or evaluating the problem.

Family violence includes four distinct forms:

- Abuse among spouses, mainly a husband's abuse of his wife
- Abuse of children by parents, mainly a mother's abuse of her child
- Abuse among siblings
- Abuse of parents by children

Two of these, abuse among spouses and parental abuse of children, have appeared throughout history. Public awareness of the abuse of parents by children has been more recent. In the 1980s, only sibling abuse has failed to stimulate significant public interest.

Family violence in the form of either spouse abuse or child abuse has aroused concern among various groups since the nineteenth century at least. But the two forms follow distinctive patterns, and, historically, they have interested different groups. Public policy on spouse and child abuse has evolved along a bifurcated path, and no unified campaign has emerged to cope with family violence in its several forms.

In the modern era the movement to curb wife abuse gathered strength both from legal advances and from a heightened concern among feminists. In England the common

law upheld the husband's right to ". . . give his wife moderate correction. For, as he is to answer for her misbehaviour, the law thought it reasonable to entrust him with this power of restraining her, by domestic chastisement in the same moderation that a man is allowed to correct his servants or children . . . ."[4] Nevertheless, the husband was limited to reasonable forms of chastisement, and by the early nineteenth century, a small number of wives were seeking protection from their abusive husbands through criminal prosecution.[5] Divorce was an alternative, but it was available, in effect, only to women with sizable financial resources. The legal proceedings were lengthy and expensive, and separation from the husband meant separation from any children in the marriage and from all forms of material support as well. Only women with independent means could afford such a drastic step. As violently abused women appeared repeatedly in court, however, the magistrates began to recognize a need for more effective protection, and in 1853 Parliament passed an act strengthening the punishments of wife and child abusers. In 1857 passage of the Divorce Reform Act eased the divorce route for some women seeking an escape, but it did not provide any alternative means of support and was used only rarely by working-class women. It was not until 1891 in *R.* v. *Jackson* that the English courts finally and clearly rejected the ancient rule that permitted a husband to physically chastise his wife.[6]

Social efforts to help battered wives also gathered momentum during the nineteenth century. The conventional view regarded wife abuse as an ancient and tolerable practice among lower-class families that was seriously aggravated by an equally ancient custom of excessive drinking.[7,8] In the upper classes, however, where family customs were more moderate, domestic violence, especially wife abuse, was indefensible.[8]

In England key feminists, both male and female, supported and sponsored legal advances that gave abused wives greater latitude in coping with their husbands' violence. John Stuart Mill was one of the first to champion the battered wife. In 1866 he submitted to Parliament a petition in support of women's suffrage, and in 1867 he succeeded in bringing the issue to the floor. There he argued that women's suffrage was a first and necessary step to abolishing wife battering. Others took up the cause, and it became a central issue in the feminists' efforts to improve the condition of women in England. Frances Power Cobbe was one of the early campaigners, and her essay "Wife Torture in England," published in 1878, was one of the first studies of family violence.[9] The feminists sponsored legislation to support battered wives, and in 1878 Cobbe succeeded in gaining passage of the Matrimonial Causes Act in Parliament. This act provided legal separation for wives whose husbands had committed aggravated assault against them and granted them child custody and separate maintenance as well.

Much the same course was followed in the United States where the courts were the first to confront the problem. From the beginning, they recognized a husband's right to chastise his wife; they also recognized that he might abuse this right. After the Civil War the courts began to reexamine the husband's right of chastisement. In 1874 in North Carolina it was specifically repudiated. Subsequently, several states included wife abuse as a form of battery in their criminal codes. However, these laws typically required a more grievous injury to a wife than to an unrelated individual before the act could qualify as battery.

The antebellum struggle against slavery in this country inspired a movement in behalf of women, and one of the feminists' goals was relief for battered wives. American laws governing family relations were written mainly in state legislatures, not in Congress, and progress in this area was possible only on a state-by-state basis. The women's movement, as it focused on wife abuse, was neither as centralized as in England nor as dramatically effective in gaining results. Accordingly, legislative relief was a less attractive avenue for reform. The main effort turned to attracting public attention and shaping public opinion.

While the movement combating wife abuse drew most of its support from the legal profession and from the women's movement, the issue of child abuse has been highlighted mainly by the medical profession. In the nineteenth century, the women's movement often fought against child abuse along with wife abuse, but it was the latter that received the strongest support. In the late twentieth century, however, pediatricians have dramatized the problem of child abuse and brought it to the public's attention.

Parental coercion of children, like a husband's chastisement of his wife, has enjoyed a legal basis since virtually the beginning of history. In modern times this parental right has been coupled with a parental obligation to avoid unrestrained cruelty. In 1874 the movement to protect children from parental abuse began in earnest when the first Society for the Prevention of Cruelty to Children was founded in New York City. The precipitating event was the case of Mary Ellen Wilson, about seven years old, who was the foster child of Francis and Mary Connolly in New York City. In 1874 Mary Ellen Wilson was brought before the local court. Her emaciated appearance and her testimony of frequent beatings and close confinement by the Connollys shocked the court; she was taken from the Connollys and placed in an asylum for orphans. As Mary Ellen's case unfolded, it became clear that an agency to protect children like her was urgently needed, and the New York Society for the Prevention of Cruelty to Children was formed. Philadelphia formed a similar organization in 1877, and Massachusetts (1878) and Chicago (1881) quickly did the same. In England the first

Society for the Prevention of Cruelty to Children was formed in Liverpool in 1883, and in 1889 the National Society for the Prevention of Cruelty to Children was established there. These societies acted through the courts to protect abused children and lobbied successfully for laws sympathetic to children.

In the twentieth century, support came from a new direction. With the perfection of the X-ray film as a diagnostic technique, physicians began to report that many of the injuries suffered by children were not accidental. In 1946 Caffey reported an association in infants of subdural hematoma (bruises to the brain) and fractures in the arms and legs,[10] and in 1955 Woolley made the startling charge that these injuries were often willfully inflicted.[11] Finally, in 1962 Kempe coined the term "the battered child syndrome" to cover the pattern of injuries that pediatricians were finding in their infant patients.[12] On this basis the effort to curb child abuse in the United States assumed a national focus in the 1970s.

The movements to curb these two forms of family violence sprang from different sources and unfolded along different paths. In England and the United States wife abuse was fought primarily by feminists and members of the legal profession, whereas child abuse was opposed primarily by philanthropic organizations and, later, by the medical profession. Their different histories probably reflect the fact that they offended different social groups with distinctive sensibilities and that different professional groups were instrumental in bringing the problem to the public's attention.

WHAT IS THE HISTORY OF FAMILY VIOLENCE?

Although there is little solid evidence, there is a broad suspicion among scholars that family violence has diminished in modern times. In the nineteenth century, the popular literature abounded with accounts of violence both between husband and wife and between parents and children. Mayhew documented the violent life-styles of English working-class husbands and wives,[13] and Dickens's accounts of parental brutality toward children completed the familial picture in striking clarity.[14] However, family life throughout Western civilization has seemingly evolved to a more tranquil and settled pattern with less of the violence so forcefully depicted in early literary accounts. The long-term subsidence of other working-class aberrations—drunkenness, prostitution, and violent crime—in the twentieth century seems to argue for a decline in domestic violence as well. And, finally, sizable segments of the working class in both the United States and England have moved into the less violent social and cultural milieu of the middle class. If the lower classes endorse a life-style and cultural perspective supportive of family violence, broad demographic shifts that decrease the prominence of these classes in society must reduce the prevalence of family violence as well.

But there are several difficulties with this conclusion. It assumes the primary factor in domestic violence is the prevalence of a subculture of violence in the lower classes. The lower classes endorse the use of violence in interpersonal relationships, and since family relationships are among the most intense of interpersonal relationships, violence is common among lower-class family members. And yet the evidence suggests that although violence among spouses is more common among lower-class families, it is not unknown among the middle class.[15] Similarly, although parental violence toward children is common in the lower classes, it is only slightly less common in the middle class.[16] Neither form of violence, incidentally, embraces a majority of lower-class family members. If a subculture of violence is typical of lower-class individuals, it is more honored in the breach than in conformity. And if the lower class is the focus of a subculture of violence, how can one explain violent behavior among the middle class?

A different explanation must also be considered. Family violence may be stimulated when the social resources of the family are inadequate to cope with the problems the family faces. Some families face more difficult trials than other families do; some family members bring fewer resources to their difficulties than other members do. The incidence of family violence need not be regarded as a phenomenon controlled solely by social class.

Although lower-class families probably face more severe trials overall than middle-class families do, an unkind fate does not respect class position. Moreover, although mental illness may be more prevalent in the lower classes, it is not unknown in the middle classes. From this viewpoint, which might be described as the existential position, family violence represents an inability of specific family members to deal effectively with the family's problems. This inability occurs either because the problems themselves are overwhelming or because the family members are not especially effective in meeting them. Thus, family violence need not be concentrated in the lower classes, although it should be more prevalent there. Moreover, family violence should be more common among family members who have other severe personal disabilities such as a psychological disturbance. This relationship between disabilities and violence need not be strong since certain disabilities may inhibit interpersonal violence.

The evidence in support of this thesis is impressive. There is research that links parental abuse of children with a variety of ailments including personal defects, straitened social or economic circumstances of the family, and even particular defects in the child. Abusive parents, for example, tend to exhibit mental illness, alcoholism, a variety of personality defects, and low intelligence.[17-22] Their social or economic condition is often unusually stressful: they are cut off from meaningful social contact outside the family; they are forced to endure severe crises, including marital conflict; and they are economically deprived.[23-29] And the children themselves often represent a special problem: they are sometimes illegitimate, malformed, or saddled with physical handicaps.[30-33] Similarly, wife abusers have been described as alcoholic, underemployed or unemployed, and socially isolated.[2] Even in the absence of a subculture of violence, it is easy to see how a parent or spouse who has personality deficiencies and who encounters severe stress could lose control and resort to violence. It is easy to see how families that do not particularly endorse violence as a legitimate form of interaction might fall into a violent pattern because of low personal resiliency or difficult social circumstances.

Suggesting that a variety of factors, including the existential, may be involved in family violence does not indicate how these factors impinge on individuals or families and affect their behavior. Clearly, they do not all affect individuals or families in the same way, and one needs a paradigm to link the discrete factors with one another and with individuals to describe the *patterning* of their behavior. A typology of family violence would permit such a description, and professionals could differentiate distinct patterns of family violence. A mature typology would also suggest appropriate remedies for each type.[34,35] A typology of family violence, therefore, is an important step in sorting out the ways in which different factors—psychological, social, and economic—combine to produce distinctive patterns of violence in the family.

A nationwide survey on child abuse found four broad patterns involving the parents.[36] The first, psychological rejection, stemmed from parental inability to love and accept the child; a second pattern was connected with an impulsive, uncontrolled style of disciplining the child. A third one was associated with personal inabilities in meeting stress; and the fourth was provoked by the child's stubbornness, willfulness, or other defects. Boisvert developed a typology which distinguished two general types: those parents who uncontrollably batter the child and those who abuse the child in a more controlled way.[19] The former is plagued with serious personal pathologies that make it difficult to restrain violence toward a child; the latter uses violence as a means to an end without regard to normative reactions.

These typologies are still vague and incomplete in their descriptions, but they point the way for future understanding of this problem. Although no two families engage in violence for exactly the same reasons, patterns do appear. It is important to describe these patterns accurately; to find their causes in the psychological, social, economic, and existential circumstances of the family; and, ultimately, to find appropriate remedies. In this way, solutions to the different types of violence that appear can be formulated.

THE LEGAL RESPONSE TO FAMILY VIOLENCE

Family violence stems from a variety of intertwined factors, and the attempt to deal with it uses a variety of methods. Perhaps the most common, but least understood, method is the legal approach.

Traditionally, the courts have been cautious about forcibly intruding into family affairs. Historically, the Western family is patriarchal; the father has authority over all its members, the wife as well as the children. For the most part, the use of force in exercising this authority has been sanctioned by custom and reserved to the father. Although the wife has enjoyed some authority over the

children and could assert it forcibly, her authority has not superceded the father's when the two disagreed. Traditionally, the Western family was not founded on an ethic of universalism or equality. The Western legal tradition, however, assumes equality before the law. Consequently, the court was placed in the awkward position of either doing violence to the traditional family structure or violating the fundamental rule of equality before the law. Thus, the courts have been reluctant to involve themselves in family disputes, except those involving severe violence, and have preferred to leave less violent disputes to other, extralegal corrective measures. They have been reluctant to confront the family's traditional patriarchal structure head-on by imposing a legal form of equality on it.

In addition, family members are often reluctant to invoke legal restraints on other family members, and complaints are often dropped when tempers have cooled and forgiveness has been extended. Frequently, these informal solutions to family crises are relatively effective, and legal intervention often only hardens and embitters an initially fluid family situation.

Nevertheless, it is only natural that victims of family violence (most often wives, since children are generally ignorant of their rights under law) should turn to the legal system since it is the ultimate force in the community, and it has the ultimate responsibility to prevent violence by one family member against another. The reluctance of the legal system to intervene in family disputes, however, surprises, shocks, and angers many plaintiffs who fear for their well-being when they urgently seek help from the courts.

There are two legal routes that a plaintiff can choose in seeking help: the criminal and the civil. Each has its strengths and weaknesses. The criminal route is useful because it does not require any prior legal action to invoke the authority of the law against a violent malefactor. The police can intervene on the basis of evidence that a felony has been committed. However, they often will not make an arrest on the basis of a simple threat to commit a felony, particularly if the threat is leveled by one family member against another. The legal system, including the police, often views a husband's or father's threat to do violence as within the law. Consequently, there is usually no arrest (even though threatening bodily harm to someone is an assault and against the law) until the wife or child has already been severely battered—until the damage has already been done.

The civil route to legal protection is similarly slippery. Violence in family settings often is associated with the separation of spouses. Sometimes it is the cause of the separation, but sometimes a result of it as well. It is possible, of course, in a legal separation, to forbid the violation of court judgments about the separation. The wife may get a restraining order that forbids her husband to threaten or harass her while the issue is being settled in court. Unfortunately, courts are usually reluctant to take decisive action against a husband who violates a restraining order until the violation becomes flagrant. Even then it is often days or weeks after the violation before punishment is imposed. All too often, a wife in danger from a violent husband receives little or no protection until she has already suffered considerable personal harm. This lack of or delay in protection is even more common for battered children. The law is not a useful method for preventing imminent violence among family members.

Informal, social methods appear much more effective in an emergency. Communal refuges, for example, where women and their children can be sheltered overnight against the abuse of their spouses, often provide more protection than the law or the police.

The law is not designed to cope with potential violators (who would not qualify here?); it is designed to identify actual offenders and to punish them. Asking the law to focus on potential violators pushes it into a hazy area where evidence is weak and conviction unlikely. Prevention of family violence by invoking the law, either criminal or civil, is not likely to prove effective.

CONCLUSION

This chapter pinpoints some of the problems involved in dealing with family violence:

1. Emergency personnel must develop a concept that defines family violence in an appropriate way. It is foolish to use a definition so broad that it includes forms of behavior, such as threatening or slapping, that are not generally regarded as serious.

2. Spouse abuse and child abuse are, for the most part, distinct problems. Concern for them was sparked in the nineteenth century in very different audiences, and the efforts to bring them before the public were sponsored by diverse groups using different approaches.

3. The apparent decline of family violence in Western societies since the nineteenth century probably reflects a decline of the lower class, though family violence seems to stem from existential misfortune and psychological imbalance as well.

4. The law cannot effectively prevent family violence. It may have some value as a general deterrence when the pressures to be violent are still weak. It should not be regarded as the primary means of coping with family violence.

The ineffectiveness of the law in preventing family violence is not a hopeful note to end on, but it does suggest that the most promising avenues for coping with family violence lie in the social and not the legal sphere. Some of these avenues are (1) molding public opinion so that family violence is no longer seen as a legitimate part of married life, (2) making psychotherapy and counseling readily available to married couples who are facing difficulties, and (3) establishing family shelters where abused spouses can gain refuge from violent home situations.

Since violence is such a natural part of family life in many segments of society, only positive measures that reach directly into the family and relieve the pressures that urge violence can have any very direct effect upon the problem. The legal approach is important, but profssionals should not believe that it can substitute for creative social programs that approach family violence with a remedial objective. The law defines and protects the rights of individuals, including those accused of violence, but it does not ordinarily spearhead social reforms—unless the reforms are geared to basic legal questions. Measures designed to relieve family violence must come from other groups with a broader mandate.

REFERENCES

1. Loizos P: Violence and the family: Some Mediterranean examples, in Martin JP (ed): *Violence and the Family.* New York, John Wiley & Sons Inc, 1978, pp 183-196.

2. Steinmetz SK: Violence between family members. *Marr Fam Rev* **1**: 1-13, 1978.

3. Gelles RJ: Violence in the American family, in Martin JP (ed): *Violence and the Family.* New York, John Wiley & Sons Inc, 1978, p 177.

4. Blackstone W: *Commentaries on the Laws of England,* London, Clarendon Press, 1770, vol I, pp 444-445.

5. May M: Violence in the family: An historical perspective, in Martin JP (ed): *Violence and the Family.* New York, John Wiley & Sons Inc, 1978, p 144.

6. *R vs Jackson,* I QB 671, 1891.

7. Godwin G: *London Shadows: A Glance at the Homes of the Thousands.* London, Routledge & Kegan Paul Ltd, 1854, p 3.

8. Warton JJS: *An Exposition of the Laws Relating to the Women of England.* London, Longman, 1853, pp 312, 468.

9. Cobbe FP: Wife torture in England. *Contemp Rev* **32**:55-87, 1878.

10. Caffey J: Multiple fractures in the long bones of children suffering from chronic subdural hematoma. *Am J Roentgenol Radium Ther* **56**:163-173, 1946.

11. Woolley PV Jr, Evans WA Jr: Significance of skeletal lesions in infants resembling those of traumatic origin. *JAMA* **158**:539-543, 1955.

12. Kempe CH, et al: The battered-child syndrome. *JAMA* **181**:17-25, 1962.

13. Mayhew H: *London Labour and the London Poor,* 4 vols. London, Griffin Bohn & Co, 1861-1862.

14. Dickens C: *Oliver Twist.* New York, Bantam Books Inc, 1981.

15. Levinger G: Sources of marital satisfaction among applicants for divorce. *Am J Orthopsychiatry* **36**:804-806, 1966.

16. Erlanger HS: Social class differences in parents' use of physical punishment, in Steinmetz SK, Straus MA (eds): *Violence in the Family.* New York, Dodd Mead & Co, 1974, pp 150-158.

17. Birrell RG, Birrell JHW: The maltreatment syndrome in children: a hospital survey. *Med J Aust* **2**:1023-1029, 1968.

18. Boisvert MJ: The battered child syndrome. *Soc Casework* **53**:475-480, 1972.

19. Dorman S: Child abuse: a review of 69 cases. *Clin Proc* **31**:256-262, 1975.

20. Green AH: A psychodynamic approach to the study and treatment of child-abusing parents. *J Child Psychiatry* **15**:414-429, 1974.

21. Green AH, et al: Child abuse: pathological syndrome of family interaction. *Am J Psychiatry* **19**:171-179, 1968.

22. Smith SM, et al: EEG and personality factors in baby batterers. *Br Med J* **3**:20-22, 1973.

23. Kent JT: What is known about child abusers, in Harris SB (ed): *Child Abuse: Present and Future*. Chicago, National Committee for Prevention of Child Abuse, 1975, pp 47–51.

24. Disbrow MA: Deviant behavior and putative reference persons: child abuse as a special case. *Nurs Res Conf* 5:322–346, 1969.

25. Kaplun D, Reich R: The murdered child and his killers. *Am J Psychiatry* 133:809–813, 1976.

26. Holter JC, Friedman SB: Child abuse: early case findings in the emergency department. *Pediatrics* 42:128–138, 1968.

27. Holter JC, Friedman SB: Principles of management in child abuse cases. *Am J Orthopsychiatry* 38:127–136, 1968.

28. Paulson MJ, Blake PR: The physically abused child: a focus on prevention. *Child Welfare* 48:86–95, 1969.

29. Wight BW: The control of child-environment interaction: a conceptual approach to accident occurrence. *Pediatrics* 44:799–805, 1969.

30. Bishop FI: Children at risk. *Med J Aust* 1:623–628, 1971.

31. O'Neill JA Jr, et al: Patterns of injury in the battered child syndrome. *J Trauma* 13:332–339, 1973.

32. Fredrich WN, Boriskin JA: Ill health and child abuse. *Lancet* 1:649–650, 1976.

33. Sills JA, et al: Nonaccidental injury: a two-year study in central Liverpool. *Dev Med Child Neurol* 19:26–33, 1977.

34. Ferdinand TN: *Typologies of Delinquency*. New York, Random House Inc, 1966, chap 3.

35. Diesing P: *Patterns of Discovery in the Social Sciences*. Chicago, Aldine Atherton, 1971, chap 14.

36. Gil DG: *Violence Against Children: Physical Child Abuse in the United States*. Cambridge, Mass, Harvard University Press, 1970.

4

CHANGING ATTITUDES TOWARD VICTIMS OF VIOLENCE

Linda Meyer Williams, Ph.D.

S tudies show that fear of crime is growing. Public frustration with preventing crime and the admitted failure of the professionals, the experts, to intervene in the criminal careers of offenders have increased. Treatment programs to reduce the likelihood of offender recidivism are cited as abysmal failures.[1] Many who previously advocated rehabilitation of the offender now take a punitive stance and rely on an incapacitation model. This model argues that convicted criminals do not threaten society while they are in prison. Yet it is noted that fewer crimes result in prosecution.

How have attitudes toward the victim changed? One would think that as fear of crime increased, support for the victims of crime, particularly for victims of violent crime, would increase also. While many changes have occurred, victims are still often subjected to insensitivity, at best, and revictimization by society, at worse.

This chapter will explore why victims are blamed for their own victimization, how society's response perpetuates and encourages victimization, and how attitudes towards victims of violence are changing.

BLAMING THE VICTIM

Assigning blame to a victim can be viewed as part of an individual psychological response and as a sociocultural response. It is difficult to divorce one from the other.

In her article on nurses' perceptions of rape victims, C.S. Alexander focused on the relationship between the psychological attributes of the nurses and the amount of responsibility they assign to victims of rape and assault.[2] Alexander concluded that the more nurses see themselves as potential victims of crime, the greater responsibility they assign to the rape victim; and the more rape victims the nurses had encountered (and, therefore, one assumes, the more vulnerable they feel), the more they blame the victim. The concept of cognitive dissonance appears to play a large role in attitudes toward victims of violence.

The theory of cognitive dissonance explains what happens when there are inconsistencies between attitudes and observations. According to this theory, dissonance is "psychologically uncomfortable," and the resulting tension motivates the individual to reduce the dissonance and achieve more consistency between the elements involved. Therefore, when nurses encounter many victims of rape and feel more vulnerable to rape or more threatened by it, they move toward blaming the victim as a way of reducing the tension created. In general, as fear of crime and feelings of vulnerability increase, people look for ways to explain why some other individual was victimized and why this victimization could not happen to them. They may blame the victim, that is, find reasons why the victim deserved to be hurt, or portray the victim as being very different from themselves.

These methods are often used by people who work with victims of violent crimes. They are a protective stance for individuals who might be overcome by anxiety if they were consciously aware of their vulnerabilities. This stance may be an impediment to effective treatment if blaming the victim eliminates empathic response.

Attitudes and behavior toward victims of violence are also fostered by societal norms, values, and belief systems that are part of the Protestant work ethic. Calvinists believe that one does not wait until one dies and goes to heaven to receive all rewards, but that good works are rewarded here on earth. Therefore, successful men or women are successful because of their good works. The socially reinforced perception is that victims of crime did something to deserve their victimization. Furthermore, a culture that places considerable value on winning has little sympathy for a victim. The heroes are Bonnie and Clyde, the successful bank robbers, not the bank tellers they shot and killed.

William Ryan pointed out that the generic process of blaming the victim is applied to almost every American problem.[3] For example, the miserable health care of the poor is explained away by saying that they have poor motivation and lack health information. When cultural mores reinforce the belief that the locus of control of events resides within individuals who receive their just desserts, the victim's plight is viewed with little sympathy.

THE VICTIMIZATION PROCESS —SOCIETY'S ROLE

Victimization is a process. It includes the preparation of the victim for the crime, the victims' experiences during the crime, and the treatment or responses victims encounter as a result of the crime. Society has a role in each step of this process.[4]

Preparation of the Victim for the Crime

In the 1970s literature on person-to-person crimes, particularly crimes against women and intrafamilial violence (child abuse, spouse abuse, and marital rape) proposed that society prepares victims for their victimization. Numerous authors have argued that cultural permission is given for these crimes, that, in fact, the culture may encourage these behaviors.[5-7] Brownmiller helped to clarify the notion of a "rape culture" that provides normative support for male aggressiveness against females;[5] Straus held that cultural norms legitimize marital violence;[6] and Rush traced historical patterns that encourage and perpetuate sexual abuse of children.[7] How religion, the media, and the law perpetuate the victimization process is the focus of these works. They emphasize the role of society in encouraging the victimization of the weak by the strong. The majority of the offenders are male; the victims are the elderly, women, and children.

Writers with a sociocultural perspective argue that males control females in most domains of social life. Men exercise power in Western society, and the exercise of power always involves coercion of the powerless— especially women and children. The exercise of male power, directed at females, can be aggressive as well as exploitative. In this context, sex offenses, particularly rape, are one method men use to dominate women. Rape becomes a symbol men use to remind women that females are powerless and to insure male dominance. Brownmiller and others attempted to uncover values and beliefs that pervade Western culture and insure the continuance of men's dominance over women. Sex offenses are considered another form of dominance behavior that exists between the powerful and the powerless.

The male role, as defined by this culture, usually shows a mixture of aggression and macho; these traits and their continual expression mark male identity. Brownmiller rejects psychoanalytic interpretations of male aggressivity; she favors a cultural or subcultural theory of violence to explain rape. Within this culture there is some normative support for male aggressiveness with females. The male role is defined in terms of aggression and conquest. Men are taught to exercise power to get what they want. The sex offender may not be the inadequate person that psychoanalysts portray. Rather, the sex offender may be someone who overidentifies with the popular male role in his dealings with all females.

This understanding of the socialization process explains how society encourages the offender's behavior and similarly prepares the victim for her victimization. Women are socialized to accept the passive role and to expect victimization. Consequently, they become part of the criminal pair (an early term for offenders and their victims).

Society's Response to the Victim After the Crime

A subcultural theory of violence argues that an individual will construct a set of beliefs that permits interpersonal violence.

This approval of violence has the strongest influence on the acceptance of rape myths.[8] These myths, which pervade the culture, blame the victim for being raped, deny the possibility of sexual assault, and claim the victim wanted to be assaulted and enjoyed it. These beliefs are part of the psychology of the social reaction to sexual assault. They make sex offenses a less serious and more frequent occurrence and protect the offender from blame.

The legal system of a society is designed to deal with all infractions of social order and to insure the continuance of a culture. Brownmiller contends that the entire power structure of the law is dominated and controlled by men. The sexual assault of the victim on the street is followed by the legal assault, termed court proceedings. In these proceedings the victim is often questioned about her previous sexual behavior and her relationship to the offender. The law requires proof of rape and evidence that the victim offered resistance. A rape case is most likely to be heard, and a conviction handed down, when there is physical evidence of sexual assault and evidence of force by the offender and resistance by the victim.[9] Many argue that the criminal justice system favors the sex offender since sexual assaults are unlikely to be prosecuted or to result in a conviction. These features of society constitute a "rape supportive culture" for some authors.[10]

Research by Sykes and Matza included three techniques of neutralization that juvenile delinquents use to justify their behavior: denial of responsibility, denial of injury, and denial of the victim.[11] Weis and Borges maintained that these same techniques play an important role in the socialization of victims and offenders and in the final stage of victimization: the response of society to the crime and the victim.[4]

Society permits and encourages denial of offender responsibility by blaming outside forces. The offender was drunk or sick or poor.

Denial of injury transforms a criminal act into a noncriminal one by declaring the action noninjurious. Sexual abuse does not harm the young child; a child forgets. Physical abuse is not serious; it is necessary for discipline. Rape does not injure nonvirgins; they have experienced sex before. Harming the elderly is acceptable; they are not part of the labor force.

Denial of the victim places the blame on victims and, in fact, converts them to offenders. Society denies a victim's position as a victim when it considers sexual chastity in cases of sexual assault, a child's "seductive nature" or delinquency or misbehavior in cases of child abuse, the obedience of a wife in cases of wife beating, or the crankiness of an old person in cases of abuse of the elderly. Stereotypes of victims—the seductive child or woman; the nagging wife; the cantankerous, worthless, old man or woman—serve to legitimize children, women, and the elderly as victims of crime. These stereotypes have pervaded the legal system as well. Special requirements for corroboration, limitations on a victim's right to sue for redress or receive compensation when a family member is the offender, and requirements for higher standards of proof all contribute to the victimization process.

CHANGING ATTITUDES TOWARD VICTIMS OF VIOLENCE

Three factors have influenced changes in attitudes and treatment for victims of crime, particularly victims of person-to-person and violent crime. First, fear of crime can no longer be ignored; it has an effect on the lives of the rich and powerful as well as the poor. Realistic fear of crime has motivated the powerful to seek changes in the way the legal system treats the victim. Second, frustration with attempts to rehabilitate offenders has changed the focus of the legal system's re-

sponse to crime. In the 1970s the failure of rehabilitation programs became more and more evident, and society became interested in standardizing punishment for offenders who commit the same crime. As a result, the focus of the criminal justice system shifted to reparation for and rehabilitation of victims.

Third, the members of groups that had formed in the 1960s realized that they were frequently the victims of crime and that their victimization was not treated seriously. Blacks, women, and the elderly began to demand redress.

Increased visibility of victims has prompted programs such as offender restitution to victims, victim compensation by the state, and new treatment programs. The media's response has been increasingly sympathetic, and victims are less likely to be blamed for their own victimization.

The status of children as victims has improved the least. Children are not surveyed in studies of fear of crime or victimization, and they do not have a voice through a children's movement or the voting booth. Children are seen and not heard. The criminal justice system has not accommodated itself to children. The courts are set up for adults. Children usually cannot seek victim compensation. They are often victims of violence by family members, and, in most states, victim compensation is not available for crimes committed by family members. In an era of fiscal austerity, programs for children will suffer, losing out to more powerful and vocal groups in the struggle for grant money. Attitudes towards victims reflect the distribution of power in society and patterns of crime. A higher level of victimization among the powerful will lead to reforms aimed at helping victims.

REFERENCES

1. Lipton D, et al: *The Effectiveness of Correctional Treatment.* New York, Praeger Publishers Inc, 1975.

2. Alexander CS: The responsible victim: nurses' perceptions of victims of rape. *J Health Soc Sci Behav* **21**:22–23, 1980.

3. Ryan W: *Blaming the Victim.* New York, Vintage Books, Random House Inc, 1976.

4. Weis K, Borges S: Victimology and rape: the case of the legitimate victim. *Issues Criminol* **8**: 71–115, 1973.

5. Brownmiller S: *Against Our Will: Men, Women and Rape.* New York, Simon & Schuster Inc, 1975.

6. Straus M: Sexual inequality, cultural norms and wifebeating. *Victimology* **3**:61–67, 1976.

7. Rush F: *The Best Kept Secret.* Englewood Cliffs, NJ, Prentice-Hall Inc, 1981.

8. Burt M: Attitudes supportive of rape in American culture. Presented at meeting of University of Minnesota Center for Social Research, January 1978.

9. McCahill T, et al: *The Aftermath of Rape.* Lexington, Mass, Lexington Books, 1979.

10. Meyer L, Romero J: *Sex Offender Recidivism: A Ten-Year Followup.* Philadelphia, Joseph J Peters Institute, 1980.

11. Sykes G, Matza D: Techniques of neutralization: a theory of delinquency. *Am Sociol Rev* **22**: 664–670, 1957.

5

FAMILY INTERACTION AND CYCLES OF VIOLENCE

Janet L. Blenner, R.N., Ph.D.

SYSTEMS THEORY AND THE FAMILY

Violence, especially violence in the family, is a complex issue. One holistic approach to understanding this issue is general systems theory. This theory offers professionals a comprehensive method for examining the interrelating factors involved both in the family and in violence.

Viewing each family member as an independent entity may lead to an invalid portrayal of family dynamics. Keen observation from the perspective of a systems theory allows more complete understanding of the network of relations within the family. Systems theory focuses on the whole rather than on parts or the summation of parts. Families are similar to all other systems; they have patterns which are dynamic, probabilistic, and developmental. In essence, a family is an open system in constant interchange with society (suprasystem) and with its family members (subsystems). A continual exchange between the subsystems and suprasystem occurs on a

daily basis. The two systems are interdependent. For example, delinquent behavior by one member of a family affects the inner functions of both the family and society. Each family member affects the total functioning of the family system. The family functions as a network dependent upon the interrelationships of its members. A change in one part of the system (subsystem) resonates and alters the functioning of the total system.

Relationships between members can often be ascertained by examining the communication network of that particular family. An examination is likely to reveal that each member assumes a particular hierarchical level within the family system. Hierarchical levels represent a member's level of power in decision making in the family.

Incorporated in each family system are rules and norms that reflect the family's goals. Goals may be covertly or overtly expressed in the family. An example of an overt goal is the explicitly stated expectation that all the children will pursue higher education. Whether this goal is conveyed or not depends on the openness of the communication network.

The family uses the mechanism of feedback to regulate the behavior of its members. Deviations from the accustomed, familiar behavior may cause an interplay between positive and negative feedback. A morphostatic system is a system ruled by negative feedback. In effect, it resists change and attempts to maintain the status quo. A morphogenic system, on the other hand, is ruled by positive feedback. It fosters growth, makes allowances for deviation, and explores new avenues for change through the exchange of information. All families use both positive and negative feedback in their attempts to cope with change. Disturbed family systems generally employ a preponderance of negative feedback, while healthy families use mostly positive feedback.

Societal changes cause both anxiety and strain in a family. The flexibility with which the family system responds to these changes depends upon the predominant feedback mechanism. For example, a family using chiefly a morphogenic system will be more flexible in coping with societal strains such as unemployment, changing definitions of sex roles, and overspending. Moreover, a morphogenic system is characterized by a more open communication process that aids in conflict resolution when societal issues interfere with the family.

The family regulates itself through rules and norms that guide the behavior both of individual members and of the family unit as a whole. Deviations from these established behaviors are generally discouraged through disciplinary action and other methods.

THE SOCIALIZATION PROCESS IN THE FAMILY

The first five years of life are crucial in the development of the basic personality structure of an individual. During this period the child acquires a set of values, norms, beliefs, and expectations toward violence through examples and reinforcement set by parents, peers, teachers, and informal social agents.[1] The family plays a central role in the child's integration of social values and norms since it is almost exclusively responsible for socialization of the young and dependent child.

Health professionals are aware of the impact of intergenerational transmission of information on child-rearing practices. Most people tend to raise their children in the same way they themselves were raised. The educational system is not structured to teach people parenting roles, and unhealthy patterns can become perpetuated from generation to generation. However, these patterns can be interrupted through psychotherapeutic techniques and education. Individuals can modify or change their views on their roles in their families or society. The more insight people have about their behavior and relationship to others in their social network, the more likely they are to contemplate and to follow alternative ways of child rearing.

Through the use of techniques such as a genogram (family mapping), the professional can elicit a comprehensive family history which illuminates preexisting patterns of behavior (Fig. 5-1). The genogram also can disclose different value systems held by each parent and points of existing or potential conflict.

The influential role that society (suprasystem) plays in the family cannot be minimized. One function of society is to define violence and violent behavior. Society may sanction certain violent acts or targets while condemning others. For instance, killing one's fellowman may be accepted and even rewarded under conditions of war but severely punished in most peaceful situations. Competitive Western societies, such as the

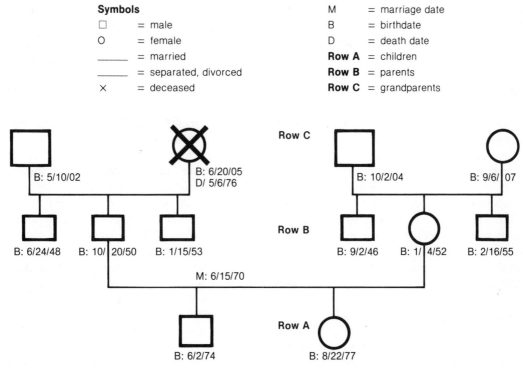

Symbols

☐ = male

O = female

_____ = married

_____ = separated, divorced

× = deceased

M = marriage date

B = birthdate

D = death date

Row A = children

Row B = parents

Row C = grandparents

Fig. 5-1   Genogram

United States, sanction and even demand a marked degree of aggressive behavior as a means of achieving success.

Society may also impose stresses on the family in the form of unemployment, inadequate role fulfillment, insecurity, isolation, or insufficient community support systems. All these conditions have been found to foster violent behavior.[2] Individuals who feel a sense of powerlessness because of societal circumstances may resort to controlling family members through abusive behavior.

DYSFUNCTIONAL FAMILY SYSTEMS AND CONFLICT

A potential point of stress may be strained relations between the family and the community. A "dysfunctional" family typifies this kind of strained relations. Bowen views a "dysfunctional" family as one so fused that conflict is not resolved between the marital dyad, and either a spouse or a child signals distress by exhibiting physical, mental, or social illness.[3] It is a common behavioral pattern of "dysfunctional" families to either exclude or be excluded in the community. Major difficulties arise in these families since the parents have so internalized the standards of the surrounding community that they have great difficulty in finding a legitimate basis for scapegoating outsiders and scapegoat their own child instead.[4]

The methods used by any family to contend with societal stresses depend on coping mechanisms, conflict resolution, and self-esteem. Direct communication may be the most effective way of resolving conflicts. However, if an individual has not acquired these communication skills or is unable to discharge inner tensions in a socially acceptable way, other outlets may be sought. Frustration may be displaced onto a target that is accessible and less personally threatening. Family members who occupy a relatively low position of power in the family often become this target. Many times a child will assume the role of scapegoat because of dependency needs and a rather low hierarchical level. Spouses also fit this description sometimes. The professional must remember that scapegoating is a two-way process. Once the cycle has begun, scapegoated members learn behaviors that encourage others to hurt them. The scapegoat serves a useful function as a vehicle for release of the family's tensions. Moreover, a unification among members is accomplished through projection of hostility. In dysfunctional families one child has become entangled in parental tension; in the functional families, parental tension was either less severe or handled in such a manner that the children did not become pathologically involved.[4] The choice of a particular child for the role of scapegoat may be dependent upon whether the child is unwanted, born at a stressful time, resembles another family member, or has physical or mental problems.[5]

who reacts to sibling fighting with physical punishment reinforces this behavior since violence generates violence. When these children mature, they use these methods, which are a firmly entrenched part of their behavior repertory,[2] to resolve conflict. The disciplinary modes they use continue the cycle by transferring this method to their children, the third generation.

Society (suprasystem) generally regards the family system as a valued social institution. According to Steinmetz and Straus, the semi-sacred nature of the family has prevented an objective analysis of the exact nature of intrafamilial violence.[6] Thus, an objective systems analysis of the family can help therapists change dysfunctional family patterns. Family therapy assists the family in repatterning its communication network and in finding new methods of conflict resolution. Since family therapy uses systems theory in its therapeutic interventions and analysis, it can stop the perpetuation of patterns from one generation to another. Since any social intervention that reduces real social oppression in a person's life also reduces the probability of violent behavior,[7] it behooves health professionals and society at large to assist the family in its everyday existence.

CYCLES OF VIOLENCE

It must be noted that even the most violent individual is not perpetually violent, and even the most passive person is likely to be incited to violence under certain circumstances.[1] Violence does elicit a feeling of catharsis for the frustrated individual; it reduces tension by providing an emotional release. This sense of emotional relief tends to reinforce the use of violence and, thereby, creates a cycle of violence. Thus, violent behavior may be used in lieu of positive coping mechanisms in dealing with conflict and frustration. The parent

REFERENCES

1. Goldstein JH: *Aggression and Crimes of Violence.* New York, Oxford University Press Inc, 1975, pp 20–21.

2. Steinmetz S: *The Cycle of Violence: Assertive, Aggressive and Abusive Family Interaction.* New York, Praeger Publishers Inc, 1977, pp 118, 119.

3. Bowen M: Use of family theory in clinical practice, in Haley J (ed): *Changing Families.* New York, Grune & Stratton Inc, 1971, pp 172–192.

4. Vogel E, Bell N: The emotionally disturbed child as the family scapegoat, in Handel G (ed):

The Psychosocial Interior of the Family. Chicago, Aldine Publishing Co, 1972, pp 425, 427.

5. Postner RS, et al: Process and outcome in conjoint family therapy: *Fam Process* **10**:451–474, 1971.

6. Steinmetz S, Straus M: *Violence in the Family.* New York, Dodd Mead & Co, 1975, p 6.

7. Chappell D, Monahan J: *Violence and Criminal Justice.* Massachusetts, DC Heath & Co, 1975, p 40.

6

COMMUNICATION TECHNIQUES FOR WORKING WITH VIOLENT FAMILIES

Patricia Spezeski Muldary, M.A.

The process of intervening in violent or neglectful families is one that attempts to give individuals an opportunity to change, resolve, restructure, and cope with problems or circumstances that are contributing to their physically or psychologically destructive behavior. Helping the victims and abusers requires an empathic understanding of the pain and trauma of the family. In a therapeutic atmosphere of genuine caring, support, and respect, family members can be helped to integrate the violent experience, to express and deal with their feelings about it, to find a place for it among all their life experiences, and to restructure their defenses so that they can begin coping with life in more positive and healthy ways.

Approaches to intervention will vary according to the setting: a hospital emergency department, a neighborhood mental health clinic, a protective social service agency, or a private medical or counseling office. Yet, a central aspect of any approach is the quality of the initial contacts, particularly the helper's ability to listen effectively, build trust, and engage clients in a therapeutic process. Caring, empathy, and effective communication are tools that go a long way in intervention.

The purpose of this chapter is not to reduce the complex and extremely difficult work of intervention to a cookbook approach but to sensitize helpers to the special needs of abusing families and to point out useful communication techniques for establishing a therapeutic relationship with these clients. The chapter is a compilation of ideas and approaches culled from the works of outstanding authors and clinicians in the areas of child abuse, incest, child neglect, rape, spouse assault, and family violence in general. It is intended to aid personnel in various roles who require certain skills to serve the abusing families they encounter.

HELPERS IN NEED OF INTERVENTION TRAINING

Pollack and Steele believe that persons from many disciplines become involved with abusing families and can be effectively used as part of a communitywide intervention effort.[1] While social workers, psychologists, and psychiatrists provide a large portion of treatment—particularly for long-term contacts—their colleagues in hospitals, clinics, and schools may be involved in the initial stages of crisis intervention when problems of abuse are uncovered. Few violent families come directly to the attention of specialized treatment teams, and many communities do not even have such teams. Persons involved in the initial uncovering and treatment of abuse include:

- Police
- Probation officers
- Social workers
- Teachers
- Physicians
- Nurses
- Clergy
- Volunteers in human service programs
- Child care workers
- Psychologists
- Marriage, family, and child counselors
- Psychiatrists
- Mental health workers

While many of these have received specialized training in abuse intervention via educational cirricula, workshops, or in-service training programs, there is much to be done in educating a wider range of people about the dynamics of family violence and its treatment. With training in basic communication skills, many community helpers could become more effective, aware, and sensitive instruments for introducing families in need to specialized intervention programs and the broader treatment network.

EXPLORING ATTITUDES TOWARD FAMILY VIOLENCE

Personal attitudes and feelings greatly influence one's response to other people and their problems. In situations that involve battering, neglect, or sexual abuse, attitudes can make a critical difference in the kind of service and treatment victims and offenders receive. The successful outcome of intervention efforts depends, in large part, on the ability to acknowledge, examine, and deal honestly with individual attitudes and feelings about violence in families.

Many individuals have mixed feelings about spouse assault, child abuse, incest, abuse of elderly parents, and other forms of family violence. Society has the ideals of loving and supportive families, devoted and understanding parents, and gentle and well-behaved children. People tend to cling tenaciously to these ideals because they evoke basic human needs for love, security, and nurturance. Images of stressed, violent families are contrary to one's idealized fantasies and are, therefore, threatening on unconscious as well as conscious levels. Feelings about the problem of family violence are further aroused by the emotion-laden terminology of the field: child murderer, wife beater, child molester. Powerful and sometimes overwhelming feelings, both positive and negative, produce a climate where biases, prejudices, and value judgments interfere with supportive intervention.[2]

How do helpers develop the means of handling their feelings? The first step is to recognize and acknowledge the feelings that occur. The initial reaction toward persons who abuse is typically outrage, triggered by the reports of what they have done to their child or spouse. Justice and Justice point out that a certain amount of intense anger is natural when one hears about an adult who assaults a defenseless child, but continuous outrage is not. Continuous rage probably has its roots in other feelings, such as wanting to deny that a parent can be angry enough to abuse a child. People prefer to believe that parents always love their children, but almost everyone knows that children can be exasperating and incite fierce anger.[3]

Similarly, husbands and wives, brothers and sisters, parents and grandparents can infuriate others when they fail to meet certain demands or live up to personal expectations. Hostile and negative feelings are common; however, they are often totally unconscious. One way to deny that these hostile feelings exist is to feel different from or superior to those persons who strike out at their families and to label them deviant, sick, crazy, or unfit.[3]

A similar process of denial occurs as people struggle to confront their feelings about incest. It is not uncommon for an adult to experience sexual feelings for a child, and yet abhorrence of these feelings causes one to strongly deny them. Sometimes very warm and physically affectionate fathers, and mothers will discourage their children's attempts to cuddle as they grow into adolescence. Discomfort with sexual feelings toward children may be expressed in a powerful taboo against even discussing the subject. Thus, people may be overwhelmed with hostility toward parents or siblings who act on their sexual feelings toward a child. One therapist wrote about the difficulty of maintaining an attitude of awareness and acceptance.[4] She found it easy to maintain an attitude of acceptance with the child and mother of the first incestuous family she treated. But when she prepared herself for the session with the father, by reading the lurid details of the father's sexual activities with the daughter, which included mutual oral copulation and sodomy at the age of ten, the compassionate, therapeutic attitude completely dissipated.

People who cannot work through their intense feelings of outrage cannot be effective helpers. They will tend to punish or to seek a "cure" or perhaps even give up on the client as being beyond help.

Caution must be taken to avoid the other extreme of rationalizing the behavior of abusive parents: "They couldn't help it. They were abused themselves as children and never learned how to become good parents."[3] Such a position is no more helpful than rejection of the persons involved. While it is important to understand the stressors and dynamics of abusing families, these stressors and dynamics do not justify their actions. Justice and Justice state that it is possible to understand how abuse occurs without condoning or dismissing it.[3] Adults who inflict violence on children must learn that they will be expected to take responsibility for themselves even if they have not done so in the past. They are not children, and no matter what their parents did to them, they now have adult responsibilities. In working with abusive persons, then, it is important to accept the *feelings* but not the behavior.

In essence, self-awareness and insight into one's feelings about family violence will help in becoming a more effective helper. Emotional hang-ups hinder the work of intervention and only add to the stresses of the families served. More positive attitudes free clinicians to offer clients a more sensitive approach. It is hoped that any initial feelings of anger will pass quickly and be replaced by an understanding of the family's pain as well as by an optimism that change is possible for them.

EFFECTIVE COMMUNICATION SKILLS

Effective helping is built on the abilities of clear communication and keen observation. In addition, the qualities of empathy, genuineness, and warmth are basic to an effective interview, counseling session, and psychotherapeutic process. The importance of these fundamental characteristics is supported by years of research.[5] The discussion that follows focuses on some of the skills that enable human service workers to more competently serve their clients. These skills include therapeutic listening (physical and psychological attending), encouragement to talk, nonjudgmental acceptance, empathy, genuineness, honesty, concreteness, and the use of questions and confrontation. The particular relevance of these skills to work with troubled families is emphasized.

Therapeutic Listening

Anderson underscored the importance of therapeutic listening in work with abusing families because of their predisposition to certain problem characteristics.[6]

Effective listening is a valuable means for altering an abusive person's chronic feelings of low self-esteem. Frequently, abusive parents and spouses were abused themselves as children and subjected to harsh punishment and psychological trauma. They are extremely vulnerable, insecure, and lack the basic feeling of being loved, which develops the inner strength to deal with life crises.

Good listening skills can give these clients the sense that someone genuinely cares about them and that, despite their problems, they are valuable persons worthy of respect. People who are helped to feel better about themselves are then more willing and able to have richer relationships with their children and partners.

Therapeutic listening allows abusive persons the chance to express their own pain and conflicts and to sort out feelings that have them trapped in destructive behaviors. Lacking the skills necessary to develop rewarding relationships with other persons, they remain defensive, isolated, and fearful of being severely judged for what they have done. For many of these persons, it may be one of the few times in their lives that someone has truly heard them out and allowed them to express their own hurt and frustration.

The helper's listening skills may positively influence the abusive person's ability to listen to and respond appropriately to others. In this regard, the counselor models good communication for persons who most probably have lacked positive parental role models in their lives. Clients are indirectly taught more functional skills to replace their dysfunctional and often destructive patterns of the past.

Egan states that the skills needed by a counselor can be summed up in the word "attending."[7] Counselors must let the client know by posture, eye contact, and relative closeness that they are "with" the client and "available" during the session. This behavior constitutes physical attending. Next, the counselor must actively listen to the client. Active listening involves perceiving both the verbal and nonverbal communications of the client. While verbal messages involve the client's choice of words, nonverbal messages are carried in the client's tone of voice, silences, pauses, facial expressions, gestures, eye contact, and posture.

PHYSICAL ATTENDING

Physical attending means doing certain things in the session and not doing others. Of primary importance is clearing one's mind of any preoccupations, either personal or related to the client. Physical attending may include arranging the physical environment so that the room is as quiet and private as possible and taking the time to have all incoming telephone calls intercepted. These seemingly minor details assume greater importance when one considers the particular dynamics of abusing families. Their extreme fragility, vulnerability, distrust of others, and feelings of low self-worth often cause them to misinterpret social stimuli and to perceive others as not really wanting to help them at all. Helpers should adopt a posture of involvement by facing the clients squarely, maintaining good eye contact (without intimidating stares), maintaining an "open" posture of uncrossed arms and legs, leaning in toward the client, and remaining relatively relaxed. A counselor who conveys a stern, controlled, cold, and aloof posture is apt to intimidate clients and heighten their anxiety and defensiveness about the discovery of abuse in their family. The skilled helper is aware of the subtle nuances of body language and uses this knowledge to ease interview tension, convey an atmosphere of trust and genuine interest, and encourage the client to risk seeking help for the family.[7]

PSYCHOLOGICAL ATTENDING: ACTIVE LISTENING

Active listening is a twofold process that involves "listening" to the client's verbal and nonverbal behavior. The effective listener pays attention not only to the words and sentences of the client but also to subtleties such as the client's choice of words, syntax, and especially to what the client chooses *not* to say. All these facets of communication provide important clues to the client's meaning and make it easier to see the situation through the client's eyes. Abusive persons can be particularly unskilled in communicating how they feel; this is part of the reason why they tend to respond physically to frustration and pent-up anger. Consequently, workers who desire to help abusing families must train themselves to "read between the lines." This lack of skill is also the reason why attending to nonverbal communication is so valuable. The eyes, face, and body are extremely communicative, and an alert helper can learn much by noticing a tensed fist, a rigid jaw, or eyes filling up with tears.

"Minimal Encourages to Talk"

Egan cites "minimal encourages to talk"[7] as another aspect of attending behavior, one that encourages clients to explore their feelings and behavior. Examples include such things as "um-hmm," repetition of one or two of the client's words, one-word questions,

nods of the head, and a variety of gestures and body postures (leaning forward or moving closer). Egan views these expressions as interjections or signs given by helpers to indicate that they are attending. These signs are particularly useful in interventions with abusive families because, as stated before, such clients tend to be more withdrawn, incommunicative, fearful, and distrustful than other persons seen in community agencies. Any tool that helps these clients feel supported and listened to and that encourages them to risk sharing their feelings is certainly well worth developing as part of one's repertoire of skills.

OTHER SKILLS

Nonjudgmental Acceptance

It is difficult to maintain a nonjudgmental acceptance when working with cases involving incest or battering, but to be effective, one must try to avoid moral and value judgments, preconceived ideas, biases, and assumptions. Abusive persons are threatened by the intervention of outsiders and fear, understandably, the legal and social consequences of their actions. A nonjudgmental attitude projected by the counselor invites openness and increased risk taking on the part of the client. When painful issues must be raised during a session (and they inevitably surface), clients are more apt to respond candidly if they feel the listener is nonjudgmental.[6]

Empathy

Conveying empathy presents another aspect of facilitative interaction. It involves responding to clients in a way that shows the counselor has listened and understands how clients feel and what they are saying about themselves. Empathy is, in a sense, the ability to see the client's world from the client's frame of reference rather than one's own. The helper must not only understand but also communicate understanding.[7]

To achieve a sense of empathy, counselors must allow themselves to walk in the shoes of the client. They must disengage personal values, expectations, and judgments and allow themselves to listen with a kind of "third ear" so that they not only hear what the client says but also experience what the client feels. The counselor sifts through and sorts the words, feelings, and moods of the client in an attempt to grasp the deepest meaning. "You seem to be saying . . . . Is this correct?" "I am hearing you say that . . . . Am I right?" By checking out personal impressions and interpretations with the client, the counselor is able to zero in on the client's inner world.

Genuineness

According to Schulman, the meaning of genuineness involves two closely related concepts: congruence (when one's words and actions correspond) and authenticity (when one is oneself, not a phony).[8]

Speaking and behaving congruently is important for establishing trust between counselor and client. Clients will easily tune in to the true attitude of a therapist who verbalizes concern and interest but whose frequent checking of the clock and out-of-focus looks indicate a lack of true involvement. Genuineness also implies sincere intention to follow up on commitments. Anderson wrote that one female client was frustrated when the listener's promise of follow-up involvement did not materialize; feeling that the therapist was feigning interest increased her wariness of future involvement with professionals.[6]

A battering or battered client will also respond more openly to helpers who are natural in their presentation of themselves, who avoid intimidating clients with their role and authority as counselors, and who approach

clients at a human being-to-human being level.

Honesty

During the initial phase of intervention, most people will have many fearful questions about what will happen to them and their family and will feel angry and powerless over the situation. Being forthright and honest with them is the most productive way to handle their questions and feelings and gain their trust. It may be necessary, for example, to tell the parents of a reportedly abused child that the law mandates filing an abuse report and to explain to them what steps are likely to be taken. Their feelings of anger and frustration can be worked through if the helper conveys a sincere interest in them and assures them of the helper's support throughout the entire process that will follow.[4] Honest answers, presented in a sensitive and supportive manner and appropriately timed, can go a long way in building trust with clients.

Concreteness

An additional task of the counselor is to ground the interview process in concrete feelings and concrete behaviors. The task is twofold: (1) to aid the client in putting words to pent-up feelings and to focus in on specifics of the problem and (2) to be sure that the counselor's language is not vague or filled with generalities and psychological jargon.[7]

These clients are typically overwhelmed and rendered helpless by their life problems. By keeping the interview concrete, the counselor is able to elicit information from the client and help the client look at the situation in a more focused and behavior-specific way. For example, a mother explodes in anger at her son who has soiled his pants at suppertime, and she punishes him by placing his hand on a hot stove. The mother's tearful admission, "I just got so angry I couldn't help it," leaves her feeling guilty and powerless over her behavior. Gently encouraging her to explore the incident more concretely may help her remember her feelings at the time and see the antecedents of her behavior more clearly: "It had been a hectic day, and I got dinner started late. Then all of a sudden there was Johnny crying because he had wet his pants. I knew I'd have to drop everything to clean him up and that my husband would be home any minute—tired and ready to yell at me because supper was late. I blamed it all on Johnny." A client's ability to connect feelings and behavior will develop slowly, but a helper's skill in using concreteness will facilitate the process. When clients can begin to make small connections between behavior and feelings or examine smaller pieces of their life situations, they can begin to deal more effectively with their problems.

QUESTIONS AND CONFRONTATION

Questions

In some types of interviews with abusive persons, it may be necessary to gather data on the nature of the physical or sexual abuse, the perpetrator, and the family history. Workers from specific agencies such as the police or hospital may be involved in documenting the nature of physical injuries or gathering evidence for prosecution of the offender. This type of interviewing is not within the scope of this chapter.

In the type of initial interviews under discussion, the use of questions must be limited and focus only on immediate issues, such as assessing the potential for recurring abuse. The central purpose of the contact is building rapport with the clients and engaging them in the therapeutic process. Listening, rather than questioning, is the task at hand.

If some questions are necessary, it is important to frame them in a genuinely suppor-

tive and concerned way. Some questions are too threatening at this stage of the intervention and should be avoided. For example, the interviewer should resist the desire to find out who actually hurt the child in cases of child abuse.[9] Newberger[10] states that the third degree or its gentlemanly equivalent often hardens the defense or promotes more primitive defenses—resistance to talking about the problem at all or angry outbursts directed at the interviewer or at the hospital. Such defenses limit both the process of gathering information and the prospects for continuing helpful professional relationships. A good interview technique allows parents and child to maintain the integrity of ego and family as it is in each case.

Questions, then, must be used appropriately and be weighed against such factors as the purpose of the interview, the role of the counselor, and the timing of the issue. Even the most painful of issues can be positively explored at the right time, in the right place, and with the right person.

Confrontation

Confrontation, like questioning, is a therapeutic technique that should be used with caution in the initial stages of work with troubled families. In general, confrontation is used by the helper to challenge discrepancies, distortions, games, and smokescreens in the client's life and personal interactions.[7] Confrontation is necessary and positive if it helps people develop the kind of insight and self-awareness that leads to positive changes in behavior.[7]

Accusations and critical questions stated in a disbelieving way are not facilitative confrontations and may be devastating to clients. Skepticism and sarcasm will only confirm their belief that they will once more be criticized and punished and that no one can understand or help them.[4] Newberger writes that denial is a prominent ego defense in almost all abusing parents, and the bizarre stories about how their children got their injuries should not be taken as intentional falsifications.[10] These odd accounts often tell how profoundly distressing it is for parents to acknowledge that they inflicted an injury or failed to protect a child from someone else's doing so.

A useful approach is to accept the inconsistencies or blatantly phony stories, for the moment. Often, after many months of treatment, abusive persons may admit their feelings of guilt and the fact that the injury was inflicted by them.[4]

Impediments to Therapeutic Intervention

Anderson cited the following as blocks and hinderances to the process of attending to the client:[6]

OCCUPATIONAL REALITIES

Severe time pressures, large caseloads that necessitate short cuts, the need to obtain information rapidly, and budget restrictions are examples of occupational realities that can hamper the treatment process.

MULTIDIMENSIONAL PROBLEMS

Frequently, clients who come to the attention of community workers for problems of abuse or neglect are also suffering from other stresses—unemployment, illness, financial crisis, housing problems, and the like. Violence or incest may be only one of many problems for these families, a factor that makes them extremely difficult to treat and complicates successful intervention. The counselor may not be able to provide all the kinds of services the family needs. Clients may become frustrated with the helper's failure to supply all their needs or may make demands that the helper cannot meet. It is, therefore, useful, at an early stage, to be clear with families about the kinds of services one can and cannot offer. An honest explanation, coupled

with a sincere willingness to help through referral and advocacy, can do much to build trust and lessen clients' frustration with social service bureaucracies.

BURNOUT

Intervention in these troubled families is demanding, frustrating, and sometimes overwhelming. "Burnout" is the tendency to become so overwhelmed by occupational stress that one becomes less effective in one's job. Signs of burnout vary among personnel, but common ones include increased physical illness, decreased interest and involvement in work, pessimism over job purpose, unrealistic anger at clients, and withdrawl from peers. Burned-out professionals are frequently too needy themselves to be effective helpers to their clients. Recognition of burnout in its early stages is important; so are building strong peer and family supports, quality supervision, and occasional "time out."

SEVERE PATHOLOGY

An additional important impediment to therapeutic intervention is the presence of severe pathology. Approximately 10 to 15 percent of abusive parents (and probably abusive spouses as well) have psychiatric diagnoses that make their potential for treatment very poor. These persons include those who are psychotic, particularly paranoid schizophrenics; those who are severely depressed; those who have sociopathic personality disorders; and people with severe alcoholism or drug addiction. Effective helpers must recognize the limits of their expertise and rely on specially trained professionals to continue the intervention effort with these clients.

A NOTE ON REFERRALS AND ADVOCACY

Optimal treatment of abusing families is a group effort, and no professional should attempt to manage such a family alone. Most programs or agencies, with rare exceptions, do not have professional counselors on staff. They are staffed instead by volunteers, para-professionals, or professionals with other kinds of expertise (police, teachers, lawyers, nurses). Therefore, it is extremely important that helpers who are "counseling" be properly trained and be aware of their *limitations* and the restraints of their role. Treatment for violent families is a long-term process to be handled by professional agencies. Appropriate counseling activities for helpers and volunteers include providing support, client advocacy, and referrals; establishing trust; and helping clients explore options, make decisions, and set goals.[11]

It is extremely important that every community helper be aware of the local options and resources that are available. Referrals will vary according to the helper's role. A teacher who is the confidant of a mother admitting child abuse will have a different role in the referral process than a physician who is part of a child abuse team. Potential referrals include hospitals and doctors, police, legal services, welfare agencies, counseling and guidance services, housing and rental agencies, employment agencies, and child care facilities. It is necessary to have up-to-date information for each of these organizations on basics such as operating hours, age restrictions, socioeconomic eligibility requirements, number of available beds, scope of services, and any pertinent data that will save clients in crisis from the "agency shuffle."

Gentzler believes that it is the responsibility of a particular program or agency to monitor the referral agencies and persons (as much as possible) to insure that they are knowledgeable about and sympathetic to the problems of abusing families.[11] Women or men who are being supported and encouraged by a helper can be devastated by an outside agency where they receive implicit or explicit negative messages: "You are a sick person for having abused your child," or

"You deserve the beatings that your husband is giving you." Knowledge about community resources, their policies, their limitations, and their personnel is integral to successful referrals. Talking to other persons (staff and clients) about their experiences with a given agency is helpful. Gentzler also suggests that programs include measures that simultaneously educate the community and gather information by having personnel visit agencies and individuals, inform them about the program, and indirectly find out what their attitudes are; the most painful way to get this information is from personal mistakes, the feedback one gets from a client who sought help and got criticism and verbal abuse instead.[11] When referral to a nonsympathetic agency is unavoidable, a counselor should prepare the clients as to what they may expect and how to handle the situation so that the consequences may be less disturbing.

IN CONCLUSION

The task of establishing and maintaining a relationship with families troubled by violence, sexual abuse, or neglect is difficult, but experience has shown that it can be done. The quality of the initial contact with the family is crucial and will set the tone of the relationship.[12] Caring, empathy, and development of effective communication skills are critical aspects of therapeutic intervention with these persons.

Helpers must recognize the need of these individuals to discuss their worries, anxieties, and anger at the events that have already taken place. The hospitalization of a child or spouse, the question of abuse or incest, the intervention of many new people are all most distressing. A person who empathizes with the pain and fear they feel and is able to help them discuss the realities of their situation will be most helpful to them.[4] The skilled helper can provide information, help them face reality, and encourage movement toward change. The clients will experience being accepted and being listened to and understood by someone who cares—a rare event in their lives.

In his book, *The New Professional,* Dugger summarizes the ingredients that contribute to successful helping relationships:[13]

- Know *why* you want to help people. Motives may vary from philanthropy to unconsciously working through one's own problems.
- Know yourself and how you feel about the people you help.
- Really mean to do what you say you will do; keep commitments.
- Have sufficient knowledge, understanding, and acceptance of the people you want to help.
- See life through their eyes.
- Have respect for them and their strengths.
- Develop communication skills.
- Let your clients tell you what they feel, what they need, and what they want from you.
- Be willing to listen and to learn.
- Involve local community resources in your treatment plan right from the start.
- Work within the framework of the setting you have chosen.
- Recognize that other people and groups are available for help.
- Be able to receive criticism.
- Evaluate what you have done and be open to change.
- Know how long you are needed.
- Really care.

During the initial crisis period, the role of the helper (policeman, social worker, teacher, nurse) is the key to engagement. Once a crisis is over (hospitalization, separation, placement in a shelter), the role of the helper will probably be a very secondary one in the long-range treatment of the family. However, if the helper has managed to demonstrate a spirit of caring for the family and,

thus, has made it possible for them to accept help from other therapists, that contribution to treatment will have been a significant one.[14]

Finally, it is important to note that new helpers are apt to experience much frustration and disillusionment. Before assuming responsibility in working with victims of violence, new helpers should read some basic texts and articles, attend lectures and workshops, and be exposed to in-service training to acquire general background information about rape and family violence and their treatment.

Rape is a violent crime which must be addressed in any discussion of social violence. All the communication and therapeutic skills discussed here are applicable to work with rape victims. However, the special needs of the traumatized rape victim must be considered separately (see chapters 14–17).

Most victims of attempted rape as well as victims of complete, forcible rape develop a pattern of symptoms that has been termed "rape trauma syndrome."[15] This trauma syndrome is a crisis reaction to a life-threatening situation, and victims usually experience an acute phase of disorganization of their lifestyle: inability to cope with homemaking or parenting tasks, disruption in or termination of employment, or disruption in academic studies, for example. Other reactions may include psychophysiological and hypochondriacal symptoms, disabling fear, fear of or lack of interest in sexual activities, nightmares, and phobias.[16]

REFERENCES

1. Pollack C, Steele B: A therapeutic approach to the parents, in Kempe CH, Helfer RE (eds): *Helping the Battered Child and His Family.* Philadelphia, JB Lippincott Co, 1972, pp 3–21.

2. Ebeling NB: Thoughts on intervention, in Ebeling NB, Hill DA (eds): *Child Abuse: Interven-*

tion and Treatment. Acton, Mass, Publishing Sciences Group Inc, 1975, pp 3-9.

3. Justice B, Justice R: *The Abusing Family.* New York, Human Sciences Press, 1976.

4. Kempe CH, Kempe RS: *Child Abuse.* Cambridge, Mass, Harvard University Press, 1978.

5. Truax CB, Carkhuff RR: *Toward Effective Counseling and Psychotherapy.* Chicago, Aldine Publishing Co, 1967.

6. Anderson GD: Enhancing listening skills for work with abusing parents. *Soc Casework,* **60**:602–608, 1979.

7. Egan G: *The Skilled Helper: A Model for Systematic Helping and Interpersonal Relating.* Monterey, Calif, Brooks/Cole Publishing Co, 1975.

8. Schulman ED: *Intervention in Human Services,* ed 2. St Louis, The CV Mosby Co, 1978.

9. Schneider C, et al: Interviewing the parents, in Kempe CH, Helfer RE (eds): *Helping the Battered Child and His Family.* Philadelphia, JB Lippincott Co, 1972, pp 55-65.

10. Newberger EH: A physician's perspective on the interdisciplinary management of child abuse, in Ebeling NB, Hill DA (eds): *Child Abuse: Intervention and Treatment.* Acton, Mass, Publishing Sciences Group Inc, 1975, pp 61-67.

11. Gentzler R: Counseling, in *The Abused . . . Pennsylvania Coalition Against Domestic Violence.* Advocacy Programs for Abuse Victims, 1978.

12. D'Agostino P: Strains and stresses in protective services, in Ebeling NB, Hill DA (eds): *Child Abuse: Intervention and Treatment.* Acton, Mass, Publishing Sciences Group Inc, 1975, pp 41-45.

13. Dugger JG: *The New Professional: Introduction for the Human Services Mental Health Worker.* Monterey, Calif, Brooks/Cole Publishing Co, 1975.

14. McDonald AE: The collaborative aspect of the hospital social worker's role, in Ebeling NB, Hill DA (eds): *Child Abuse: Intervention and Treatment.* Acton, Mass, Publishing Sciences Group Inc, 1975, pp 55-59.

15. Burgess A, Holmstrom L: Rape trauma syndrome, *Psychiatry* **131**:981–986, 1974a.

16. Walker MJ, Brodsky SL: *Sexual Assault.* Lexington, Mass, DC Health & Co, 1976.

SUGGESTED READINGS

Helfer RE, Kempe CH (eds): *Child Abuse and Neglect: The Family and the Community.* Cambridge, Mass, Ballinger Publishing Co, 1976.

Schmitt BD (ed): *The Child Protection Team Handbook; A Multidisciplinary Approach to Managing Child Abuse and Neglect.* New York, Garland STPM Press, 1978.

Shapiro D: *Parents and Protectors: A Study in Child Abuse and Neglect.* Washington, DC, Research Center, Child Welfare League of America, 1979.

7

EDUCATIONAL APPROACHES TO MANAGEMENT AND PREVENTION OF FAMILY VIOLENCE

Jill Waterman, Ph.D.
Janet Young, M.D.

Several factors have emerged from investigations of child abuse and other forms of family violence. Depending upon the theoretical position, these factors lead to different methods of intervention and prevention. There seems to be reasonable evidence or theoretical underpinnings for four factors: (1) adults who engage in family violence tend to have experienced violence, neglect, or other forms of pathological parenting in their families of origin;[1-5] (2) there is some correlation between types of family violence; there tends to be a higher than expected relationship between child abuse and marital violence,[5,6] and there is a correlation between the use of physical aggression and verbal aggression within the family;[7] (3) abusive families tend to be socially isolated and lack support systems to call upon in times of stress;[2,3,8-10] (4) abusing parents have poor knowledge of norms of child development and have unrealistic expectations of their children.[3,8,11,12]

MODELS OF FAMILY VIOLENCE

The main theoretical models are psychodynamic, sociological, and social learning.

Some models combine different aspects of these three.

Psychodynamic Models

Psychodynamic models include both descriptive and dynamic formulations. Descriptive approaches include personality descriptions of abusing adults and diagnostic labeling of child or spouse abusers. Mere descriptions add little to the understanding of the mechanisms of family violence,[13] and diagnostic labeling has not been very fruitful since most physical and sexual abusers are nonpsychotic.[14,15] Psychodynamic explanations tend to center on the poor parenting that abusers received themselves. Because of a lack of "empathic mothering,"[1] the child never learns basic trust in people and does not have basic needs met. Parents place unrealistic expectations on a child, and the child may develop a poor self-concept as a result. As adults, the abusers have many unmet needs for nurturance, and they place these needs on the child in a reversal of roles. The child can not gratify the parents' overwhelming needs and is, therefore, abused. In addition, parents may demonstrate impaired impulse control because of exposure in early childhood to harsh punishment.[5]

SPOUSE ABUSE

A similar mechanism can be postulated to explain spouse abuse. Each spouse may have tremendous unmet needs, because of inadequate or abusive parenting, and may strike out at the other spouse when that partner fails to meet the unrealistic demands. Steele points out that abusers tend to marry people with a similar history of inadequate parenting.[1] Justice and Justice speak of the shifting symbiosis and fusion in the marriages of child abusers where each spouse seeks to be taken care of and nurtured by the other.[8] Since neither spouse's needs can be completely met, the parents turn to the child and attack the child when the youngster fails to meet the parents' needs. The child is the scapegoat; however, the parents may, at times, strike out more directly at the spouse who is perceived as frustrating and withholding.

Dynamics in spouse abuse may also relate to spouse selection.[16] Because of a history of abuse or lack of nurturance, the woman may seek protection and caring and feel she is most likely to receive this from a strong, "macho" male. However, the male's own insecurity causes him to rigidly adhere to traditional sex roles, exhibit a hostile-dependent style toward his wife, and hit her. The wife is also likely to be locked in to traditional sex roles including a passive-aggressive manner of expressing anger. Social sex-stereotyping may perpetuate a complex mythology of wife abuse that intensifies the victim's denial and need to protect her husband and to manage at the expense of her self-esteem and autonomy.[17,18]

Pfouts[19] uses a scheme based on the exchange theory of Thibaut and Kelly to explain the dynamics of wife abuse. This theory asserts that behavioral outcomes depend on the satisfaction the individual experiences in the existing situation relative to the satisfaction offered by available alternatives. In the case of wife abuse, the outcome involves comparing the payoffs of marriage (high versus low) with the payoffs of alternatives (high versus low) and results in four basic coping responses.

When a payoff of marriage is low, but the payoff of the alternative is perceived as lower, the wife becomes a "trapped victim." She remains in this seemingly intolerable position for a variety of reasons: her experiences in childhood provided a strong role model for her to be a victim, cultural or economical factors, and low self-concept. These women have a high incidence of anxiety and seldom seek help; as many as one-fourth of their children may have emotional disturbances.

When the payoffs of marriage are high, and those of available alternatives are low, the abused wife is an angry aggressor, a contributor to as well as a victim of marital abuse. Many also abuse their children. They are frequently impulsive, immature, and alcoholic, much like the men to whom they are attracted. Their violence seems to stem from childhood socialization to violence, and such women seldom seek help. As many as one-half of their children may be emotionally disturbed. Such women are difficult to treat as they seem to live in a violence "high."

When the payoffs of marriage are low, and the alternatives are high, there is early disengagement. Such women typically have better employment potential, and the strong support from relatives suggests that those from nonabusive backgrounds are more likely to find abuse unacceptable and to seek help early.

Finally, if the payoffs of marriage are high, but those of the alternatives higher, there is a pattern of reluctant or late disengagement. These women tend to come from the first group (victims or self-punishers) and never from the second (aggressors) and finally decide that there cannot be "one more chance."

INCEST

While incest is clearly a form of abuse, perceptions of the violence involved vary greatly. Sometimes sexual abuse within the family is seen as a loving act by family members; in other cases it is viewed as the ultimate violent act. Most theoretical explanations of familial sexual abuse use a psychodynamic framework; instead of the emphasis on the individual's dynamics described previously for physical abusers, the focus is on family dynamics that lead to incest.[14,20,21] Father-daughter incest is by far the most common type reported,[15,22] and the dynamics involved are generally quite different from the patterns seen in physical abuse or wife battering. A few multiproblem families in which incest and physical abuse coexist probably follow patterns similar to physically abusive families.

While various distinctions occur among incestuous families,[15,23] the most common dynamic appears to involve a married father who is concerned about his sexual identity and sexually estranged from his dependent and, perhaps, depressed wife. The mother may unconsciously collude in the incest and abdicate her role of wife to her teenaged daughter in the classical role reversal found in other types of abuse.[14,24,25] Almost all researchers stress the importance of looking at all three members of a triad and considering the incest "a family affair."[26] Conditions that can lead to father-daughter incest are the following:[27] (1) the daughter is the central female figure in the home and takes over some aspects of the mother's role; (2) the parents are sexually incompatible; (3) the father is unwilling to look for a sexual partner outside the nuclear family; (4) the mother unconsciously fosters or condones her daughter as-

suming a sexual role with the father. In a study of 12 fathers convicted for incest, the most common psychological findings were nonpsychotic paranoid traits and unconscious homosexual strivings.[28] Others have reported high rates of alcoholism in the fathers and depression in the mothers.[25]

According to the National Center on Child Abuse and Neglect, several factors influence the severity of the child's reaction to incest.[29] The effects appear to be more serious if the victim is an adolescent or preadolescent, rather than a young child; physical violence or the threat of such is used; and the incident or relationship is handled insensitively by police and legal or medical personnel.

Implications for intervention follow clearly from the psychodynamic model of family violence. The adults need psychotherapy to help them deal with their own deprived and unfulfilling childhoods. They also need a nurturing relationship with an accepting, gratifying adult who can, in some aspects, parent them.[5,30] Individual psychotherapy or casework, lay therapy programs, and nurturing residential treatment for the adult are interventions compatible with this model. Treatment for incest almost always involves a family systems approach to psychotherapy,[21,29,31] and individual counseling may or may not be done within this framework. Prevention of abuse can come only from breaking the generational cycle of poor parenting that leads to adult violence that leads to poor parenting, and so on.

Sociological Models

Several investigators have postulated that environmental stresses such as poverty, large family size, and unemployment are the causative factors in family violence. Gil hypothesized that some of these factors lead families with little education and low socioeconomic status to use more corporal punishment than middle-class families.[9] While family violence is more prevalent (or is reported more often) among lower-class families, the phenomenon certainly occurs in all social classes.[13] Gil hypothesized that the increased concrete and psychological stresses and frustrations of poverty may be the mediators that link poverty and child abuse.[32] Intervention strategies stemming from this approach tend to be societal and preventive. They include elimination of poverty; national health service; and readily accessible homemaker, day-care, and family planning services.[9]

A second model attributes causative power to the unfortunate legitimization of physical violence as a method for socialization and problem solving. On television as well as in real life, Americans are exposed to violence as an appropriate way to resolve conflict.[13] Violence within the family is likely to be seen as acceptable by family members and by society. Consequently, the family serves as a training ground for violence. Violence within the family is often justified as necessary for moral development; parents feel that a child *needs* and *deserves* to be hit in order to learn a lesson.[33,34] Two-thirds of the educators, police, and clergy questioned in a survey condoned physical discipline by spanking as a proper method for child discipline.[35] A culturally approved, permissive attitude toward the use of force in parent-child interactions and the lack of legal prohibitions against this type of violence are probably central factors in the high incidence of child abuse in America.[9] The same tacit approval of abuse exists for spouse abuse.[36]

According to this sociological perspective, intervention must come through public education and law. Systematic public education and attempts to change families' attitudes toward physical violence as a problem-solving and child-rearing technique have been advocated. A preventive program would include education for family life in public schools that stresses the use of alternative methods of child rearing that do not involve physical force. A somewhat different approach would strengthen legal prohibitions against family violence and outlaw corporal punishment in institutions such as schools and residential treatment centers.[9]

Social Learning Models

In the social learning model, family violence occurs because hitting is the only method known by family members to control behavior. Parents who use physical punishment provide their children with an aggressive model which the children imitate.[37] Since parents are powerful and control many reinforcements, they are highly effective models for a variety of behaviors, including aggression.[12] Because the child has seen and experienced the use of aggression as a way to express anger and control others, the same behavior is used for the same purposes when the child becomes an adult. Additionally, experiencing physical punishment in the home is associated with high levels of aggression outside the home during both childhood and adulthood.[38] It is well established that the majority of abusing adults were abused themselves as children.[1,3] Using the type of discipline one was exposed to in childhood perpetuates the cycle of child abuse and family violence, and the inconsistent discipline given by most abusive parents tends to perpetuate the undesirable behavior of the child through the learning principle of partial reinforcement.[13] Abusive parents may be predisposed to be abusive because of behaviors they learn in their own childhood: uncontrolled aggression, avoidance of social interaction, fear of authority, and low self-esteem.[12]

A second model of social learning focuses on the expectations of the parents. Abusive parents frequently do not know the basic stages of child development and what behaviors are to be expected at different ages,[11,39] and they tend to either underreact or overreact to their child's behavior.[3] Consequently, parents tend to expect behaviors from a child that the child is developmentally incapable of and then physically punish the child when the child fails to perform. These ineffective methods of discipline cause the child to continue undesired behaviors and, in turn prevent the parent from feeling more positive toward the child. The result is a cycle of abuse that promotes undesirable behavior that elicits more abuse.

Educational approaches to both treatment and prevention cover two main areas. First, parents are educated about appropriate behaviors and expectations for children of various ages and developmental stages. Second, methods other than physical punishment are explored as ways to decrease undesirable behaviors and increase desired behaviors in children. A third possible focus for intervention involves teaching techniques of anger control to violent adults.[13] Educational approaches based on the model of social learning are probably compatible with most theories of family violence. Psychodynamic theorists would agree that, in addition to personality change in abusive adults, changes in methods of child rearing and conflict resolution are needed to prevent further abuse or violence. Justice and Justice commented that unless parents learn what a child needs at different stages of development and how the child's behavior can be managed without the use of physical force, all the therapy in the world is unlikely to prevent the recurrence of abuse.[8] Similarly, sociological models suggest educational approaches that advocate alternative child-rearing methods that do not involve physical violence.

There are two educational approaches to intervention in cases of abuse: primary, those aimed at prevention, and secondary, those instituted after abuse has occurred. These approaches can also be considered in terms of the person who is educated: the abuser or potential abuser (parent or spouse), the abused (child or spouse), professionals working with children or families, or the community at large. In this chapter, examples of specific approaches will focus primarily on child abuse because of the paucity of literature on educational approaches to marital and sexual abuse.

SECONDARY EDUCATIONAL APPROACHES

Approaches That Focus on the Personal Needs of the Abusive Adult

Treatment of abusive families usually involves learning and education since it provides individuals an opportunity to learn about themselves, about what motivates their behavior, and about relationships. Such opportunities are imperative for abusive persons who wish to alter their behavior.

CASEWORK AND INDIVIDUAL THERAPY

Casework and individual psychotherapy have been the traditional modalities available to the abusive parent (or spouse). However, these have certain limitations. Individual treatment is slow and often inefficient, and professionals frequently do not like working with abusive parents. Provision of both a nurturing role and parent modeling are extremely important in working with abusive adults. Individual therapy provides adequate nurturance but limited parent modeling, an equally important part of adult rehabilitation.

THE LAY THERAPIST

Because of these shortcomings of traditional therapy, Kempe and his associates developed the concept of the lay therapist.[40] This concept is based on the premise that some people who have been adequately parented are naturally able to provide nurturance. The lay therapist goes into the home and provides a warm parent model for the abusing parent; the therapist provides the parenting and nurturing that the abusive parent never had. The primary focus of lay therapy is to provide nurturance rather than to facilitate insight. Objective assessment of this type of program is obviously difficult, but subjective reports have mentioned parents' growth in ability to cope with and enjoy life as well as in relationships to their children. A study by the Berkeley Planning Associates of 11 federally funded demonstration projects showed that clients who received lay treatment as a supplement to other services were most successful in improving their daily functioning and in reducing the tendency for future abuse and neglect.[41] Although lay therapy was considered most effective because lay workers have more time and energy than professionals to devote to the family, can help reduce the family's isolation, and are friends to the parents, even these lay services produced only a 10 to 20 percent decrease in the occurrence of additional incidents of abuse.

GROUP THERAPY

Other therapeutic models have also been developed as attempts to resolve some of the shortcomings of individual therapy. These focus on meeting the needs of parents by providing them a nurturing environment in which they can begin to understand their behavior. Group methods for meeting parental needs may be more desirable than individual therapy; they are less anxiety producing and threatening,[42] and they tend to lessen the social isolation of abusing families.

Using principles of transactional analysis, Justice and Justice organized a group therapy program around six areas of concern common to abusive parents:[8]

- Symbiosis
- Isolation
- Talking and sharing with mate
- Impatience/Temper
- Child development and management
- Employment

These areas touch on psychodynamic, sociological, and social learning models.

Cantoni used a group approach that centered on education of the whole person.[43] The therapists modeled relating behavior and helped parents relate to each other. They taught methods of problem solving, helped parents to understand and accept normal human emotions, and provided factual information about human growth and development and human interactions. Some time was spent on specific parenting skills, but these were not a major focus.

SELF-HELP GROUPS

Self-help groups are another type of group available not only to parents who physically abuse their children but also to perpetrators of spouse and sexual abuse.[44] Some self-help groups remain independent of professional help; others use professional help to various degrees. Mothers Anonymous, founded in 1970 in California by an abusive parent, was the first such organization. It functioned as a crisis intervention group to prevent damaging relationships between mother and child. A number of such groups were formed; they are most commonly referred to as Parents Anonymous. Similar groups for parents who sexually abuse their children are called Parents United.

Parents model their behavior after others who have proved it is possible to change abusive behavior. Self-help groups teach the members ways to deal with anger and to express feelings without destroying relationships. Members feel they gain much support from the groups. The study by the Berkeley Planning Associates concurs on the relative efficacy of Parents Anonymous.[41] A possible shortcoming of such groups, especially if used alone, is that parents lack a model of healthy parenting. Behavior toward the child may improve, but feelings and relationships may not change. For example, one parent reported, "I don't hit Johnny anymore, but I still don't like him." Groups that use professional support are perhaps less subject to this potential shortcoming.

EFFECTIVENESS

It has been difficult to assess the effectiveness of therapy designed to meet the needs of parents because it is seldom used in isolation from other interventions or educational approaches. This type of therapy, in combination with other interventions, is thought to produce recognizable short-term results and permit earlier return of the abused victim(s) to the home environment. Galdston of the Parents Center Project, which combines a therapeutic day-care setting with the parent-need approach, reported improvement in the growth and development of the children but much less improvement in the domestic functioning of the parents.[45] Most interventions based on fulfilling the needs of the parents seem to have developed from psychodynamic models.

Approaches That Focus on Developing Parenting Skills

Most educational approaches that deal with issues of behavior management are formulated around one of three different child management systems: Parent Effectiveness Training (PET), social learning theory, or Rudolf Dreikurs's Adlerian approach. These systems are summarized in Table 7-1.

PARENT EFFECTIVENESS TRAINING

PET focuses on feelings of parents and children and on ways to assure open and honest communication between parent and child.[46,47] The basic premise is that parents should allow themselves to be real with their children. This premise involves telling the child what behaviors the parent accepts and does not accept and allows for parental inconsistency. As an attempt to develop open communication with children, a technique

Table 7-1   Child Management Systems and Key Concepts

1. Parent Effectiveness Training (Thomas Gordon)
   - Active listening
   - Sending "I" messages
   - No-loss conflict resolution

2. Social Learning Theory (Gerald Patterson)
   - Positive and negative reinforcement
   - Behavioral contracting
   - Time-out
   - Contingency management

3. Adlerian Approach (Rudolf Dreikurs)
   - Identifying goals of children's misbehavior: attention, power, revenge, display of inadequacy
   - Disengaging from struggles
   - Use of natural and logical consequences
   - Shared decision making

called "active listening" is used when the child has a problem. The parent listens to the child accurately and acceptingly, decodes the child's feeling, puts this understanding into the parent's own words, and feeds it back to the child; for example, "You're feeling sad because Johnny won't play with you."

Gordon[46] proposes that parents must have certain attitudes to successfully use active listening. These include the ability to genuinely accept the child's feelings, no matter what they are; a deep sense of trust in the child's capacity to handle feelings and work them through to solution; awareness that feelings are transitory and not permanent; and the ability to see children as people who are separate from the parent and who have their own identities. Some of these attitudes may be difficult for abusing parents to achieve.

When the parent has a problem with a child's behavior, the concept of "I messages" is used to help children listen to parents.

Rather than telling the child what to do or criticizing or blaming the child, I messages tell the child how an unacceptable behavior makes the parent feel.

The third major area addressed in PET is power struggles between parent and child; in this case the problem is in the relationship. The idea is that parents inappropriately use the power available to them because of their control of rewards and punishments and that parents should neither win nor lose power struggles. A "no-loss" method of conflict resolution is advocated: the parent asks the child to work with the parent to find a solution to the problem that is acceptable to both. Together, the parent and child generate possible solutions and critically evaluate the alternatives until they decide on one that is mutually agreeable. The child is trusted to carry out the decision, as opposed to negotiating penalties in case the child does not follow through.

SOCIAL LEARNING THEORY

Social learning theorists advocate a very different approach to parenting and use principles of operant conditioning for managing a child's behavior.[48,49] The management techniques are based on principles of reinforcement. A behavior that is positively reinforced will be strengthened; a behavior that is not reinforced or is negatively reinforced will be weakened. The behavior will be weakened more quickly through negative reinforcement than through nonreinforcement. For most people, social reinforcement (smiles, attention, praise, hugs) is highly effective as a positive reinforcer. For some children, other reinforcers such as riding a bike, playing with friends, or getting a new toy may be necessary.

When trying to weaken a behavior through nonreinforcement or negative reinforcement, positive reinforcement of a prosocial, competing behavior is helpful. When using negative reinforcement, it is important to be con-

sistent and remain calm. Physical punishment, nagging, and criticism are unacceptable negative reinforcers.

One specific behavioral technique, "behavioral contracting," involves negotiation between parent and child so that a child can earn a reward that is mutually agreed upon. This approach is frequently used in connection with children's household chores but might be used to modify a wide variety of behaviors. Generally, a child earns points, and the points are accumulated until there are enough to earn the reward. To be effective, contracts must involve specific behaviors and rewards and be written down, and points must be recorded soon after they are earned.

A second popular technique and frequently advocated alternative to physical punishment is "time-out." Time-out is a mild, effective punishment that removes the child from positive reinforcement (both social and tangible) and places the youngster in a separate place without other people or toys for a short period of time (usually one to five minutes). In most homes, time-out usually occurs in the bathroom. The child is sent to time-out *each time* the undesirable target behavior occurs, and data are kept about the frequency of the undesired behavior. Patterson feels that time-out works best with children 2 to 12 years old and with behaviors that occur frequently.[48]

A third technique is contingency management. A child is told that the child will receive positive reinforcement after performing a behavior desired by the parent. For example, "First you hang up your coat, and then you can have your snack,"[48] or "You can watch television as soon as your room is clean." These contingencies are given firmly and without debate or argument. To be effective, consistent follow-through is necessary.

ADLERIAN APPROACH

Dreikurs's approach to child management[50] is based on principles of Adlerian psychology. This approach focuses on understanding the child's motives and needs to be important and respected. Dreikurs feels that parents' ideas of their own responsibility for child rearing prevent them from sharing those responsibilities with their children and cause the children to feel discouraged and inadequate. A child's misbehavior is seen as an attempt to feel important in the world, to find a place in the family in some way. A child's misbehavior has four specified goals, and parents are encouraged to figure out which goal may be operating in particular problem situations. The goals are as follows:

- Attention—the child wants to be heard and responded to
- Power—the child wants to be the boss
- Revenge—the child wants to hurt the parents
- Display of inadequacy—the child feels worthless and hopeless and wants to be left alone

Once the goal of the child's misbehavior has been determined, the parent has cues for understanding the child's feelings and for successful interventions to change behavior. Parental responses allow the child to feel important and respected by sharing responsibility with the child and allowing the child to participate in decision making.

Some principles of child management based on the goal of the child's misbehavior are given here. If the child is seeking attention by misbehaving, the misbehavior is ignored, and the child is given extra attention during pleasant times in the parent-child relationship.

If the child's goal is power, parents attempt to avoid the power struggle by disengaging themselves from conflict (often by withdrawing to the bathroom or other private place) or by allowing natural consequences to follow. For example, if a child refuses to get ready for school on time, the child must deal with the natural consequence of being tardy. In this way, the responsibility is placed on the child for the child's actions, and a power struggle with the parent is avoided. When

natural consequences are not available, logical consequences may be used. For example, the mother may suggest that the family may go swimming after the children's rooms are clean because the housework has to be done before she can leave. Children are also encouraged to share power; they are given choices by their parents and allowed to follow through on their choices. For example, "You can finish cleaning your room and go outside to play now, or you can continue to play in your room and finish cleaning later. It's up to you." All choices given must be acceptable to the parent, and when the *child* makes the decision, a power struggle is avoided.

When the child seeks revenge, it is usually the result of an intensification of an ongoing power struggle. To help the child, the parents must be very encouraging and help the child feel understood; they use the same principles of natural and logical consequences and choices cited before.

A child who feels completely discouraged may display inadequacy. To help this child, a parent encourages the child when mistakes are made, praises the child for attempts and efforts in difficult tasks, and communicates faith in the child's ability to do things independently by not taking over and doing things for the child. This is frequently a goal for handicapped children.

ADVANTAGES AND DISADVANTAGES

These three systems of child management were developed to help relatively intact patients deal with problems encountered in child rearing. All of the approaches have been used with abusing parents, but some aspects may need to be modified to accommodate the special needs of abusing families. The active listening techniques proposed by PET are specific measures to help children of abusing parents develop a positive self-concept and a sense of trust in people. However, the abusive parents' own needs may be so overwhelming that giving to the child in this way may be impossible unless the adult is getting the same empathic response and nurturance from someone in the adult's environment. Similarly, it may be difficult for abusing parents to use the "no-loss" method of conflict resolution because their authoritarian style dictates that they should be in charge, be strong parents, and guide their child firmly. PET may be more successful later in a treatment program when the parents' self-esteem is higher and changes in attitude may have already occurred.

The principles of behavior management advocated by the social learning approach are more compatible with abusing parents' attitudes because this approach maintains the parent in a position of power. However, the possibility of misuse of negative reinforcement must be considered. In addition, this approach gives very little attention to understanding the child's feelings or encouraging growth in the child. These and other issues involving the child's self-esteem must be addressed if the generational cycle of family violence is to be interrupted.

Although Dreikurs's Adlerian approach is probably more intrinsically appealing to abusive parents than PET, because of the former's greater emphasis on behavioral management, it has some of the same drawbacks as PET. Shared responsibility between parent and child for decision making, avoidance of power struggles, and withdrawal of the parent from conflicts run counter to the abusive parent's needs to provide strong guidance and to demand obedience. Providing encouragement to the child and respecting the child as an individual may be difficult for abusing parents who themselves are discouraged and have low self-esteem.

Each of the systems of child management is potentially beneficial to abusive parents by helping them learn child-rearing techniques that do not involve use of physical punishment. However, educators and therapists who use these systems must remember the special needs of the abusing parents. The systems will probably not be successful unless the parents also receive much support and nurturance themselves. Additionally, extra work with the parents will probably be necessary to help them understand and consider the child's feelings and motives.

EFFECTIVENESS

A few parenting programs have been set up especially for abusive parents or have reported results with this population. Patterson developed a program for parents of aggressive children.[51] One-fourth of the parents in the program were classified as abusive. The treatment is based on principles of social learning, particularly concepts of operant conditioning. The first phase involves studying a programed text[49] on child management. In the second phase, the parents are taught to define, track, and record the consequences of deviant and prosocial child behaviors. The third stage is a parent training group that uses modeling and role playing of appropriate techniques to teach the parent to reinforce prosocial behaviors and to reduce the occurrence of deviant behaviors. Evaluations of this program reported a significant decrease in deviant behavior which remained relatively stable over one year. Stability was attributed partially to the improvement of the child's behavior and partially to an improved parent-child relationship. This program, and others based on the same principles, may serve as a methodological model for future parent education programs since it demonstrates the feasibility of using adequate evaluation procedures as part of an intervention program.

The child abuse project at the University of Pennsylvania Presbyterian Medical Center also used social learning theory as the basis for group work with parents.[52] The center reported an 80 percent success rate in changing parental attitudes about child-rearing practices.[53]

An increase in positive interactions with the child was the main finding of a social learning training program by Burgess and Conger.[54] However, follow-up indicated that the gains were not always maintained, and Burgess suggests that families who are successful in maintaining treatment progress are those who are more socially involved. Hughes used a programed text and monetary incentives to encourage abusive parents to do well on tests of the child-rearing curriculum.[55] After passing the five unit tests, the parents were involved in a home project. This project was designed to provide an opportunity for parents to pinpoint undesirable behaviors and then alter those behaviors by using what they learned from the curriculum. The parents were pleased with their successes, and Hughes considered his parent performance training program to be a useful adjunct to other treatment.

Approaches That Combine a Focus on Parental Needs and on Developing Parenting Skills

Thistleton developed a parent education program specifically for abusive parents.[56] The program is designed to provide learning opportunities in child growth and development and techniques of home management in the context of a nurturing environment. The sessions are divided into two phases preceded by a nurturing session directed at helping the mother learn something about personal grooming. In the first phase, the parent is paid for coming. In the second phase, this concrete giving to the parent is replaced by the giving of help and support by the parent education. Thus, an integral and important part of the program is nurturing the parent. Anecdotal reports indicate that the program is helpful to some abusive parents.

Martin's goals of treatment with abusive parents are similarly broad ranging.[30] One goal involving parent-child interaction has two components: (1) helping the adults change their feelings toward the child and (2) helping them change their behavior toward the child. A second major goal is help for the adult in several areas: improving self-esteem, increasing pleasure in activities that are not centered around direct gratification of needs, learning more appropriate ways to show anger, developing lifelines for times of stress, and helping with problems such as money and employment. Such multifaceted approaches provide a broad base for intervention.

Both individual and group approaches may include techniques to help the abusing adult cope with anger. Traditionally, anger and hostile feelings have been dealt with by in-depth individual psychotherapy, but some investigators have suggested more direct, behavioral approaches for teaching violent adults to control anger. Suggested techniques include reinforcement of nonangry responses to provocation, role playing and modeling of nonangry responses, and desensitization in the presence of the anger-evoking stimuli.[13]

Designers of curricula for the abusive parent must consider several factors. Abusive parents, who have typically never had normal parenting experiences, need a curriculum and experiences that meet their own needs before they can benefit from the parenting information. Educators must remain nonjudgmental and permit the abusive parents to use the education-oriented sessions to meet the parents' own needs. A nurturing format must be included in any attempt to provide parent education. It will tax the skills of the educator to help abusive parents give up the parenting models they experienced as children.

Approaches That Focus on the Needs of the Child

Any educational model that alters the parents' behavior and feelings toward the child will obviously have a secondary effect on the child. There are, however, many educational interventions directed primarily at the child, often with secondary educational gains for the parents.

Any setting that provides respite for the child from an abusive environment is likely to be beneficial. Several crisis nurseries exist for this purpose; placement in foster care homes offers the same respite. When the child is able to remain at home, there are several options. Day-care placement or nurseries give the child the opportunity to be in a more stressfree environment and to interact with other children and adults; the child can learn to play and to trust. This process can be facilitated by placement in a therapeutic day-care or nursery setting designed to focus on the needs of abused children. Most try to demonstrate the modeling of healthy child care and management by combining the therapeutic setting for the child with the opportunity for the parents to observe their child and other children.

A demonstration project in Colorado, the Circle House Therapeutic Preschool established in 1974, offers an intensive therapeutic environment to the abused preschooler.[57] The goals of the program are to promote development of a positive self-image, a sense of trust of other people, and a sense of autonomy by providing a safe environment with warm, accepting adults. Emphasis is not placed on parent involvement. There is no objective evidence that these approaches are effective; like parent groups, they are usually combined with other forms of therapy and are difficult to assess.

A program that combines child-oriented with parent-oriented education is the residential treatment program. This approach guarantees the child's protection without total separation from the parent and promotes therapeutic and educational role modeling for the parent. It permits more intensive involvement with all members of the family. For example, Park Hospital for Children in Oxford, England, uses parent-oriented therapy in a residential setting.[58,59] The parents live in bungalows, and the children are initially hospitalized. Later, the children spend increased periods of time with the parents. Emphasis is on helping the parents feel secure and loved through group, individual, and marital therapy. The therapists observe parent-child interactions and, in addition to helping parents learn to play with their children, help them understand and cope with their children's behavior. Much of the parent's learning is by "precept and example." There is also emphasis on creating a stable bond between parents and hospital staff. Lynch and Ounsted reported that 80 percent of the children in their families-in-residence returned home.[58] In the 40 families involved, one serious injury and one death (of a severely brain damaged child) occurred. Perhaps the greatest shortcoming of residential approaches is their great expense. It has been difficult to justify such an approach, partly because of the problems in demonstrating effectiveness. Other programs[45,60] have placed more emphasis on the child. They used therapeutic day care or foster care in conjunction with individual or group therapy for the parents.

Approaches That Focus on Marital Abuse

A growing number of intervention programs focus on marital abuse, but most are relatively new, and few are reported in the literature. Most are concerned with crisis intervention and not education. Residential centers as temporary havens for the abused spouse had their advent in England in 1971 with the establishment of Chiswick Women's Aid, a total communal living model.[61] Independence is encouraged as the woman slowly assumes responsibility for herself and others in a sheltered, protected environment. From Chiswick, she can move out into secondary, smaller, independent living centers. Finally, she can move out into the community or elect to remain permanently in the communal living center. The safe house movement in the United States provides a sense of community and a support system for battered women. As in child abuse, role modeling by staff and other women is used heavily.[36] A variety of educational and therapy settings can be combined with the safe house concept. The York Street Center in Denver, Colorado, arranges for out-of-town housing while providing short-term psychological, educational, and legal counseling to the abused spouse.[62] Marital counseling is available, and the Center will arrange for (but does not provide) ongoing, long-term individual therapy for the abusing spouse and for the abused spouse.

As many as 50 percent of women who stay one week or longer in a safe house do not return to the abusing spouse, but this percentage can be increased if the safe house remains open to women who return home and want to come back to the refuge.[63] Refuges or safe houses have several shortcomings, however. They provide an artificial sense of community that does not exist outside itself; as a result, the women have difficulty in coping in the real world without support. Many groups are beginning to strengthen potential support systems in the community to help offset this shortcoming. There is limited potential for educational or vocational training; most have their hands full dealing with the basic physical and emotional needs of the women and the women's children. Many of the children have emotional problems or learning difficulties, and there is little available time or energy to devote to these problems. The crowded conditions of many safe houses only serve to intensify emotional issues and perpetuate the violent behavior exhibited by some of the children, particularly adolescent males. The crowded conditions also contribute to illness. Most safe houses do not have facilities or programs for the men. These men are often left alone and experience depression, psychosis, or involvement in an abusing

relationship with another woman. Finally, safe houses are expensive and difficult to operate and have frequent turnover in staff. In spite of their shortcomings, safe houses serve an important and effective role in the treatment and prevention of wife abuse.[64]

Therapy for these battered women emphasizes understanding the psychodynamics of the abuse as well as an explanation of the "mythology" involved.[17,18,36] There are advantages to a "feminist" approach that emphasizes termination of the relationship with the abuser rather than attempts to change his behavior.

Approaches That Focus on Sexual Abuse

Intervention strategies for treatment of sexual abuse generally take a family system approach. Incest or other familial sexual abuse is the result of dynamics involving the triad of father, mother, and child,[24,31,65] and each member of the triad must be considered when planning treatment.

Giarretto has provided the most comprehensive description of a treatment approach for sexual abuse.[21] His program, based on a humanistic growth model, is one of the very few that reports any data on the outcome of treatment. The Child Sexual Abuse Treatment Program (CSATP) provides comprehensive services to incestuous families. Counseling proceeds in a generally fixed order, from individual counseling for each member through mother-daughter counseling, marital therapy, and father-daughter counseling to family counseling and group therapy. An important component of the program is the availability of self-help groups for both the parents (Parents United) and the daughters (Daughters United). In Giarretto's view, the marital relationship is the key factor because incest is unlikely if the marriage is satisfactory. High self-esteem is a prerequisite to a satisfactory marital relationship and a major focus in counseling. Preliminary results of the

CSATP showed no recidivism among over 250 families who completed the program; 90 percent of the marriages were saved. Treatment of the offender was more successful when counseling was begun soon after arrest and continued during and after incarceration. The authority of the criminal justice system is needed to ensure treatment, and fathers need to admit guilt and take responsibility for their actions rather than laying blame on the daughter.

Other clinicians agree that a major therapeutic goal is to help the parents admit guilt and let the daughter know that she is a victim of poor parenting[15,29] and not the cause of the incest. Pittman asserts that therapy should restore appropriate role relationships: the mother and father have appropriate parenting functions, sex occurs between the mother and father, and the child can be a child without maternal or marital functions.[20] Similarly, Walters sees the long-range goal of treatment as bringing about a healthier familial relationship where sex is not used as a controlling mechanism in the parent-child interaction.[31] If the incest is due to alcoholism or psychosis in the father, Pittman suggests treating the father separately and giving therapy to the rest of the family to allow them to work through their reaction to the trauma.[20]

Tormes focused on the mother as the key to preventing further incest since the mother can control incest by restructuring the family to assure that the daughters are protected.[66] Counseling and support services such as homemaker services and self-help groups are advocated for the mother. Treatment mainly for the father is difficult because of his completely deviant understanding of the father role and his use of denial or rationalization to justify the act.

A very different approach to sexual abuse was reported by Harbert et al.[67] They used the behavioral technique of covert desensitization to reduce incestuous behavior in a man who had had sexual interaction with his daughter for five years. After the man was relaxed, he was asked to imagine scenes of himself and his daughter in sexual activity that were followed by noxious consequences such as his wife discovering them. He also imagined scenes of neutral interactions with his daughter with pleasant consequences. At a six-month follow-up, the man had not engaged in any incestuous behavior and was relating appropriately to his daughter.

Trends in treatment of sexual abuse have been summarized by the National Center on Child Abuse and Neglect.[29] They include helping the victims understand that the adults, not they, were responsible for the abuse; helping the mothers make decisions about their marriages; using group therapy and self-help groups; installing 24-hour sexual abuse hotlines; and developing sensitive and minimally intrusive legal and medical procedures to decrease the harm suffered by the victim and the family because of society's response to incest. While some legal action is probably required to guarantee treatment, the process of prosecution and splitting up families often leads to chaos and disorganization that may be more harmful than the incest itself. Because incestuous family configurations tend to repeat themselves in generational cycles,[29,65] successful treatment of incest is partly preventive.

PRIMARY EDUCATIONAL APPROACHES

Primary educational approaches are aimed at prevention and early detection of family violence. These logically fall into four categories: (1) approaches that attempt to prepare young people for parenting and family roles; (2) approaches that provide ongoing support or role modeling for families at risk; (3) approaches that educate professionals in the early detection, prevention, and treatment of family violence; and (4) approaches that educate the community about the issues of family violence.

Parenting and Family-Life Education

It has been proposed that education that provides parenting skills would serve as a deterrent to inadequate parenting. To be effective, such a program must combine didactic classroom experience with "laboratory" experience or opportunities to care for children under supervision. When the opportunities for acquiring knowledge and firsthand experience are supplemented with group sessions that promote discussion of the students' feelings and responses to working with children, the teenager may be in a position to really appreciate what parenting may be like.[30] Brazelton urges exposure to infants and young children even before the teen years to capture the excitement of child development.[68] The later school years seem to be the appropriate time to provide formal courses in child development, family planning, and management and opportunities to work with and directly care for young children. These experiences should be available to boys as well as to girls.

EDUCATION FOR PARENTHOOD (EpF)

One project developed to meet the preparenting needs of children and teenagers is Education for Parenthood.[69] The program is designed to give teenagers the opportunity to develop more positive attitudes about children and parenting; to increase their knowledge of and skills in child development and the social, medical, and emotional needs of children; to aid their understanding of the family's role in child development and socialization; and to stress important factors in prenatal care and the early months of infancy.

Three major components of EpF are development of parenthood education curriculum for schools, development of parenthood edu-

cation programs for nonschool settings, and provision of technical assistance from the Office of Education for setting up these programs. EpF is being used in over 3000 settings throughout the country.

The EpF curriculum for schools is called *Exploring Childhood.*[70] This program has four underlying values: (1) to view the present, whether adolescence or childhood, as an important time of being as well as becoming; (2) to demonstrate that insight can be learned and can be an important influence on behavior; (3) to help students and children develop confidence in their own identities; and (4) to legitimize the view that anyone responsible for the care of children has worthwhile experiences to share. The program attempts to promote growth by combining classroom instructions with practical experiences in a one-year course for teenagers that is adaptable to various cultural backgrounds. Students spend a part of their time in classes learning about child development, family relationships, and child-rearing practices in different cultures. Several additional hours per week are spent working directly with children under the supervision of preschool teachers. A variety of materials are used, including workbooks, films, and audio cassettes. Teacher guides and a manual for school administrators are also available. Materials include special units on families under stress and single parenthood. No information is available on the effectiveness of this curriculum.

The nonschool component of EpF has been developed and field-tested by seven national volunteer organizations,[69] and evaluation information is available. Preliminary data suggest that the participants, as compared with a control group, showed small gains in their opinions about children and themselves as persons. Gains were greatest in self-ratings on knowledge of child-care skills. Similarly, many pupils who completed the Inner London Education Authority course in child development and the family showed a marked increase of maturity and acceptance of personal responsibility.[71] This course emphasizes the young child's need for a loving and secure relationship, for communication through talking and being listened to, for play as a means of learning and relating the child's own inner world to the world outside, and for acceptance as a person from birth.

VOLUNTARY VERSUS REQUIRED EDUCATION

There is often a question of whether education for parenthood should be required or voluntary. The family structure is changing along with a rapidly changing society so that supports for parents such as small communities and proximity of the extended family are no longer available, and many parents need help with the task of rearing children. Some feel it is the responsibility of the schools to teach persons how to cope with their future lives as adults and parents and handle their children appropriately.[71] If courses are optional, self-selection may well result in the lack of participation of potentially poor parents who may abuse. Many abusing parents do not have adequate knowledge of child development and management, and some recognize this deficit.

IMPORTANCE OF NURTURING

The question is whether one can teach parenting skills to the potentially abusive parent at the high school level without providing the nurturing relationship that abusers need to benefit from education for parents. Many potentially abusive parents are so lacking in basic nurturing qualities that they may be unable to benefit from the teaching of parenting skills. Many persons other than those recognized as abusing parents lack nurturing qualities as well. It would seem beneficial to develop programs for increasing nurturance as well as preventing abuse. If these educational programs are to be successful, they must be presented in a nurturing setting. Simply requiring all high school students to take parenting courses is not enough. If, as postulated, the dynamics of spouse abuse are similar to those of child abuse, it is even more important that family-life education include material on personal growth and understanding as well as on child development. Family-life education should be available to all students. The courses should include didactic material as well as practical experiences that prepare students for the various roles they must fulfill if they are to be happy, productive adults. These approaches to preventing abuse are compatible with both sociological and social learning models of family violence.

Approaches to Support Families "At Risk"

Several investigators have reported systems for recognizing families at high risk for abuse.[12,72,73] Screening and early recognition presuppose that effective intervention and educational techniques are available for minimizing the potential for abuse in the population at risk. A model for comprehensive, ongoing support is outlined in Table 7-2.

Table 7-2 Support of Families at Risk

1. Screening and early recognition

2. Prenatal support
   - Through obstetrical clinics
   - Through public health nurses

3. Support in the delivery room and hospital
   - Promote bonding
   - Provide ongoing role model of nurturance
     Lay health workers
     Specialized nurses
   - Comprehensive medical follow-up

PRENATAL INTERVENTION

Intervention can begin in the prenatal period. Public health nurses can encourage participation in prenatal care, provide a nurturing support system to the family, and educate the family about the pregnancy and approaching delivery and birth. In the obstetrical clinic or office, prospective parents can receive printed materials on the pregnancy and birth process and on parenting and family relationships as well. Obstetrical clinics are also convenient places for courses in parenting that help parents prepare for the initial impact of the infant. One approach[74] uses hospital nursing personnel to provide greater continuity of care and, subsequently, increases the opportunity for providing nurturing to the family at risk.

POSTNATAL INTERVENTION

Beginning at birth, from the first interaction in the delivery room, bonding behavior can be facilitated.[75] Hospital personnel can be taught to provide suitable experiences so the parent can learn to interact appropriately with the new infant. Lay health workers can assure that the basic health needs of every child are met.[76] These workers are successful mothers who can form a communication bridge between the family at risk and the health care system. They visit the home; look at the mother, the child, and the setting; and determine how the family is coping and what problems may exist. In addition to nurturing the parents, they help educate the family about basic immunizations, good nutrition for the whole family, and periodic medical examinations. They attempt to be nonthreatening and available when needed.

A model for comprehensive medical follow-up was described by Newberger and McAnulty.[77] Their Boston clinic provides continuity of medical care to abusive families as well as to families at risk. At the University of Colorado Medical Center, a Pediatric Mothers Clinic provides health maintenance care to the infants and children of high-risk families; many of these families include teenage mothers. The clinic attempts to nurture the parent by providing a warm, nonthreatening atmosphere and conveying genuine interest in the parent and in the infant as developing and worthwhile human beings. Few parents fail to return after an initial visit to the clinic.

A lay health worker and comprehensive pediatric care were the only resources used in one program for intervention with a group of families recognized to be at risk.[73] Five children in the "high-risk non-intervene" group required hospitalization for serious injuries that were thought to be secondary to abnormal parent practices; no such hospitalizations occurred in the "high-risk intervene" and "low-risk control" groups. The conclusion was that perinatal assessment and simple intervention with families at risk significantly improves the infant's chance of escaping physical injury. There are several common elements in these programs designed to help families at risk: provision of a nurturing figure to the parent, guaranteed medical follow-up, and decreased isolation of the new family unit. The emphasis on providing nurturance is most congruent with a psychodynamic model.

Infants who are premature or deformed and children who are mentally retarded, who have other chronic illnesses, or who are difficult to manage are at greater risk for abuse; it may be necessary to place extra emphasis on helping the parents cope with these children. When an infant requires prolonged hospitalization as a newborn, it is important to promote early parental contact and provide educational counseling to the parents about the kinds of difficulties they can expect to encounter. Information about crisis and respite care should be given to the parents along with invitations to ask for help if needed. Public health nurses can provide follow-up care to the whole family.

Education of Professionals Who Work With Children or Families

SCHOOL PERSONNEL

Most children spend the largest portion of their day at school where the effects of abuse or neglect can be recognized and appropriate steps taken toward intervention. School personnel are often reluctant to report suspected abuse, partly because they are uncertain of how to accurately recognize it and partly because they are afraid of potential legal repercussions.

"Lift a Finger"

The "Lift a Finger" program developed in Texas[78] trains school personnel to recognize and refer suspected cases of abuse and neglect. This program includes two autotutorial packages. The first package is designed for the administrator; it includes information about reporting laws, immunity laws, and the misdemeanor penalty for failure to report and a suggested procedure for referring suspected cases. The administrator's manual contains a sample policy statement and suggested administrative procedures for reporting which could be modified to meet the needs of an individual district. The second package is for the teacher and consists of three slide tapes. The first is an overview; the second tells school personnel how to recognize and refer suspected cases and defines the teacher's role in working with the child and the parents after the referral has been made; the third deals with the legal aspects. The teacher's manual gives instructions for conducting in-service sessions with teachers, nurses, and counselors and contains follow-up activities and supplemental discussion material.

Project PROTECTION

Montgomery County, Maryland, has also developed a school-based program to detect and prevent child abuse and neglect. This program, Project PROTECTION,[79] which trains educators in the recognition and referral of suspected victims of child abuse and neglect, can be a model for other school systems. A major objective of the program is to protect children by assuring that all school staff members are trained to recognize child abuse and neglect, are aware of their obligations to report, and know the procedures for doing so. There are four phases. The first phase, policy revision, promotes a policy that requires all school staff to refer any suspected victim of child abuse or neglect to proper authorities, emphasizes that any doubt about reporting a suspected situation should be resolved in favor of the child, and explains immunity laws. The second phase, staff development, informs local administrators and staff of their legal responsibility to report, their immunity guaranteed by law, and proper referral procedures. The third phase provides information on child abuse and neglect to each nonpublic school in the county. The fourth phase, curriculum development, presents information about child abuse to the student population. Project PROTECTION has demonstrated that a school-based program can have a significant impact in the early detection of child abuse and neglect. There was a marked increase in reporting of abuse after inception of the program.[79]

Requirements for Success

Ultimately, the success of any school program depends upon those who are in daily contact with the children. If staff members are familiar with the syndrome of abuse and neglect and can recognize the signals of a child at risk; if they know they must report suspected abuse and neglect and that they have legal immunity when they do so; if they are familiar with required referral procedures; and if they are convinced that their referrals will be handled promptly and intelligently—they will become a vital force in the detection and prevention of abuse and neglect. Education of school and community personnel to increase reporting of abuse and neglect is compatible with most theoretical approaches.

PROFESSIONALS IN THE FIELD OF FAMILY VIOLENCE

Professionals who come in contact with abuse and neglect must be aware of the various factors involved. The Children's Trauma Center of Oakland, California, has developed a series of programs for training professionals. These consist of separate units for physicians, administrators, social workers, public health workers, and mental health workers. The major objectives are to provide information about recognition, management, treatment, and prevention of child abuse; to develop awareness of feelings and attitudes about child abuse; to understand the necessary components for delivering comprehensive services to abusive families; and to become successful community models for working with child abuse. The Minnesota Child Welfare Training Project has also developed a training series for workers in child welfare and related fields.[80] Unfortunately, very little evaluation of such programs is available.

Ten regional training centers are funded by the federal Office of Child Development to serve as educational resource centers (see Appendix). They sponsor a variety of conferences, symposia, and training workshops for child protection teams; assist with a variety of educational programs; develop audiovisual training materials; and serve as sources of training information.

An educational program on spouse abuse has been instituted for law enforcement officials by the York Street Center for Victims of Crime and Family Disturbance in Denver, Colorado.[62] Classes are held for police, sheriff's officers, and state patrol personnel. The training includes material on techniques for investigating sexual assault, interviewing vic-

tims, crisis intervention, and family disturbance. Role playing is used to present this information to the officers. Walker emphasizes the importance of prompt police protection, rights of arrest, and equalization in obtaining and enforcing restraining orders.[36] She urges hospitalization of the abused spouse for protection and for emphasis on the seriousness of the incident. By viewing the abuse as assault and not simply a "domestic incident" and by making appropriate arrests, the state, not the woman, becomes involved in pressing charges. This model of a criminal justice system is already effective in incidents of child abuse. Walker also suggests requirements for reporting spouse abuse, similar to those for child abuse, and financial support (social security) for the victim. The latter already exists in England.[63]

Community and Public Education

Education of the public about family violence, whether it be child or spouse abuse, must involve awareness of the problem, understanding of the dynamics, methods for early recognition and intervention, and awareness of treatment alternatives.

Various communications media have been used to make the public aware of the problem of abuse within families and have dramatically portrayed some of the dynamics involved. Television is a powerful force in American society. In fact, many feel that television may perpetrate violence by providing aggressive models. It can be used equally well to model more positive behaviors. To be effective, however, it should not emphasize the spectacular and the gory; it should show people how to avoid becoming abusers by modeling how they can meet their psychological needs, get along better within their family relationships, manage children without undue physical discipline, relax in times of stress, and make use of community resources. These same educational principles can be presented through other news media and through the popular literature.

Community education may be sponsored by a variety of agencies including regional resource centers, hospitals, and schools.[81] For example, the York Street Center in Denver[62] is extensively involved in community education. The major purpose of the education is to encourage reporting and prosecution of serious criminal acts and to inform the public about the impact of crime on the individual and the community. Some of the topics of their workshops are Family Violence and Wife Abuse, The Victimization of Women and Children, and Crime Prevention in Your Home. Another phase of their program shares expertise with professionals such as physicians, nurses, counselors, attorneys, and social workers to develop more resources for referral and advocacy. Some of the more commonly requested topics include Clinical Issues in Treating Family Violence, Clinical Issues in Treating Battered Women, Crisis Intervention as a Treatment Modality, and Incest and Sexual Abuse of Children. There is a continuing demand for workshops, prevention programs, professional training, and media reviews. This demand and direct posi-

Table 7-3 Intervention Strategies Derived from Theoretical Models of Family Violence

PSYCHODYNAMIC	SOCIOLOGICAL	SOCIAL LEARNING
Secondary Educational Approaches		
Individual Psychotherapy or Casework	Community Support Services (day care, homemaker, caseworker)*†	Education about Child Development* (group or individual)
Group Psychotherapy		Education about Behavior Management‡* (group or individual)
Lay Therapy		Anger Control Techniques‡*
Supportive Residential Treatment		
Self-help Groups		
Primary Educational Approaches		
	Family-Life Education Courses in Schools†	Education about Child Development‡
	Community and Public Education	Education about Behavior Management‡
	Education of Professionals Involved in Treatment of Family Violence	
	Legal Sanctions	

*Techniques also compatible with psychodynamic models
‡Techniques also compatible with sociological models
†Techniques also compatible with social learning models

tive feedback from participants have indicated that the community regards the project's educational programs as highly valuable and informative.

Community education approaches to preventing family violence follow most directly from sociological models.

CONCLUSIONS

Various models of family violence and educational interventions that are compatible with them have been explored.[73] The models of domestic violence are not mutually exclusive, and educational approaches draw from several models (Table 7-3). The time of intervention emphasized, however, is partially dictated by the tenets of the models. Psychodynamic models, with the focus on treating pathology, seem to fit with successful secondary educational interventions. Since the cause of family violence is, according to these models, a lack of adequate parenting in the abuser's past, educational approaches that emphasize the need for provision of nurturance should be most successful. On the other hand, sociological models seem most compatible with primary educational approaches. Since these models see the cause of family violence as society's legitimization of violence as a means to control children, educational approaches that focus on changing the attitudes of young people and the community to favor nonviolent methods of child rearing and problem solving should be effective. Social learning models seem to have some applicability to both secondary and primary educational approaches. Developing skills for nonviolent parenting and relationships is necessary for successful education after abuse has occurred. Similarly, teaching of both parenting skills and child development are heavily used in primary prevention approaches.

While many programs have been developed for both secondary and primary education, few have reported data that can be used to evaluate the effectiveness of such approaches. Some of the difficulties involved in research on educational approaches to family violence are the overlapping, multifaceted nature of the intervention and the lack of skilled research involvement in the projects. Assessment is imperative to help define directions for future programs to both treat and prevent family violence. Systematic data are also necessary for determining the relative practical importance of the various theoretical models.

APPENDIX

CHILD ABUSE AND NEGLECT— REGIONAL RESOURCE CENTERS

(These projects are funded by grants from the federal Office of Child Development for the purpose of assisting individuals and organizations in the area of child abuse and neglect. Services offered are different from project to project.)

REGION	PROJECT NAME AND LOCATION	AREAS SERVED
I	Judge Baker Guidance Center 295 Longwood Avenue Boston, Massachusetts 02115	Connecticut Maine Massachusetts New Hampshire Rhode Island Vermont
II	College of Human Ecology MVR Hall Cornell University Ithaca, New York 14853	New Jersey New York Puerto Rico
III	Howard University Institute for Urban Affairs and Research P.O. Box 191 Washington, D.C. 20058	Delaware District of Columbia Maryland Pennsylvania Virginia West Virginia

REGION	PROJECT NAME AND LOCATION	AREAS SERVED
IV	Regional Institute for Social Welfare Research P.O. Box 152 University of Georgia Athens, Georgia 10601	Alabama Florida Georgia Kentucky Mississippi North Carolina South Carolina Tennessee
V	Graduate School of Social Work University of Wisconsin Milwaukee, Wisconsin 53201	Illinois Indiana Michigan Minnesota Ohio Wisconsin
VI	Graduate School of Social Work University of Texas at Austin Austin, Texas 78712	Arkansas Louisiana New Mexico Oklahoma Texas
VII	Institute of Child Behavior and Development University of Iowa, Oakdale Campus Oakdale, Iowa 52319	Iowa Kansas Missouri Nebraska
VIII	The National Center for the Prevention and Treatment of Child Abuse and Neglect University of Colorado Medical Center 1205 Oneida Street Denver, Colorado 80220	Colorado Montana North Dakota South Dakota Utah Wyoming
IX	Department of Special Education California State University 5151 State University Drive Los Angeles, California 90032	Arizona California Hawaii Nevada
X	Western Federation for Human Services 157 Yesler Way, #208 Seattle, Washington 98104	Alaska Idaho Oregon Washington

REFERENCES

1. Steele BF: Violence within the family, in Helfer RE, Kempe CH (eds): *Child Abuse and Neglect: The Family and the Community.* Cambridge, Mass, Ballinger Publishing Co, 1976.

2. Solomon T: History and demography of child abuse. *Pediatrics* **51**:773-776, 1973.

3. Smith SM, Hanson R: Interpersonal relationships and child-rearing practices in 214 parents of battered children. *Br J Psychiatry* **127**:513-525, 1975.

4. Baldwin JA, Oliver JE: Epidemiology and family characteristics of severely abused children. *Br J Prev Soc Med* **29**:205-221, 1975.

5. Green AH: A psychodynamic approach to the study and treatment of child-abusing parents. *J Am Acad Child Psychiatry* **15**:414-429, 1976.

6. Flynn JP: Recent findings related to wife abuse. *Soc Casework* **58**:13-20, 1977.

7. Straus MA: Leveling, civility and violence in the family. *J Marr Fam* **35**:13-19, 1974.

8. Justice B, Justice R: *The Abusing Family.* New York, Human Sciences Press, 1976.

9. Gil DG: *Violence Against Children: Physical Child Abuse in the United States.* Cambridge, Mass, Harvard University Press, 1970.

10. Smith SM, et al: Social aspects of the battered baby syndrome. *Br J Psychiatry* **125**:568-582, 1974.

11. Lystad MH: Violence at home: a review of the literature. *Am J Orthopsychiatry* **45**:328-345, 1975.

12. Helfer RE, et al: Arresting or freezing the developmental process, in Helfer RE, Kempe CH (eds): *Child Abuse and Neglect: The Family and the Community.* Cambridge, Mass, Ballinger Publishing Co, 1976.

13. Parke RD, Collmer CW: Child abuse: an interdisciplinary analysis, in Hetherington EM (ed): *Review of Child Development Research.* Chicago, University of Chicago Press, 1975.

14. Sarles RM: Incest. *Pediatr Clin North Am* **22**:633–642, 1975.

15. Summit R, Kryso J: Sexual abuse of children: a clinical spectrum. *Am J Orthopsychiatry* **48**:237–251, 1978.

16. Ball M: Issues of violence in family casework. *Soc Casework* **58**:3–12, 1977.

17. Elbow M: Theoretical considerations of violent marriages. *Soc Casework* **58**:515–526, 1977.

18. Hilberman E, Munson K: Sixty battered women: a preliminary report. Prepared for special session, Battered Women: Culture as Destiny, American Psychiatry Association Meetings, Toronto, 1977.

19. Pfouts JH: Violent families: coping responses of abused wives. *Child Welfare* **57**:101–117, 1978.

20. Pittman FS III: Counseling incestuous families. *Med Aspects Hum Sex* **10**:57–58, 1976.

21. Giarretto H: Humanistic treatment of father-daughter incest, in Helfer RE, Kempe CH (eds): *Child Abuse and Neglect: The Family and the Community.* Cambridge, Mass, Ballinger Publishing Co, 1976.

22. DeFrancis V: *Protecting the Child Victim of Sex Crimes Committed by Adults.* Denver, American Humane Association, 1969.

23. Weinberg SK: *Incest Behavior.* New York, Citadel Press, 1955.

24. Langsley DG, et al: Father-son incest. *Compr Psychiatry* **9**:218–226, 1968.

25. Browning DH, Boatman B: Incest: children at risk. *Am J Psychiatry* **134**:69–72, 1977.

26. Machotka P, et al: Incest as a family affair. *Fam Process* **6**:98–116, 1967.

27. Lustig N, et al: Incest: a family group survival pattern. *Arch Gen Psychiatry* **14**:31–40, 1966.

28. Cavallin H: Incestuous fathers: a clinical report, in Shiloh A (ed): *Studies in Human Sexual Behavior: The American Scene.* Springfield, Ill, Charles C Thomas Publisher, 1970.

29. *Child Sexual Abuse: Incest, Assault and Sexual Exploitation,* Publication (OHDS) 79-30166. US Dept of Health, Education, and Welfare, National Center on Child Abuse and Neglect, 1978.

30. Martin HP: Working with parents of abused and neglected children, in Abidin RR (ed): *Parent Education Handbook.* Springfield, Ill, Charles C Thomas Publisher, 1980.

31. Walters DR: *Physical and Sexual Abuse of Children.* Bloomington, Ind, Indiana University Press, 1975.

32. Gil DG: Unraveling child abuse. *Am J Orthopsychiatry* **45**:346–356, 1975.

33. Gelles RJ: *The Violent Home: A Study of Physical Aggression Between Husbands and Wives.* Beverly Hills, Calif, Sage Publications Inc, 1974.

34. Gelles RJ, Straus MA: Family experience and public support of the death penalty. *Am J Orthopsychiatry* **45**:596–613, 1975.

35. Viano EC: Attitudes toward child abuse among American professionals. Paper presented at International Society for Research on Aggression, Toronto, 1974.

36. Walker LE: *The Battered Woman.* New York, Harper & Row Publishers Inc, 1979.

37. Bandura A: *Aggression: A Social Learning Analysis.* Englewood Cliffs, NJ, Prentice-Hall Inc, 1973.

38. Erlanger HS: Social class differences in parents' use of physical punishment, in Steinmetz SK, Straus MA (eds): *Violence in the Family.* New York, Dodd Mead & Co, 1974.

39. Spinetta J, Rigler D: The child-abusing parent: a psychological review. *Psychol Bull* **77**:296–304, 1972.

40. Kempe CH, Helfer RE: Innovative therapeutic approaches, in Kempe CH, Helfer RE (eds): *The Battered Child and His Family.* Philadelphia, JB Lippincott Co, 1972.

41. Cohn AH: Essential elements of successful child abuse and neglect treatment. Paper pre-

sented at Second International Congress on Child Abuse and Neglect, London, 1978.

42. Caskey OL, Richardson I: Understanding and helping child-abusing parents. *Elem Sch Guid Counsel* 9:196-207, 1975.

43. Cantoni L: Family life education: a treatment modality. *Child Welfare* 45:372-381, 1975.

44. Reed J: Working with abusive parents: a parent's view—an interview with Jolly K. *Child Today* 4:6-9, 1975.

45. Galdston R: Preventing abuse of little children: the parents' center project for the study and prevention of child abuse. *Am J Orthopsychiatry* 45:372-381, 1975.

46. Gordon T: *P.E.T.: Parent Effectiveness Training.* New York, Wyden Books, 1970.

47. Gordon T, Sands JG: *P.E.T. in Action.* New York, Wyden Books, 1976.

48. Patterson GR: *Families: The Applications of Social Learning to Family Life.* Champaign, Ill, Research Press, 1971.

49. Patterson GR, Gullion ME: *Living with Children.* Champaign, Ill, Research Press, 1968.

50. Dreikurs R: *Children: The Challenge.* New York, Hawthorn Books Inc, 1964.

51. Patterson GR: Intervention for boys with conduct problems: multiple settings, treatments and criteria. *J Consult Clin Psychol* 42:471-481, 1974.

52. Tracy JJ, Clark EH: Treatment for child abusers. *Soc Work* 19:338-342, 1974.

53. Tracy JJ, et al: Child abuse project: a follow-up. *Soc Work* 20:398-399, 1975.

54. Burgess RL, Conger RD: Family interaction in abusive, neglectful and normal families. *Child Dev* 49:1163-1173, 1978.

55. Hughes RC: A clinic's parent-performance training program for child abusers. *Hosp Community Psychiatry* 25:779-782, 1974.

56. Thistleton K: The abusive and neglectful parent: therapy through parent education. *Nurs Clin North Am* 12:513-524, 1977.

57. Mirandy J: Preschool for abused children, in Martin HP (ed): *The Abused Child: A Multidisciplinary Approach to Developmental Issues and Treatment.* Cambridge, Mass, Ballinger Publishing Co, 1976.

58. Lynch MA, Ounsted C: Residential therapy: a place of safety, in Helfer RE, Kempe CH (eds): *Child Abuse and Neglect: The Family and the Community.* Cambridge, Mass, Ballinger Publishing Co, 1976.

59. Ounsted C, et al: Aspects of bonding failure: the psychopathology and psychotherapeutic treatment of families of battered children. *Dev Med Child Neurol* 16:447-456, 1974.

60. McBogg P: Circle House: a residential treatment program. Paper presented at International Congress on Child Abuse, London, 1978.

61. Pizzey E: *Scream Quietly or the Neighbors Will Hear.* England, Penguin Books, 1974.

62. Saltzman K: *Victim Support System: Final Report.* Grant 77-DF-08-0007, Law Enforcement Assistance Administration, 1977.

63. Walker LE: Treatment alternatives for battered women, in Chapman J, Gates M (eds): *The Victimization of Women.* Sage Yearbooks in Women's Policy Studies. Beverly Hills, Calif, Sage Publications Inc, 1978, vol 3.

64. Martin D: *Battered Wives.* San Francisco, Glide Publications, 1976.

65. Rosenfeld AA, et al: Incest and sexual abuse of children. *J Am Acad Child Psychiatry* 16:327-339, 1977.

66. Tormes YM: *Child Victims of Incest.* Denver, American Humane Association, Children's Division, 1968.

67. Harbert TL, et al: Measurement and modification of incestuous behavior: a case study. *Psychol Rep* 34:79-86, 1974.

68. Brazelton TB: Early parent-infant reciprocity, in Vaughn VC (ed): *The Family: Can It Be Saved?* Chicago, Yearbook Medical Publishers Inc, 1976.

69. Morris LA (ed): *Education for Parenthood: A Program Curriculum and Evaluation Guide.* Pub-

lication (ODHS) 77-30125, US Dept of Health, Education, and Welfare, Office of Human Development Services, Administration for Children, Youth, and Families, Children's Bureau, 1977.

70. *Exploring Childhood: Program Overview and Catalog of Materials 78/79.* Newton, Mass, Education Development Center, Inc, 1978.

71. Reynolds C: Can good parenting be taught?, in Franklin AW (ed): *Child Abuse: Prediction, Prevention and Follow-up.* London, Churchill Livingstone, 1977.

72. Lynch MA, et al: Child abuse: early warning in the maternity hospital. *Dev Med Child Neurol* 18:759-766, 1976.

73. Gray J, et al: Approaches to prevention of child abuse and neglect. *Int J Child Abuse Neglect* 1:45-58, 1977.

74. Kowalski K, et al: Team nursing coverage of prenatal-intrapartum patients at a university hospital: an innovation in obstetrical nursing. *Obstet Gynecol* 50:116-119, 1977.

75. Klaus MH, Kennell JH: *Maternal-Infant Bonding: The Impact of Early Separation or Loss on Family Development.* St Louis, The CV Mosby Co, 1976.

76. Kempe CH: Approaches to preventing child abuse. *Am J Dis Child* 130:941-947, 1976.

77. Newberger EH, McAnulty EH: Family intervention in the pediatric clinic: a necessary approach to the vulnerable child. *Clin Pediatr* 15: 1155-1161, 1976.

78. *Lift a Finger: The Teacher's Role in Combating Child Abuse.* Houston, Tex, Education Professions Development Consortium, 1975.

79. Broadhurst DH: Project PROTECTION: a school program to detect and prevent child abuse and neglect. *Child Today* 4:22-25, 1975.

80. *"If the Bough Breaks"* . . . *A Training Series for Workers in Child Welfare and Related Fields.* Minnesota Child Welfare Training Project and The School of Social Work, Center for Urban and Regional Affairs, University of Minnesota, Minneapolis, July 1975-June 1976.

81. Roy M: *Battered Women: A Psychosocial Study of Domestic Violence.* New York, Van Nostrand Reinhold Co, 1977.

8

CONCEPTS IN TEACHING THE VICTIM AND FAMILY

Carmen Germaine Warner, R.N., M.S.N., F.A.A.N.

The practice of teaching patients evolved in the 1970s as a means of familiarizing individuals with the process of their disease and its impact on their lives. This evolution has been beneficial for the patient, family members, and practicing clinicians. It has enabled the patient and family members to gain a working knowledge of the disease, become actively involved in intervention and recovery, develop a respect for the concept of wellness, and actively pursue techniques of preventive health maintenance.

These principles can also be applied to intervention, recovery, and regrowth and are an integral part of the teaching-learning process. This teaching-learning concept involves more structure, active participation, and feedback than traditional counseling sessions, and it can be a valuable tool throughout intervention. However, sensitive guidance, support, and listening must still be integral parts of the process of recovery and regrowth because of the probable existence of guilt, fear, hostility, shame, and denial.

In addition to the benefits of teaching during the acute posttrauma stage, there is need for follow-up teaching and reinforcement be-

cause victims frequently experience a lack of recall during the posttrauma period. This follow-up intervention is critical in order to reinforce the learning process and to reassess the sequence of recovery and regrowth.

INFLUENCING FACTORS IN THE TEACHING-LEARNING PROCESS

Professionals working with victims of violence can carefully assess the situation and be adequately prepared with teaching techniques and specific knowledge, but they will be unable to transfer the information and facilitate the learning process unless the victim is open and willing to learn.

Understanding the factors that influence the learning process is as important as understanding the nature of the violent behavior itself. These factors should be considered during preparation of the teaching-learning program.

Sex

If a female victim has been sexually abused by a male perpetrator, her interaction with a male investigator, physician, nurse, or counselor may not be as spontaneously open and trusting as it would be with a female. Likewise, should a male be physically abused by his female mate, his interaction with a female who commands a position of leadership or authority may be threatening for him. It is important to note, however, that once a trusting relationship has developed, the professional's sex becomes irrelevant.

Culture

Some victims are raised in a culture that respects personal and family privacy. They tend to remain closed to outsiders and profess that their problems are to be dealt with as they choose. Other individuals may pour out their concerns and problems to anyone who listens. This latter communication can be unrelated to the present situation, and the desire to share problems can block attempts to teach and to resolve conflict.

Language

English as a second language may present some difficulties for the victim and the victim's family members. Words that have multiple meanings or that might change meaning during translation could inhibit communication. Victims should be asked to repeat important ideas and factors in an attempt to assess their level of understanding.

Physical Impairments

Poor eyesight or hearing difficulties frequently influence one's ability to fully comprehend verbal communication. The importance of clear, slow enunciation along with thorough exposure to visual aids may markedly assist comprehension. Professionals should be aware of body language such as frowning, squinting, tilting the head, peering, and leaning forward. These behaviors

are excellent indications of visual or auditory impairment.

Education

The patient's knowledge of certain terminology used by the professional and the professional's knowledge of terminology used by the victim should be assessed at the onset of the teaching session. If difficulties exist, alternative words must be selected and initial instructions changed in an attempt to establish a mutual foundation of understanding.

Physical or Emotional State

Physical and emotional trauma that accompany cases of abusive trauma affect the victim's physical capability and general interest in learning and listening. Feelings of fear, anger, guilt, hostility, embarrassment, and denial may produce a strong protective wall that can not be penetrated in a medical or counseling setting. In this situation, it is imperative that emergency and social service professionals remain as supportive as possible and still be gentle. This behavior will be remembered even though the professional's name and face may not. If professionals place a business card or instructions for follow-up care in the victim's pocket, purse, or wallet, there is an excellent chance that communication may be reestablished later on.

Past Experiences

If the victim has experienced or witnessed episodes of abuse in the past, the present situation may be influenced by past memories. Anxieties that may appear inconsistent with present trauma may be a response that is the result of past accumulative incidences. It is critical that teaching techniques always begin at the victim's individual level of comprehension.

Possible Threat to the Victim's Well-Being

Even if the aforementioned barriers to effective learning are nonexistent, the victim may still resist attempts by professionals to provide teaching. Changed behavior occurs only if victims perceive a possible threat to their well-being. These changes may be influenced by the victim's personal perception and acceptance of the seriousness of the act of violence, how vulnerable the victim feels, how much importance the victim places on tranquility and wellness, and the possibility of future acts of violence should counseling and intervention not begin.

PURPOSE OF TEACHING THE VICTIM AND FAMILY

The concept of practicing preventive health maintenance, achieving optimum levels of wellness, and participating in one's own intervention and recovery is essential in developing a personal interest and responsibility toward one's own life. This is an important philosophy for victims to understand. It not only encourages their own optimum state of wellness but also helps them regain and maintain the self-respect and self-confidence that are frequently shattered by the trauma of violence. Feelings of self-worth and the ability to recognize, design, and attain personal and professional goals are an essential foundation for effective regrowth.

Respect of self and a holistic approach to life are valuable factors for victims of violence. They have the right to understand and be guided through the stages of recovery and regrowth.

Professionals who recognize this right must direct their teaching toward the

- Determination of specific processes of intervention and investigation, their purpose, impact, and procedural steps

- Realistic presentation of the problem
- Determination of the rate of incidence for each form of violence (to avoid feelings of isolation and aloneness on the part of the victim)
- Development of intervention based on the violent situation as a whole, rather than on the victim or perpetrator alone
- Pursuit of rebuilding, believing in, and living a meaningful, valuable life.

PLANNING PROCESS

Professionals working with victims of violence must understand the dynamics of violent behavior. Building on this understanding, the professional should assess the needs of each particular victim and modify teaching techniques accordingly.

Once the victim's personal needs and general knowledge of a particular violent behavior have been determined, the information can be applied to a particular blueprint for teaching that victim. There are five possible individual components in this teaching blueprint (Fig. 8-1):

1. Designing behavioral objectives
2. Assessing the victim's level of knowledge of the incident
3. Implementing specific teaching strategies
4. Evaluating the teaching blueprint
5. Filtering information through the feedback circle

Designing Behavioral Objectives

Professionals who design behavioral objectives should consider certain factors.[1]

- What type of behavior is anticipated of the victim and the victim's family after the teaching sessions?
- What specific information will be presented during the teaching sessions?

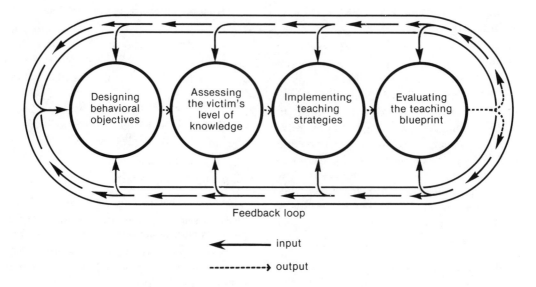

Fig. 8-1 Blueprint for teaching the victims of violence.

- Under what circumstances would change be expected?
- For whom are the teaching sessions prepared?
- What specific criteria are established to determine change in behavior, attitude, or environment?

Objectives may be modified as the victims' needs change and they progress through the stage of recovery and regrowth.

Assessing the Victim's Level of Knowledge

To facilitate effective learning, professionals must determine what the victim and family members already understand about the particular act of violence. They must

- Assess how motivated the victim is to change a particular living situation
- Determine how eager the victim is to reconstruct the victim's perception of self and future goals
- Evaluate the level of attention exhibited by the victim at any particular time

- Analyze the victim's level of maturity and stage of development necessary to understand the trauma of violence
- Interpret the victim's personal attitudes and beliefs concerning violence in general.

Implementing Specific Teaching Strategies

The focus of implementing specific teaching strategies focuses on the actual information that will facilitate learning. The critical point is that specific information must be correlated directly with the original behavioral objectives. Handouts to reiterate and clarify points of information are most valuable since the victim's level of concentration immediately after an assault is very low. Once the acute emotional stage has subsided, there will be a higher level of attention and more effective learning.

Evaluating the Teaching Blueprint

The entire teaching-learning process is only as effective as its potential for transmission, understanding, and implementation.

Teaching tools should be evaluated and modified constantly.

Because the evaluation process is a direct corollary to the behavioral objectives, the original objectives must be stated in terms that are measurable and observable, with specific, built-in requirements for performance.

A critical portion of the evaluation is the witnessed ability of the victim to apply the information learned. The teaching sessions are only as effective as the supportive attitude of the professionals and their available openness for continued verbal interchange.

Filtering Information Through the Feedback Circle

As indicated in Fig. 8-1, the feedback circle encompasses the entire process; an opportunity for direct input occurs at each stage. In this fashion, the information gained through evaluation may be directed to the appropriate segment and that segment modified and changed. This manner of updating can help maintain the most effective method of presenting information to both the victim and concerned family members.

CONSIDERATIONS FOR SUPPORTIVE WRITTEN MATERIALS

During the planning process, emergency and social service professionals should develop a resource bank that will enable them to speak knowledgeably and comfortably about all aspects of social and domestic violence. This information will help the professional understand and respond appropriately to each type of violent behavior.

Even with the most effective communicator, the probability that a victim will retain factual information is remote. The emotional trauma caused by violence is characterized by disrupted periods of concentration, misinter-

pretation of material, lack of recall, and total blockage of all verbal interchange.

Therefore, written material should be designed and used. These will enable the victim and family members to

- Refer to pertinent facts about their particular situation
- Clarify specific points of information
- Reinforce the teaching-learning process
- Answer certain questions for themselves
- Correct misinformation
- Use a self-teaching mechanism when the victim is more receptive to learning
- Have a list of warning signs and symptoms for which medical or social service personnel should be alerted
- Have information about community resources and follow-up care.

Printed material, designed as a teaching aid, is often described as frozen language.[2] This material can be useful to both the victim and family members if the following factors are applied:

- Present the information on a sixth-grade reading level.
- Explain the terminology in simple, lay terms.
- Design specific examples the victim can relate to.
- Provide an accompanying glossary for clarification of certain words.
- Arrange the material so that important facts can be easily recognized (consider the bullet style of outlining used in this chapter).
- Do not use too many words; full sentences are not always necessary.
- Reinforce learning with simple diagrams, illustrations, or tables.
- Organize material into sections that are clearly labeled and self-explanatory.

This method of organizing written material will complement the preparation of oral material and reinforce the victim's continued growth of understanding.

SUMMARY

Professionals who come in contact with victims of violence should explain each phase of intervention and guide the victim toward a deeper and more thorough understanding of the entire process of recovery and regrowth. A formal learning mechanism may not evolve, but through the continued attempt to communicate, share, and listen, victims will gain confidence, develop a sense of trust, and be able to openly discuss their lives and their future.

REFERENCES

1. Huckabay L: A strategy for patient teaching, *Nurs Admin Q* **4**:47–54, 1980.

2. Redman BK: *The Process of Patient Teaching in Nursing,* ed 3. St Louis, The CV Mosby Co, 1976, p 132.

SUGGESTED READINGS

DeCecco J, Crawford W: *The Psychology of Learning and Instruction: Educational Psychology,* ed 2. Englewood Cliffs, NJ, Prentice-Hall Inc, 1974.

Fletcher SW: Improving emergency room patient follow-up in a metropolitan teaching hospital. *N Eng J Med* **291**:385–388, 1974.

Gagne R: *The Conditions of Learning,* ed 3. New York, Holt Rinehart & Winston, 1976.

Glaser R: Psychology and instructional technology, in *Training, Research and Education.* Pittsburgh, Pa, University of Pittsburgh Press, 1962.

Korsch BM, Negrete VF: Doctor-patient communication. *Scientific American,* August 1972, pp 66–75.

Zander KS, et al: *Practical Manual for Patient Teaching.* St Louis, The CV Mosby Co, 1978.

9

INTERACTION WITH THE LEGAL SYSTEM

Gilbert Geis, Ph.D.

The law can be a significant aid to medical personnel who work with physically and emotionally abused persons. For one thing, legal codes that define powers, demand actions, and delineate obligations clearly establish the differences between legitimate undertakings and actions that might incur legal liability. In this sense, the law serves as a superordinate source of legitimation; it categorically defines mandatory actions regardless of one's personal preferences or those of a patient. Presumably, the law's position is rooted in reasoned judgment about what is best for the common good; often, however, more mundane considerations have fashioned the form of legal codes.

If necessary, persons and agencies charged with upholding the law will stand behind legal demands; they will use force, injunctions, fines, and, ultimately, imprisonment against those who fail to obey legal requirements. In general, the goals of medical personnel who deal with emotionally or physically abused patients are in close harmony with those of the law. At times, however, legal requirements can conflict with one's concept of professionally proper or personally acceptable behavior. This chapter considers dilemmas that may arise from legal demands upon medical personnel and suggests possible ways to solve such problems.

SUBSTANTIVE AND PROCEDURAL LAW

Medical personnel should thoroughly acquaint themselves with both the substantive laws and the procedural processes for enforcing these laws in the jurisdiction in which they work. Different jurisdictions in the United States have considerably different statutory enactments and case law as decreed by appellate court justices. Within a given state, cities and counties may use different methods to enforce the law.

Child Abuse

A particularly important legal requirement for medical personnel who see cases of child abuse is reporting such cases to the authorities. Mandatory reporting laws were first enacted in the 1960s and were largely confined to physicians. After passage of the federal Child Abuse Prevention and Treatment and Adoption Reform Act of 1974 (42 U.S.C. §5102), states expanded the reporting duty to cover, among others, teachers, dentists, police officers, nurses, social workers, and school officials. Today all 50 states, the District of Columbia, the Virgin Islands, and Puerto Rico have mandatory reporting laws,[1,2] and 20 states oblige "any person" to report instances of child abuse.[3]

Twenty-four states can impose criminal penalties upon persons who fail to comply with the reporting statutes (see, for instance, Delaware Code, title 16, §909). The offense is normally a misdemeanor, and the penalty can range from a minimum fine of $100 and/or five days imprisonment to a maximum $1000 fine and/or a year in jail.

Either by statute or through application of the negligence principles of common law, persons who fail to report cases of child abuse may become liable for damage suits. A typical liability imposed by statute is the Iowa requirement:[4] a person obligated to report who suspects that child abuse has occurred and knowingly fails to make a report is liable for any further injuries to that child "proximately caused" by the failure to report (Iowa Code §232.75). Although California imposes no specific liability on people who fail to report child abuse, the courts have held a physician and the hospital in which he worked liable, on the grounds of common-law negligence, because they did not notify the authorities as required. In that case, Gita Landeros, then 11 months old, had been brought to the hospital suffering from injuries which included a comminuted fracture of the right tibia and fibula, back bruises, and a nondepressed linear skull fracture. The mother could not adequately explain the infant's condition, and when approached, the child was fearful and apprehensive. Author-

ities later concluded that she had been abused by her mother and the mother's common-law husband.[5-7]

An investigation among medical personnel—physicians, nurses, and social workers—in 10 Iowa counties found that 63 percent of the social workers, 60 percent of the physicians, 46 percent of the registered nurses, and 33 percent of the licensed practical nurses were aware of the state law on reporting child abuse. Nonetheless, the researchers concluded that the statute was a "success" because the number of reported cases was increasing and medical personnel could easily pick out the "proper" cases for referral.[8] Other writers,[1] however, insist that the laws on reporting child abuse have diverted too much attention from effective approaches for primary prevention because they favor the identification of cases of abuse only after the abuse has taken place.

Domestic Violence

The law is rather ineffective in dealing with cases of domestic violence involving adults, usually cases of husbands assaulting their wives. The use of civil protection orders (CPOs) has become the most recommended tactic in such cases; about 60 percent of the states provide for the judicial issuance of CPOs. The orders generally impose one or more of the following conditions upon the offending party: (1) that he immediately move out of the family residence and have no further contact with his wife or cohabiter, (2) that he desist from any further abusive behavior against his wife or cohabiter, (3) that he take part in counseling sessions. Civil protection orders may be used also to establish custody arrangements for children, and they may specify support payments or sums to be paid in restitution for damages or medical expenses incurred by the victim.[9]

A few states permit a victimized woman to file for a protective order by herself, thus bypassing the need to pay an attorney's fees or to apply for free legal aid services. Other jurisdictions waive filing fees so that financial considerations will not prevent an abused party from seeking court-dictated protection and assistance.

A major difficulty with CPOs is the frequent lack of adequate enforcement. The stipulations are often flaunted with impunity by persons upon whom the orders are imposed. Judges are usually uncertain about what steps to take next when someone disobeys a CPO, particularly if there has been no other assaultive episode.

Criminal laws can be applied to cases of domestic violence involving married or cohabiting parties, usually by leveling charges of assault or attempted murder, if the facts warrant. But these cases are not favored by district attorneys, who possess virtually unlimited authority to reject any prosecutions they wish to disregard. Prosecutors sometimes explain that they are not interested in cases of domestic violence because women who initially press the charges more often than not withdraw them later or fail to cooperate in the prosecution. The true extent of such behavior has never been clearly documented, but there is anecdotal evidence that it is not uncommon. Women may renege because they cannot support themselves financially without the aid of their mates or because they are fearful of further violence. One effort to cope with this problem has been to discard the requirement that the beaten victim herself sign a complaint before any formal action will be undertaken. This change was dictated by the belief that an assaultive person who can no longer accuse his wife of bringing him to grief will not use the complaint as an excuse for violent retaliation. If the wife has not signed the complaint (medical personnel may have to decide if they care to do this for her where it is permissible), she legitimately can point out that the case is not being pressed by her, but rather by the state. In addition, such a maneuver may serve as a tactic for reducing guilt.[5,10-14]

Changes in the law in 20 states permit entries and arrests without warrants in cases of domestic abuse if the act of physical abuse is creating an immediate emergency. Five states—Maine, Minnesota, North Carolina, Oregon, and Utah—make arrest mandatory under specified conditions; the Oregon law adds the clause that the arrest may be made only if the victim offers no objection.

The mandatory use of arbitration procedures in instances of domestic violence is sometimes a particularly useful legal option, especially for women who are reluctant to take more drastic actions without prior attempts to reach a peaceful solution—such as having a third party mediate the case.[15]

A growing body of research deals with killings committed by women who maintain that they were driven to their lethal act only after a long and terrible history of physical and emotional abuse by their spouses. According to legal doctrine, the acts constitute self-defense only if there is an honest and reasonable expectation of unavoidable harm. Often the charges are reduced from murder to manslaughter on the grounds that the offender was so overcome by passion that she could not cool down in the interval between the abusive provocation and her death-dealing act.[16] There are no satisfactory statistics on the trials of wives who claimed they were abused by their husbands, but the common belief is that prosecutors and juries are sympathetic to their situation and that the women do not often receive the penalties that a cold-blooded, literal reading of the legal codes might dictate.

Rape

The legal position on rape has altered dramatically since the feminist movement first became actively interested in the problem.[16,17] More than 30 states now exclude questions about the complainant's previous sexual history, and most jurisdictions have eliminated the ancient cautionary instruction that directed the jury to remember that rape was easy to charge and difficult to defend against.[18] Most jurisdictions no longer require that a woman bringing a rape charge undergo a lie detector test at the request of the accused or that a rape charge must be corroborated in order to obtain a conviction. Furthermore, the legal definition of rape has been extended to include both men and women as victims and to incorporate any form of bodily penetration, not just genital violation. Despite these extensive changes, it remains notably difficult to secure convictions in rape cases. The evidence often comes down to the word of the accuser against the word of the accused, and it is an esential element of Anglo-Saxon jurisprudence that the defendant must be proven guilty "beyond a reasonable doubt." American law also has the rule epitomized by the *Mayberry* case:[19] a person accused of rape can use the defense that, given the circumstances, he acted as a "reasonable man" would have acted.[20]

Although spousal exemption from rape allegations dates back to medieval times in Anglo-Saxon law, about a dozen states permit a wife to file a rape charge against her husband. Charges pressed under the new provisions face problems common to all rape cases plus the compounding difficulty of social resistance against interfering when the matter involved concerns a married couple or a pair with a long-standing relationship.[21-23]

Compensation For Victims of Crime

Medical personnel should be conversant with statutes that provide state funds to persons who have been injured by criminal actions.[24] About 80 percent of the states have such laws. A number of jurisdictions restrict recovery to persons who can demonstrate an absence of personal financial resources to cover expenses or loss of earnings suffered because of criminal victimization; many do not have such a "need" requirement. Most jurisdictions, however, bar victims from compensation for acts committed by persons in their family or by persons living with them. This rule is based on the legal principle of "unjust enrichment," which maintains that a person should not benefit from a meretricious act committed by another who is legally related. In part, the doctrine rests on the dubious proposition that allowing such a recovery might encourage one family member to harm another in the same family so that the victimized individual could collect state funds.

PROBLEMS POSED BY THE LAWS

As noted earlier, legal obligations rarely cause problems either for medical personnel or for their clients. Difficulties can arise, however, when laws impose imperatives and burdens that conflict with the personal or professional standards of medical personnel or with the expressed interests of their patients.

Perceptions of the Victim

A major problem can be the different ways the legal system and medical personnel regard victims of physical and emotional abuse. The law views victims in a rather indifferent manner; its major concerns are trying to convict the offender and observing due process requirements.[25] Enormous state resources are poured into the preparation and prosecution of criminal cases, but virtually no heed is accorded the victim's needs or wishes. Indeed, one of the uglier aspects of the criminal process may come into play when victims of sexual abuse decide not to proceed with a case, and the district attorney threatens to bring an action against them if they continue to be "intractable." At the trial, victims can be humiliated, insulted, and otherwise revictimized as part of the few-holds-barred method that criminal trials often follow in the United States. Children in particular can be severely traumatized by insensitive courtroom proceedings. Take, for example, the following instructions in a manual for defense attorneys, and imagine the impact of such tactics upon a victim of physical or emotional abuse:

When you have forced the witness into giving you a direct answer to your question you really have him under control; he is off-balance, and usually rather scared. This advantage should be followed up with a few simple questions such as, "You did not want to answer that question, did you?" If the witness says that he wanted to answer it, ask him in a resounding voice, "Well, why did you not answer it when I first asked you?" Whatever his answer is you then ask him, "Did you think that you were smart enough to evade answering the question?" Again, whatever the answer is, you ask him, "Well, I would like for the jurors to know what you have behind all this dodging and ducking you have done!". . . This battering and legal-style "kicking the witness around" not only humiliates but subdues him.[26]

Legal Obligations Versus Medical Judgment

The idea that medical personnel who report cases of abuse might be partly "responsible" for subjecting a victim to such harassment might be thought of as compounding the original felony against the victim. What, then, is the proper posture for medical personnel who confront a legal obligation that they believe runs contrary to the best interests of their patient? The question is not simply a topic for philosophical discourse; it raises quite common dilemmas, and resolution can take a variety of forms.

Sometimes, the law will bend a little in the face of demands that medical judgment take precedence; thus, there are statutes that guarantee confidentiality between physician and patient. In the absence of such exceptions, medical personnel are obligated to adhere strictly to the law, even though they believe doing so may jeopardize the well-being and best interests of their patient. The greater the possible trauma for the patient, the more pronounced the dilemma becomes. If only convenience is involved, that is one

thing. However, when adherence to the law seems likely to produce serious health problems for the patient, the matter assumes much greater importance.

One fact that must influence any decision is the matter of employment. A person who accepts a position as a state employee implicitly or explicitly agrees that state requirements have precedence. As Halleck has argued, a psychiatrist working in a state prison must try to persuade an inmate to cease criminal activities, even if those activities are in the best interests of society (such as a black who stages forceful, but illegal, civil rights demonstrations) or in the best interests of the person (such as a young woman who thrives financially and emotionally on a career as a prostitute).[27]

The problem may be more severe for medical personnel who operate under private auspices. The easiest resolution is rote adherence to legal requirements; in most ways this course is assuredly the safest. On the other hand, the law is not always supreme; certainly the record of Nazi Germany argues for a citizen's self-judgment as the final arbiter of right and wrong. State authorities are not apt to move against medical personnel if their offense was one of omission based upon a professional judgment that it was in the best interest of their client. At times, such moral positions have persuaded courts that inflexible rules that infringe upon professional expertise should give away to that expertise. Perhaps the best illustration is the case of *R. v. Bourne.*[28] Bourne, a British physician, was prosecuted for performing an illegal abortion on a woman who, in his professional judgment, would suffer serious harm if she was not relieved of the fetus. The British courts not only reversed his conviction but also suggested that he might have been successfully prosecuted as a criminal had he not provided such medical assistance.

The problem, then, for medical personnel, is the need to balance responsibly the dictates of the law and the demands of the medical profession. At heart, the matter is one of conscience.

REMAINING IMPARTIAL

Another topic of concern is the extralegal interference of medical personnel in matters that are exclusively legal. Most fundamental is the occasional tendency of medical personnel to overstep their area of responsibility, medical expertise, by making moral and legal judgments.

A good illustration of this situation is a study by Geis et al. which questioned police surgeons in Great Britain about their handling of rape victims.[31] British police departments (constabularies) all have attached to them, usually on a fee-for-service basis, one or more physicians who examine victims that come to the department's attention. The presumed advantage of this system is that these police surgeons are specially trained in the gathering and packaging of evidence for subsequent criminal proceedings. In addition, they acquire considerable experience in testifying in court and in combating cross-examinations.[29]

It is arguable whether the British system, in contrast to the more entrepreneurial American one, serves the purpose of providing the best treatment for victims of crime.[30] But the point of interest in the study was that the British physicians had assumed duties normally associated with law enforcement[31] and justified their activities by labeling them medically relevant.

The physicians were asked if they believed that a police surgeon should offer an opinion to the police or prosecuting authorities before the trial about the legitimacy of a rape complaint. More than one-half, including the five female surgeons, thought such advice always should be offered. The major justification for this position was the belief that the police surgeons, who were among the first at the scene of a crime, secured evidence and formed insights that would not be so apparent to the authorities later on.

A majority of the respondents also believed, on medical grounds, that it was desirable to ask a rape victim if she had had previous sexual experience with the alleged rapist or with other persons besides her husband. They also thought it medically important to inquire about induced abortions and venereal diseases. Such information, if recorded, can be subpoenaed. And, although most American and British jurisdictions no longer allow questions about a rape victim's prior sexual history, except with the accused, the matter can sometimes be circuitously introduced if it is gleaned from official hospital reports.

There is no corresponding study of American personnel, but the tendency, at times, to play detective or to overstep professional boundaries is probably no different in the United States.

CONCLUSION

If laws were written by medical personnel rather than by legislators, they would undoubtedly be different than they are now. Understandably, medical people are sometimes impatient with the intricacies and esoterica of judicial considerations when such considerations interfere with what they regard as the proper performance of their job. Medical people, like policemen, often see the casualties of life first hand, and they may yearn for speedy and efficient redress. The law has other concerns besides suitable punishment for the guilty and proper protection for the innocent. At its very best, the law can be ennobling. At its worst, it can be shabby indeed. This chapter has presented some of the ways, both good and bad, used by the law in response to cases of emotional and physical abuse, and it has suggested some solutions for problems that exist because of the nature of legal mandates.

REFERENCES

1. Sussman A: Reporting child abuse: a review of the literature. *Fam Law Q* **8**:245-313, 1974.

2. Sussman A, Cohen SJ: *Reporting Child Abuse: Guidelines for Legislation.* Cambridge, Mass, Ballinger Publishing Co, 1975.

3. Fraser BG: A glance at the past, a gaze at the present, a glimpse of the future: a critical analysis of the development of child abuse reporting statutes. *Chicago-Kent Law Rev* **54**:641-686, 1978.

4. Besharov DJ: The legal aspects of reporting known and suspected child abuse and neglect. *Vill Law Rev* **23**:458-520, 1978.

5. Clymer JN: Torts: the battered child—a doctor's civil liability for failure to diagnose and report. *Washburn Law J* **16**:543-551, 1977.

6. Kohlman RJ: Malpractice liability for failure to report child abuse. *Cal State Bar J* **49**:118-123, 1974.

7. *Landeros vs Flood,* 17 Cal 3d 399, 551 P 2d 389, 1976.

8. Frischmeyer LE, Ballard DD: Iowa professionals and the child abuse reporting statute: a case of success. *Iowa Law Rev* **65**:1273-1385, 1980.

9. Orders of protection in family court disputes, note. *Colum J Law Soc Prob* **6**:164-175, 1966.

10. Field M, Field H: Marital violence and the criminal process: neither justice nor peace. *Soc Serv Rev* **42**:221-240, 1973.

11. Freeman M: The vice Anglais—wife battering in English and American law. *Fam Law Q* **1**:199-251, 1977.

12. Parnas RI: Judicial response to intrafamily violence. *Minn Law Rev* **54**:585-644, 1970.

13. Parnas RI: Prosecutorial and judicial handling of family violence. *Crim Law Bull* **9**:733-768, 1973.

14. Prosecutors discourage battered women from dropping charges. *Response Violence Fam* **6**:1-2, 1978.

15. Stulberg JB: A civil alternative to criminal prosecution. *Albany Law Rev* **39**:359-376, 1975.

16. Field HS, Biene LB: *Jurors and Rape: A Study in Psychology and Law.* Lexington, Mass, Lexington Books, 1980.

17. Chappell D, et al: *Forcible Rape: The Crime, The Victim and The Offender.* New York, Columbia University Press, 1977.

18. Geis G: Lord Hale, witches and rape. *Br J Law Soc* **5**:26-44, 1978.

19. *Mayberry vs People,* 15 Cal 3d 143, 542 P 2d 1377, 1975.

20. Bienen L: Mistakes. *Philos Pub Affairs* **7**:224-245, 1978.

21. Barry S: Spousal rape: the uncommon law. *Am Bar Assoc J* **66**:1088-1091, 1960.

22. Geis G: Rape in marriage: law and law reform in England, the United States and Sweden. *Adelaide Law Rev* **6**:284-302, 1978.

23. Glasgow JM: The marital rape exemption: legal sanction of spouse abuse. *J Fam Law* **18**:565-586, 1979-1980.

24. Edhelhertz H, Geis G: *Public Compensation to Victims of Crime.* New York, Praeger Publishers Inc, 1974.

25. Geis G: Victims of crimes of violence and the criminal justice system, in Chappell D, Monahan J (eds): *Violence and the Criminal Justice System.* Lexington, Mass, Lexington Books, 1975, pp 61-74.

26. Lake L: *How To Win Lawsuits Before Juries.* Englewood Cliffs, NJ, Prentice-Hall Inc, 1954.

27. Halleck SL: *Psychiatry and the Dilemmas of Crime.* New York, Harper & Row Publishers Inc, 1967.

28. *Rex vs Bourne,* 3 All Eng R 615, 1938.

29. Paul DM: The medical examination in sexual offenses. *Med Sci Law* **15**:154-162, 1975.

30. Clark LMG, Lewis DJ: *Rape: The Price of Coercive Sexuality.* Toronto, Canadian Women's Educational Press, 1977.

31. Geis R, et al: Police surgeons and rape: a questionnaire survey. *Police Surg* **14**:7-14, 1978.

Unit III

Adult Abuse

10

DYNAMICS OF FAMILY VIOLENCE

Ashley Walker-Hooper, B.A.

Many interchangeable terms are used to refer to domestic violence. "Battered wives," "abused women," and "family disturbances" all conjure up the same image. The victim is usually a female who is intimidated, threatened, and assaulted within the confines of her home, often within "plain view" of her children and within earshot of neighbors, family, and friends.[1] The involvement with the assailant has been or presently is an intimate one. Dependence upon the relationship is emotional as well as financial.

The difficulty for many people is understanding why a man who is involved with a woman could violently attack and harm her. Of equal difficulty is understanding why women stay and endure this physical and psychological abuse—some until death.

MEN AND WOMEN: VICTIMS OF DOMESTIC VIOLENCE

Viewing the woman as victim is relatively easy. She is physically harmed and often must seek medical attention. She is a prisoner in her own home and suffers loss of friends, family, and control of her life. Accepting the fact that men are also casualties is not as easy. Men often are abused as children and grow up in homes without role models for communication, nurturing, or support. Men are socialized to be always strong and to have their total environment under their control. Many watch their fathers abuse their mothers and learn violence as a means of communication. Hitting "tells" people whether one is happy or not. The masculine stereotype of strength, control, and family provider is difficult for many men to live up to.

General Characteristics

Table 10-1 is a comparison of characteristics of men who batter and women who are their victims. A portion (items 1 to 9) is taken from Walker's *The Battered Woman*.[2] Note the similarities and contrasts.

Four Types of Abusers

Elbow characterized abusers into four syndromes based on emotional needs central to each syndrome.[3]

Table 10-1   Characteristics of Men Who Batter and Women Who Are Their Victims

MEN	WOMEN
1. Has low self-esteem.	1. Has low self-esteem.
2. Believes all myths about battering relationships.	2. Believes all myths about battering relationships.
3. Is a traditionalist believing in male supremacy and stereotyped masculine sex role in the family.	3. Is a traditionalist about the home; strongly believes in family unity and prescribed stereotype of the female sex role.
4. Blames others for his actions.	4. Accepts responsibility for the batterer's actions.
5. Is pathologically jealous.	5. Suffers from guilt, yet denies the terror and anger she feels.
6. Presents a dual personality.	6. Presents a passive face to world, but has strength to manipulate enough to prevent further violence and to prevent being killed.
7. Has severe stress reactions; during them he uses drinking and wife battering to escape.	7. Has severe stress reactions with psychophysical complaints.
8. Frequently uses sex as act of aggression to enhance self-esteem in view of waning virility; may be bisexual.	8. Uses sex as a way to establish intimacy.
9. Does not believe his violent behavior should have negative consequences.[2]	9. Believes that no one will be able to help her resolve her predicament except herself.[2]
10. Has a low frustration threshold; poor impulse control; violent, explosive temper; external locus of control.	10. Martyrlike behavior; often long-suffering.
11. Emotionally dependent on wife and children.	11. Emotionally and/or economically dependent on partner.
12. Family history of domestic violence.	12. Family history of domestic violence.
13. Accepts violence as a viable method of problem solving; sees it as an acceptable means of maintaining an intact family.	13. Accepts violence in hopes of someday being able to change mate and solve family's problems and because she thinks she provoked anger and violence.
14. As a control mechanism, frequently abuses or threatens to abuse household pets and children.	14. Gives in to mate's demands to protect life of children and pets.
15. Was physically and/or sexually abused as child or saw ''significant other'' abused (usually mother by her mate).	15. Was physically and/or sexually abused as a child or saw violence at home.
16. Has high level of job dissatisfaction, underemployment, or unemployment that leads to feelings of inadequacy and inability to provide for family according to cultural stereotype.	16. Often employed but not allowed control of any finances.
17. Maintains close contact with his own family.	17. Loses contact with her family out of embarrassment or forced isolation; maintains contact with mate's mother.
18. Expectations of relationship are unrealistic; expects wife to conform to his definition of her role, but his expectations are often unspoken.	18. Has traditional expectations of husband as provider; of self as mother, wife, and mate.
19. Has preoccupation with weapons.	

THE CONTROLLER

The controller has a history of getting his way by persuasion, threats, or force. He is viewed as confident and in control of his emotions and life situations. He is never to blame. What he wants is his because it is due him. He appears generous and surrounded by friends and gives to those who give favors in return. People are used as objects to get what he wants. Relationships lack emotional reciprocity. He discounts the needs, desires, and feelings of his mate. He has unyielding control of his mate's activities and finances. Violence occurs when the controller cannot dominate or his authority is questioned. Terminating relationships means loss of control, not emotional ties. He can leave her, but she cannot leave him.

THE DEFENDER

The defender is attracted to women he sees as less powerful. He is afraid of being harmed. He wants his mate to cling to him and depend on him so he can feel strong. He has rigid standards and operates in the role of "forgiver." He associates his assertiveness and sexuality as something to be feared. He keeps his mate powerless so he will not have to fear attack. He is the "giver" and wants his wife to rely *only* on him. If his wife leaves, he has no helpless being to protect. Some women are attracted to the defender because they want someone they can lean and depend on.

THE APPROVAL SEEKER

The approval seeker is a high achiever who is seldom satisfied. He gets depressed when criticized but can be caring and sensitive. His self-esteem depends on the approval of others. When he is low, he expects rejection; he reacts by attacking verbally first and then physically when his mate denies the accusations or seeks to protect herself. He can be supportive and nurturing in nonfamilial situations. His mate is not allowed autonomy, and withdrawal is seen as disapproval.

Drinking and his feelings of inadequacy with authority figures are part of the pattern. Some women are attracted because he is achievement oriented and dependable. His need for emotional support and nurturing is seen as attractive, and his self-demeaning may be seen as honesty and humility.

THE INCORPORATOR

The incorporator is potentially dangerous. Desperation is his predominant feeling, and it is manifested as clinging to his mate, public displays of anger, threats to kill, depression or suicidal thoughts, and heavy use of alcohol and drugs. The desperation stems from his need to incorporate the ego of another in order to feel whole. He desires a close family tie, but he cannot give support and comfort. His wife is not allowed to leave, have friends in, or, sometimes, work. He fears she will leave. Leaving him causes ego eruption; he threatens, begs, pleads, and is violent. He frequently abuses or neglects children.

Why Women Stay in Abusing Relationships

Some reasons women stay in violent and unhappy relationships are discussed here.[4] Explanations of societal and interpersonal conditions help explain why separation from mates who are abusers is difficult. Some reasons include

- Guilt, embarrassment, and self-blame
- Fear of loss of sanity
- Fear of loneliness
- Fear of reprisals
- Economic dependency
- Emotional dependency
- Lack of resources
- Learned helplessness.

Women who believe in the traditional female sex roles of wife, mate, and mother are often embarrassed when the family nucleus is in jeopardy. They accept the blame for the emotional, physical, and psychological upset of the family. They feel guilty for not being able to make a go of the marriage. The violence is felt to be their fault because of some incompetence in their roles.

Loss of sanity is a fear because women, through self-imposed and forced isolation, have no one to validate their sanity. Over time, with continued abuse, they exhibit survival behaviors which, if viewed in isolation, appear to be manifestations of a psychological problem. Living under constant fear and stress takes a psychological and physical toll.

The fear of being alone and unwanted cannot be underestimated. The woman has been verbally abused and told she is incompetent, unwanted, and not lovable. She stays in the relationship hoping to be cared for; she cannot face being alone.

The precedent for reprisals has already been set, so when a mate threatens to kill her, to take the children, to hurt friends or relatives, or to hurt or maim her, she believes him. She has felt his rage before and knows the power of his retaliation. She also believes no one can help her.

Economic and emotional dependency are primary reasons why women stay. Women believe mates when the mates promise to change because the women love them and have invested a lot of emotional energy to make the relationship a success. Without funds, women cannot make choices about independent life-styles. Men encourage this dependency by cutting off outside contacts or refusing to let women work. Lack of personal or community resources also has kept women in abusive relationships.

Learned helplessness is a sense of powerlessness. Women believe there is no way to escape the domination of the batterer. They have been subjected to imprisonment and punishment. Even when an escape route is offered, many women feel it is no use trying to escape because the batterer will overpower them and force them to return (as he often has in the past). The powerlessness and loss of control has been generalized to their whole environment. They feel inadequate and incapable of helping themselves. Often helpers encounter battered women at this stage and respond without sensitivity to their predicament.

REFERENCES

1. Walker-Hooper A: Domestic violence: Assessing the problem, in Warner CG (ed): *Conflict Intervention in Social and Domestic Violence.* Bowie Md, RJ Brady Co, 1981.

2. Walker LE: *The Battered Woman.* New York, Harper & Row Publishers Inc, 1979, pp 26, 30.

3. Elbow M: Theoretical considerations of violent marriages. *Soc Casework,* **58**:515–526, 1977.

4. Walker LE: Battered women and learned helplessness. *Victimology* **2**:41–48, 1977–1978.

11

BEHAVIORAL ASSESSMENT OF THE PHYSICALLY ABUSED

Wendy G. Goldberg, R.N., M.S.N.

The staff of an emergency department is in a particularly good position to assist in recognizing physically abused persons, to conduct research on effective treatment modalities, and to determine community resources required to assist victims of violence. These departments usually offer 24-hour availability and accessibility without regard to cost as well as a certain degree of anonymity and the crisis-focused treatment of traumatic injury. It is understandable that victims of violence would choose these centers over other community resources, as they are frequently the most accessible resource when injuries occur.[1-3]

Medical Rationale for Treatment

The physically abused patient experiences both psychological and physiological trauma. Since the treatment of trauma is one of the raison d'être of emergency departments, it follows that treatment of physically abused persons should be given a high priority by departments of emergency medicine. Some would argue that the emergency department should confine its activity to trauma that could result in immediate loss of life or limb; this approach would mean treating only the life-threatening injuries and referring the patient to ambulatory agencies for mental health and medical care. There are three major problems with such an approach. First, victims of violence often do not return for follow-up appointments. Fear, embarrassment, lack of predictability in life-style, and sometimes the victim's age (coupled with deficits in the young victim's parental figures) impede the victim's ability to comply with scheduled follow-up appointments. In one emergency department study, for example, only 35 percent of the women requesting help for problems related to domestic violence actually returned for follow-up appointments.[4] Therefore, treatment that cannot be completed during the initial contact is not likely to be rendered at all. Efforts must be made to develop intervention strategies that can be successfully completed during a single visit to an emergency center and still meet the changing needs of the patient if this person should return for subsequent visits.

A second problem with delaying behavioral assessment and treatment of patients is that poorly timed intervention can be therapeutically ineffective or lead to serious aberrations and even mortality.[2,4,5] On the other hand, intervention during the acute phase of a crisis can prevent serious morbidity and promote resolution of the crisis to the premorbid level of functioning or above.[5] Victims of violence who come to the emergency center are in a state of crisis. During this time they have the greatest potential for change and are most responsive to therapy.

A third problem with delaying treatment is that physically abused persons may be experiencing an acute threat to loss of life or limb even though their physiological "vital signs" are normal. This threat may become a reality if the victim is discharged to a lethal home environment. If potential threats to the victim are inadequately explored, the victim's next visit may be to the morgue.

Sociopolitical Rationale for Treatment

In addition to the therapeutic reasons for treating victims of violence in the emergency department, there are several coexistent sociopolitical factors that intensify the need to provide service to these victims. A depressed economy, a decrease in the per capita income a drastic reduction in publicly funded projects, and a high rate of unemployment all contribute to an increase in family violence and mental health problems. For the victim, these factors mean limited employment opportunities, stringent requirements for public assistance, the closing of protective shelters, and the termination of human service programs or a reduction to a state of ineffectiveness. For the health care professional, these factors mean an innundation of patients whose primary complaints are rooted in social dysfunction rather than in organic etiology. Additionally, emergency centers can no longer look to community agencies or shelters to provide either the

volume or scope of services once available to victims of violence.

If the physically abused person is treated in the emergency setting, there are two possible approaches. One option is to focus on assessment for the sole purpose of gleaning information needed to guide the health care professional in developing a treatment plan. The patient is irrelevant in this process except as a source of information. Supporters of this particular approach suggest that the process of assessment should not be encumbered with therapeutic or treatment issues. An alternative approach is to begin therapy with the initial patient contact. Assessment in this case is an integral part of the therapeutic plan, and the patient works cooperatively with the experts (The author believes that the assessment process is best served by active patient involvement). Treatment of victimized persons should avoid further dehumanization and victimization of the patient caused by placing the patient in a passive, helpless role. Rather, health care professionals should urge the patient to take as active a role as possible. This latter approach attempts to maximize the therapeutic benefit of each patient contact. One does not first complete the assessment and then begin therapy. Assessment and therapy occur simultaneously but not always with equal emphasis. The process of intervention is dynamic and oscillates between the two aspects.

RECOGNIZING VICTIMS OF VIOLENCE

Emergency departments that treat victims of violence need a systematic way of recognizing the treatment population. Some victims overtly identify themselves as battered (by spouse, parents, other family members, or unknown assailants), and they request some form of assistance.

Many victims of sexual assault identify themselves initially, but may leave the emergency department prematurely if personnel are not compassionate or sensitive. If the patient does remain for treatment only to have health care professionals reinforce the self-demeaning myths of sexual assault, the patient's recovery will most certainly be hindered. The real challenge in the case of sexually abused persons is to provide adequate medical and psychological treatment that meets not only the victim's immediate needs but future medical, psychological, and legal needs as well.

Direct Questioning

The abused spouse presents special problems of recognition and treatment by emer-

Table 11-1   Determination of Domestic Violence Through Direct Questioning — Sample Questions

----

- Have you ever been in a relationship where you have been hit, punched, kicked, or hurt in any way? Are you in such a relationship now?

- How does your husband act when he is drinking? Is he verbally abusive? Is he physically abusive?

- Have there been any times during your relationship when you have had physical fights?

- You have mentioned your husband loses his temper with the children. How are things between you and your husband?

- You seem to have some special concern about your husband. Can you tell me more about this? Are you fearful? Has he ever hurt you?

- Do your verbal fights also include physical contact?

- Many women tell me that they argue with their boyfriends and later state they have been beaten. Could this be happening to you? Are you being beaten?

- Sometimes when husbands are overprotective and as jealous as you describe, they react strongly and use physical force. Is this happening in your situation?

- I notice you have a number of bruises. Could you tell me how they happened?

gency department staff. Since the victims rarely speak of themselves as abused, the health care professional must take a more active role.[3,6] One approach is to question patients directly. Research has demonstrated that nonjudgmental, direct, supportive questioning is both informative to the health care professional and a relief to the patient.[6] Many victims of domestic violence could be discovered simply by asking patients if they have had certain experiences (Table 11-1).

Battered Spouse Syndrome

Knowledge of the battered spouse syndrome can also aid in victim recognition (Table 11-2).[7-9] Since the syndrome is still in the formative stages of description, its components should be used as a guide in assessment and not as diagnostic criteria. Many of the

Table 11-2   Components of the Battered Spouse Syndrome

- Repeated visits to an emergency department for minor injuries

- History of being "accident prone"

- Soft tissue injuries

- Injuries on areas of the body normally covered by clothing

- Implausible explanations for injuries

- Simplistic or vague explanations for injuries

- Psychosomatic complaints

- Depression

- Pain—especially chronic

- Substance abuse in patient or spouse

- Suicidal gestures or attempts

- Psychiatric history in patient or spouse

- Previous marriage counseling

- History of physical abuse

- History of observing someone else being abused

- History of sexual abuse

guidelines are applicable to victims of other types of battery besides domestic violence.

Some physical injuries sustained during domestic assaults may cause pain without much evidence of visible trauma, while other injuries may be confined to areas of the body normally concealed by clothing. Therefore, a complete examination of the disrobed patient must be performed if there is any suspicion of domestic violence. Victims of domestic violence usually sustain repeated injuries over time. Hence, even if the cause of the injury seems plausible, the medical history should be reviewed to determine if the patient is reporting an inordinate number of "accidents." If so, this pattern should be discussed with the patient. This pattern of "hidden injuries" has been associated with the battered child syndrome as well.[10]

The victim of domestic violence is a person under chronic stress. It is understandable, therefore, that victims might have psychosomatic or functional complaints secondary to the stress of their violent relationship. In addition, it is more "acceptable" to seek treatment for headaches, loss of sleep, or depression than to acknowledge domestic violence. Explanations for the development of pain, suicidal gestures, and problems of substance abuse have been offered by two theories. One theory asserts that victims learn to hate themselves and seek sources of self-punishment.[10-13] For example, in some cases the intensity of chronic pain has increased after the termination of a violent relationship. Apparently, some victims learn that they are worthless and deserving of punishment. This group may subconsciously seek punishment when it is not provided for them. Nevertheless, masochism is not a unilateral explanation for domestic violence. Another theory suggests that self-destructive behaviors such as substance abuse and suicide attempts represent victims' efforts either to dull the noxious experience or to extricate themselves forever from repeated assaults.[3] Evidence suggests that substance abuse and suicide attempts are not primarily disorders but behaviors that occur after participation in violent relationships. These self-destructive efforts occur in victims too oppressed and depressed to seek more constructive alternatives.

Victims of sexual assault and victims of assault and battery may also be blamed for their attacks, particularly when the victim knows the assailant. A victim who has not revealed the traumatic experience to anyone or has suppressed critical aspects of the attack may come to the emergency department with an array of psychosomatic symptoms. Abusive or potentially abusive parents have also come to the emergency department with psychosomatic or minor complaints about themselves or their children during especially stressful periods. If these patients' behaviors can be accurately assessed, there is a great potential for therapeutic intervention and prevention.

BARRIERS TO RECOGNITION AND TREATMENT

Recognition and treatment of victims can be hindered by stereotypes and misconceptions about domestic violence which are unconsciously accepted by professionals and victims.[1,3,4,6,8,14,15] Successful treatment depends on understanding how barriers impede the therapeutic process (Table 11-3) and on developing alternative therapeutic behaviors.

Sanctity of the Family

Historically, the family's right to privacy has been rigorously protected in educational, legal, medical, and religious spheres. Health care professionals are reluctant to "invade" family boundaries, and family members hesitate to reveal problems as family centered,

Table 11-3   Barriers to Recognition and Treatment of Victims of Domestic Violence

- Sanctity of the family
- Rationalization
- Definition of violence
- The victim
- Blaming the victim
- Professional impotence
- Overreaction
- Excusing the assailant

choosing instead to handle domestic disputes within the home. Consequently, health care professionals who are confronted with a domestic problem may succumb to the dangerous belief that the sanctity of the family system dictates a position of noninvolvement. A healthier approach would be to recognize that a dysfunctional family may not be able to help itself without assistance from a skilled outsider.

Rationalization

There is historical precedent for wives being treated as property or children. As such, wives become an acceptable target for corporal punishment. Accordingly, the abused woman is not viewed as having a problem other than her unwillingness to fulfill her obligation to please the man who "owns" her. Health care professionals who excuse violent occurrences because one of the spouses "asked for it" unwittingly sabotage treatment. The professional must help the victim distinguish between violent acts (always totally unacceptable) and contributing factors within the victim's behavior over which the victim has some control.

In some cases, violent outbursts are rationalized on the basis of cultural stereotypes; the assumption is that violence within a particular group of people is the norm. While some groups may express themselves physically more often than others, the misinformed belief that violence is to be tolerated within certain groups falsely excuses professionals from intervening with the very people whose need may be most acute. A therapeutic distinction must be made between the prevalence of violence and its acceptability.

Definition of Violence

Individuals who are chronically exposed to extreme forms of violence, either in their job or personal milieu, tend to become impervious to lesser forms of violence. A slashed arm seems minor compared to a gunshot wound. Likewise, a kick in the abdomen may be perceived as trivial compared to the slashed arm. A person who has been roughly shaken and demeaned repeatedly by a spouse may not be perceived as a victim of violence at all. This dulled state of perception is pathological, particularly in terms of prevention, early recognition, and treatment of domestic violence. A corollary of a dulled state of perception is the victims' tendency to use nonspecific descriptors and minimizing language to deny the seriousness of the situation to themselves and others. Common examples are "He hit me" and "We were fussing." These phrases do not activate the health care professional's suspicion that the patient may be a victim of severe, ongoing violence. Although there are many psychosocial reasons for the victim's denial, the important point is that victims use imprecise language. Health care professionals must anticipate it, recognize it, interpret it, and validate it with the victim. A classic example is the woman who reported, "I yelled at my husband, and then we had a fight." After persistent questioning, which required the victim to specify the details of her experience, it was learned that the victim yelled obscenities at her husband after he chased her from room to room threatening to kill her. The "fight" consisted of his kicking and punching her in the head, chest, and abdomen.

The Victim

Victims of domestic violence often impede helping agencies from mobilizing on their behalf. Along with requests for assistance, they simultaneously exhibit overwhelming dependency, passivity, and even open resistance to change. These behaviors can infuriate professionals who are independent, self-motivated, and efficient at solving problems. The thought of leaving a known but oppressive environment produces a state of ambivalence within the victim, a situation which may be interpreted as disinterest or laziness, rather than immobilizing psychic conflict. The female victim may fear leaving the relationship because she believes she is incapable of surviving outside it; she dreads retribution by the assailant; the thought of single parenthood is intolerable; or perceiving her partner's fragility, she fears his self-destruction if she leaves. Simultaneously, the victim may fear remaining in the relationship because she can no longer cope with its chronic unpredictable stress, she values her children's well-being, or she dreads continuing a potentially lethal relationship. Victims of domestic violence are often psychologically and physiologically debilitated by the time they openly seek professional help. They lack the energy to objectively reflect on the severity of their past history and cannot conceptualize an improved future. It is only through persistence and tenaciousness on the part of the health care professional that victims of domestic violence can sufficiently restore their resources and actively choose healthy alternatives to their current situation.

Blaming the Victim

Most people believe that "you get what you deserve" and "you reap what you sow." Unfortunately, the world is not always a rational or logical place. People find it unsettling to believe that events beyond their control could influence their lives in severely destructive ways. For example, events that include the components of high coercion and high control inherent in brainwashing, kidnapping, and domestic violence cause people with normal psychological profiles to behave in a bizarre or irrational manner.[13,16,17] Adopting the "it-could-never-happen-to-me" philosophy is a defense against the realization that everyone is susceptible to bad fortune and bad judgment. Believing that people get what they deserve and denying that the "innocent" may be victimized leads to the rationalization that victims must be blamed for their misfortunes. This concept has broad application to victims of circumstance and even of disease. People are socialized to exhalt those who overcome great obstacles, but are not well-versed in understanding or aiding the temporarily defeated.

The health care professional must assist the victim and others to distinguish between "blame-ability" and "response-ability." For example, a woman is more likely to choose abusive partners if, as a child, she observed her mother being beaten.[8,18,19] The fact that this woman chooses a series of abusive mates is not cause for blame. Each abusive encounter will reinforce the woman's own sense of worthlessness and the worthlessness of women in general. Masochistic behavior should not be reinforced by subtly inferring that it is the victim's fault for choosing such partners. Rather, professionals must communicate that she and other victims can get help in regaining control over their lives and in assuming responsibility for their actions.

Professional Impotence

A lack of education and training in current useful approaches, the general underdeveloped "state of the art," and a lack of community resources contribute to the professional's feelings of inadequacy in treating victims of domestic violence. Feelings of help-lessness may be particularly strong when treating a victim who has been in a violent situation for years, who has already made several unsuccessful attempts to get help. While this victim might appear to have a poorer prognosis than the victim seeking help for the first time, many who eventually get out of abusive relationships are older, have been involved in abusive relationships longer, and have sought help before. Once the people who provide health care receive adequate education and training in this area, their feelings of inadequacy in treating victims of domestic violence should decrease.

Overreaction

Situations of domestic violence can be extremely affectively laden and may produce strong responses from the well-meaning but naive care giver. Overreaction by the helping person may frighten victims into silence or, even worse, into defending the assailant. This situation prevents victims from assessing their own feelings and needs. The victims' task is to recognize, express, and channel their anger constructively. Therefore, treatment must remain focused on the victim, not the outraged professional.

Excusing the Assailant

Incidents of spouse abuse too often evoke pity and compassion for the assailant. Observation of the assailant's solicitous concern and apologetic behavior toward the victim may lead the health care professional to encourage the couple to continue the relationship despite evidence of a long history of abuse. One can accept the sincerity of assailants' apologies and their belief that they love the victims and, at the same time, understand that without a change in the assailants' coping mechanisms, the violence will continue. Recommending counseling while a couple continues to live together is a risky option at best. Most often assailants do not

consent or follow through with counseling. Certainly, the assailants require professional help, but this requirement in no way diminishes the victims' need to extricate themselves from abusive situations.

A common mistake, when trying to comfort the assault victim, is emphasizing the sickness of the attacker. If done prematurely, the victim is forced into a compassionate, almost protective attitude toward the assailant, thus blocking the victim's anger and rage which need to be expressed.

Acceptance on the part of any physically abused person shortly after the assault is a pathological behavior that should be investigated. A legitimate goal of brief or long-term therapy is sufficient integration of the attack into the person's experience so that the patient emerges whole and functional. Acceptance cannot occur immediately after the attack without compensatory action by the victim. These fragile defensive maneuvers will most surely break down and result in delayed, but probably more severe, symptoms for the victim such as depression, rage, and various forms of chemical or physical abuse. While attempts to understand the assailant may aid the victim, excusing the assailant is never a component of therapy.

RATIONALE FOR THE INTERVENTION MODEL

The intervention model presented in Table 11-4 can be used in emergency departments as a guide for providing comprehensive treatment to victims of domestic violence. The model's effectiveness depends upon applying the principles of interaction described in this chapter and understanding the rationale for the model's construction.

Function of the Model

The model's function is to serve the needs of both the professional and the victim. For the professional, this model can promote the

Table 11-4 Assessment and Treatment Report for Victims of Domestic Violence

PHYSICIAN'S REPORT

1. Date of Assault _____.

2. Statement of Complaint (use patient's own words)

3. Description of Assault (use patient's own words)

    a. Specific detail and chronology of assault:

    b. Pain and symptoms mentioned:

4. Check physical findings.

	Contusions	Abrasions	Lacerations	Bleeding	Fracture	Other (Specify)
Head						
Ears						
Nose						
Cheeks						
Mouth						
Neck						
Shoulders						
Arms						
Hands						
Chest						
Back						
Abdomen						
Genitalia						
Buttocks						
Legs						
Feet						

Table 11-4 (Cont'd)   Assessment and Treatment Report for Victims of Domestic Violence

PHYSICIAN'S REPORT

5. Describe presence of trauma. Indicate location, appearance, and size. Indicate possible source such as teeth, cigarette burns, etc.

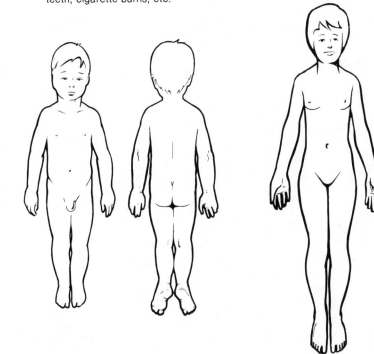 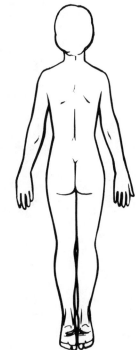

6. Internal Injury:

7. Previous assaults (describe injuries and treatment):

8. Additional comments:

9. Assessment:

10. Consultations (service and consultant):

_____   _____

_____   _____

Table 11-4 (Cont'd) Assessment and Treatment Report for Victims of Domestic Violence

MENTAL HEALTH CONSULTANT

I. *History of Current Abusive Relationship*	SPECIFIC COMMENTS

A. Relationship to assailant (circle):
 	
Married   Friend
Divorced   Ex-friend
     Separated
 	
B. Living arrangement (circle):
 	
Cohabit   Separate
 	
C. Length of relationship:
 	
D. Onset of abuse:
 	
  1. How often
  2. Abuse pattern is (circle):
 	
    Increasing   Staying the same
     Decreasing
 	
F. Types of abuse (circle):
 	
Verbal   Mobility Restriction
Battering   Phone Restriction
Sexual   Economic
    Other (specify)
 	
G. Instruments of abuse (circle):
 	
Gun   Fire
Knife   Hot substance
Blunt object Cord
    Other (specify)
 	
H. Descriptive quality of assault (circle):
 	
Ritualistic   Slow rise in tension
Impulsive   Other (specify)
 	
I. Coincidental Factors:	

	Victim	Assailant
Alcohol		
Drugs		
Argument		
Omission		
Commission		
Other (specify)		

Table 11-4 (Cont'd)   Assessment and Treatment Report for Victims of Domestic Violence

MENTAL HEALTH CONSULTANT

I. *History of Current Abusive Relationship*	SPECIFIC COMMENTS

J. Behavior after assault(s) (circle):

    Reconciliation   Terminate relationship
    Leave scene   Contact friend
    Contact relative Other (specify)

K. Attempts to leave relationship (describe):

L. Supportive resources (circle):

    Family   Employer
    Friends   Other (specify)

M. The overall relationship is changing in the following way (circle):

    Much worse   Better
    Worse   Much better
       Same

II.   *Education Level (circle highest):*

   1 2 3 4 5 6 7 8 9 10 11 12

   General Education Degree (GED)

   Post High School (specify) _____

   Graduate Education (specify) _____

   Other Education (specify)_____

III.   *Employment Summary*

   Current: _____

   Past: _____

IV.   *Children*

NAME	SEX	DATE OF BIRTH	PLACE OF RESIDENCE	WELL BEING	COMMENTS

Table 11-4 (Cont'd) Assessment and Treatment Report for Victims of Domestic Violence

MENTAL HEALTH CONSULTANT

V. *Summary of Past Abusive Relationships*

    A. Adult: _____

    B. Child: _____

VI *Mental Status* (circle):

Above average intelligence average intelligence below average intelligence mentally retarded
alert disoriented short-term memory intact long-term memory intact depressed elated fearful
angry flat passive demanding manipulative labile apathetic agitated bizarre poverty of ideas
flight of ideas loose associations delusional paranoid suicidal homicidal drug abuse alcohol abuse

Additional comments:

VII. *Alternative Place(s) of Residence*   _____Yes _____No

    Name: Name:

    Address: Address:

    Telephone: Telephone:

VIII. *Contact Person(s)*

    Name: Name:

    Address: Address:

    Telephone: Telephone:

    Relationship: Relationship:

IX. *Victim's Goals*

    A. Short-term:

    B. Long-term:

X. *Assessment*

    A. Present danger: D. Readiness for intervention:

    B. Problem-solving ability: E. General impressions:

    C. Needs:

XI. *Recommendations*

XII. *Victim's Plan* (if known)

XIII. *Final Disposition*

_____

                                  Signature

Reprinted from *Topics in Emergency Medicine 3:4* "Domestic Violence Victims in the Emergency Setting" by Wendy Goldberg and Anne L. Carey by permission of Aspen Systems Corporation • January 1982.

systematic acquisition of salient information, reduce the incidence of prejudicial responses, and provide a mechanism for collecting research data. Completed assessments should allow the health care professional to:

- Diagnose and treat patients' physical injuries
- Evaluate victims' strengths and deficits
- Determine what actions patients can take on their own behalf
- Promote patients' self-growth
- Provide needed information to victims
- Make appropriate referrals.

Although patients should be urged to function as independently as possible, there may be times when the professional will have to share or take over necessary tasks on behalf of a patient. For example, the professional might sit with a patient while the patient telephones helping agencies. In this way, the professional provides support and guidance while offering victims an opportunity to experience independent functioning as they develop the skills necessary to interact with the bureaucratic jungle.

Application of the Model

Application of the model benefits the victim because it facilitates the critical components of crisis intervention:

- Provision of a safe environment
- Opportunity for improved understanding of self
- Immediate medical and psychological treatment
- Assistance with establishing future goals
- Information about services patients cannot provide for themselves

The model includes very specific questions about the nature of the abusive situation. It is believed that as patients are assisted to recall the details of the immediate crisis, they will begin to break through their own denial about the seriousness of the assault. As they are able to make historical links with past episodes of abuse, they will be able to recognize their ongoing pattern of victimization. These two insights, insights into the depth and breadth of their situation, foster the victims' ability to view themselves seriously enough to institute constructive steps to change their plight. If they continue to view each attack as an isolated, unpleasant, but tolerable episode, their chances of getting out of the role of the victim are minimal. Likewise, the model provides opportunities for the patients to examine their own strengths by reviewing their achievements, skills, activities in solving problems, and support network. Through a collaborative process between health care professionals and the patient, these strengths are then incorporated into a treatment plan specific for the individual victim.

VICTIMS OF ASSAULT AND BATTERY

Victims of assault and battery have been virtually ignored by mental health professionals because it has been assumed that the psychological consequences of this experience are minimal. If such a victim should come to the emergency department, the focus is on immediate treatment of physical injuries and follow-up for any medical sequelae. Yet, health care professionals would do well to recognize the developing science of victimology which describes the devastating effects a victimizing experience can have on a person.

For purposes of behavioral assessment, victims of assault and battery can be divided into two major groups. The first group includes persons who do not know their assailant, and who usually experience a single, isolated attack. These persons are victims of opportunity and are not seen as participants in the crime. Examples are shoppers attacked in a parking lot, pedestrians attacked during daylight on a busy street, and elderly or otherwise infirm persons attacked in a park. These persons are similar to victims of sexual assault; the fact of an attack is often overt, but their fears and psychological needs may be quite covert. Both types of victims report fears of dying during the attack regardless of the actual severity of the assault. These patients may engage in ritualistic behavior or make life changes similar to those made by victims of sexual abuse. Health care professionals must assist these persons to uncover masked concerns and help them plan for future psychological and social service needs such as the ventilation of anger, recognition of vulnerability, and planning for personal safety. Unlike victims of sexual assault, these patients are spared the trauma of being forced to intimately participate in their attack.

The second group of victims is more like victims of domestic violence. These persons usually know their attackers or experience multiple attacks. Examples of patients in this category are persons attacked at night while walking along a deserted street, persons attacked while intoxicated or using drugs, and persons who are presumed to have prior knowledge of the aggressiveness of their attacker. These patients tend to arouse little sympathy from emergency department personnel and may even elicit hostile responses for "deserving what they get" since they should have "known better." Patients in this second group respond to techniques similar to those described for recognizing and assisting victims of domestic violence.

CONCLUSION

Victims of violence are a significant population in hosptial emergency departments. There is substantial reason to provide treatment to these victims in the department, and the treatment should be comprehensive. Victims of several types of violence have been discussed. A guide to recognizing victims and barriers to effective interaction has been provided. An assessment and treatment report (Table 11-4) facilitates coordinated, comprehensive intervention by a multidisciplinary team of nurses, physicians, mental health consultants, and other specialists as needed.

Unfortunately, many facilities that provide acute care for victims of violence do not have the luxury of onsite mental health consultants, and those that do tend to underutilize the consultants' services. The incidence of underutilization can be reduced by teaching personnel that much can be done for physically abused persons in the emergency department and by establishing protocols to ensure that these patients are referred to the mental health consultant. Emergency departments that do not have an onsite mental health consultant may choose to retain a mental health specialist on a contractual basis. Nevetheless, physicians and nurses still have a primary role in addressing the needs of physically abused persons. It takes little time to overtly acknowledge the overwhelming nature of patients' experiences and to communicate the belief that, with help, patients can not only survive the current trauma but also make significant positive changes in their lives.

Specialists in emergency medicine and emergency nursing face the continued challenge of developing comprehensive approaches for treating the physically abused person. It is clear that services to the population can no longer be restricted to the treatment of physical injuries. A current understanding of the nature of the problem and of the benefits derived from timely intervention mandates a comprehensive approach. Gaps in existing research and practice provide exciting opportunities for emergency care specialists to benefit all victims of violence and abuse and to contribute to the theoretical understanding of physically abused persons.

REFERENCES

1. Friedman KO: The image of battered women. *Am J Public Health* **67**:722-723, 1977.

2. Rounsaville B, Weissman MM: Battered women: a medical problem requiring detection. *Int J Psychiatry Med* **8**:191-202, 1977-78.

3. Stark E, et al' Medicine and patriarchal violence: the social construction of a "private" event. *Int J Health Serv* **9**:461-492, 1979.

4. Rounsaville BJ: Battered wives: barriers to identification and treatment. *Am J Orthopsychiatry* **48**:487-494, 1978.

5. Aguilera DC, Messick JM: *Crisis Intervention: Theory and Methodology,* ed 3. St Louis, The CV Mosby Co, 1978.

6. Parker B: Communicating with battered women. *Top Clin Nurs* **1**:49-53, 1979.

7. Star B: Comparing battered and non-battered women. *Victimology* **3**:32-44, 1978.

8. Star B, et al: Psychosocial aspects of wife battering. *Soc Casework* **60**:479-487, 1979.

9. Appleton W: The battered woman syndrome. *Ann Emerg Med* **9**:84-91, 1980.

10. Kempe CH, et al: The battered child syndrome. *JAMA* **181**:17-24, 1962.

11. Shainess N: Vulnerability to violence: masochism as process. *Am J Psychother* **33**:174-189, 1979.

12. Straus MA: A sociological perspective on the prevention and treatment of wifebeating. *Nurs Dimensions* **7**:45-62, 1979.

13. Symonds A: Violence against women: the myth of masochism. *Am J Psychother* **33**:161-173, 1979.

14. Seminar gives guidelines on how to handle family abuse cases. *Registered Nurses Assoc BrC News* **10**:26-28, 1978.

15. Lesse S: The status of violence against women: past, present and future factors. *Am J Psychother* **33**:190-200, 1979.

16. Steinmetz SK: *The Cycle of Violence: Assertive, Aggressive, and Abusive Family Interaction.* New York, Praeger Publishers Inc, 1977.

17. Singer MT: Coming out of the cults. *Psychology Today,* January 1979, pp 72-82.

18. Price J, Armstrong J: Battered wives: a controlled study of predisposition. *Aust NZ J Psychiatry* **12**:43-47, 1978.

19. Gayford JJ: The aetiology of repeated serious physical assaults by husbands on wives (wife battering). *Med Sci Law* **19**:19-24, 1979.

12

MANAGEMENT OF SPOUSE ABUSE

Ashley Walker-Hooper, B.A.

Because of self-imposed and forced isolation, many battered women make few ventures into the outside world. One of the few places the women are allowed to visit is the physician or hospital when they seek treatment for the injuries inflicted by the "significant other" during a violent episode. For many battered women, the hospital emergency department is the only contact they will make with an agency or system after the battering incident. How the woman is treated is a crucial issue in a discussion of her ability to obtain and maintain contact with other important systems such as legal, criminal justice, health-related, and social service. The sensitivity and comprehensiveness of care is important.

Time is at a premium in an emergency department, but the failure to recognize and acknowledge domestic violence as the cause of even a moderate percentage of women's medical complaints reinforces their feelings of helplessness and isolation. Thousands of women have called the hotline, attended support groups, or sought shelter from the YWCA's Battered Women's Services in San Diego, California. When asked about their medical histories and interactions with medical personnel, an overwhelming number stated that physicians were distant and single-minded in treating only the injury, did not establish enough mutual trust and interest for women to discuss their "personal dilemmas," or did not inquire, in some instances, or did not believe the circumstances of the injuries. Some women, because of guilt, shame, fear, or embarrassment, did not tell the truth about the origin of their injuries. In situations where the injury obviously did not fit the explanation, the old classic line, "I ran into the door!" was not questioned as an inadequate explanation for injuries to the face, back of the neck and head, chest, or lower back. A high index of suspicion is the first tool necessary for recognizing the abused wife.[1]

Most women do not seek medical attention at the time of the injury unless the injuries are life-threatening or another system (police, social service agency) has intervened to assist her and has insisted that she get help. Often there is not only a delay in seeking medical assistance but also a discrepant explanation and numerous other visits for vague symptoms. Often there is a history of discomforts and, in a significant number of cases, evidence of earlier injury.

One cannot underestimate the need of women to pretend that their lives and family interactions are all right (especially since many are accompanied by their husbands). Many, however, if queried in a straightforward and caring manner, will truthfully tell the cause of their injuries. They are relieved that someone asked and will readily unload this terrible secret. The battering situation makes most people uncomfortable, and it is easier to feign unawareness of the suffering and concentrate on treating individual injuries. Although there is no open acknowledgement that battering is an issue in a substantial number of medical histories, in a 1979 study Stark et al. found that though medical personnel failed to recognize that women were battered, these women were treated differently than nonbattered women.[2] Records of 481 female clients (clinic records, previous visits to the emergency department, social and psychiatric service records, and hospitalizations) were analyzed. These women had sought treatment for injuries during a sample month at a major urban emergency department. Over 1,400 cases of trauma were examined; the frequency ranged from 1 to more than 20 per patient. Physicians positively diagnosed battering in 14 women (2.8 percent) even though another 72 (16 percent) had injuries described as *probable* (at least one injury caused by a punch, kick, or similar assaultive act) or *suggestive* (at least one injury inadequately explained by medical history). When full medical histories were analyzed, almost 10 percent of the 481 women could be positively classified as battered and another 15 percent had histories that suggested trauma and pointed to abuse. Physicians recognized fewer than 5.5 percent incidents of abuse in more than 1,400

injuries. An additional 24 percent were "probable" or "suggestive." Almost 50 percent of the "probables" and 25 percent of the "suggestives" were classified by other agencies as abuse. Women recognized by physicians as battered (positives) were injured three times as often as nonbattered women (6.35 injuries versus 1.83 injuries). The battered women and "probable" women had almost identical records of trauma; "suggestives" had similar incidences of injury (0.82 compared to 1.13 and 0.97 incidents per year). The interpretation of "suggestive" statistics is that it includes women who are just beginning abusive relationships.

In sum, although physicians saw 1 out of 35 of their patients as battered, a more accurate approximation is 1 in 4. They acknowledged that 1 injury out of 20 resulted from domestic abuse, but the actual figure approached 1 in 4. What they described as a rare occurrence was, in reality, an event of epidemic proportions.[2]

MEDICAL CONSIDERATIONS FOR BATTERED WOMEN

Immediate Treatment of Acute Injuries

Battered women often seek medical attention for bruises and contusions. Typical and frequent complaints are somatic complaints, conversion symptoms, and psychophysiological reactions. There are frequent clinic visits for headaches, choking sensations, hyperventilation, asthma, chest pains, gastrointestinal symptoms, pelvic pain, back pain, and allergic phenomena. Most have been treated intermittently or chronically with sedative hypnotics, tranquilizers, or antidepressants.[3]

Violence usually increases during pregnancy; battered women are three times more likely than nonbattered women to be pregnant when injured.[2] Consequently, they experience a significantly higher number of miscarriages. Rounsaville found that 16.2 percent of battered women had been beaten by their partners when the women were pregnant.[4]

Since many batterers become adept at inflicting injuries that are not readily noticeable, a thorough examination is often necessary to ascertain the full extent of injuries. Injuries to the back, stomach, breast area, and the part of the head covered by hair often require close scrutiny to determine the extent of injuries.

Victims of domestic violence often return home with numerous medications that treat the physical symptoms but without any acknowledgement of spousal or intimate assault. Drugs maintain the victim's dependence and often reduce her ability to respond to her situation in a clear and rational manner. Reduction of a woman's understanding, determination, and problem-solving ability because of the use of the drugs is often a problem. The most frightening aspect of the use of medications is that the drugs are often abused by women who seek to escape the relationship by numbing their senses or by committing suicide. Again, there is evidence that battered women (24 percent) are more likely than nonbattered women (9 percent) to be given medication.[2]

Battered women are also most likely to get psychiatric referrals.[2] For nonbattered women, referrals for psychiatric or mental health consultation were 4 percent compared to 15 percent for largely unrecognized victims of domestic violence. The mental health label (pseudopsychiatric) reduces the client's chances of sympathetic, quality health care within the emergency department or hospital. Psychiatric referrals without mention of domestic violence as an issue or to therapists who are unaware of or insensitive to the causes and consequences of this violence often do the patient irreparable damage. The victim is in an unequal power relationship with her husband and often with the physician and the therapist. Consequently, the victim may be isolated in three relationships in which she has no control, power, or independence. The label is a handy excuse and reinforces her inability to cope. The situation and her mate are not sick, she is.

Documentation of Injuries in the Case Record

Notations in the case record are important even though the pattern of injuries over time rarely leads to a clear diagnosis. The typical injuries of battered women are often not symptomatic of an illness that can be diagnosed and treated. Involvement in cases of domestic violence is not a particularly rewarding or pleasant experience, but the victim can seldom take the steps necessary to change her life situation without some assistance from concerned helpers. Fear of being sued by the assailant, of losing time attending court hearings, or of making things worse by open discussion with the victim makes many medical personnel avoid any meaningful contact with the victim.

Clear, concise chart notations are a necessity for many reasons. Since personnel often change stations and shifts, the record may become a returning patient's only constant in the emergency department. The record is the tie that binds one assaultive incident to another. It is also possible that the records may be subpoenaed at a much later date. A careful description of injuries prefaced by a statement from the patient about the cause of her injuries is crucial. Subjective information should be carefully weighed. General statements about the physical condition and emotional state should be free of personal prejudices, values, and judgments. Statements about what one sees are better than what one feels or thinks. For example, "Ms. X was crying and unable for several minutes to answer my questions. She stumbled and had problems standing without assistance." This approach is preferable to "Ms. X was hysterical. She appeared to have been drinking because she could not stand without assistance and stumbled about."

Photographs should be taken. The photographs and a signed and witnessed permission form should be placed in an envelope marked *confidential.* Information relevant to the photograph should be noted on the back (who took the photograph, day, date, time, who is in the photograph, and patient's signature). Photographs become crucial during criminal and civil litigation.

Reduction of Trauma and Emotional Upset

The battered woman in the emergency department is a unique patient. These women need their presence acknowledged as soon as they arrive. Their injuries are not different from other "accident" victims, but their behavior certainly is. Sensitive nursing and secretarial staff are important. The victim is experiencing a crisis. She often has little energy and is physically and psychologically drained. Many feel helpless and worthless. Many have long ago accepted the blame for the violence; they are trapped and they feel responsible. The woman is usually very anxious. She often judges herself harshly and looks for signs from medical personnel that verify her feelings of inadequacy, shame, guilt, and embarrassment.

Reactions of medical personnel may increase or decrease a victim's anxiety and crisis. What she needs is objective, immediate assistance uninfluenced by personal inclinations or feelings. Any negative, nonverbal behavior that is sensed by the patient magnifies her feelings of worthlessness. The battered woman, especially if this is not her first visit, is shocked, dismayed, and disconcerted. She is feeling used and betrayed. She transfers these negative feelings to the emergency department personnel at any sign of hostility or inattention. She feels that the staff must feel the same way about her as she feels about herself.

NONVERBAL COMMUNICATION

Touch

Communication with the patient should be continuous. Verbal communication is only a small part of what one says to others. Positive nonverbal communication is learned. Awareness that communication is a continuous process is the first step. One of the most positive nonverbal interactions is touch. The way one touches a person is as important as where one touches. Touching can transmit understanding, reassurance, and empathy in a more caring and compassionate manner than words, regardless of intonation, ever can. Conversely, feelings of hostility, fear, rejection, animosity, and distain can be conveyed just as easily. The communication of touch is reciprocal and simultaneous, as are facial expressions. If used at appropriate times and in appropriate ways, touching can be a vital tool. The battered woman has just experienced the ultimate invasion of body space. Physical abuse tears down the facade of "wholeness" and "impenetrability" that everyone has. Physical abuse says that the woman is vulnerable and incapable of taking care of and protecting herself. The abused body is sensitive to "touching messages"; it quickly discerns positive and negative communication.

Touching as a rote experience is often viewed by the patient as patronizing and demeaning. Health care professionals must examine their personal feelings about touching because those feelings are transmitted to the patient. The appropriate time and circumstance are critical. The issues of invasion of personal space, embarrassment, and taboos are important. Knowledge of cultural and ethnic differences prevents embarrassing and offensive gestures that inhibit the flow of communication.

Silence

Silence is an effective form of nonverbal communication. Many people cannot remain silent because they become too uncomfortable. They feel the need to fill the void with conversation. To a woman in crisis, meaningless, idle chitchat can be very anxiety provoking. To a person physically injured, talking is sometimes painful. In order to focus on what is being said, the woman must concentrate, and this concentration increases the tension and often the discomfort. Silence can be soothing and calming. Talking to the patient should be for the specific purpose of gathering information and comforting.

Active Listening

Active listening is difficult. It requires silence, concentration, patience, and attention. Active listening is a learned skill. It requires that one not interrupt, not assist by finishing sentences or paraphrasing feelings, not make judgments about what is being said, and not express anger in any form.

While the woman is talking about the incident or her partner, it is inappropriate to express shock, dismay, disgust, or any sign of judgment. These reactions can make the woman feel worse about herself because she is unable to extricate herself and her children from a situation that someone else perceives as intolerable and grotesque. Judgmental gestures and statements block communication because the woman may still have positive feelings about her assailant. If medical personnel express disapproval of the assailant, she can no longer talk openly to them because they have expressed indirect disapproval of her.

Often victims will make "loaded" statements; these statements are often tests to see where the listener stands. What is needed is an objective acceptance of information; it is not necessary to agree with it. On the surface, judgmental replies such as "You are right, men can be animals" may appear to be supportive. The problem arises as the woman attempts to process the situation. She will have difficulty changing her statements if she thinks that she will offend the listener or, more likely, that the listener will see her as unstable and indecisive. Active listening prevents the intrusion of subjective, judgmental data.

The act of listening is very special for the victim. It may be the first time she has ever dared to tell anyone or the first time anyone believed what she is saying. Knowledge of the psychodynamics of battering will reduce gestures that are inappropriate or block communication. Facial expressions are a television screen for the emotions. As the victim talks, she is judging the listener's reactions by watching facial expressions. As in touching, facial cues are reciprocal and often simultaneous. It is not enough simply not to make verbal judgments; health care personnel must also be aware that they may be making facial judgments.

Mutual Trust

Establishing mutual trust is the ultimate goal for medical personnel if they wish to have the victim share difficult and embarrassing information. The women must feel that the staff care about them and understand their dilemma; they hope for genuine sympathetic feelings toward them. Trust is established through mutual sharing and disclosure. Medical personnel are not expected to share intimate, personal problems but should allow the warm, caring, humanitarian side of their personalities to emerge.

Other Nonverbal Communicators

Body movements; lack of eye contact; movements of the hands, eyes, feet; and vocal expressions such as clearing the throat, sighing, inarticulate sounds, moans, and groans all send messages to the victim. The victim has a Pandora's box of emotional reactions (anger, fear, anxiety, loss of control, shame) that may be opened by nonverbal behavior. Communication with the victim should *never* stop whether the messages are spoken or not.

Factors Influencing Quality Care and Communication

Health care professionals must examine their personal feelings about the issues of battering in general and battered women in particular. The personal feelings and prevailing attitudes of the helper affect the quality of care that patients receive. If a professional feels that these women do not warrant any special consideration because they deserve or ask for violence, that feeling will be shown in the care given. Cultural and ethnic stereotyping of victims also affects care.

Quality care is often influenced by three factors: personal inclination, circumstances, and experience. One's own life stresses and situations determine, at any given time, whether one is inclined to empathize with others or simply to give the minimum amount of care necessary. The circumstances of the situation also influence how much care can be given. If the patient enters the emergency department when things are less hectic, and she represents the "crisis" of the moment, obviously she will receive more intensive, sensitive care than if she is preceded by several accident victims. Personal experience is also important. Treating any patient in a generalized fashion because of perceived "typical client behaviors" or stereotyping a victim because of a previous bad experience leads to false assumptions about the patient: "I went out of my way, and she went smiling back home"; "They are always angry and cursing and demanding attention. She should take out her anger on her partner." Nonjudgmental acceptance of values, attitudes, and life-styles different from their own is the basic requirement for all objective helping professionals.

A large emergency department takes care of many people, and the additional stresses of patient documentation, administrative duties, and insufficient staff can often be overwhelming. However, giving adequate support and information to victims can be the beginning of preventive social action. Violence is cyclical and generational. Helping a woman deal with the violence of an abusive partner is an important step out of the violent interaction. When meaningful assistance is offered to the victim, her ability to cope with her own needs and the needs of her children are increased. With quality medical care, appropriate referrals, and follow-up, victims can begin, while in the emergency department, to redirect their energy into strategies and ideas that they never before thought possible. This is an important time to interact with the victim. Her immediate situation is out of her control and untenable. Her defenses are down, and she is emotionally quite accessible. Sensitive, knowledgeable assistance from medical personnel may help victims begin to regain their self-esteem, self-control, self-reliance, and positive self-image.

VERBAL COMMUNICATION

Verbal communication with the victim is obviously necessary to gather accurate information. However, negative and demeaning statements about the patient or her situation should be avoided since they will effectively block all channels of communication. Another situation to avoid is the constant use of technical language. Many people do not know simple abbreviations and expressions, such as PRN, NPO, vital signs, that medical personnel take for granted. This language is appropriate when addressing another health professional, but when used with patients who do not understand, it serves to isolate, intimidate, and frighten them. It sets up an unequal power relationship and makes the patient feel inferior. The patient is no longer free to question or interact for fear of appearing ignorant and inadequate.

A professional's use of a patient's first name while only the professional's last name is given is often seen as a put-down and an attempt to establish control and a hierarchy. It makes the patient feel as if she has not earned the respect to be addressed by her last name. It establishes an adult-to-child flow of communication. The flow is one-way, from the knowledgeable person of control and power to the incompetent, needy, powerless patient.

GATHERING INFORMATION

Information should be obtained in as quiet and nonthreatening a manner as possible. The victim should be placed in a quiet waiting area that affords her some privacy. Being forced to yell one's private affairs at the medical secretary through the little hole in the glass will not prompt very many confidential disclosures. Embarrassment plays a large part in women's reluctance to seek assistance; it should not be discounted. Constant interruptions are a way of life in an emergency department. Since these situations can seldom be changed, success or failure may hinge on the expertise of the nurse or medical secretary in helping the woman focus on her story. They must let her know that they are listening, accept what she is saying without judgment, and give her the emotional and physical security to speak without fear. Physical security and privacy are important because often the assailant is in the emergency department or very close by.

In addition to general medical history, the following information is important to establish the safety of the immediate situation. These questions should be asked even if a social worker is available.

1. Do you have children? Where are they now?

2. Are the children safe? (A simple affirmation is not sufficient. Inquire about the kinship, age, and accessibility to alleged assailant.)

3. What is the present location of the assailant? (Watch for nonverbal behavior.)

4. Who accompanied you here?

   • If police, they can usually assist in transporting the victim to safety at some place other than her home. They will also inform the patient of her legal rights and the legal process if she wishes to prosecute. If the police did not inform the patient, medical personnel should be knowledgeable enough to do so.

   • If an advocate or escort from a referral source, a relative, or a friend accompanied the victim, their emotional state should be ascertained. If they appear calm, are willing to obey the hospital rules, and appear to be of comfort to the victim, they should be allowed to enter. Since the victim is now under professional care, the professional should determine whether the presence of the accompanying individual is helpful or harmful.

5. Where will you go when you leave here?

6. Have you used our emergency or other medical services in the past? (This question is necessary for a record search).

These questions help the woman focus on the apparent danger of her present situation. They must be answered satisfactorily before inquiring about her life-style and living situation. Safety issues are the first consideration. Questions about life-style and personal resources are discussed in the next section on the role of social service and other personnel.

Physicians are extremely important in the life of a battered woman. Their knowledge of medicine should be coupled with knowledge of community resources. For many battered women, the only link to the outside is the clinic, emergency department, or physician's office. They are not allowed to seek counseling and very often are completely unaware of any other resources. The batterer is the woman's only reality, and he tells her that it is her fault and that no one will help her. Concise and relevant information provided by the physician can save battered women from years of physical and psychological abuse.

An article in the *Journal of the American Medical Association* states that whatever the consequences of the changing physician-patient relationship may be, it is clear that the law expects physicians to actively intervene in situations where violence has erupted or may erupt. Intervention may come to include the responsibility of recognizing the effects of violence. Thus, physicians are not only responsible for the well-being of their patients but also to society. They should be aware not only that wife abuse exists and is probably more prevalent in their practice than they currently recognize but also that community resources are available for dealing with the problem once its existence is discovered.

Friedman discusses the importance of health professionals interacting and coordinating with legal assistance, therapeutic counseling, and community service resources.[5] Referrals are seen as a way to prevent the recurrence of injury; they acknowledge that there is a victim of a crime who deserves assistance and protection. Recognizing the social pattern of violence does not diminish the responsibility of health professionals. Hospital emergency departments are frequently the only medical resources when injuries occur as a result of intrafamily abuse. Like the police, who are on the front line of crisis intervention, hospital staff are in a position to note and document the incidence of battered partners. Health care agencies can play a major role in increasing public awareness of the problem. Health professionals are asked to increase their knowledge of and sensitivity to the issues of domestic violence and become a leading community force that seeks research, legislation, and the development of alternative treatments.[5]

Community Resources

Updated knowledge of community resources is vital in work with victims of domestic violence. Women who have been isolated for prolonged periods of time often depend on the person who gives them information to verify its accuracy and appropriateness. In extreme circumstances, false information can lead to increased mental and physical harm.

If only one referral will be made in the emergency department, it should be to the hospital's department of social services. The woman can always use the excuse that she has another physician's appointment. In an ideal situation, a social worker on call would assist the woman with crisis counseling and the acquisition of temporary housing if the woman desires it. If the woman does not require emergency housing, the telephone number of a crisis hotline should be given to her for future use. Violence escalates, and without some outside intervention into their family system, battered women are seldom able to stop the violence.

Making referrals in crisis situations does not mean giving the woman a series of telephone numbers and access to a telephone. Many women are too physically and mentally exhausted to complete the calls. They say that they will call later, and later never comes. Whenever possible, making the initial call for the woman and paving the way shows her that the health care system will respond to her needs. Numbers that the woman needs immediately are for crisis hotlines, police, and emergency shelters. If possible, and if the woman is willing, a call to the crisis hotline should be made immediately. Hotlines are available to women 24 hours a day, seven days a week, and a victim can call when her partner is not around. She can call when she is lonely or when she needs help or information. Making the initial contact is important because to battered women, busy telephones may mean "hopelessness."

Hilberman listed the following community resources that might be needed by professionals who assist battered women:[3]

- Medical institutions for birth control, abortions, tubal ligations, and good medical and mental health care for the victim and her children

- Social service agencies for financial aid for the woman and her children, child protection services, food stamps, clothing, day care, housing, and emergency shelter

- Criminal justice agencies for protection against further violence

- Legal aid for assistance with warrants, court procedures, separation, and divorce agreements

- Vocational rehabilitation agencies for employment counseling and for financial assistance and information about educational pursuits and job training

- Women's groups for information, support, and shelter

The Role of Social Service and Other Personnel

SHARING INFORMATION

Safety issues for the battered woman and her children are usually handled by the medical secretary or nurse before the social worker is summoned. This information is necessary; if the woman is not safe, she cannot begin to discuss issues of life-style, personal resources, or other therapeutic issues. Since medical care is the victim's immediate concern, the social worker must acquire the available medical information. The physical condition and whether medical follow-up is required are vital information and a logical point of departure for the discussion of other issues. Information gathered by the medical staff should be shared with the social worker to prevent repetitive questioning of the victim and to give the social worker a sense of the woman's emotional state and what she is willing to share. The information gathered by the social service should include, where possible, a review of hospital records.

THE INTERVIEW

A logical point of departure is the most recent incident that precipitated the need for emergency care.

The Victim's Responses

The victim's response to the incident should be noted. Is she angry? If so, this righteous indignation can be channeled into some positive attempts to stop the violence. Is she lethargic or despondent? If the woman feels that her situation is hopeless, it will be difficult to generate any enthusiasm. Is she submissive or passive? She may have internalized the incident and accepted it as her fault.

The victim should be assisted in focusing on her current life situation and problems. Discussing the patterns of the violence helps to stimulate the cognitive process. She is usually very ambivalent, often confused, and unusually vulnerable. Her ambivalence is easy to understand. She lives, in essence, with two different men in one body. One is often sensitive, protective, and concerned. The other is cruel and verbally and physically abusive. It is difficult to separate the two as she speaks. The ambivalence should be acknowledged.

Options and Consequences

Social workers must have a sense of their own personal experiences and values. Care must be taken to ask the victim what she wishes to do. The social worker should not look for opportune moments to accomplish the hidden agenda of "what is best for the patient." It is important to discuss options and consequences. The woman can then make a clear choice and begin to experience some decision-making power and the consequences of those decisions. Utmost, and most anxiety provoking for many women during their visit to the emergency department, is the fact that their partner will be angry that they have stayed so long. Establishing options at the first visit is important. The woman can leave the relationship and attempt to make it on her own; she can return home and attempt to get her partner to change; or she can return home and surrender all hopes that her partner will change. The options of leaving, staying and hoping for change, and staying without hope of change each have a distinct set of referrals and actions. By making a conscious choice, the victim begins the long process of accepting and taking control of her own destiny.

Dispelling Myths

Along with discussing options should be the dispelling of myths. Whether the victim returns home or not is her decision alone. All victims should, however, leave with an increased knowledge about domestic violence and a clear statement that no one deserves to be beaten. A woman should leave knowing that she is not to blame for the violence and that if she wishes a cessation of the violence, *she* must take some actions. The plan must be the woman's plan. She must invest her own time, energy, and self in carrying it out. She must deem herself and her children worthy and capable of obtaining and maintaining a violence-free environment. The plan begins with a realistic assessment of her current situation.

Assessing the Current Situation

Appropriate questions and considerations are as follows:

1. Describe the incident that brought you here. (Brief narrative in the woman's own words.)

2. Were weapons involved?

3. Is this a recurring situation? If weapons are involved, are they the same each time?

4. Were police called? What action was taken?

5. What is the length of your relationship with the assailant?

6. Was there abuse in prior relationships? Weapons?

7. Was there abuse of alcohol or drugs or both during this or prior relationships?

8. Children.

   • Ages and sex

   • Did they witness the abuse?

   • Are they experiencing any physical or psychological problems (bedwetting, stuttering, nightmares, insomnia, fears, separation problems, for example)?

   • Are they being abused?

   • Are they experiencing school problems, (poor grades, fights, lack of concentration, few or no friends, for example)?

9. Have photographs been taken? Has permission been given?

10. Safety issues.

    • Are your children safe? Where are they?

    • Where is the assailant?

    • Where do you plan to go when treatment is complete? (This can be an appropriate place to discuss options and personal resources as many victims do not realize that they have either.)

Personal Resources

Personal resources need to be assessed regardless of the victim's immediate plans. The next time the woman appears for assistance, needed information will be available. Acceptance of the victim's assessment of her resources is important. Even though a woman may feel more in control by being able to call upon her own resources, very often she may hesitate because she does not wish to subject her family and friends to the rage and danger of her partner. Often family and friends are not an adequate deterrent to a partner's violence because of fear or their desire to maintain congeniality. In some instances, strangers offer the best protection because their response is more objective, and they can usually offer enlightened, immediate assistance to both parties. Strangers' expectations for the woman and her partner are different from the expectations of family and friends. The intervention of others (shelter staff, counselors, hospital personnel, police, legal and law encorcement officers) offers partners a neutral territory for working through their problems.

The nature of domestic violence includes a hesitancy to explore outside the protective sanctuary of family and friends. The batterer's response to strangers is usually his "public" facade of great husband, father, and provider. He wishes to have people see him as a great guy who lives with a woman with problems. There are instances of batterers who have threatened and attacked "helping" professionals, but this percentage is small and, in most instances, involves women (as in shelter systems) whom he generalizes as weak, inferior, or a threat or men who have encountered him while he is still in a state of rage and out of control (as with police officers). Most professionals are more likely to invoke cultural sanctions (calling the police, pressing charges for assault and battery, making citizen's arrests) than are friends and family.

Transportation

How a woman travels from one place to another is as important as where she goes. Transportation is a crucial issue, especially when the woman does not wish to return home. Whether she is injured or not, often someone must assist her in reaching her destination. Taxis require money which a majority of battered women do not have. The bus may be inappropriate if the woman is injured, has several children, or must travel long distances to reach safety. Transportation is an important consideration when making referrals because shelter services usually do not have ample personnel or a vehicle to transport clients from the hospital to the facilities. Many a referral falls apart because there is no means of transportation. Appropriate questions:

- Do you drive and have a valid driver's license?
- Do you own or have access to a car?
- Do you have someone with a car who will come and get you?
- Do you have taxi or bus fare?

FAMILY

In today's mobile culture, many women are separated from their immediate families and do not have relatives nearby. If relatives do live nearby, some inquiries must be made about their family life-style, finances, and personal interactions. If relatives are involved in domestic violence; are experiencing personal stress because of employment, family relationships, or finances; or have assisted the family before and the woman has returned home, sending the victim into that environment is often more detrimental than helpful. In developing personal resources, it is important that the resource offer the woman emotional and physical security. Families who are experiencing great stress or similar problems may openly or subtly encourage the woman to return home. They often reinforce the woman's negative self-image and feelings of blame.

If the woman has family nearby and has chosen not to inform them because of embarrassment, fear, or lack of support, these issues must be pursued before "dumping" the woman (and children) onto unsuspecting relatives. Often the haste to get the woman out of the office or hospital results in poor and inappropriate referrals. From personal experiences, most people have some relatives that they would rather not "bother." In some cases, they probably would prefer going to strangers. Battered women are no different.

Battered women often lose touch with their own families and seem to maintain contact with their partner's mother or family. The victim has often been discouraged from or forbidden interactions with her family. Often a jealous partner promotes estrangement between the woman and her family whom he perceives as the enemy. Information, support, and encouragement from her family will only drive the woman away from him. A similar pattern is observed with friendships. The pattern of self-imposed and forced isolation is rampant.

If the woman chooses to go with her family, social workers should try to involve family members in the supportive social service system. Usually neither the woman nor her family understands the dynamics of battering. If the family is given some information and helped to understand that the woman does not stay because she likes it or is beyond help, they can be more supportive. The woman's behavior needs to be understood; the quality and amount of family assistance depends upon it. They attempt to help the woman by rescuing her and giving her "sound" advice. Families often give the woman exactly what she does not need. They pour out their love and caring and, in the end, feel rejected and a failure. They often turn against the woman because she makes them feel inadequate. The family as a resource, without additional supportive referrals, is seldom enough to sustain the victim.

Appropriate questions are

1. Do you have family nearby?

2. Have you maintained contact with them? Why? Why not?

3. Does your family know about the violence?

4. Have you sought help from them before? If yes, when? Results?

5. What kind of assistance can they give you?
   - Place to stay
   - Financial assistance
   - Emotional support
   - Pipeline to other family members

6. What is the stability of the household as a referral? (Can it withstand the increased stress of additional members and problems?)
   - Drug and alcohol use
   - Violence
   - Economics and employment
   - Number of household members
   - Size of household dwelling

7. Can your family be used as a temporary or overnight referral?

8. Will your partner contact or harass them in his search for you? What will be their response to his threats or violence?

FINANCES

Over 70 percent of the women who contacted the YWCA's hotline for battered women in San Diego, California, in the fiscal year 1980 to 1981 did not depend upon their spouse's income as their primary means of support. These women either worked full or part-time or received unemployment benefits, social security, public assistance, or family support. Control of money is an issue in domestic violence. Many women earn or receive money that they do not control. It is not uncommon for a woman to work and yet not have access to the checking or savings account. The partner controls the finances because money equals power. Many women cannot, in one session, separate finances that legally belong to them from the finances of their husbands. The immediate answer for most women is that they have *no* finances.

If the woman depends on her partner's income, it is almost certain that she has no money. Immediate access to money is important for placement of women in hotels, emergency housing facilities, or shelters that charge a fee.

Many women return home because they see their plight as hopeless. Many have already spent any available income on food and shelter, and the thought of starting over with no money is frightening.

Some appropriate questions:

- Do you have any money on your person?
- What is your source of income?
- Do you have access to any money?

TELEPHONE

This may seem inappropriate, but it has a major impact on the social worker's ability to maintain contact and the victim's ability to establish and maintain a link outside the home. Rounsaville stated that most battered women in an emergency room situation enthusiastically accepted follow-up social service appointments. However, the women who followed through were substantially older and more likely to be separated or divorced, to have medical coverage, to be working and not dependent on their spouses, to have more children, and to have a telephone in the home.[4]

Many victims do not have telephones because excessively jealous, abusive husbands have sought to limit the women's outside contact with acquaintances, friends, and relatives. A telephone lifeline in the home or through acquaintances needs to be established along with some code for communication, if the situation warrants it.

FRIENDS, ACQUAINTANCES, NEIGHBORS

It is important to know if the victim has anyone outside her immediate family who can help her. The questions are the same ones used to assess the suitability of family members as a referral source. As a short-term referral (emergency) source for safety, almost any place is better than the home. However, if the outside people do not understand the issues of violence and know how to assist, the victim often must return, within days, to the violent home.

SUMMARY

Medical and social service personnel are important in increasing the awareness of and assistance to battered women. Medical assistance is often the only help an abused woman has. If the violence is not acknowledged and treated as part of the problem, the silence reinforces the woman's sense of helplessness and worthlessness. Increased sensitivity to the victims and adequate knowledge of resources are a minimum requirement for all who assist abused women. Hospital personnel must become a vital link in an organized community effort to assist victims of spouse abuse and to educate the public about this violent crime.

REFERENCES

1. Petro JA, et al: Wife abuse: the diagnosis and implications. *JAMA* **240**:241, 1978.

2. Stark E, et al: Medicine and patriarchal violence: the social construction of a private event. *Int J Health Serv* **9**:461–492, 1979.

3. Hilberman E, Munson K: Sixty battered women. Paper prepared by special session of the American Psychiatric Association Meetings on Battered Women: Culture as Destiny, Toronto, 1977.

4. Rounsaville BJ: Battered wives: barriers to identification and treatment. *Am J Orthopsychiatry* **48**:487–494, 1978.

5. Friedman KO: The image of battered women, editorial. *Am J Public Health* **67**:722–723, 1977.

13

DOMESTIC ABUSE AND NEGLECT OF THE ELDERLY

Richard L. Douglass, M.P.H., Ph.D.
Patricia Ruby-Douglass, M.S.W.

Medical and nursing training and practice have traditionally focused on the cure of illness, the repair of trauma, and the care of the sick. Until the late 1970s, the geriatric aspects of medicine and nursing were taught to only a small fraction of medical personnel. A still smaller fraction of professionals who specialize in emergency care are schooled in the special needs and issues of geriatric patients.

This situation is not unique; it reflects the general disregard of the aged in our society. The social attitude toward the elderly has begun to change, but the reason for the phenomenon is the swelling numbers of the old among us, rather than any enlightened social awareness.

Robert Butler, the Director of the National Institute on Aging, stated that old age in America is often a tragedy. It demands our energy and resources, frightens us with illness and deformity, and is an affront to a culture with a passion for youth and productive capacity. At best, the living old are treated as if they were already half dead.[1] This chapter will focus on what is perhaps the most disturbing tragedy of being old in America, the neglect or abuse of the elderly by those upon whom they depend. The emergency medical team is in a critical position to provide immediate aid to older persons who have been neglected or abused and to recognize such victims when their plight is first exposed outside the home. The role of the emergency team is vital to those older people whose last hope of care at home has turned against them.

The elderly patient who visits the emergency department is not very different from other adults. Circulatory or respiratory crises resulting from chronic conditions; adverse drug reactions, interactions, or dosage problems; physical trauma; and other problems are generic to older people as well as to people 20 to 60 years old. The geriatric patient, however, responds to these emergency conditions differently than younger adults, and when the crisis is the result of neglect or abuse, the task of the emergency team is greatly complicated. Neglect and abuse of the elderly in domestic settings are realities in this society. The medical aspects range from severe dehydration and malnutrition to all forms of trauma. Many kinds of neglect and abuse of the elderly are life-threatening.

As the population of aged persons increases, and alternatives to living with or being dependent upon family members diminish, more and more older people will be cared for primarily by people who are ill-equipped for such responsibility. Thus, the prevalence and incidence of neglect and abuse of the elderly will certainly increase.

The present chapter has five specific objectives. The first is to alert emergency personnel to the known facts of domestic abuse and neglect which will influence their response to geriatric emergency patients. The second is to create an awareness of this problem which will facilitate the recognition of victims of neglect and abuse. The third is to suggest roles for medical and nursing emergency personnel outside the hospital and for other professionals such as social workers and referral staff. The fourth and fifth objectives are to initiate the development of standard operating procedures for recognizing and handling abused or neglected geriatric patients at local hospitals and to stimulate further inquiry into the problem.

RESEARCH ON DOMESTIC ABUSE AND NEGLECT OF THE ELDERLY

Social commentators, novelists, and some journalists have noted domestic abuse and neglect of the elderly for decades, even centuries, but health professionals and social scientists did not become involved in the treatment, intervention, or study of the problem until the late 1970s.

In the years 1977 to 1981, significant research on the problem was done in the United States. None of these studies is comprehensive or definitive, but the main findings and conclusions are consistent. The characteristics, etiology, and implications for practice in these studies have been widely acknowledged by protective service workers and numerous state and federal authorities.

Between 1977 and 1978 three studies indicated that older adults were more frequently mistreated by adult children or other caretakers than was previously imagined. Steinmetz at the University of Delaware examined reported cases of neglect and abuse of the elderly and found a surprisingly high incidence of physical beatings at the hands of adult sons and daughters.[2,3] Rathbone-McCuan, who studied cases from social and geriatric agencies and hospital emergency departments, also discovered numerous cases of physical abuse, forced confinement of aged parents, and verbal and emotional assault.[4]

Lau and Kosberg conducted a case review of clients who had been seen at a chronic-illness center in Cleveland, Ohio, during the year June 1977 to June 1978.[5] The study included data from the agency's records and recollections from the assigned case workers. All cases with clients aged 60 years and older were reviewed with the intention of determining instances of physical, psychological, and material abuse. A total of 404 new cases fit the age specifications. Among these they found 39 cases of abuse.

Three larger studies have been reported since mid-1979. O'Malley et al. surveyed 1044 Massachusetts professional and para-professionals with mail questionnaires.[6] The respondents were selected from mailing lists, agency staff, and selected lists provided by community agencies that had routine contact with the elderly. A 34 percent response (355 returned questionnaires) yielded 183 cited cases of abuse in the previous 18 months. Of the responses included in analyses, only 42 percent reported seeing no abuse of the elderly during the previous 18 months.

Two other studies, funded by the federal government as a response to public concerns raised by previous investigations, confirmed the existence of the problem. Block and Sinnott surveyed samples of the membership of the American Psychological Association, the Gerontological Society, and the American College of Emergency Physicians who reside in Maryland.[7] They used a mailed questionnaire as well as direct requests to agencies for case reports.

Douglass et al. personally interviewed a mixture of community practitioners and professionals in five Michigan locations.[8] The sample included police officers, lawyers, physicians, hospital nurses, public health nurses, social workers, nutrition site aides, clergy, judges, morticians and coroners, mental health counselors, and protective service workers. This study also analyzed data on 1977 crimes against the elderly that involved relatives of the victims, a personal interview survey of nursing home staff, and patient data from nursing homes.

The Problem is Real

When the initial clinical and research findings on child abuse were presented to the medical and social service communities, their response was frequently doubt, skepticism, or outrage. Eventually, repeated research and compelling evidence convinced community professionals and paraprofessionals that children are sometimes abused and neglected. One can expect a similar response to domestic abuse and neglect of the elderly. The consistent findings of the scientific research cited here are, therefore, of great importance. All of the studies mentioned describe a pattern of circumstances, victims, and responsible parties. Steinmetz,[2,3] Lau and Kosberg,[5] and O'Malley et al.[6] have reported a high incidence of physical abuse such as beatings, burnings, cutting, or bat-

tering with fists or objects that caused physical injuries including superficial wounds, dislocations, bone fractures, and many fatalities. Physical restraint and forced confinement have also been reported. Block and Sinnott[7] and Douglass et al.[8] verified physical abuse of the elderly but found that verbal and emotional abuse were more common. All studies have agreed that physical abuse is usually found in association with verbal or emotional abuse.

Each major study has reported financial exploitation or the misuse, theft, or fraudulent use of a dependent elder's finances and assets. Respondents in one survey raised the issue of financial abuse voluntarily.[8]

Neglect of the elderly takes many forms. It includes the lack of attention to personal care, essential services, goods, or assistance required by a frail, dependent older adult. Douglass et al. distinguished between active neglect and passive neglect.[8] In active neglect, assistance, personal care, food, medicine, or other needs are purposely withheld. In passive neglect, the caretaker is unable to provide what is needed because of ignorance, impairment, or the caretaker's own disability. Some caretakers are elderly and frail themselves and physically unable to meet the needs of still older and more disabled parents. Neglect in any of its forms can be devastating and is just as likely as physical abuse or emotional abuse to require emergency medical care. In fact, among the elderly, problems such as diabetic crises or dehydration are more probable causes for emergency treatment than small lacerations or bruises. Such problems are likely consequences of neglect.

Who Are the Abused and Neglected?

The population at risk can be most simply defined as those elderly who are most vulnerable because of their advanced age, frailty, chronic disease, or physical or mental impairment. Victims of abuse and neglect are those who are least capable of independent living and, thus, most dependent on others. They are generally less aware of alternative living arrangements or means of support than others their age, they generally have two or more ongoing physical disabilities, and they are more likely to be women.

Neglect or abuse should not be ruled out, however, if an older patient without impairments appears for treatment. Unlike children, who survive domestic violence, vulnerability of the aged *increases* over time. Isolated incidents of neglect or abuse are relatively uncommon. In a specific family, episodes of neglectful or abusive behavior can be expected to continue and increase in frequency as a dependent older person ages, unless some form of intervention changes the family's circumstances. Racial, socioeconomic, or other social criteria that define segments of the population at higher risk of being neglected or abused have not been found.

The Causes

Just as the varieties of neglect and abuse are numerous, so are the causes. The most common ones include the consequences of adult caretakers becoming overtaxed by the requirements of caring for a frail, dependent adult. Physical, economic, or emotional limitations of the caretaker can prohibit adequate recognition of the needs of an older person and prevent the caretaker's responsiveness to those needs. The burden for caring, without occasional relief, can lead to despair, anger, resentment, or violence among some caretakers. A family that is already at the brink of crisis, for any reason, will only be thrown more quickly into a disastrous chain of events when a frail and dependent parent imposes unexpected problems and demands on the family's physical, emotional, and financial resources.

Long-term hostility between a child and parent may erupt into abuse and neglect when the parent becomes dependent on the adult child. Douglass et al. found some support for the hypothesis that abused children grow up to become abusive adults; the abusiveness becomes manifest when the formerly abusing parent becomes dependent on the adult child.[8]

There are several theories and observations on the causes of the abuse and neglect of the elderly:

1. Malicious neighbors or greedy relatives have exploited an older person's finances.

2. Alcohol abuse by the victims or abusers has been reported, particularly when the form of mistreatment is physical abuse.

3. Caretakers may be unaware of social supports and community services or, out of fear or disinclination, fail to use existing services to assist their efforts to care for an older person.

4. A frail older person might be unaware of housing and other services as alternatives to living in the care of family members who cannot or will not provide the kinds of care that are required.

Like child abuse and spouse abuse, some cases of neglect or abuse are clearly criminal and intentional. Some cases involve caretakers with unresolved emotional or psychotic problems. Also, victims have been known to provoke abuse or neglect through unacceptable, hostile, or confused behavior.

Barriers to Recognizing, Reporting, and Helping Victims

There are several barriers to the recognition of cases of abuse or neglect when victims enter health or social service systems. Most medical or entry-level staff see the victims' symptoms and problems in the abstract and do not interpret them as the consequence of inflicted trauma or as the result of neglect.

Elderly victims of neglect or abuse cannot be expected to reveal the true circumstances and causes of their physical signs and symptoms. Many researchers agree that fear of reprisals by the abuser, embarrassment, shame, mistrust of agency or hospital staff, or rationalizations that the mistreatment was justified all influence the hesitation of elderly victims to tell strangers how injuries or other problems came about.[2,3,6-8] Few victims of neglect or abuse make their plight known to anyone.

Many helping systems have built-in barriers to proper recognition of the problem. Respondents in one study indicated that few medical units or social agencies have standard training, reporting or response procedures, or policies.[8] This situation suggests a lack of awareness or sensitivity to the existence of abuse and neglect of the elderly. Police officers in the same study reported that their ability to respond to neglect and abuse is limited to cases in which a crime is reported and the victim is willing to prosecute the offender, even when the offender is a son, daughter, grandchild, or the last remaining relative or friend. Reporting cases is difficult at best in states with no mandatory reporting laws; and even when a voluntary case-reporting system does exist, few community practitioners are aware of its appropriateness for mistreated elderly. Douglas et al. asked the physicians in their study what they would do if confronted with a case of domestic mistreatment of an elderly person.[8] The most typical response was "call a social worker." Few of these respondents, however, knew *how* to "call" a social worker if given the opportunity.

Referral of cases of abuse or neglect of the elderly often becomes complicated by poor interagency communication, jurisdictional overlaps, and even institutionalized hostility to suggestions that elderly people are being abused or neglected. This situation is analogous to the initial reactions to child abuse in the early 1960s and to spouse abuse a decade later. Only a great increase in our knowledge of abuse and neglect of the elderly and intensive public and professional education will increase the ability or willingness of health and other systems to respond appropriately.

FIVE ILLUSTRATIVE CASES

These case studies illustrate the points discussed in earlier sections. They were reported by respondents in a 1979 project[8] but have not been previously published. It is clear from these cases that the manifestation of mistreatment of the elderly, the causes, and the appropriate professional responses are often multiple and complicated. These five cases were selected because the victims required emergency care; they do not, however, represent the full range of neglect or abuse.

Mrs. W.

This case, reported by a metropolitan police detective, involves an 84-year-old widow of Eastern European origin who immigrated to Michigan in 1921. Mrs. W. speaks no English. She is very obese and is somewhat impaired because of her weight and associated circulatory and respiratory problems. For six years Mrs. W. lived with her son, a 48-year-old factory worker and an alcoholic.

Mrs. W.'s son became abusive and violent toward her during the six-year period. At one point, in December, 1978, he brought one of his friends home to demonstrate that his mother was impervious to pain when he hit her. He demonstrated that her large legs resisted bruising even when hit with a variety of objects; one object, however, a crowbar, broke both of Mrs. W.'s kneecaps.

Mrs. W.'s son took her to a nearby emergency department several hours later. He explained to the staff that his mother fell on the ice, and the fall produced the injuries. Mrs. W. was treated and admitted for two weeks. During that time she remained silent.

Several weeks later Mrs. W. discovered her son in the yard dead from exposure. He had apparently collapsed and died from the subzero temperature. At autopsy he had a very high blood-alcohol level. At this point, Mrs. W. informed a neighbor of the circumstances of her frequent bruises and the truth behind her many "falls." Her neighbor notified the police, and the story was documented.

At no point did the emergency care team question the explanation provided by Mrs. W.'s son, even in the absence of any reported difficulties with her hands or wrists or other injuries that might be expected from a "fall on the ice." Nor did the bilateral symmetry of the injuries or the fact that Mrs. W. was dressed in only a housecoat arouse any suspicion. No involvement with a social worker was initiated, and no attempt was made to provide an interpreter to allow Mrs. W. to speak for herself.

Mr. C.

A probate judge in a county of great socioeconomic and urban-rural diversity reported the case of Mr. C. Upon the death of his wife in an automobile accident, Mr. C., aged 71 years, who suffered minor injuries in the same accident, moved into the home of his daughter and son-in-law. Mr. C. liquidated all of his assets, including a small home, some stocks, and other properties, and gave the entire amount to his daughter and her husband in return for a promise to care for him. The situation was pleasant for several years.

Mr. C., however, was plagued by severe boredom and depression. While physically healthy, he came to be viewed as "in the way" or "a nuisance," and the family activities rarely included him. Eventually Mr. C. lost contact with his friends and peers. He stayed in his room and became virtually isolated. After overhearing his daughter remark, "It is almost like he's dead," Mr. C. attempted suicide. An investigation by the county social service department recommended that Mr. C. be included in more family activities and be reunited with his peer group. The family, however, responded to the incident as an embarrassment and actively isolated Mr. C. thereafter. Mr. C. successfully committed suicide by drinking a large quantity of isopropyl alcohol one year later, after being excluded from his daughter's birthday celebration.

The probate judge who cited the case pointed out that suicide is a major cause of death among the elderly, particularly widowed men who have lost their economic or social independence. In this case, the caretaking family failed to recognize the despair and depression that Mr. C. experienced.

Recommendations by the county social service were ignored, and no agency follow-up took place. Mr. C.'s thwarted suicide attempt was followed by an action calculated to succeed, an important point for emergency department staff; suicide attempts by the elderly are more likely than those of youth to be serious efforts at self-destruction rather than "calls for help" or attention. The need for efficient emergency procedures is essential. In addition, discharging an elderly survivor of a suicide attempt to the same living situation that led to the attempt should be considered only if meaningful follow-up and personal and family assistance services are initiated.

Mrs. R.

Mrs. R. was an 80-year-old who lived alone in an apartment. After her husband died, she became involved in several volunteer programs in her community but decided to discontinue these activities in winter months when transportation became a problem. Mrs. R.'s case was reported by an adult service caseworker who had known her as a volunteer for the agency.

Mrs. R. was frequently beaten by her son whenever he became temporarily unemployed or laid-off, usually during the winter. Mrs. R.'s son would demand money and would become belligerent if it were, at first, refused or if it were insufficient. Only after several visits to the emergency department did Mrs. R. indicate that she had been assaulted by her son rather than an unknown street criminal as she had reported in the past. The hospital involved local police and social services, and a degree of protection was provided for Mrs. R. No criminal charges, however, were initiated by Mrs. R.

This case illustrates that seasonal factors and situational influences, on both the victims and the perpetrators, can be important. Victims can be expected to hesitate or fail to report the involvement of relatives or caretakers. Criminal charges are unlikely, a situation which severely limits the potential for police intervention, and the elderly victims are not always more isolated, frail, or dependent than the majority of older people in the community.

Mrs. O.

Mrs. O. was admitted through a hospital emergency department for severe dehydration. She also received treatment for multiple skin decubiti and complications of very poor personal hygiene. A hospital nurse reported that Mrs. O. lived with her sister and brother-in-law who were responsible for her care. The situation, however, was complicated by the ages of the people involved. Mrs. O. was 88 years old, her sister was 72, and her brother-in-law was over 80. Simultaneous with Mrs. O.'s increasing disabilities, including being fully bedridden, her caretakers became overwhelmed by the deterioration of their own physical health. The caretakers could barely care for themselves, and their inability to provide personal services to Mrs. O. led to her hospitalization because of neglect.

This type of case is likely to become increasingly common as the population ages. Appropriate use of existing community services can easily prevent this problem and, thus, preclude the role of emergency care.

Mrs. S.

The case of Mrs. S. was reported by three independent respondents in the field study, an adult services worker, a hospital nurse, and a clergyman. After falling and suffering a fractured hip at the age of 71, Mrs. S. became highly dependent on her daughter and approved a voluntary consent agreement that made the daughter her mother's legal guardian. The daughter, who was single and employed, resented the demands and inconveniences of caring for her mother. Mrs. S. required at least two daily visits for personal care, food preparation, and management of household affairs, but the caretaking daughter rarely appeared more than twice a week and rejected outside services.

A neighbor discovered Mrs. S. tied to her bed, incontinent, and dehydrated. Her many prescriptions had not been filled for several months, and she was malnourished. Although clearly responsible, the caretaking daughter told one reporter that she had to "slap Mom to make her eat," and decided not to visit for a full week to "punish Mom for giving me such a hassle."

This case is an obvious example of an ill-suited, resentful caretaker who took advantage of a situation. The daughter gained access to her mother's finances by becoming a guardian and then became abusive and neglectful when the required level of care increased. Mrs. S. was placed in a nursing home, and the issue of guardianship was referred to the courts.

SPECIAL CONCERNS OF THE GERIATRIC PATIENT

Geriatric patients present special medical concerns. Elderly people are generally more prone to illness and injury than younger people, and the direct effects of neglect or abuse are compounded and exacerbated by physical and emotional conditions prevalent among the aged.

The severity of injury, expected physiological responses, and perception of pain are frequently depressed in elderly patients. Consequently, emergency personnel may underestimate the severity of injury or make an inaccurate diagnosis. If a patient responds with confusion rather than severe pain, or if expected bleeding is not observed, attending personnel may misjudge the patient's actual state of health unless they are sensitive to the special conditions of geriatric patients.

In old age, normal responses to infections are often not obvious on physical examination. For example, external conditions have direct effects on the elderly. Elevated temperatures normally associated with infections are often depressed if the patient has been exposed to a cold room or the outdoors. On the other hand, exposure to relatively minor heat can cause heat exhaustion in a susceptible aged patient. Many medical professionals consider confusion in geriatric patients a sign of normal, expected "senile" deterioration. However, in the elderly, confusion may be a sign of blood loss, coronary heart failure, heat or cold exposure, dehydration, or acute, traumatic fear. Emergency personnel should never assume that confusion among geriatric patients is normal (Alzheimer's disease, one of the most common causes of progressive emotional problems and confusion, may be prevalent, but it is *not* universal among the aged). Adverse home conditions, which certainly include neglect or abuse, are leading contributors to emotional problems and instability of geriatric patients.[9]

Other factors of the aging process can confound the initial examination of a geriatric victim of abuse or neglect. The signs and symptoms of injury or illness may be more generalized, less localized, and less acute than those of younger patients. Fluid losses, chronic borderline dehydration, and untreated chronic conditions all present a diagnostic challenge to emergency personnel. This challenge will be complicated by the suspicion that the emergency problems were the result of domestic neglect or abuse. The patient is likely to be fearful of the medical team, an unfamiliar place, and the abusive or neglectful caretaker who might have accompanied the patient to the emergency department. Older patients frequently have reduced visual, auditory, or communicating abilities that can make it difficult to take a proper history.

The elderly in America are more likely than any other group to be taking numerous prescribed and over-the-counter drugs and medications. These medications are frequently not taken in proper dosage or on proper schedules. The expected effects of the drugs can be radically altered by drug interactions, alcohol intoxication, poor nutritional status, the traumatic events surrounding the neglect or abuse, or a frightening trip to the emergency department.

Transporting older patients to a hospital emergency department is also problematic because aged patients have preexisting conditions that are unlikely in younger patients. Nixon cites debilitating arthritis, common in old age, as a frequent problem.[10] Kyphosis, lordosis, or scoliosis can interfere with transporting the patient or with procedures such as resuscitation. Practical problems, including efforts to make a patient comfortable in transit, can be frustrating unless the transportation team is sensitive to the special needs and conditions of the elderly. The most frail and dependent aged are apparently at a higher risk of mistreatment than their more vital and independent peers. Victims of abuse or neglect may have permanent indwelling tubes, prostheses, or essential medical equipment that require special care and attention.

Finally, unlike a minor child, an aged victim of neglect or abuse can refuse any and all help. This refusal can pose the most difficult challenge to any emergency personnel and can be overcome only with a compassionate and understanding relationship with the patient; a rapport must be established quickly. Permission to treat an unconscious patient often comes from the adult caretaker or an available relative. If abuse or neglect is suspected, the person giving permission for treatment may later be proved culpable. In all cases, the legal rights of the elderly patient must be strictly honored.

THE EMERGENCY TEAM'S RESPONSE

The purpose of this chapter is to make emergency medical personnel aware that domestic neglect and abuse *probably* involve a larger proportion of geriatric patients in their care than they currently recognize. There is no need to underscore the necessity of providing first-class medical care except to outline some of the complications that staff may encounter. Certain actions are warranted, however, regarding geriatric patients; these are probably not standard policies or procedures for emergency staff. All emergency personnel should develop a heightened level of suspicion. Outside the hospital, staff should be alert to signs of abuse or neglect and take mental notes to be documented later. Unsanitary conditions, filth, obviously neglected indwelling tubes, isolated living conditions, and cooperation and attitudes of adult caretakers should be noted. A propensity of adult caretakers to talk for a geriatric patient or to treat the patient like a child may be a common practice, but it is especially prevalent in cases of domestic abuse or neglect. Personnel who deliver the patient to the emergency department should be aware of and record any evidence that the patient has been brutalized or is uncommonly fearful. It is not their role, however, to initiate contacts with police or social services. There is usually too little time for such secondary procedures before the patient reaches the emergency department.

Staff in the emergency department should be alert to the possibility of neglect or abuse with any geriatric patient who is injured, malnourished, dehydrated, traumatized, or in a drug crisis. It is in the emergency department that the suspicion of neglect or abuse should be recognized, documented, and acted upon.

If a hospital social worker is on staff or assigned to the emergency care unit, this person should be involved at the earliest opportunity. Observations by the delivery team should be included in the case documentation along with the medical history, physical examination, photographs, and any remarks made by the patient. Documenting the affective and emotional status of the patient is essential.

If the emergency department is in a jurisdiction that has mandatory reporting laws, someone must report the case immediately to the designated authority. If reporting is voluntary, someone should notify the closest adult protective services agency, usually part of a state or county department of social services. If criminal mistreatment such as assault or attempted homicide is suspected, it is the responsibility of the emergency department to notify local police authorities immediately. When the patient is not admitted to the hospital as an inpatient, the advisability of releasing a possible victim to the place where suspected mistreatment occurred should be carefully weighed. Whenever possible in such cases, alternative housing, admission for observation, or immediate involvement of protective services should be considered.

Referral of a case to community agencies and services does not end the role of emergency personnel. Their initial observations of the geriatric victim of neglect or abuse will provide the basis for any future improvement in the victim's circumstances. They should remain involved with the case to assist protective services, police investigations, arrangements for alternative housing, or the provision of supportive services to the caretaking family, and they should determine if referrals are acted upon. Adequate availability and utilization of community services such as nutrition sites, respite or relief care for caretaking families, home health services, chore services, or financial assistance to caretaking families could prevent the majority of cases.

The ultimate resolution of this problem requires an increased awareness by individuals of the aging process, a basic understanding of the debilitating effects of chronic illness, and a fundamental belief that the elderly have a right to live in dignity. Meanwhile, the elderly population is steadily increasing, and cases of neglect or abuse will probably show up in emergency departments with increasing regularity. The responsibilities for initial recognition and appropriate management of severely abused or neglected elderly people, therefore, remain with emergency personnel.

REFERENCES

1. Butler R: *Why Survive?* New York, Harper & Row Publishers Inc, 1975.

2. Steinmetz SK: *The Cycle of Violence.* New York, Praeger Publishers Inc, 1977.

3. Steinmetz SK: The politics of aging: battered parents. *Society* **15**:54–55, 1978.

4. Rathbone-McCuan E: Intergenerational family violence and neglect: the aged as victims of reactivated and reverse neglect. Read before the International Congress of Gerontology, Tokyo, 1978.

5. Lau EE, Kosberg JI: Abuse of the elderly by informal care providers. Presented to the 31st Annual Meeting of the Gerontological Society, Dallas, Tex, November 1978.

6. O'Malley H, et al: *Elder Abuse in Massachusetts.* Boston, Legal Research & Services for the Elderly, 1979.

7. Block MR, Sinnott JD: The Battered Elder Syndrome: An Exploratory Study. Final report to the US Administration on Aging, University of Maryland Center on Aging, College Park, Md, 1979.

8. Douglass RL, et al: A Study of Maltreatment of the Elderly and Other Vulnerable Adults. Final report to the US Administration on Aging and the Michigan Department of Social Services. The Institute of Gerontology, University of Michigan, Ann Arbor, Mich, 1980.

9. Garvin JM: Caring for the geriatric patient. *Emerg Med Serv* **9**:75-76, 1980.

10. Nixon RG: Some problems in the care of the geriatric patient. *Emerg Med Serv* **9**:45-47, 1980.

BACKGROUND LITERATURE

Elder Abuse: The Hidden Problem. Committee publication 96-200, Select Committee on Aging, US House of Representatives, Ninety-Sixth Congress, 1980.

Harden M: The abused elderly. *Ohio Magazine,* March 1980.

Press RM: Battered grandparents: hidden family problem. *The Christian Science Monitor,* December 5, 1979.

Renvoize J: *Web of Violence: A Study of Family Violence.* London, Routledge & Kegan Paul Ltd, 1978.

SUGGESTED READINGS

Frazier CA: Drug emergencies among the elderly. *Emerg Med Serv* **9**:71-73, 1980.

Wilder RJ: Trauma in the elderly. *Emerg Med Serv* **9**:61-63, 1980.

Unit IV

Sexual Violence and Adults

14

MANAGEMENT OF THE ADULT FEMALE RAPE VICTIM

G. Richard Braen, M.D.

Increasing numbers of women are seeking medical attention after rape and sexual assault. Some of these women receive care in emergency departments while others prefer the relative anonymity of a private physician's office. In either setting, knowledge regarding the physical and emotional treatment for sexual assault and an ability to apply that knowledge are essential for the examining professional. This chapter deals with the initial physical and emotional treatment of the rape victim as well as the evidentiary and legal aspects of the examination.

Rape is unlike the great majority of cases seen in emergency departments or physicians' offices and requires special care. Even though several articles have been published about the needs of rape victims,[1-11] many professionals in primary and emergency care remain unaware of them. These needs, listed below, will be considered in the following sections.

- Consent
- History
- Physical examination

- Collection of specimens
- Chain of evidence
- Treatment of injuries
- Initial care of emotional trauma
- Disease prevention
- Pregnancy prevention
- Follow-up

INITIAL CONTACT

When a rape victim comes to an emergency department or private office for treatment, the initial contact may set the tone for the remainder of that visit. The victim immediately becomes a patient who deserves all of the rights granted to any patient. Unlike many patients, however, she should be given some priority and should be escorted to a private room as soon as possible. If the initial contact itself is dehumanizing or accusatory, the patient either may not cooperate fully with the examination or may not return for follow-up care at a later date. This initial contact may be the first step in the patient's return to emotional stability, and clerical and nursing personnel should be trained to deal with rape victims who are at this crucial stage.

CONSENT

Informed, written, witnessed consent for examination, treatment, and the obtainment of legal samples or photographs is essential. The patient may choose to have medical attention only, but she should be urged to give consent also for an evidentiary examination since she may later choose to seek prosecution of her assailant.

HISTORY

The purpose of the history in a rape examination is to document when and where the event took place, what trauma may have resulted from the rape, what areas of the body should be most closely examined for seminal deposits, what events occurred that may cause the victim to need psychological support later, and what physical aspects of the victim herself may alter the findings in the rape examination or subsequent treatment. The history should include the following:[7,8]

A. HISTORY OF THE RAPE

1. Time, date, place

2. Use of force, threats of force, etc.
   a) Type of violence used
   b) Threats of violence
   c) Use of restraints
   d) Number of assailants
   e) Use of alcohol or drugs
   f) Loss of consciousness

3. Type of assault and frequency
   a) Fondling
   b) Cunnilingus
   c) Vaginal penetration or attempted penetration
   d) Oral penetration or attempted penetration
   e) Anal penetration or attempted penetration

   f) Ejaculation—on or in the body? Where?
   g) Use of a condom
   h) Did assailant tell the patient that he was sterile or had a vasectomy?

B. GYNECOLOGICAL HISTORY

1. Use of birth control? During the rape?

2. Last normal menstrual period

3. Date of last voluntary coitus before the rape
   a) Use of condom
   b) Postcoital douche
   c) Did partner have a vasectomy?

4. Gravidity and parity

5. Recent gynecological surgery

6. Recent venereal or genital disease

C. MEDICAL HISTORY

1. Current medications

2. Status of tetanus immunization

3. Allergies

D. ACTIVITIES AFTER THE RAPE

1. Douching or bathing

2. Urination or defecation

3. Gargling

4. Ingestion of alcohol or medications

Forms which address each of these points may be used, but some examiners prefer narrative formats that address the same historical elements. Whether forms or narratives are used, many examining physicians lack the skills needed to ask these embarrassing questions without contributing to the patient's discomfort. Some institutions use trained nurses or counselors to obtain the detailed history, and it is then reviewed by the physician. This method may not only be time-saving for the physician but also more comfortable for the patient.

PHYSICAL EXAMINATION

The physical examination of a rape victim will help determine her emotional status and her need for medical or surgical intervention and will provide the setting for the collection of evidence.

Medical History

Much of the success of the physical examination depends on the care used to obtain the medical history. Without the knowledge that there was forced fellatio, for example, the physician might miss a torn frenulum of the mucosal surface of the lower lip. Without the knowledge that drug use contributed to the rape, the physician might attribute a mild state of disorientation purely to the emotional trauma of the rape. The physical evaluation begins while the history is being obtained. During this time, the physician should observe the patient's emotional state. The manner in which she responds to specific questions may yield clues to her feelings about the event. Also, her ability to understand and appropriately respond to questions will help the physician determine if the victim was able to give consent for intercourse. Some victims of rape are not capable of consenting to intercourse because of mental retardation, immaturity, or intoxication with drugs or alcohol. If mental retardation is suspected, the examiner may recommend a formal examination of the patient's mental status at a follow-up visit.

Examination of Clothing and Body

The clothing worn by the patient when she was attacked may reveal seminal stains, foreign material, tears, blood, and other evidence. Seminal stains, blood, and other body fluids may contain blood group antigens attributable to the assailant. Eighty percent of people secrete blood group antigens in their body fluids, and these antigens may be used to trace the assailant. To avoid contamination by blood group antigens that may be present in the sweat of the hands of hospital

staff members, the patient should remove her own clothing and should place each article in a separate paper bag. Moisture-retaining plastic bags may promote molding of some stains and should be avoided. Before the removal of clothing, particularly if the patient was wearing the clothing when she was attacked, photographs should be taken.

It is difficult to perform a pelvic examination on a patient with a full bladder; if the patient needs to urinate, pubic hair combings and semen-matted hair should be collected before urination. Urine samples should be collected for drug and pregnancy screening tests. At this time, wiping of the perineum and defecation should be discouraged.

The entire body should be examined for bruises and scratches, particularly about the mouth, throat, wrists, breasts, thighs, and back. The skin and head hair should also be inspected for the presence of foreign material.

Up to 30 percent of rape victims will show external evidence of trauma.[12] This trauma may range from abrasions and contusions to major lacerations and facial fractures. The trauma may be documented in a variety of ways including photography or drawings on full body diagrams. All photographs should be given to the police for use as evidence.

Dried semen may be found on the skin or in the hair. Seminal stains appear as crusted, flaking areas of various sizes. These crusted areas may be removed with saline-moistened swabs. Fingernail scrapings should be obtained from the victim since bits of the assailant's skin, blood, or facial hair may be present. Other evidence from the rape site, such as dirt or sand, may also be present under the fingernails.

Pelvic Examination

After this initial examination, a pelvic examination should be performed. Once again, the inner thighs and perineum should be inspected for signs of seminal stains and trauma. The pubic hair should be combed to remove foreign material, and combings should be preserved as evidence. If semen is encrusted in the pubic hair, these areas of encrustation should be trimmed out and preserved as evidence.

A careful vulvar and vaginal examination is essential. The vulva should be examined for signs of trauma, semen, and other foreign material. Water should be used as the lubricant when inserting a vaginal speculum because other lubricants may adversely affect either the acid phosphatase or sperm motility test. The introitus and the hymen should be examined for signs of trauma. Later, a simple statement should be made about the condition of the hymen: The hymen was present, intact, and free of evidence of trauma; the hymen was present, intact, and showed old scarring; the hymen was present and recently ruptured; or the hymen was absent. Recent trauma to the hymen is commonly associated with bleeding or fresh clots. The vaginal wall should be examined for lacerations. Sexually inactive patients who have been raped may have lacerations in the area of the lower vagina near the introitus. Patients who are sexually active tend to have lacerations, when present, higher in the vagina near the posterior fornix, particularly on the right side. All except the most superficial vaginal lacerations should be treated by a gynecologist.

The cervix should be inspected for signs of existing pregnancy, menstruation, trauma, and preexistent infection. The cervix itself is rarely injured during rape except when foreign objects have been placed in the vagina.

Collection of Specimens

After the vagina and cervix have been inspected, secretions in the posterior fornix should be aspirated or removed with sterile cotton swabs. These secretions may contain motile sperm and acid phosphatase.[13,14] If the patient had a vaginal tampon in place when she was assaulted or inserted a tampon after the assault, it should be retained as evidence because it may also contain sperm and acid phosphatase. Swabs from the posterior fornix should be smeared onto two glass slides; one will be used for an examination of sperm motility and the other for acid phosphatase. The slide for sperm motility should first have a drop of normal saline placed in its center. Then the sample suspected of containing sperm should be added to the saline and covered with a glass coverslip. Bacteriostatic saline should not be used because it may immobilize the sperm.

A Papanicolaou (Pap) smear should be obtained from the cervix. It may reveal intact sperm for several days after the assault. Another specimen from the cervix should be immediately streaked onto a Thayer-Martin culture plate to test for gonorrhea.

The anal area should be examined even if the patient denies anal intercourse. Signs of trauma, blood, or semen may be present even when anal intercourse did not occur. A specimen to test for gonorrhea should be routinely obtained from the rectum. If the patient has reported anal intercourse, the hub of a syringe should be used to wash the rectal vault with 5 to 10 milliliters of normal saline. Samples obtained this way should be checked for motile sperm, immotile sperm, and acid phosphatase.

When fellatio is reported, the patient's oral cavity should be inspected for signs of trauma. These signs may include bruises about the mouth or inside the mouth, a torn frenulum beneath the lips or tongue, and broken teeth. Tests for acid phosphatase on specimens from the oral cavity are seldom positive, but careful swabbing of the oral cavity, particularly between the teeth, occasionally will recover sperm.

Saliva samples, on swabs, can be used to determine if the patient secretes blood group antigens. Blood samples should be obtained for drug and alcohol screening, blood typing, and a baseline serological test for syphilis. Some institutions now take blood for a serum pregnancy test which uses the beta subunit of human chorionic gonadotropin (β-HCG). This test detects pregnancy as early as one week after implantation of a fertilized egg. If it is positive within a few hours of the assault, then the victim was probably pregnant at the time of the rape. If the test becomes positive at the two-week follow-up visit, it may be assumed that the patient became pregnant during or near the time of the rape.

CHAIN OF EVIDENCE

A chain of evidence refers not only to the custody of evidence but also to the transfer of that evidence from one authority to another. This evidence must be accounted for during each step of its transfer to ensure that samples taken from the victim are exactly the same samples examined in the crime laboratory. This chain of evidence should be written and witnessed; each person who gives samples to another should sign them out, and each person who receives samples should sign them in.

Each sample must be labeled with the patient's name, hospital number, the date and time of collection, the area from which the specimen was collected, and the collector's name.

MANAGEMENT OF THE RAPE VICTIM

The medical and psychological problems of the rape victim include physical trauma, the potential exposure to venereal disease, the possibility of pregnancy, and psychological trauma. With the exception of physical trauma, which is managed in the rape victim the same as in any patient, each of the other problems needs special consideration.

Prevention of Venereal Disease

It has been estimated that 1 in 30 rape victims develops gonorrhea after the attack.[12] Some examiners routinely offer victims treatment for gonorrhea since follow-up visits by rape victims cannot be assured. These patients are treated as if they had been exposed to a known case of gonorrhea. Many victims prefer prophylactic treatment for gonorrhea, and this treatment may be psychologically beneficial. The treatment may follow any one of several modalities (Table 14-1).

It has been estimated that only 1 of every 1,000 rape victims develops syphilis after an attack. A positive serological test for syphilis at the time of the initial examination indicates that the patient had syphilis before the rape (if supporting tests do not prove that the serological test for syphilis was a biological false-positive). If the serological test for syphilis is negative, the patient should have the

Table 14-1   Treatment of Gonorrhea

Dose regimens of choice
  (1) *Aqueous procaine penicillin G (APPG):* 4.8 million units injected intramuscularly at two sites, with 1.0 gram of probenecid given orally.
or (2) *Tetracycline hydrochloride:* 0.5 grams given orally four times daily for five days, with a total dose of 10.0 grams.*
or (3) *Ampicillin:* 3.5 grams given orally with 1.0 gram of probenecid.**
or (4) *Amoxicillin:* 3.0 grams given orally with 1.0 gram of probenecid.**
or (5) *Spectinomycin hydrochloride:* 2.0 grams in one intramuscular injection.***

---

*All tetracyclines are ineffective as single-dose therapy.
**These regimens are less effective than other recommended regimens.
***Patients allergic to penicillins (including ampicillin and amoxicillin) or probenecid should be treated with tetracycline. If they are allergic to penicillins or probenecid and also intolerant to tetracycline, spectinomycin should be used.
Note: Patients with incubating syphilis (seronegative, without clinical signs of syphilis) are likely to be cured by all of the above regimens except spectinomycin.

Source: *Morbidity Mortality Weekly Rep* **28**:13–16, 1979.

test repeated at a follow-up visit six weeks later. If the patient was prophylactically treated for gonorrhea with 4.8 million units of aqueous procaine penicillin with probenicid, this regimen will also treat incubating syphilis.[15]

Prevention of Pregnancy

Pregnancy because of rape develops in about one percent of raped patients. A careful gynecological history should be obtained by the examiner since 90 to 95 percent of conceptions that are the result of a single act of intercourse occur between 120 hours before ovulation and 10 hours after ovulation. If the time of ovulation can be estimated, the examiner may be able to advise the patient about the need for pregnancy prevention.

The examiner must also determine that pregnancy did not exist before the attack. The results of a pregnancy test should be available before any "morning-after" postcoital therapy is given. The most accurate pregnancy test is the radioimmunoassay for β-HCG. Before giving any type of postcoital treatment to prevent pregnancy, the physician not only should know for certain that the victim is not pregnant but also should obtain written, formal consent from her. Alternatives to pregnancy prevention include those suggested in Table 14-2.[16] Since only 1 in 100 rape victims becomes pregnant from the assault, the examiner may choose to offer a suction curettage abortion to that one victim rather than "morning-after pills" to many.

Other Treatments

Some types of treatment may be beneficial both medically and psychologically. For example, a cleansing douche or a mouthwash (particularly if the victim was forced to engage in fellatio) may not only help the victim feel more clean but also help eliminate some disease. An antiscabies lotion or shampoo

Table 14-2 Alternatives to Pregnancy Prevention

Diethylstilbestrol (DES)	25 mg given orally twice daily for 5 days
Conjugated estrogens (Premarin)	50 mg given intravenously once daily for 2 days, or
	50 mg given intravenously once, or
	30 mg given orally once daily for 5 days
Ethinyl estradiol	5 mg given orally once daily for 5 days

may also be offered. Many victims may be asked to remain at a police station for several hours after the examination, and they will feel more comfortable if they are given an opportunity to clean themselves and change into fresh clothing.

Psychological Help

Psychological help for the rape victim begins in the emergency department. An empathic, concerned emergency staff will begin to help the victim realize that she is safe again and among caring people. This is only a beginning, however, and further psychological help may be necessary. For those who are severely disturbed, professional help may be needed, but many victims may profit from volunteer help provided by rape crisis centers and similar organizations.

Follow-up

Follow-up of rape victims is essential. A minimum of a two-week and a six-week follow-up visit is recommended. At the two-week follow-up, the patient's psychological status should be evaluated, and an examination should be performed to rule out gonorrhea. If a beta subunit test for pregnancy is available, this test should also be done. At the six-week follow-up visit the patient's emotional status should be evaluated again, and there should be a repeat test for syphilis. If a pregnancy test that requires urine is being used, it should be repeated at this six-week visit.

CONCLUSION

Trained, organized medical staffs can have a significant impact on the management of rape victims. These victims immediately become patients with special needs when they come to the emergency department or private office. With adequate planning, understanding, and caring, the emotional, physical, and forensic needs of these patients can be met.

REFERENCES

1. Schiff AF: Examining the sexual assault victim. *J Fla Med Assoc* **56**:731–739, 1969.

2. Schiff AF: Rape needs a special examination. *Emerg Med* **3**:28–29, 1971.

3. Massey JB, et al: Management of sexually assaulted females. *Obstet Gynecol* **38**:29–36, 1971.

4. Breen JL, et al: The molested young female. *Pediatr Clin North Am* **19**:717–725, 1972.

5. Evrard JR: Rape: the medical, social and legal implications. *Am J Obstet Gynecol* **3**:197–199, 1971.

6. Braen GR: *The Rape Examination.* North Chicago, Abbott Laboratories, 1976.

7. Braen GR: Physical assessment and emergency medical management for adult victims of sexual assault, in Warner CG (ed): *Rape and Sexual Assault.* Rockville, Md, Aspen Systems Corp, 1980, pp 47–66.

8. Schiff AF: How to handle the rape victim. *South Med J* **71**:509–515, 1978.

9. South Carolina Committee on Sexual Assault: guidelines for the treatment of sexual assault victims. *J SC Med Assoc* **74**:331–335, 1978.

10. Halbert DR, Jones DED: Medical management of the sexually assaulted woman. *J Reprod Med* **20**:265–274, 1978.

11. Daniels JS: Emergency department management of rape. *Ohio State Med J* **75**:351–352, 1979.

12. Schiff AF: A statistical evaluation of rape. *Forensic Sci* **2**:339–349, 1973.

13. Gomez RR, et al: Qualitative and quantitative determinations of acid phosphatase activity in vaginal washings. *Am J Clin Pathol* **65**:423–432, 1975.

14. McCloskey KL, et al: Prostatic acid phosphatase activity in the postcoital vagina. *J Forensic Sci* **21**:630–636, 1975.

15. Schroeter AL, et al: Therapy for incubating syphilis: effectiveness of gonorrhea treatment. *JAMA* **218**:711–713, 1971.

16. Hunt G: Alternatives to pregnancy prevention. *Am Fam Physician* **19**:27, 1979.

15

EXAMINATION AND MANAGEMENT OF THE MALE RAPE VICTIM

G. Richard Braen, M.D.

Sexual assault of males is generally perpetrated by other males; cases of females assaulting male victims are extremely uncommon. *Webster's New Collegiate Dictionary* defines rape as sexual intercourse with a woman by a man without her consent and chiefly by force or deception. In common usage today, however, "rape" of a male may occur and includes forcible anal or oral intercourse.

The incidence of homosexual rape is not known.[1-5] It is felt that rape of adult males occurs primarily in jails and prisons, and these cases frequently go unreported unless the victim is severely injured physically. Cases of male rape reported to emergency departments generally involve children and early adolescents, and there still remains a great deal of underreporting in this type of sexual assault.

As with females, the rape of males is an act of aggression. In prison, where it has been conservatively estimated that one-half to three percent of those incarcerated are subjected to sexual assault, the most aggressive rapes have been conducted by lower-class inmates against middle-class inmates.[6] The average age of a man who rapes another man in prison is 23; the victim's average age is 21. Usually the assailant in this type of rape is a person who has been incarcerated for a violent crime such as murder, rape, or robbery.

Like female victims, male victims have psychological, medical, and legal needs and should be given the same consideration that female victims receive. These considerations include the right to be escorted into a private room and to be interviewed away from the police and prison officials.

CONSENT

As with any victim of sexual assault, the male rape victim should sign consent forms for the obtainment of the history, physical examination, collection of evidence, photography, and treatment. Since many victims are brought from jails or prisons under court order, the examining physician should make sure that each type of consent is specified in that court order.

HISTORY

The history should include the time, date, and place of the event; the use of force and its type; the use of threats of violence; the use of restraints; the number of assailants; the concommitant use of alcohol or drugs; and any loss of consciousness. The type of assault should also be noted and should include the occurrence of oral penetration or attempted penetration, anal penetration or attempted penetration, the use of lubrication, if and where ejaculation occurred, and the use of a condom. The general medical history should include the current use of medications, the status of the victim's tetanus immunization, and allergies. The examiner should also question the victim about the history of recent venereal disease and any recent anal or rectal surgery.

PHYSICAL EXAMINATION

The victim's airway, breathing, and circulation should be assessed upon his arrival in the emergency department. Active bleeding should be stopped by local pressure, when possible. While the history is being obtained, the physician should note and record the victim's general emotional state.

General Survey of Clothing and Body

Signs of violence and traces of semen may be present on the victim's clothing, and these should be sought. The examiner should pay particular attention to underwear when looking for evidence of ejaculation or blood from rectal penetration. Garments should be placed in individual paper bags, appropriately labeled, and turned over to the police along with an appropriate form for the chain of evidence.

The unclothed victim should be thoroughly examined for signs of trauma such as bruises and scratches. If the victim was forcibly held by the arms or neck, these areas should be carefully examined for signs of bruises that may outline the marks left by constricting hands. It is not uncommon for an adult male to fight with his assailant or assailants before submitting, and signs of trauma may be found from being beaten about the head or kicked while on the floor. The physician should look for fractures; if found, they should be treated appropriately.

Examination of Oral, Genital, and Anorectal Areas

After this general body survey, attention should be turned to the mouth, genitals, and anorectal areas. The mouth should be examined for tears, lacerations, bruises, and broken teeth, all signs which might indicate that the mouth was forced open. The pharynx should be examined for exudates, lacerations, and contusions. If the victim was repeatedly forced to perform fellatio, there may be local swelling of the pharynx which could later lead to occlusion of the upper airway. Samples should be obtained from the pharynx and cultured for gonorrhea. Careful swabbing between the teeth has occasionally turned up sperm, but the presence of acid phosphatase in the oral cavity is uncommon.[7]

The male genitals should be examined for signs of trauma including bruises, bites, and lacerations. The perineum and rectum should be inspected for signs of trauma; these include rectal fissures, tears, and rectal bleeding. If it is difficult to perform a digital rectal examination because the victim has intense rectal and anal pain, he should be put under anesthesia for the examination. When possible, rectal washings should be collected: the hub of a 10-millimeter syringe filled with normal saline should be inserted into the anus, the liquid injected, and the contents aspirated after 5 to 10 minutes. This sample can be used in the analysis for acid phosphatase or sperm. Blood in the rectum, whether occult or fresh, is an indication for proctoscopy. Any deposits on the buttocks that may be semen or lubricant should be removed and submitted to the police for analysis.

Collection of Specimens

The examining physician should inspect rectal swabs or washings for motile sperm. If there are blood or feces mixed with the suspected semen, and spermatozoa cannot be identified, a drop of a supravital urine stain may be added to the mixture to stain the sperm.[5]

The hospital laboratory should process all specimens that are important for the treatment of the victim. These include blood for serological testing for syphilis, serum or urine for drug screening, and urine for a urinalysis to detect things such as renal contusions. All other samples can be sent to the police crime laboratory: air-dried slides of material from the rectum and oral cavity, rectal washings, swabs of any skin area that showed traces of semen, fingernail scrapings, and photographs. The crime laboratory should be able to analyze specimens that might contain semen for acid phosphatase and immotile sperm.

MANAGEMENT

If oral or anal intercourse was forced upon the victim, the physician should consider treating the victim as if he were a contact of a known case of gonorrhea. (See Chapter 14 for treatment regimens.) Pharyngeal gonococcal infections are difficult to treat and generally do not respond to ampicillin and spectinomycin. An alternative regimen for the treatment of pharyngeal gonorrhea would include four tablets of either tetracycline or trimethoprim-

sulfamethoxazole (320 milligrams trimethoprim and 1,600 milligrams sulfamethoxazole) given orally twice daily for two days. The treatment with trimethoprim-sulfamethoxazole results in a 95.3 percent cure rate.[8]

Incubating syphilis (seronegative cases without clinical signs of syphilis) can be cured by tetracycline, aqueous procaine penicillin G, ampicillin, or amoxicillin.[9] Treatment with tetracycline or trimethoprim-sulfamethoxazole will also eliminate coexisting chlamydial infections.

Psychological support for the male rape victim is important and can be begun while the victim is still in the emergency department. Both older and younger men may need formal psychiatric treatment. Many rape crisis centers now have trained male counselors who may themselves have been victims of sexual assault and who may help provide psychological support for the victim. Unfortunately, many of the male victims of rape must return to the prison setting where the assault occurred, only to be confronted by the same assailants with the future possibility of repeated or intensified abuse.

SUMMARY

Reports of sexual assault on males by other men are increasing. Treatment begins by providing the patient privacy and protection from further humiliation, if possible. Proper consent forms must be signed and witnessed. The physical examination should include a general body survey followed by specific examinations for trauma and the collection of specimens.

Treatment of these victims should include stabilization of life and limb, treatment of trauma, and prophylaxis against venereal disease. Follow-up care is important both for the psychological recovery of the victim and for the prevention of venereal disease.

REFERENCES

1. Josephson GW: The male rape victim: evaluation and treatment. *JACEP* **8**:13-15, 1979.

2. Orr DP, Prietto S: Emergency management of sexually abused children. *Am J Dis Child* **133**:628-631, 1979.

3. Raybin JB: Homosexual incest. *J Nerv Ment Dis* **148**:105-109, 1969.

4. Dixon KN, et al: Father-son incest—underreported psychiatric problem? *Am J Psychiatry* **135**:835-838, 1978.

5. Braen GR: The male rape victim: examination and management, in Warner CG (ed): *Rape and Sexual Assault*. Rockville, Md, Aspen Systems Corp, 1980, pp 67-71.

6. Moss CS, et al: Sexual assault in a prison. *Psychol Rep* **44**:823-828, 1979.

7. Enos WF, Beyer JC: Spermatozoa in the anal canal and rectum and in the oral cavity of female rape victims. *J Forensic Sci* **23**:231-233, 1978.

8. Sattler FR, Ruskin J: Therapy of gonorrhea: comparison of trimethoprim-sulfamethoxazole and ampicillin. *JAMA* **240**:2267-2770, 1978.

9. Gonorrhea: CDC recommended treatment schedules. *Morbidity Mortality Weekly Rep* **28**: 13-21, 1979.

16

COUNSELING AND FOLLOW-UP INTERACTION FOR THE ADULT RAPE VICTIM

Carmen Germaine Warner, R.N., M.S.N., F.A.A.N.

The dynamics of a rape attack are unpredictable, sudden in onset, and explosive in nature. These elements, in addition to the violent, hostile nature of the attack, are very disruptive. They leave the victims disorganized, disassociated from the present, and unable to refocus and rebuild their lives. This process is experienced by both male and female victims irrespective of their educational, economic, or social status.

It is essential that emergency care professionals, social workers, and community counselors work toward the common goal of recovery and regrowth during both the counseling and follow-up phases of intervention.

COMMON REACTIONS TO RAPE

The impact of rape, on both men and women, manifests itself in feelings of loss, a realization that the assault was a life-threatening act, and feelings of helplessness and vulnerability. These manifestations generally result in a crisis, and emergency and social service personnel are needed to clarify the relationship between the rape and its subsequent reactions. Victims experiencing a crisis may respond in a manner totally inconsistent with routine behavior. They may experience a disruption in cognitive, affective, and behavioral mannerisms and create situations that are both frustrating and disruptive to themselves and others.

In addition, victims may verbalize feelings of both threats and losses and be anxious and depressed. A classic reaction consists of two specific phases during the postassault period.[1] These phases are immediate and subsequent reactions.

Immediate Reactions

The phase of immediate reactions occurs immediately after the assault and is usually seen in an emergency department. This phase is brief and generally focuses on the initial emergency. Personnel must realize that psychological defenses are frequently present and assist the victim in coping with the rape and its impact.

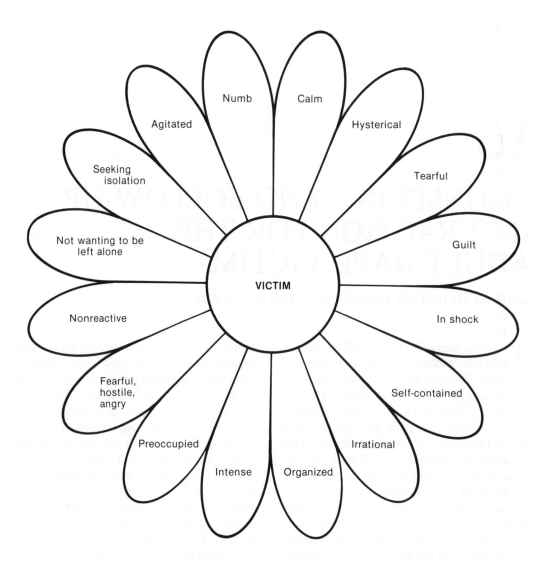

Fig. 16-1 Responses of rape victims during the immediate reaction phase.

Fig. 16-1 portrays the dynamic meshing of immediate reactions commonly experienced by rape victims. Any combination of these reactions may evolve concomitantly, and emergency personnel should be aware of this behavioral pattern.

It is not uncommon for victims to either completely deny the assault, consequently resisting all attempts to even discuss it, or to behave in a very controlled, rational manner.

This behavior is significant for three reasons: (1) it is contrary to the belief and expectations of most emergency personnel; (2) it masks the victim's real emotional trauma; and (3) in the absence of visible physical trauma, it reinforces the tendency to disbelieve the victim. When emergency professionals begin to be supportive, the victim may then begin to release inner restraints and express personal feelings.

Emotional intervention may begin once the victim acknowledges the incident. It is important for professionals not to initiate the interview or physical examination before establishing this rapport.

ASSESSMENT OF THE EMOTIONAL STATUS

Victims can be aided significantly by guiding them in defining the problem and identifying various alternatives. Professionals should record the victim's present level of anxiety and inquire how previous crises have been handled.

It is also valuable to record whether the victim is showing signs of alcohol or drug use. These signs may be important in determining the victim's initial ability to resist or may reflect the introduction of such agents by the perpetrator.

INTERPRETATION OF EXISTING RESOURCES

Emergency and social service personnel should interpret the victim's strengths and potential coping mechanisms. They should also inquire about the availability of family, friends, or significant others.

It is essential to meet the victim's basic human needs during this early phase of readjustment. Frequently, victims may be too overwhelmed to do so on their own.

Familiar coping strengths useful in the past may prove most inadequate after a rape. Rape advocates from community centers are valuable in assisting the victim to formulate and resolve many questions and concerns. These advocates play a vital role in bridging the gap between initial management and long-term recovery and in initiating the transition period from immediate to subsequent reactions.

INTERPRETATION OF INFORMATION

Emergency personnel should be aware of the need for information and explanations throughout the process of assessment and intervention. Required medical procedures must be carefully pointed out and any personal consequences reiterated. Specific notation must also be made to fully explain each procedure described in Chapters 14 and 15. Personnel should stress the importance of follow-up intervention and inform the victim of resources for obtaining such care.

The thoughtfulness of little things such as the availability of a telephone, facial tissue, cigarettes, and clean clothing will mean a great deal. After the physical examination, the victim may welcome bathing facilities, oral hygiene, a comb or brush, something to eat or drink, and personal privacy. Many of these may be requested before the physical examination, but personnel should carefully explain why they are not permitted at that time.

The general level of cooperation and response will be impressive if professionals take time, show courtesy, and explain everything.

Subsequent Reactions

The second phase of reactions deals with the days, weeks, and years that follow discharge from the hospital. Many of the immediate reactions may continue to be expressed during this second stage, and new concerns—physical, emotional, spiritual, social, and economic—may also develop.

Because victims are frequently unable to foresee the need for follow-up intervention, emergency personnel should encourage and initiate this process. The ultimate goal is to help victims resume their previous levels of functioning as quickly and as realistically as possible.

Professionals should recognize that many victims may continue to have somatic symptoms regardless of the severity of their physical injuries. Some of these symptoms are disrupted sleep patterns, loss of appetite, fatigue, soreness, aches, and genital or urological problems. Other problems requiring attention during this follow-up period include fear, guilt, depression, developmental problems, preoccupation, and withdrawal from sexual relationships.

FEAR

The feeling of fear continues long into the period of regrowth and recovery. This feeling may be general, concerning areas of well-being, or it may be specific, relating to the rape incident itself. Victims consistently fear being alone.

GUILT

One of the most important issues to be dealt with is guilt. Victims constantly ask why the act was ever committed and must be helped to realize that they were not responsible for and did not seek the assault.

DEPRESSION

Depression usually occurs when the individual begins to relive the incident and attempts to resolve personal feelings about the trauma. Depression should be dealt with by a professional to restore the victim's sense of security and trust.

DEVELOPMENTAL PROBLEMS

Recovering victims frequently express a need for security, achievement, recognition, and love. The victim's age and stage of development frequently determine relevant issues. For example, young adults may fear that the rape will create problems in interpersonal relationships; adults may be concerned about how the rape will affect others and existing life-styles; older adults are likely to fear death and the impact of the trauma.[2]

PREOCCUPATION

Victims may spend considerable time wondering, "Why me?" They relive the incident over and over again and try to see how they could have escaped the attack, even if an escape was virtually impossible. This preoc-

cupation may be an attempt to undo what happened as well as an attempt to regain control. If victims can establish how and why the assault happened, they may be able to prevent a recurrence.

WITHDRAWAL FROM SEXUAL RELATIONSHIPS

Withdrawal from sexual relationships is a complex issue, and existing problems may stem from numerous sources: individual differences that existed before the assault and existing and subsequent relationships with others.[1] Flashbacks may occur if the victim engages in sexual relationships; consequently, the victim may choose to withdraw. Despite the need to abstain from sexual closeness, the victim still has an intense need to receive comfort and personal closeness from a loved one. Regardless of one's choice of recovery, it is imperative that professionals help the victim restore and regain feelings of self-worth and pride. It will be difficult for victims to develop closeness with a mate unless they have regained love and respect for themselves.

TECHNIQUES IN COUNSELING

Emergency professionals and counselors working with victims of rape have the ultimate goal of assisting the victim to deal with existing physical, emotional, social, legal, and economic concerns. The specific techniques and skills used will depend upon the working tools advocated by the counselor, the response of the victim to the counseling, and the type of communication required for mutual understanding of the process.

Assessing the Effectiveness of Counseling

Emergency personnel should constantly assess the effectiveness of the counseling by measuring the following behavioral outcomes:

- Ability of the victim to begin formulating a trusting relationship

- Evidence of the victim's ability to express personal feelings, fears, responses, and concerns related to the rape

- Evidence of the victim's increased feelings of self-love and acceptance

- Ability of the victim to conceptualize the loss the victim has felt

- Evidence of the victim's decreased level of agitation and anxiety

- Capability of the victim to incorporate individual coping and problem-solving skills

- Evidence of a workable solution for regrowth and recovery

- Admission by the victim of the potential long-term results of the rape

- Degree of comfort shown by the victim in seeking out and analyzing information on alternatives for a future life-style

Guidelines for Counseling Victims of Rape

After an initial assessment, each professional will be able to modify the sequence of the first interview and make it appropriate for that particular victim. Irrespective of the format, there are guidelines to be considered and applied throughout the counseling session:

- Introduce yourself to the victim.
- Select a room that is quiet and private.
- Explain your role and specific responsibilities.
- Acknowledge your awareness of the rape.
- Encourage the victim to talk about the rape.
- Facilitate an open discussion of the victim's personal feelings about the rape.
- Validate the specific feelings expressed.
- Encourage assessment of feelings about short-term and long-term implications of the rape.
- Repeat and clarify concerns expressed by the victim.

- Summarize the content of the counseling at periodic intervals.

- Assist the victim to identify each concern.

- Encourage the victim to assign priorities to these concerns.

- Assist the victim in setting goals.

- Help the victim with decision-making and problem-solving techniques.

- Determine existing coping skills.

- Encourage the victim to apply specific coping skills and to develop others.

- Inform the victim of possible outside reactions, both short-term and long-term.

- Assist the victim to develop techniques for dealing with outside reactions.

- Determine the value of support from family and friends.

- Encourage an initial communication session between the victim and family and friends.

- Teach the victim about psychological and medical concerns and the importance of follow-up intervention.

- Initiate a follow-up visit.

- Begin to work with outside community agencies for ongoing follow-up intervention

The length of time required to complete this initial counseling session may differ among victims. Multiple sessions may be needed to accomplish everything. Regardless of the time required, the essential factor is to guide the victim in the direction of regrowth and recovery.

TELEPHONE COUNSELING IN THE EMERGENCY DEPARTMENT

Since rape usually occurs when an individual is alone, it is recommended that the victim contact someone as quickly as possible once the perpetrator has gone away.

Whether the victim contacts law enforcement personnel, community crisis advocates, counselors, friends, family, or emergency personnel, it is important that the victim receive immediate support and reassurance.

The victim may be in shock and unable to respond to specific recommendations. Therefore, it is imperative that the victim gets help as quickly as possible. This process may require that a professional telephone the victim's neighbor or family member as quickly as possible.

In the meantime, the professional should

- Talk to the victim in a distinct, slow, calm voice
- Reassure the victim that help is on the way and tell the victim not to leave
- Provide brief, clear instructions for some simple task that will help the victim gain control
- Repeat over and over again, "I will help you," and "You will be okay"
- Remind the victim that people care.

The initial response provided by this telephone contact is essential to establish the foundation for continued intervention. If the telephone counselor is supportive and comforting, the rape victim will be more willing to cooperate with other medical and law enforcement personnel.

It is imperative that both telephone counselors and personnel who provide immediate care to the victim be informed of the measures that *must* be taken to preserve the evidence. Table 16-1 lists DO NOTs that are essential if prosecution is to be possible.

If victims who have been informed of the purpose and validity of these requests insist that they must clean up, their wishes should be respected. The ultimate goal is to minimize the results of the rape, not intensify them.

The telephone counselor should continue talking to the rape victim until help arrives. Those who come to help should also be informed of the DO NOTs. The more people

Table 16-1 DO NOTs for Preservation of Evidence[3]

- Change clothes
- Eat
- Drink
- Take medication of any kind
- Gargle
- Brush or floss teeth
- Urinate
- Defecate
- Douche
- Shower
- Delay getting to the emergency department

who become involved in the victim's care and support, the easier it will be for the victim.

COMMUNITY AGENCY COUNSELING

It is important that emergency personnel develop a network between the emergency facility and various community crisis and advocacy agencies. One of the most effective means of accomplishing this goal is to include community agency personnel in the transition period from hospital to home. Rape victims will be much more willing to continue followup counseling if an initial introduction and communication session has occurred in the hospital.

In a study conducted by Sexual Assault Resource Service (SARS), 67 percent of the victims seen by a nurse from SARS in the emergency department returned for followup care; only 31 percent of the victims not seen by a SARS nurse returned.[4]

Responsibilities of a Community Counselor

Community counselors can come to hospital emergency departments on a 24-hour-a-day call basis. These community agencies offer a source of support to rape victims as long as support is needed and in any area of need. Emergency personnel should use this resource to link the victim with the community and to assist personnel with intervention during the immediate postassault period.

Services available through community rape counseling centers include the following:

- Immediate support for the victim in the hospital and during the examination process

- Counseling and support for family and friends

- Education on venereal disease, pregnancy, physical injuries, emotional trauma, and legal concerns

- Establishing communication with community agencies

- Long-term emotional support for the victim, as well as the victim's family and friends

- Informing victims of the importance of their return visits to the clinic

- Answering all questions related to follow-up visits

- Support for the victim during legal proceedings

Emergency personnel and community counselors should remember the following points in their support sessions:

- Recognize the victim as a man or woman with special needs.

- Remain sensitive and open to both verbal and nonverbal communication.

- Practice active listening.

- Respond to the incident and its effect only; do not attempt to analyze why it happened.

- Guide the victim to rise above the rape incident and deny the rapist the satisfaction of traumatizing the victim.

- Help the victim regain self-control and develop and use coping skills.

- Encourage the victim to take responsibility for the victim's care.

- Encourage the victim to focus on the future, including life-style, location, employment, educational pursuits, social and athletic interests.

Guide to Goals[4]

Professionals must realize that setting goals is not only a specific step during the intervention process but also an integral part of both short-term and long-term counseling.

An excellent example of treatment that includes setting goals has been used by the SARS program in Minneapolis, Minnesota. This treatment approach, called "Guide to Goals," is an adaptation of Kiresuk and Sherman's Goal Attainment Scaling (GAS) method.[4] At its simplest, "Guide to Goals" involves the setting of goals, implementation of a program for change such as counseling, determination of subsequent attainment of the previously set goals, and use of this information to modify future activities. "Guide to Goals" varies from the original GAS format because the guide is used by persons to set their own goals. In SARS's application, goal-oriented counseling and feedback were used as interrelated aspects of the overall treatment approach.

Although the reasons why "Guide to Goals" is so effective have not been determined, SARS staff believe the method's client-centered orientation might be particularly useful with victims of sexual assault. Rogers stresses the importance of therapy never taking the power and control away from the client.[5] This dictum seems especially true for victims of rape, for whom issues of control are central. The counselor should not rescue victims and try to solve their problems for them, but should provide information and remove obstacles so that the victims can move forward at their own pace. These procedures help victims grow and cope with both past and future problems in a more integrated fashion. Clients who are setting goals and making choices are not passive recipients of services; they remain the center of activity and decision making.

Additionally, the counselor must learn to trust clients to decide on their own treatment goals and direction, just as counselors have, for so long, stressed the importance of obtaining a client's trust. The counselor's expectations can set the tone for victims' responses, but it is essential to stress the victims' capacities, their right and ability to set personal goals, and their ultimate responsibility for themselves and the care they will receive.

Kopp has suggested the arrogance of a counselor who takes on the role of "caretaker" for "helpless victims," who may in turn relinquish complete control of their lives to the counselor.[6] The counselor cannot possibly do enough and, as a result, will also feel helpless. Maintenance or regaining of control in many ways is an educational process, but it is an especially essential element for the victims of sexual assault. "Guide to Goals" is a treatment model that can facilitate this process and help the rape victim cope with stress in a more adaptive fashion. An example of "Guide for Goals" is found in Table 16-2.

FOLLOW-UP INTERVENTION

Follow-up care extends beyond the first clinic revisit. It extends beyond the three-month to six-month period of personal counseling and guidance. In fact, it should continue for the remainder of the victims' lives, until they are finally able to *love and accept themselves again as very special human beings.*

Professionals should intensify the value of each follow-up visit and minimize the length of time required for regrowth and recovery. Situations that must be dealt with during regrowth and recovery include disruptive patterns in life-style, flashbacks and nightmares, and fears and phobias.

Disruptive Patterns in Life-style[7]

When the pretrauma life pattern is disrupted, some or all of the victim's daily routines may change. Even the most basic aspects of daily patterns may be difficult to resume. Familiar, out-of-home activities such as work or school may be attended with little or no interest or may be dropped completely. In these cases, the victim frequently remains at home with only occasional departures, and then only in the presence of a family member or friend.

If immediate family members reside some distance away, the victim often makes an unscheduled, unexplained visit. The need to get away from horrible memories is a very intense feeling. This change of environment is made in the hope that memories will dissolve during the absence. The blatant reality is that the victim just postpones the ultimate discomfort of regrowth and recovery.

Physical relocation is frequently considered. This is especially true when the rape occurred in the victim's residence. The victim is motivated by two factors: a concern over safety and a desire to escape bad memories.

A desire to be removed from outside communication often results in a new telephone number, sometimes unlisted. The thought of a repeat confrontation, even over the telephone, is frightening. Because the thought of living alone produces fear, family or friends often reside with a victim in order to provide companionship, comfort, and safety. Even if the arrangement is on a short-term basis, the initial support is essential.

Flashbacks and Nightmares

The phenomenon of flashbacks or nightmares is very common and occurs throughout the period of regrowth and recovery. The actual flashback portrays the incident itself; the nightmares depict either the rape, a close proximity of the rapist, or variations of physical trauma.

Table 16-2   Goal Attainment Follow-up Guide[4]

Guide to Goals	CONCERN 1: *Wants to be unattractive* IMPORTANCE = 2	CONCERN 2: *Trusting people* IMPORTANCE = 3	CONCERN 3: *Does not like compliments* IMPORTANCE = 2	CONCERN 4: *Talk with boyfriend* IMPORTANCE = 1	CONCERN 5: *Sex* IMPORTANCE = 1
Much Less Than Expected Results	Is doing two or more things to make herself unattractive, e.g., gained weight, does not set hair, wears baggy clothes.	Feels uncomfortable in the company of strangers or acquaintances all of the time.	100% of the time feels irritated, angry, upset, etc. when given compliments.	Has not talked with boyfriend about rape, feelings, or related subjects for two weeks.	Has not had sex within past month or since assault.
Somewhat Less Than Expected Results	Is doing one thing to make herself unattractive.	51–99% of the time feels uncomfortable in the company of strangers or acquaintances.	51–99% of the time feels irritated, angry, upset, etc. when given compliments.	Has had one talk with boyfriend about rape within past two weeks.	Has had sex 1–2 times within past month or since assault.
Expected or Most Likely Results	Is not doing anything to make self unattractive, but wishes she were.	26–50% of the time feels uncomfortable in the company of strangers or acquaintances.	26–50% of the time feels irritated, angry, upset, etc. when given compliments.	Has had two talks with boyfriend about rape within past two weeks.	Has had sex 3–4 times within past month or since assault.
Somewhat More Than Expected Results	Wants to be unattractive only occasionally.	1–25% of the time feels uncomfortable in the company of strangers or acquaintances.	1–25% of the time feels irritated, angry, upset, etc. when given compliments.	Is in process of resolving issues about rape—because of talks with boyfriend.	Has had sex 5–6 times within past month or since assault.
Much More Than Expected Results	Does not think about wanting to be unattractive.	Does not feel uncomfortable.	Does not feel upset at all when given compliments.	Has resolved some of issues about rape—because of talks with boyfriend.	Has had sex 7 or more times within past month or since assault.

Constantly reliving the trauma only intensifies the impact and prolongs regrowth and recovery. It is imperative that the victim recognize the commonality of this occurrence, be truthful about its content, and seek appropriate professional assistance.

Fears and Phobias

Previously common, comfortable situations may become fearful and phobic experiences after an assault. Certain phobias may appear to be very logical, while others may appear, to the nonvictim, to have little or no association with the rape. Some frequently associated phobias include the following:

- Association with crowds
- Being left alone
- Previously ignored sounds
- Poorly lighted areas
- Seeing a man who may even vaguely resemble the rapist
- Odors associated with the attack, such as the smell of alcohol or gasoline
- The feeling that a crowd of people knows of the rape and is talking about it
- The occurrence of another disruptive experience, one unrelated to the rape
- A general fear of people
- The thought of sexual relations

It must be remembered that the victim finds these phobias very real and frightening.

Other Areas of Concern

Aftercare entails two-way communication. Some posttrauma manifestations are reactive responses recognized by the victim; other problems may be experienced unconsciously. It is imperative that professionals recognize and explore all possibilities throughout the process of intervention. Victims usually do not appreciate specific questions about the actual rape itself. Instead, open communication should be encouraged by general questions about how the victim feels and by an expressed, genuine interest in the victim. During the intervention, professionals should remember some of the basic postassault actions and reactions of victims:

- Overwhelming feeling of powerlessness
- Memories of the rape that interfere with normal pleasurable experiences
- Varying degrees of depression
- Frequent reliving of the actual attack
- Intense feelings of anger, fear, and revenge
- Guilt feelings which lead to self-blame and seeing the rape as just punishment
- Loss of control of feelings and actions
- Rejection of thoughts concerning the future
- Need to organize thoughts of self, relationships, and the environment

TEACHING THE VICTIM ABOUT REGROWTH AND RECOVERY

The effectiveness of regrowth and recovery is only as good as the planning, implementation, and evaluation of the process of assessment. Part of this process is to design a teaching tool and implement a way to test its appropriateness.

Since rape victims will not remember verbal information introduced during their visit to the emergency department, it is valuable to consider using a victim's informational packet. One example is the "Self-Help Guide" designed by the City of San Diego.[8]

Follow-up Medical Care

After the initial examination in the emergency department for collection of evidence and emergency medical treatment, the patient may still need basic medical care for general bodily injury, prevention of pregnancy, prevention of venereal disease, and psychological reactions.

This section is designed to present medical problems encountered by other victims of sexual assault, to describe methods of care, and to provide resources for ongoing care at various levels of expense, from low-cost clinics to private care.

GENERAL BODILY INJURY

Injuries sustained as a result of the sexual assault could require x-ray films, laboratory work, dressing changes, minor surgical care, and medications. The counselor or physician should be sure the patient understands how these injuries are to be cared for at home and when to return to the hospital or other community resource for follow-up care. Patients should be given appointment cards and written instructions before they leave the hospital.

PREVENTION OF PREGNANCY

A female patient may have become pregnant as a result of the sexual assault. *Emergency personnel should discuss the probability of pregnancy with the patient.* Three alternatives are available to avoid pregnancy if it is determined that the patient is at risk:

1. Diethylstilbestrol (DES), the "morning-after pill"
2. Abortion or menstrual extraction (early abortion)
3. Conjugated estrogens (Premarin)

The "Morning-After Pill"

A large dose of diethylstilbestrol, synthetic estrogen, prevents implantation of the fertilized egg in the wall of the uterus. A full course of 25 milligrams taken orally two times a day for five days must be started with-

in 24 hours of the sexual assault if the drug is to be effective. However, DES is associated with a rare form of vaginal cancer in *daughters* who were exposed in utero when their mothers took DES. From 1945 to 1970 DES was used to prevent miscarriages. (Should the patient become aware that she is a DES daughter, she should seek medical advice for thorough testing.) The choice to take DES is the patient's, and she should be made aware of the possible side effects before signing the consent form:

- Danger to the fetus if the patient was already pregnant at the time of the assault, but was unaware of it
- Danger to the fetus if the patient remains pregnant as a result of the rape (Counseling regarding abortion is recommended in the first two cases.)
- Nausea and vomiting, possible vaginal spotting, breast tenderness, insomnia, or rash during treatment

Abortion

A pregnancy test done at the time of the sexual assault will show if the patient is already six or more weeks pregnant. If the patient should miss her period after the sexual assault, a second pregnancy test should be done approximately six weeks after the first day of her last period. Legal abortions and menstrual extractions are available in doctors' offices, clinics, and hospitals. Health facilities where pregnancy tests are done provide referrals for abortions.

Conjugated Estrogens

Conjugated estrogens may be administered intravenously in 25 milligram doses—once upon admission and once again in 12 hours. This drug is unfavorable for many because of the high incidence of nausea and vomiting. However, more women complete treatment with conjugated estrogens than with DES.

Sixty percent stop taking DES after they suffer two to three days of nausea and vomiting.

PREVENTION OF VENEREAL DISEASE (VD)

Testing

It is recommended that a specimen to be cultured for gonococci be taken immediately and again 7 to 14 days after the sexual assault or treatment. If oral or rectal penetration has occurred, specimens should be taken from those areas as well as from the vagina. Gonorrhea is more difficult to detect in the female than in the male, regardless of the tests used, and active cases can go unrecognized and untreated. Preventive antibiotic therapy is strongly recommended. Blood to be tested for syphilis should be drawn immediately, and the test should be repeated four to six weeks later.

Treatment

Preventive antibiotic treatment may be given at the time of the sexual assault to prevent possible infection from the attacker. If the cost is prohibitive, there are many clinics where VD treatment and testing are available at low cost. The patient who chooses to be treated *may not* know for sure whether VD has been contracted, but it is *imperative* that the patient have follow-up examinations to ensure that treatment has been effective.

If a female patient chooses to be treated for VD at the time of the sexual assault, antibiotic therapy may disrupt the normal balance of bacterial organisms in the vagina. A yeast infection may develop but is easily treated. In addition, the assault itself may have an irritating effect on the genital tissues, or the attacker may have transmitted another kind of infection to the patient. Consequently, a female patient may develop other venereal vaginal infections such as trichomonas, genital herpes, venereal warts, or crabs.

Urinary tract infections can result from irritation or injury, and intercourse may become painful. If a female patient experiences an unusual or heavy discharge from the vagina, sores, a burning sensation during urination, vaginal itching, or painful intercourse, she should seek medical attention promptly. Again, low-cost care is available if the cost of private care is prohibitive.

PSYCHOLOGICAL REACTIONS

In most crisis situations, people can become upset and may be faced with unexpected changes in their lives. Since sexual assault may present a serious threat to the patient's safety and well-being, it is understandable that the patient may experience mental or emotional stress as an aftereffect of such an assault. In addition, the patient's family and friends may also be affected by what has happened. The patient needs to be around people who can be supportive and sympathetic. Some women's antirape groups offer woman-to-woman support throughout the procedures that follow a sexual assault. They are available to assist the patient.

The patient may also wish to seek short-term or long-term counseling. Members of the patient's immediate family may also benefit from counseling assistance. Sexual problems arising as a result of sexual assault are also treatable. The patient should be aware that many victims experience nightmares, phobias, fear of going out alone, fear of the dark, and a general suspicion of men. All these symptoms can be alleviated with proper care and support from friends, family members, and counselors.

SUMMARY

The process of regrowth and recovery requires the dedicated effort of many professionals, not just those actually participating in the follow-up period of intervention, but everyone who comes in contact with the victim. In essence, it is the total level of trust that the victim places in all helping professionals that influences the ultimate rate and success of recovery. This need for a team effort reiterates the fact that an understanding of the role and function of each professional is imperative in order to reinforce previous care. Professionals must relate to the victim in every aspect of the victim's care, including the critical linkages among and between other personnel. The ultimate images victims have of themselves reflect a total team effort of care and counseling.

REFERENCES

1. Abarbanel G: The roles of the clinical social worker: Hospital-based management, in Warner CG (ed): *Rape and Sexual Assault: Management and Intervention.* Rockville, Md, Aspen Systems Corp, 1980, pp 144-145, 148.

2. Schaefer JL, et al: Counseling sexual abuse victims. *Am Fam Physician* **18**:89, 1978.

3. Warner CG: Emergency management of rape and sexual assault, in Kravis TC, Warner CG (eds): *Emergency Care.* Rockville, Md, Aspen Systems Corp, 1982.

4. Ledray LE: *A Nursing Developed Model for the Treatment of Rape Victims.* A paper presented before the American Academy of Nursing, Washington, DC, September 21, 1981, pp 8-9.

5. Rogers C: *On Personal Power.* New York, Delacorte Press, Dell Publishing Co Inc, 1977.

6. Kopp S: *If You Meet the Buddha on the Road, Kill Him.* New York, Bantam Books Inc, 1972.

7. Warner CG: Aftercare: A lifetime follow-up, in Warner CG (ed): *Rape and Sexual Assault: Management and Intervention.* Rockville, Md, Aspen Systems Corp, 1980, pp 222-224.

8. *A Self-Help Guide: Taking Care of Yourself.* Subcommittee on Sexual Assault and Intrafamily Violence of the Advisory Board on Women. City of San Diego, 1979-1980.

17

COUNSELING AND FOLLOW-UP INTERACTION FOR THE GERIATRIC RAPE VICTIM

Adele Hale, B.A., M.S.W.

Rape has long been recognized as a violent act against another human being. It is not perceived as a primarily sexual act, and certainly the component of caring for and showing loving interest in another human being is conspicuously absent, as is the factor of consent. Victims of rape experience it not only as an assault on their bodies, which may cause actual physical damage, but also as a significant onslaught to their sense of self and their perception of themselves as autonomous persons with rights over their own bodies and their most immediate environment. In addition, there may be concerns about possible pregnancy, venereal disease, and general contamination. Further, the stages of life and life experiences of the victims can have profound impact on how they respond to the assault, what help they need to survive it, and how they are able to reconstitute their lives and reassess themselves and their futures. Elderly rape victims are, therefore, a unique population as well as unique individuals.

CHARACTERISTICS OF THE ELDERLY VICTIM

Senior citizens are not a homogeneous group except in terms of chronological age and in the commonality of world events and social mores to which they have been exposed during their lives. Chronological age is related to physical status. The elderly rape victim is potentially more susceptible to bodily injury, and physical changes associated with aging increase the likelihood of permanent damage from physical assault. Tissues are more tender, bones more brittle, healing somewhat slower. Recuperation is retarded and movement which has been gradually slowing down for natural reasons may be further restricted after trauma.

Elderly women realize that they are well along the continuum of life which leads ultimately to death. They are acutely aware of the normal gradual changes in their bodies, and they recognize the potential limitations to their activities that abrupt further damage can bring. They rightfully fear the results of assault which can mean disability or death. In addition, aging brings increasing frailty and, consequently, increasing vulnerability to victimization. In short, the elderly woman knows that she is less able to protect herself against physical attack, and this realization increases her perception of herself as being unprotected and a potential victim.[1] A rape reinforces these feelings and increases her anxiety about her environment and contacts. These fears alone can exacerbate aging and can lead to further isolation and removal from the mainstream of society. To the already aging, but productive, woman, being a victim or perceiving herself as a potential victim can be not only physically but also psychologically damaging.

World events and social mores influence what individuals expect of the world around them, how they expect to be treated by society and by members of the citizenry, and what they expect their roles to be in current times. The elderly woman has lived through many eras of change; the contrast between what she saw her grandmother's and mother's roles to be and what hers may be today is vast. The influences of these examples and experiences on her as an individual and on her life-style as an older woman are important factors.

The elderly female may have one role in society or a combination of several. Medical advances make it possible for people to be productive longer. It used to be considered remarkable if aged men and women could live independently, and now they embark on second careers. Menopause is no longer considered an automatic first step toward the symbolic rocking chair or the waning of interest in all things sexual. Today, a woman may choose to place less emphasis on the "number" aspect of her age and more emphasis on how she feels about what she wants to do with her remaining years.

It is important to note, however, that no matter how much she may choose to "go with today," she cannot forget or discard what she knows of yesterday. Her life experiences are part of the emotional and intellectual baggage that she carries with her to the end of her days. She grew and matured when divorce was less acceptable, abortion almost unavailable, contraception difficult. Sex was not a topic for parlor discussion. People rarely said the things that today are openly discussed and about which reams are written for public consumption. An elderly female may choose one or a combination of several roles for her later years, and she may adapt her experiences to a life-style she adopts with efficiency and superficial ease and grace, but underneath there is likely to be a struggle to maintain this new set of standards and modes. This struggle brings to the older woman a strain unknown to a younger female, and any severe trauma can threaten the equilibrium. Hence, an elderly woman may be the successful professional female, the contented grandmother-housewife, the independent spinster, the aging widow, the forlorn baglady, or any combination thereof. Nevertheless, if she is subjected to trauma such as rape, her vulnerability will be significant and unique because of her special physical status and her special life history.

The sexual aspect of rape can be particularly traumatic. She is likely to have a sexual orientation that differs greatly from that of the younger woman. Some older women think they left this aspect of life behind when they passed their sixth decade. They see sexual activity as inappropriate to their age. For them the sexual assault is experienced as a massive attack on their perceived role and status in the community. To be regarded in any way as a sexual object may seem as impossible to them as to be regarded as a candidate for the space program. It shakes their idea of how society views them and is willing to deal with them. The specifics of the rape may be particularly significant since the older woman is likely to have some very rigid ideas about what is "normal" sex and what is perverted. These ideas may range from the advice on marital sex attributed to Queen Victoria, "Grit your teeth and think of England," to the current notion that anything that two consenting adults do within the privacy of their own environment is acceptable. When the rape includes acts that the elderly woman would never have thought were acceptable or even suggestible with a beloved spouse, let alone a total stranger, the resultant feelings can be devastating.

INTERACTIONS IN THE EMERGENCY DEPARTMENT

For the elderly rape victim, the emergency department is likely to be her first prolonged contact after the assault. The neighbors or passersby who first find her will be upset for her, feel threatened themselves, and be intent on getting her immediate assistance from medical and legal authorities. The police are likely to be sympathetic and kindly, but their prime purposes will be to obtain the necessary medical care for the victim and all available evidence that can assist their apprehension of the perpetrator. At the emergency department the victim is faced with a strange environment and unfamiliar faces. Her shock from trauma is fresh; her discomfort, anxiety, and emotional pain are raw; her perception of herself as a victim with little control of herself and her environment is terrifying. Her need for reassurance may be enormous and seemingly bottomless. Emergency department personnel have the unique opportunity to set her in the direction either of reconstituting her life or of giving up. The initial assessment of this victim and her needs is, therefore, very important. It is essential to have some understanding of what her functional capabilities were before the rape. Many older women are already struggling with diminishing faculties. If they have been

coping with these difficulties on a day-to-day basis, their abilities to do so need to be reinforced at times of stress. One needs to differentiate between what is shock from the rape and what is the status quo. Communication may be slower because there are consistent current difficulties that have been exacerbated by the newness of the situation.

The victim requires prompt diagnosis of physical damage and emergency medical care. It is important to determine the amount of care the patient will require and where it can best be obtained. Whether the care should be inpatient or outpatient should be carefully considered, and the patient should be involved in these considerations. Involving the patient will help her feel that she is in control of her life and still functioning despite the humiliating and denigrating event she just experienced. She may require reassurance that medicine can, if necessary, deal with problems of venereal disease. It is important to handle any anxiety the patient may have about this kind of contamination and her fears about being unclean and a menace to others, particularly those near and dear. Such feelings can lead to increasing isolation —a wish to keep one's dirtiness to oneself and away from others lest they also be damaged or sullied.

It is particularly important to recognize the elderly victim's need to regain her feelings of dignity. A sexual assault on an older woman who perceives herself as past the age of sexual activity may be experienced as more than intrusive and denigrating. She may find it particularly insulting to her concept of herself as a dignified senior citizen who has earned the right by age, as well as by humanity, to be treated with respect and courtesy, without any hints of vulgarity. Emergency department personnel must be prepared to deal with her in a nonjudgmental and accepting way, even if her responses seem very different from what they feel their own might be. They need to understand how she feels about what happened and if she is dealing with the rape as a violent episode, a sexual one, or a combination. The patient must be given an opportunity to talk about her experience and to react without any embargo on her feelings. Although the emergency department may not be a convenient place for venting these feelings, the patient who is not given this option may feel she is more a body than a person; this situation reinforces the feelings aroused by the rape itself. This venting can be particularly difficult for some to cope with. The violence of rape seems to be particularly ugly and horrifying when its victims are either very young or very old. Both extremities of age are seen as people who require special protection and shielding from the nasty aspects of life, and their maltreatment produces feelings of helplessness and sadness that can make involvement with these patients particularly painful. It is important to recognize that the elderly victim's response to the physical trauma may be extreme but still very appropriate to her. She understands her potential physical limitations and knows how easily she can be moved closer to incapacitation or death.

Follow-up care is very important, and the patient should have the major role in its planning. If she can meet her own needs and wishes to do so, her wish should be respected. Options for help should be explored and made available. The issue of where the rape occurred and how this affects future living arrangements must be examined. Can she return home, or is this unreasonable because of fear, actual inappropriateness, or some combination thereof? Does she have some support available within the circle of her friends or family? If so, who among these should be notified, and by whom? Arrangements for follow-up care must be definite and not left to chance.[2]

It is obvious that once physical problems have been dealt with, the focus of care moves to the emotional area. Nevertheless, the es-sential point is that recognition of and dealing with emotional needs must begin at the first moment of contact and must underlie all physical treatment.

ROLE OF SOCIAL SERVICES AND OTHER COUNSELING PERSONNEL

Some tangible issues come up almost immediately after a rape. The police are always concerned about apprehension of the assailant, and they want contact with the victim as soon as possible. The routine of questions, identifications, descriptions, and repeated retelling of the episode can be a source of great anxiety and discomfort to the victim, no matter how eager she is to cooperate and no matter how open and uncomplicated her story. There is also the added discomfort and embarrassment of discussing the specific details of the assault. For some victims, the questioning and requestioning has many of the aspects of an inquisition. They may come to feel that they are being treated as if they were the offender rather than the victim and are indeed being punished. For elderly rape victims, the need to describe in detail what actually transpired may be a particular embarrassment; they are not likely to be comfortable discussing sexual particulars. In effect, they may be describing sexual acts, imposed upon them by a stranger, that they had never even considered with a life-long, beloved sexual partner. Consequently, participation in the legal process, beginning with the police and culminating in the day in court, may require much support. For many victims apprehension of the perpetrator and the ensuing legal process is helpful in finally putting an end to the entire episode, but it is fraught with many emotional issues, and strong and empathic support is essential throughout the whole process. Another issue is victims' compensation, an increasingly available option for rape victims in some jurisdictions. In addition to the possible monetary benefits, there are the emotional aspects, the recognition by society and the law that such victims should have recourse. Elderly rape victims should be supported and advised on how to use this recourse wherever appropriate. Counselors and social workers can assist also with whatever financial problems stem from the assault. For many elderly persons their living and financial arrangements are so tightly fixed that any crisis can drastically alter the situation and make it nonviable.

A practical and emotional issue is housing. The victim of an "anonymous" rape, a victim unknown to the assailant either by name or residence, does not have to worry that he will return. She may feel quite comfortable remaining in her present abode because it was not the scene of the rape and is not likely to bombard her with unpleasant memories. For this victim, housing may not be an issue. However, when the victim is known to the offender, and the assault took place in her house, and he may even have told her he would be back, she is faced with the problem of moving or staying. This issue needs to be carefully explored.[3] Younger people may be angry that they need to move to feel safe, but they are also more able to make the shift. The senior citizen is likely to be much more fearful of change. She does not perceive herself as being able to make new friends easily or to learn about the shopping, transportation, and social amenities of a new location. She is frightened by the aspect of "starting all over again." This fear may be even greater than the fear of remaining at the scene of the assault. In addition, she is likely to fear being alone anywhere on the street, as well as at home. In short, her view of herself as an independent adult has been severely shaken, perhaps permanently. For example, consider the very independent 67-year-old widow who had been living alone, who had a satisfactory lifestyle, including some social life, and little need for help from her grown children. After a rape in her home, she became fearful of being alone, both at home and away, felt she did not remember things as well as before, and felt less able to care for herself. Living with her married children did not suit her or them, but she was afraid to live alone again. For her, a satisfactory halfway solution was a living arrangement with relative peers; each took care of the others, and all maintained some semblance of independence. But, for the widow, it would never be quite as before, and she perceived herself as having lost much.

The woman who has been raped outside the home may feel that "outside" can never be safe again. She puts extra locks on her doors, does not go out, and maintains contact with only a few trusted friends. She becomes a prisoner of her fear, increasingly withdrawn and isolated. She has less confidence in herself to judge people on the outside and to protect herself, and she may feel the fault is hers. For example, a 65-year-old single lady who left her car door open and was subsequently abducted and raped sincerely thought her "rider" was only demanding a ride. Her concept of herself as a competent, efficient member of society was shaken. Her pattern of trusting others, previously perceived as a virtue, was now deemed a foolishness.

The elderly victim struggles not only with how she feels about the rape but also with what she thinks others may think of it. She may feel there is a stigma attached to being a victim of a sexual assault. She worries whether others see her as soiled or damaged, impure. A 70-year-old victim who had been involved in a loving and happily intimate relationship with another senior citizen wondered if it was allowable to continue this fine relationship after she had been the unwilling participant in a sordid rape. A 72-year-old lady who opened the door for her assailant because she thought he was a repairman not only felt guilty and stupid for letting herself be duped but also was angered and saddened by neighbors who implied that perhaps she had not been totally unwilling.

In short, the elderly rape victim suffers not only from what happened to her during the rape but also from feelings engendered by being a victim. Senior citizens seem to be natural subjects for victimization. Frequently they are not physically strong enough to protect themselves; they perceive themselves as being at the mercy of others. They are easily bombarded by fast talk and by threats. They share some of these characteristics with the very young, and like the very young they can easily be misused and abused. They sense this vulnerability as they age, and when it becomes a reality, they know it.

The social worker or counselor needs to help the elderly victim work through her feelings about being a victim so that she does not reconstitute her life-style on the basis of over-determined reaction. (For example, an elderly woman wore old worn clothes, contrary to her previous life-style and economic status, in hopes she would not attract attention. In the process, she insulted her own self-concept and was severely damaged.) She can be aided in dealing with her feelings of helplessness so that they do not encompass her entire life but are contained in appropriate areas. She can be helped to develop prudent precautions so that she maintains herself in situations where she feels reasonably free of fear rather than a victim whose life is ruled by it. Counseling also involves helping her devise an appropriate and gratifying life-style that recognizes the realities of frailty. If she needs to make some changes in her situation because of the rape, she should be helped to make these with minimal bitterness and anger.

In summary, the social worker or counselor must assist in three broad areas: the tangible aspects of dealing with the law, the legal process and financial problems, and coping with the emotional problems and conflicts that arise from the assault. Referrals to appropriate agencies help make the recovery less traumatic.

The time required to accomplish the foregoing will vary with the circumstances of the assault, the associated physical and emotional trauma, and the individual's situation and condition. Short-term intervention may be all that is necessary for the patient who has a good personal support system in her own life, but intervention is advisable. Including the persons who comprise that support system can be very helpful. It provides support for them, as well as for the victim, and an opportunity for all to vent their anger and hurt openly, rather than trying to suppress their feelings lest they upset each other. For the more solitary victim, the professional who is prepared to engage in long-term counseling can provide a needed rehabilitative service by helping the victim regain as much of her previous independence as seems reasonable and avoid the inroads of further isolation.

SUMMARY

The elderly victim of rape feels the impact of her latent mortality, her increasing frailty, her potential helplessness, and her growing isolation and loneliness. Each individual who has contact with her after this assault on her physical body and emotional sense of self has an opportunity to reassure her of her value as an individual and as a member of society. This reassurance and reaffirmation of worth can greatly counteract the emotional damage caused by the attacker.

REFERENCES

1. *Rape and Older Women: A Guide to Prevention and Protection.* Publication (ADM) 78-734,

US Dept of Health, Education and Welfare, 1979, p 9.

2. Holmstrom LL, Burgess AW: *The Victim of Rape: Institutional Reactions.* New York, John Wiley & Sons Inc, 1978, p 101.

3. McCahill T, et al: *The Aftermath of Rape.* Lexington, Mass, Lexington Books, 1979.

SUGGESTED READING

Nass DR: *The Rape Victim.* Dubuque, Iowa, Kendall/Hunt Publishing Co, 1977.

Peters JJ: The psychological aftereffects of rape. *Comtemp OB/GYN* 7:105–108.

Victims of Rape. US Dept of Health, Education and Welfare, 1976.

18

MANAGEMENT OF FAMILIES OF SEXUALLY ABUSED CHILDREN

Renée S. Tankenoff Brant, M.D.

A family-centered approach is necessary in the management of sexually abused children. An approach that focuses on the child alone and excludes other family members may fail in many respects.

A child's capacity to resolve a crisis in a positive manner is a function of both the adaptive capabilities of the child and the support provided by parents and other important adults. In some well-functioning families, the family itself can serve as the major support to a child in crisis, and therapeutic support and guidance for the family can assist them. In other situations, resolution of the crisis may be hindered by unsupportive, maladaptive, or even destructive family reactions. Sexual abuse of a child usually precipitates a crisis for child and family. Strengths and weaknesses of the family and child must be assessed, and intervention must be structured to meet the needs of both the child and the family.

The role of the family is important in yet another way. Because of the bonds and feelings that link family members, an assault upon a child usually generates strong reactions in at least some family members. Family members other than the child may develop symptoms of stress or anxiety or strong reactions of guilt, anger, or sadness. In this respect, although the child may have been the victim of an assault, the entire family or certain family members in addition to the child may become patients.

In some cases, the family is not merely an innocent bystander reacting to the child's victimization. In fact, studies reveal that in the majority of cases of sexual abuse, the perpetrator is a family member or someone outside the immediate family who is known to the child.[1-3] When the perpetrator is someone known to the family, the situation becomes more complex therapeutically because of the preexisting relationships and the feelings that child and family have toward the perpetrator. The most complicated and therapeutically difficult situations occur when a parent or parent-figure has abused or exploited the child. In these situations, the protective function of a family has failed, and the family cannot be relied on as a support. The sexual abuse is frequently a symptom of underlying family pathology, and the family must be treated as a unit.

The siblings of the victim must also be considered. In situations where a child was assaulted, siblings often bear strong feelings of guilt that they were spared. Sometimes siblings are "kept in the dark" about a sexual assault in the family because parents hope to protect them. Yet they know something has happened and may experience anxiety or create fantasies about what happened. More than one sibling in a family may be abused. For example, in incestuous families, fathers may be serially or simultaneously involved with more than one daughter. Thus, one must assess whether siblings other than the recognized victim are at risk physically or psychologically and assure protection to all children in the family.

FAMILY REACTION TO SEXUAL ABUSE OF CHILDREN

The reaction of family members to sexual assault of a child is affected by many variables. The family's values and cultural background, strengths and vulnerabilities, and other stresses which a family is facing may color their reaction to such a crisis. The age and role of a child within the family and the preexisting relationship between the parent and child affect the reaction of a parent. An assault on an infant or young school-age child may cause parental disbelief, rage, and protectiveness. If an adolescent who has been provocative and sexually acting out reports sexual abuse, parental reaction may be quite ambivalent. Parents may blame the teenager, and support may be minimal.

Family history, the psychological state of the parents, and the state of the marriage affect parents' reactions. Often the mother of a child who has been sexually assaulted was

herself sexually abused as a child. In situations where a mother has not resolved her own feelings about her trauma, she may be psychologically unavailable to support her own child in a similar crisis and unconsciously may have contributed to creating a situation in which the child becomes vulnerable to this kind of abuse. Strengths and strains within the marriage also affect family reaction. In an optimal situation, parents can be supportive to one another and thus enhance their mutual support of the child. If there is marital stress, the family crisis may exacerbate marital tensions. In extreme situations, marital stress can directly contribute to the evolution of incest.

Details of the nature of the sexual abuse exert a powerful influence on family reaction.[4] Who was the abuser? Was the abuser a stranger, someone known to the family, or someone within the family? Was the abuse a single incident, or did it occur over a period of time? What was the nature of the abuse? Was force or violence used? In general, when an assault comes from a stranger, it is easier for the family to unambivalently direct anger and hostility toward the assailant while protecting and supporting the child. Sometimes parental feelings are so intense that a counselor must advocate some restraint to prevent parents from directly seeking revenge against the assailant. When the assailant is someone outside the family, yet someone to whom the child might be entrusted, such as a school teacher or day-care worker, parental reaction may be more complicated. On occasion, parents may disbelieve a child's report that a teacher, for example, abused the child. If parents do believe a child's accusations, they may experience distrust and a sense of betrayal in addition to more typical reactions. It is often difficult to confront institutions such as school systems with such an accusation because of fear of public stigma and because of disbelief or resistance on the part of institutional officials. Sometimes parents take legal actions against institutions under these circumstances. These actions can create additional strains for family and child and can complicate social relationships as larger segments of the community become involved.

The most complicated situation occurs when the abuser is someone within the child's family. Usually the abuse has been going on secretly for some time. Revelation of intrafamily abuse threatens the basic integrity of the family, and all family members, including child and parent, may band together to protect the family and to preserve their secret. Denial, avoidance, and flight are typical reactions in incestuous families. When one or some of the family members do not deny incest, the reaction of other members is contingent on preexisting family attachments and dependencies. Family members ally with or against the primary protagonists and experience the push and pull of divided loyalties.[5] Potential gains and losses will influence the family dynamics of who allies with whom. For example, an adolescent daughter accuses her father of incest. Mother and the entire family are totally dependent on the father economically. Does mother side with the daughter and risk economic disaster, or does she side with the father? In another family, the mother may feel quite removed from her husband and may have considered separation or divorce. An accusation of incest in this family could result in mother readily allying with her daughter and taking action to force her husband out.

GENERAL PRINCIPLES IN FAMILY ASSESSMENT AND MANAGEMENT

Interdisciplinary Team Approach

The disciplines involved in managing sexually abused children will depend on the setting in which they are seen. Ideally, an interdisciplinary team with knowledge of the physical and psychosocial indicators of sexual abuse and with expertise in pediatrics, gynecology, and psychosocial diagnosis and management can best serve the needs of these families and can provide a comprehensive psychobiological assessment and treatment plan. Legal and protective considerations are prominent in many cases. Therefore, team members or consultants should have expertise in these areas as well. For example, a physician, social worker, and nurse could be the core assessment team in a pediatric emergency department. An attorney, psychiatrist, and protective service worker might be available as consultants. While the details of team structure will vary, the roles of the different disciplines in assessment and management should be clear to all team members. The tasks at hand include medical and psychological assessment of both the child and the family. In addition, a protective assessment must be made, and medical and legal responsibilities must be carried out. Accurate records must be kept for both medical and legal purposes; in most states, reports of suspected sexual abuse must be made to authorities. Team functions should include education of the child and family about the process of assessment and follow-up, provision of support to the child and family during the assessment, and coordination of assessment and follow-up.

Family-Child Orientation

The initial contact should be structured to include family members as well as the child. Having one or more team members designated for primary contact with the child and another primarily assigned to the family can facilitate this approach. Team members then have the flexibility to see the child and other family members alone or together as the needs of the situation dictate. Even when only one person has initial contact with both child and family, the contact can be structured to allow time for meetings with the child alone, the adults alone, and the child and adults together.

The initial contact could include a brief joint meeting with the adults and child to allow all the family to voice their problems and concerns, then individual assessment meetings, and finally a joint meeting to review findings and plan future contact. This structure communicates the message that all family members are relevant to the assessment and that they have a place in the process both as individuals and as family members. Depending on the family situation, a team may decide to vary the use of individual and joint assessment meetings. Regardless of the details of the approach, the goal is a family assessment that will enable team members to begin developing a plan that can address both individual needs and family issues. During the initial contact, inquiry should be made about other family members; they should be included in the assessment-management process as early as possible. When feasible, the alleged "abuser," if a family member, should be included also. Usually this individual will not be present at the first contact.

Professional Reaction to the Family

Cases of sexual abuse generate strong emotional responses in professionals. It is advisable that personnel in an emergency department or other "front-line" setting have an opportunity to anticipate and discuss their reactions ahead of time; this preparation diminishes the possibility that their feelings will interfere with the services the family receives.[6] Working with parents can be very difficult, especially when there is evidence that the parents have overtly or covertly played a role in abusing or neglecting the child. Feelings of anger and disgust and a blaming, accusatory attitude toward such parents are not uncommon. Directly or indirectly communicating such feelings to parents, however, will either complicate or make impossible the provision of services to the family and will make it difficult to build a working alliance with the parents. Professionals must have an opportunity to review both their actions and feelings about family members with team peers or supervisors. Clinical and emotional backup and support are essential for smooth team functioning.

Professional Stance Toward the Family

Families of sexually abused children are often tentative and ambivalent in seeking help from professionals, especially if intrafamily abuse has occurred. The nature of the family's initial contact with providers in a crisis may determine whether they flee from service or decide to keep a follow-up appointment. In general, a respectful, nonjudgmental, supportive, professional attitude is desirable. A well-organized systematic approach that is explained to the child and family helps to relieve some anxiety in what often feels like an out-of-control situation to them. When necessary, the professional must be firm and straightforward in dealing with difficult issues like the need to report the case to government authorities or the need to temporarily hospitalize or place a child in foster care to assure the child's protection. Compassion can be combined with a firm, authoritative stance.

While suspected sexual abuse is a serious concern, providers should avoid overreacting to this potential problem area and neglecting other equally important concerns. Emotional reactions sometimes make it difficult to maintain a balanced clinical approach to the family's problems. Professionals should remember that sexual abuse is often a symptom of more basic underlying family pathology; it sometimes occurs in families facing multiple problems and stresses. Sometimes, seeing sexual abuse as "the" problem in a family does them a disservice.

On the other hand, emotional reactions can also cause professionals to avoid, minimize, or deny the possibility of sexual abuse when there is evidence to the contrary.[6] Often a family member will voice very explicit concerns about possible sexual abuse and then retract or deny the concerns out of fear. The professional must recognize and understand this clinical pattern and persist with appropriate concern about the issue.

In summary, professional overreaction and underreaction to sexual abuse are common clinical issues because of the complicated reactions to issues of child and adult sexuality and the incest taboo. Although assessment and management of sexual abuse does call for some expertise and variations in clinical approach, the clinical tools are not dramatically different from those used to approach other difficult clinical problems. With some education, practice, and soul-searching, clinicians can integrate a balanced approach toward sexual abuse into their repertoire for dealing with serious family problems.

GOALS OF FAMILY ASSESSMENT AND ACUTE MANAGEMENT

Building Alliances

One of the major goals of initial contact with the family members is to begin building a working alliance with them. In a crisis people are quite open to entering a working relationship that will benefit them and that promises to help them out of the crisis. Usually some need on the part of the parent, as well as the child, has precipitated their request for help at a particular time. During early contact, the professional must listen carefully to the voiced and unvoiced needs of the parent. Building a contract or working relationship around the parents' needs as well as the child's will provide some leverage in engaging a family.

In cases of sexual abuse, especially cases of intrafamily abuse, building alliances is complicated by individual and family dynamics. These lead families to deny and avoid acknowledgement of the abuse when they are in a crisis and in desperate need of help and results in a very ambivalent family attitude. Families may want help, yet act in a hostile, distrustful manner. They may demand services on one visit and forget about the follow-up appointment. This kind of family behavior can be very irritating to professionals, especially in busy emergency departments where service demands are high. It can be easy to "forget" about these cases, both because of the professional's unconscious or conscious desire to avoid them and because of the family's behavior. Professionals must realize that this behavior is clinically consistent and to be expected. It is often impossible to get families to return on a voluntary basis for assessment or treatment beyond one or two visits. The nature of the family's first encounter and their feelings about it can influence their ambivalence one way or the other. In addition, mandated reporting of cases of suspected sexual abuse to protective or legal authorities can be a vital force in assuring that families are strongly encouraged to follow through with adequate assessment. Authorities will either collaborate with hospitals, clinics, and other facilities in investigating suspected cases of sexual abuse or will instigate their own investigation. In the interest of assuring protection for the family and child, professionals must reach out to these families and must report suspected cases. Frequently, voluntary alliances cannot be built, in spite of the professional's best efforts, and assessment and management must proceed on a mandated basis.

Family Assessment

There are four parts in a family assessment: medical, psychosocial, protective, and legal.

MEDICAL

Medical assessment includes determining the parents' and child's medical concerns. A pediatrician should do a complete medical examination. If the victim has venereal disease, parents or other adults and adolescents in the home should be screened both to uncover untreated disease and to provide evidence of possible contacts who may have infected the child. Siblings of infected children should be screened also. Although the issues of public health and protection dictate these screenings, parents and other family members may be quite resistant. Some tact is needed in negotiating these matters. Protective service workers and legal consultants may have to assist.

Appropriately planned treatment and follow-up for medical and gynecological conditions are also important parts of the medical assessment.

PSYCHOSOCIAL

Psychosocial assessment is used to determine immediate psychosocial problems and stressors for parents, child, and family. Counselors should obtain the following information about the parents' knowledge of the suspected sexual abuse and about the parents' feelings:

1. How did the parents discover the abuse?
   - Did the child come directly to the parents?
   - Did they get the information secondhand?
   - Do they have suspicions only?
   - Did they directly witness the abuse?

- Did something happen that permitted the parents to reveal concerns they have had for some time?

2. What details can the parents offer about the abuse and on what basis?

3. Do the parents have fears about the consequences of disclosing their concerns and speaking to professionals about these concerns?

4. Do the parents know the suspected "abuser"? What role did family members play in the abuse? (Is the "reporting" member of the family conscious of any role that member played?)

5. What is the parents' emotional reaction to the abuse?
   - What are their feelings toward the child?
   - Toward the suspected abuser?
   - With whom do they ally themselves?

6. Do the parents feel guilty, sad, angry, or nervous?
   - On what basis?
   - Have the feelings affected their capacity to function?

The counselor should also secure relevant family historical information in the following areas:

- Are past or recent family stresses associated with the onset or disclosure of the abuse?
- Is there a prior history of abuse or neglect in the family?
- Have either of the parents ever suffered abuse? At what age? What are the details?

It is also important to secure the developmental history of the child, including information about the parents' reactions to and feelings about the child now. Assessing the nature of the family's past and present coping mechanisms will prove helpful. Available support systems for the family and involvement with other social agencies and institutions should be analyzed.

Family patterns of interaction should be assessed, especially as they relate to the parents' capacity to cope with the present family problems and to help and protect the child. Parents and children should be screened for serious psychopathology, such as psychosis, depression, suicidal ideation, drug or alcohol addiction, and impulse disorder, that may require psychiatric consultation and specialized management.

While gathering information about the child's and family's acute problems, the counselor can also begin to find out about the child's general development and performance and about the family's structure and functioning. In particular, information about the parents' functioning as spouses and parents is important in planning treatment strategies.

PROTECTIVE

Protective assessment is valuable in determining the family's capacity to protect the child from sexual and physical assault or exploitation inside or outside the family. Consultation with protective service workers may be necessary.

In general, if a child has been assaulted outside the family, and if parental neglect was not a contributing factor, parents respond with a very protective attitude. When sexual abuse within the extended or immediate family is suspected, determination of a family's capacity to protect a child is more problematic. Factors that contribute to situations of inadequate protection include psychosis, delusions, or a serious problem in controlling impulses in a parent or other adult member of the household. Alcohol or drug use may contribute to these problems. Other factors are a strong denial of abuse by the parents or caretakers when there is significant evidence to the contrary and overt anger or a blaming attitude toward the child. Intimidation and threats by one member of the household toward other children or adults may impair the capacity of adults to protect

the child and may leave others in the family, including adults, at risk for physical harm. Other considerations are a prior pattern of parental abuse or neglect and the child's expressed fear of remaining in the family. When there is significant suspicion of sexual abuse, reports should be filed according to relevant state laws.

Measures should be instituted to assure protection of the child and family during the period of assessment and acute management. Protective service workers and legal counsel may be needed to advise and assist with these matters. For example, if there is serious concern about a child's immediate protection, placement in a foster home may be advised, or legal measures may be taken to remove an alleged assailant from the home.

LEGAL

The fourth part of an evaluation is legal assessment and support. It is important to determine whether the family is engaged in or contemplating legal action related to the alleged abuse. (In some states, when reports are made to protective service agencies, the information is automatically reported to the district attorney or police.) Counselors should inquire about the family's knowledge of relevant laws and legal processes. Ideally, the resources of legal counsel, police, personnel in the district attorney's office, and support programs for families in court should be available for referral in accordance with family needs.

Members of the assessment team should realize that a family's involvement in legal processes may prolong and complicate family reactions and that family members engaged in a court process may need support throughout the legal proceedings.[7]

Follow-up and Referral

Professionals must inform the family of medical and clinical findings and recommendations for medical and psychosocial treatment. The role of protective service and legal authorities as well as clinicians should be clarified.

Appropriate referrals for medical treatment and follow-up should be made and their purpose clearly explained. Appropriate referrals should also be made for psychosocial assessment and management. Follow-up soon after initial contact and ongoing availability of professionals to the family are important; they provide support for the family during the crisis and foster building alliance and trust. Optimally, some person or persons from the team who first saw the family will continue to work with the family throughout the initial crisis or longer. If they cannot, referral and contact with follow-up caretakers should take place as soon as possible. Liberal use of telephone contact and frequent visits during the crisis will promote the family's sense that someone is really "there" for them. Outreach will be necessary to insure that families follow through on referrals. Community resources are valuable for the long-term management of cases of sexual abuse. These include specialized treatment programs, protective service departments, and mental health clinics.

MANAGEMENT OF EXTRAFAMILY ABUSE

Theory of Child-Family Crisis Reaction

Although studies have delineated the length and nature of the "rape trauma syndrome" for adult women,[8] there is little data about the nature and length of a child's and family's crisis reaction to an incident of extrafamily sexual abuse. It is not known, in fact, if there is a characteristic syndrome. Clinical experience suggests that in a reasonably well-integrated family, an acute assault on a child may cause a state of disequilibrium that lasts

four to six weeks, longer if there is court involvement. Symptoms of the child, including heightened separation anxiety, sleep and eating disturbances, fears, phobias, nightmares, and regression, are, to a large extent, age dependent.[9,10] Typical family reactions may include extreme protectiveness and a vengeful attitude toward the alleged abuser. In addition, a crisis is likely to intensify any preexisting tensions, conflicts, and vulnerabilities within the family. Families may also develop symptoms that interfere with optimal functioning.

There are no long-range prospective studies, but clinical experience suggests that the trauma may never be entirely resolved.[11] After a quiescent period of months or years, a developmental issue or some internal or external change in child or family may precipitate recurrence of symptoms in the child or family and necessitate a reworking of issues related to the trauma. For example, a child and family were seen in a treatment program for sexual abuse after the daughter was raped by a stranger when she was nine years old. The child and family were seen in short-term crisis intervention. The mother developed significant anxiety and there was considerable marital tension; the daughter did relatively well. Tensions eased during the crisis period. The mother contacted the clinic again when the child was 13 years old and requested that the child be reevaluated. Investigation revealed that the mother had become acutely anxious again when her daughter began to show serious interest in a boy for the first time. The daughter was again doing well. The mother's symptoms involved conflicts relating to her own sexuality and marriage and feelings and memories about her daughter's rape.

Management

The general goals of family assessment and management enumerated in the previous section apply to cases of extrafamily sexual abuse. Both the child and the family should have a psychiatric evaluation. In uncomplicated cases, management can follow a crisis intervention model. To the extent that parents are able to maintain an adequate level of functioning themselves, much of the counseling can be directed toward helping them understand and cope with their own reactions and toward enhancing their ability to protect and emotionally support their child during the crisis. Direct therapeutic work with a child may vary depending on the parents' capacity to provide this support.

Parents will wonder how they should act toward the child. Should they initiate discussion of issues relating to the assault? Should they avoid speaking about it at all to help the child forget? How should they respond when the child starts talking about the rape? With guidance, parents can sort out their own feelings and worries from those of their child. As they become comfortable with their own feelings, they can be assisted in creating a situation at home that helps the child feel comfortable bringing fears, feelings, or questions to the parents, and the parents can be helped to respond in a manner appropriate to the child's development.

Parents can be educated about the likelihood that both they and their children will experience intense feelings and behavioral reactions for a month or so after the crisis. They can learn that this is an important time to share thoughts and feelings and fears and to work out a constructive method of dealing with the problems at hand. They can also be reassured that their feelings will gradually return to normal and they will think about the assault less frequently. Finally, they can be told that memories or feelings about the assault may recur for them or their children. If they have trouble managing then, they might consider obtaining focused help for the problems troubling them.

Complications

The following considerations may complicate crisis management of extrafamily abuse and necessitate alteration of the treatment plan for a child and family. Experienced mental health practitioners may be consultants when these complications arise or may treat these cases directly.

1. Has the child developed symptoms of a severe nature (depression, withdrawal, suicidal ideation, psychosis) or have symptoms that interfere with the child's functioning continued beyond the crisis period?

2. Are parents preoccupied by their own needs and unable to discern or respond to the needs of the child?

3. Is there a prior history of physical or sexual abuse or neglect in the family? If so, a short-term crisis intervention may not be sufficient.

4. Is the family involved in legal action? Although the purpose of the legal process is to apprehend, try, and punish the assailant, children and families often feel that they are "on trial," too. Court processes, which are often sporadic, prolonged, and delayed, can prolong family reactions to an assault. Court involvement can sometimes be viewed as an additional family crisis. Families must be educated about legal processes and must be supported in confronting difficult legal situations such as testifying; confronting the assailant in a courtroom; and facing postponement, delay, and frustration.[7]

5. Is the parent unable to give emotional support to the child? The causes of such a situation may include

   • Prior sexual abuse of the parent and its associated unresolved feelings and conflicts

   • Preexisting difficulties in the parent-child relationship

   • Preexisting parental conflict

   • Parental feelings about the abuser or circumstances surrounding the abuse

MANAGEMENT OF INTRAFAMILY SEXUAL ABUSE

Theory of Family Dynamics in Incest

Incest deserves special mention. It explicitly involves family members in the abuse and represents one of the most difficult situations to deal with clinically. Individual and family dynamics of incestuous families are discussed in detail elsewhere.[3,12,13] However, some of the basic hypotheses will be reviewed here to facilitate understanding of therapeutic maneuvers useful in the acute management of incestuous families.

Father-daughter incest will be used as the paradigm because it is the most frequent form of incest. This does not imply that male children are never abused within families or that mothers do not abuse their children. Incest is viewed as a family symptom, a family response to underlying stress and pathology. The most important hypothesis states that father-daughter incest involves the mother as well as the father and daughter.[12,13] Certainly the father must play an active role as perpetrator of the incest. However, in most cases, the mother also plays an essential role, although it may be a passive one. At some level, often unconsciously, she is aware of the incest and contributes to its continuation through denial, avoidance, and withdrawal from certain aspects of her role as a wife and mother. Usually the marriage is stressed by difficulties in the couple's relationship to one another as well as in their parenting roles. An additional stress, such as threat of abandonment or separation, may strain the delicate balance within the family. If there is no strong bond within the marriage and fear of family disintegration, the family may respond by creating a secret incestuous bond which holds the family together. All three participants, father, mother, and child, unconsciously act together to keep the secret and to maintain the situation. Although dynamically the child is viewed as a "participant," this does not mean that she is viewed as a consenting, willing participant. Most authorities feel that strong coercive factors act on the immature daughter to trap her in the situation and that the adults are ultimately responsible.

Goals and Methods of Acute Management

A therapeutic approach that labels the father as bad and does not confront the mother's role would be inappropriate. Ultimately, the therapeutic goal is to assure protection for all family members, to support the child and relieve her of the tremendous burden the family has placed on her, and to refocus attention from the incestuous relationship to the serious difficulties within the marital and parent-child relationships. These goals are pursued in family-oriented treatment;[14,15] usually many clinical problems must be surmounted before treatment can be initiated in appropriate situations. During the phase of acute management, the goals are engagement of the family in the evaluative process, in the face of tremendous resistance, and the assessment of treatment needs.

A minority of reported incest cases are "one time only" incidents, a symptom of an acute family stress. In some of these situations, family-oriented crisis intervention can help alleviate the immediate stressors and assist the family in achieving better coping mechanisms.

In the majority of cases of intrafamily sexual abuse, disclosure of the problem reveals a situation of chronic or intermittent abuse. The disclosure itself precipitates a family crisis and threatens to upset a long-standing family equilibrium. The disclosure may be accidental or the result of a transitional event that threatens the family. One of the family participants may undergo internal changes that prompt them to try to extricate themselves from the family situation although other family forces may operate to maintain the status quo. While transient family instability may have promoted disclosure, usually there is a strong tendency for the family to regroup in the old fashion to resist threatened dissolution and the stigma and legal consequences that the family fears will accompany revelation of the family secret. The clinical results are revelation of the secret by a family member followed, within a few hours or days, by retraction of statements, strong denial, and resistance to continued professional contact or intervention. Family reactions of this type have convinced many professionals that a "mistake" was made. In fact, the family dynamics described previously predict a sequence of disclosure followed by retraction and denial. This clinical sequence is in keeping with the diagnosis of intrafamily sexual abuse. A simple crisis intervention does not suit these cases. While the families are usually in an initial state of crisis precipitated by the disclosure and open to help, this situation is quickly counterbalanced by dynamic forces that compel the family to retreat and avoid outside contacts. Participation of legal and protective services in coordination with sophisticated clinical intervention is necessary to engage the families and overcome their initial resistance.

Steps Toward Engaging the Incestuous Family

REPORTING CASES

Cases of suspected sexual abuse should be reported to mandated protective service agencies or other designated government authorities as soon as possible. In the end, the legal authority of the state to require investigation and assessment of alleged sexual abuse will be the most important factor in keeping families in the assessment process. The state may directly participate in the investigation or delegate responsibility to clinical facilities.

The powers of the state also provide mechanisms to assure the safety and protection of children and other family members during the assessment process. These mechanisms include temporary protective placement of the child and restraining orders. Clinical facilities are advised to use legal counsel in these matters and to closely coordinate their efforts with protective service agencies.

DISCLOSURE BY THE CHILD

Often the child is instrumental in disclosure of the abuse. Clinical access to the child is very important. As elaborated in Chapter 16, one must create a supportive, nonthreatening situation to facilitate the telling of the child's story. The child is the one who may most intensely experience the burden of keeping the family together because the family dynamics have, in fact, designated that role for the child. Under the best of circumstances, children will experience great guilt and ambivalence as they reveal the secret. In addition, children may have been threatened with further harm to themselves or others should they disclose the secret. The clinician must empathize with the children's position and question them directly about specific fears they may have about the consequences of their disclosure. Statements by the clinician that the parents and not the child are responsible for the family situation, that supports are available to help the child and family stay together without hurting one another, and that mechanisms are available to protect family members may ease some of the children's fears and promote their capacity to share their feelings and thoughts. If a child's disclosure is followed by retraction or denial, it is important that clinicians maintain their belief in what the child initially said and not forget or collude in denying it as the family members have. Contacts should be made with the child's allies inside and outside the family to facilitate creating a support system for the child beyond the clinical team. Protective mechanisms should be in place or available before the family is confronted with the allegation. Presentation of the complaint should be made to both parents in a manner that does not jeopardize or endanger the child. For example, it would be inappropriate to call parents into an interview room immediately after a child disclosed possible incest, ask the child to restate to the parents what was said to the clinician, and then send the family home. Revelation can create a volatile family situation. A preferable approach might include having a professional rather than the child confront the parents, having individual and joint meetings with parents to determine their reaction and their capacity to protect the child, making a report to protective authorities, and determining what measures are needed to assure family and child protection at that time.

DISCLOSURE BY SOMEONE OTHER THAN THE CHILD

When someone other than the child asks for help and discloses a situation of possible sexual abuse, the clinician should consider other problems and concerns expressed by the family member and the nature of that member's role in the family and motivation in disclosing the information. Understanding the family dynamics can help a clinician's understanding and management of the family member. If, for example, a mother voices concerns, one should inquire why she revealed the information now rather than earlier. She may be looking for a way to divorce her husband. This situation does not mean the complaint should not be taken seriously, but investigation should proceed with knowledge of circumstances and motivations. Custody battles pose a setting in which allegations of sexual abuse are made to justify one parent's incapacity to care for a child compared to the other's. Again, while allegations may be true, a parent's strong desire to possess a child can lead to false accusations. In such a circumstance, it is extremely im-

portant to see the children and search for information that corroborates the parent's allegation. Family members, in addition to children, may first disclose information about family sexual abuse and then deny their statements. Here, too, clinicians should avoid colluding with the family member's denial. The clinician should determine what problems besides possible abuse prompted the family member to seek help and then pursue these issues in addition to investigating possible sexual abuse.

MEANS OF DISCLOSURE AND THE EFFECTS ON TREATMENT

The means of disclosing suspected intrafamily sexual abuse will affect the ease with which one can begin to work with a family.

Intentional Disclosure

When a family member has made a conscious decision to seek help, the door has been opened to building an alliance with this person, enhancing this person's supports, and taking steps to involve other family members. Even in this situation, the family member may experience ambivalence and some denial. The clinician must stick with the patient and reiterate the request for help.

Disclosure During a Transitional Crisis

A transitional situation such as an argument or threatened abandonment may prompt a family member to impulsively report incest and subsequently deny the charge. A clinician will find this case more elusive than one of intentional disclosure. Clinical concern should focus both on the immediate crisis and on investigation of possible sexual abuse.

Accidental Disclosure

In the course of assessing a family or individual problem seemingly unrelated to sexual abuse, a clinician may discover signs or symptoms that suggest sexual abuse or may, unexpectedly, hear a statement from a family member that arouses suspicion.[6] Clinically this is the most difficult situation for engaging a family in an assessment since all dynamic factors are operating to maintain the status quo and resist any change. The clinician should respond to the presenting problem. If suspicion of sexual abuse is strong enough, a report should be made to protective authorities who can legally require an assessment.

TREATMENT OF INTRAFAMILY SEXUAL ABUSE

One of the goals of acute assessment and management is to determine the treatment needs of the family and to link the family to community resources that can meet their needs. Quality treatment involves careful coordination of medical, mental health, protective, and legal services. Details of the method of treatment of intrafamily sexual abuse are beyond the realm of a chapter devoted to acute management, but literature on treatment methods is available.[14,15] Although methods vary from program to program, the primary focus is usually on family-oriented treatment; particular treatment goals include restructuring the marital and parent-child relationships. Adjunctive use of individual treatment, meetings of family subunits, and self-help groups for parents and children complement the family treatment and provide additional support for family members.

In communities where specialized treatment programs for sexual abuse do not exist, it is best to work through protective service agencies or to work out collaborative arrangements with mandated authorities. Professionals involved in the acute management of these cases can serve an important role by advocating the development of treatment resources in their own community.

REFERENCES

1. DeFrancis V: *Protecting the Child Victim of Sex Crimes Committed by Adults.* Denver, The American Humane Association, 1969.

2. Finkelhor D: *Sexually Victimized Children.* New York, The Free Press, 1979.

3. Geiser RL: *Hidden Victims: The Sexual Abuse of Children.* Boston, Beacon Press, 1979.

4. Sgroi SM: Child sexual assault: Some guidelines for intervention and assessment, in Burgess, AW, et al (eds): *Sexual Assault of Children and Adolescents.* Lexington, Mass, Lexington Books 1978.

5. Burgess AW, et al: Divided loyalty in incest cases, in Burgess AW, et al (eds): *Sexual Assault of Children and Adolescents.* Lexington, Mass, Lexington Books, 1978.

6. Brant RST, Tisza VB: The sexually misused child. *Am J Orthopsychiatry* **47**:80–90, 1977.

7. Burgess AW, Holmstrom LL: The child and family during the court process, in Burgess, AW, et al (eds): *Sexual Assault of Children and Adolescents.* Lexington, Mass, Lexington Books, 1978.

8. Burgess AW, Holmstrom LL: Rape trauma syndrome. *Am J Psychiatry* **131**:981–986, 1974.

9. Lewis M, Sarrell PM: Some psychological aspects of seduction, incest and rape in childhood. *J Am Acad Child Psychiatry* **8**:606–619, 1969.

10. Peters J: Children who are victims of sexual assault and the psychology of offenders. *Am J Psychother* **30**:398–421, 1976.

11. Sutherland S, Scherl D: Patterns of response among victims of rape. *Am J Orthopsychiatry* **40**:503–511, 1970.

12. Machotka P, et al: Incest as a family affair. *Fam Process* **6**:98–116, 1967.

13. Meiselman KC: *Incest: A Psychological Study of Causes and Effects with Treatment Recommendations.* San Francisco, Josey-Bass Inc Publishers, 1978.

14. Eist HI, Mandel AU: Family treatment of ongoing incest behavior. *Fam Process* **7**:216–232, 1968.

15. Giaretto H: The treatment of father-daughter incest. *Child Today* **5**:2–5, 34, 35, 1976.

19

SEXUAL HARASSMENT

Kimberly Kathryn Greene, B.A., M.S., J.D.

THE SEXUALLY HARASSED WOMAN

Andrea worked on the construction crew of a multimillion-dollar commercial urban project. She was the only woman on the job and had been interviewed for newspaper and television human interest stories about "the new working woman." Andrea also received a lot of attention from her supervisor and her co-workers. They thought nothing of slapping or pinching her buttocks or making lewd remarks about her physique or her sexuality. Her supervisor assigned her the least desirable jobs because the "crews can't get along with no lady." When she requested a job assignment that was comparable to that of male workers, her supervisor suggested she could persuade him by spending the night at his apartment. Andrea did not want to quit this job but did not know how much longer she could put up with the sleeplessness, the irritability, and the constant anxiety she experienced because of it.

After graduating from law school, Betty accepted a job with a male trial attorney who was well known for his liberal position on major social issues. The first week on the job Betty's boss began calling her "honey" and "mamma," standing too close, or resting his hand on her thigh when they conferred on a case. After three weeks he began demanding sexual favors. When Betty replied she wanted to keep their relationship professional, he berated her: why did she think he hired her anyway, for her brain? While Betty suffered severe migraine headaches, her boss boasted about receiving the public praise of women's groups for being one of the few attorneys in town who was open-minded enough to hire a woman.

Carolyn was the office manager of a small company. Until her boss was promoted, she enjoyed considerable responsibility and took pride in her work. Her new boss, however, brought a new set of working conditions. He called Carolyn into his office to talk about her "loyalty" and his sexual fantasies about her. He hung "playmate pinups" on the office walls, and every day he placed a sexually graphic photograph or cartoon on her desk. After she had asked him several times to stop, he began to degrade her before her co-workers. When Carolyn went to her former boss for help, the new boss put a poor performance report in her personnel file. Her former boss was skeptical about the truth of Carolyn's stories (after all she was a 48-year-old woman), even though he had never before doubted anything she told him. Carolyn was the sole support of her two teenage children and desperately needed her income, but after she complained, her boss's behavior worsened. She was finally forced to quit. After seven months of searching, Carolyn was unable to find a job commensurate with her skills.

Women of every race, age, description, and occupation experience sexual harassment on the job every day. The public is beginning to perceive sexual harassment as a problem, thanks to the courageous women who have spoken out about it, often to the detriment of their jobs. There are very few documented instances of sexual harassment of working men by female supervisors or bosses. The reason for this fact will be discussed later.

What causes sexual harassment, and why does it exist in the work place? Why has the problem only recently received public attention? To understand the answers to these important questions, one must first comprehend the meaning of the term.

WHAT IS SEXUAL HARASSMENT?

Sexual harassment is unwanted, unreciprocated attention from male bosses, managers, clients, or co-workers. It takes a myriad of forms—staring, leering, touching, pinching, rubbing against, grabbing, lewd or suggestive comments, repeated invitations to date despite rejections, sexual propositions, attempted rape, and rape itself—and it exists always as a condition of work. It can be either a series of "petty offenses" that must be tolerated as part of the job or a serious ultimatum to comply with certain terms or suffer

the consequences—unnecessarily burdensome work assignments, demotion, loss of raise in salary, or loss of job.

Sexual harassment has nothing to do with mutual office flirtations and dating or with truly consensual romantic relationships between people who work together. Instead, sexual harassment is coercive and has very little to do with sex at all. Put very simply, sexual harassment is a power play.

EFFECTS OF SEXUAL HARASSMENT

The impact of sexual harassment touches every aspect of a woman's life. In addition to the obvious economic impact, there are emotional and physical repercussions.

Economic Impact

Sexual harassment makes a woman's job depend on something other than the competent performance of her duties. Refusing to concede to sexual demands or to endure more subtle, but equally demeaning, conditions on the job can result in denial of advancement or loss of job. Choosing to comply with sexual demands *may* yield job advancement, but more often it leads to the same ignominious result. Even if she is not actually fired, a woman may find that quitting is the only way to evade intolerable working conditions. All of the alternatives—losing a promotion, a raise, or a job—involve severe economic hardship for a working woman.

In times of rampant inflation, the few jobs that are open to women become flooded with applicants, many of them overeducated and overqualified. This situation permits employers to be extremely selective in their hiring. As a result, the derogatory reports that may be found in the personnel records of the sexually harassed woman, the refusal of a former boss to give a positive recommendation, and an employment record that indicates short stays at a number of different jobs can prevent a woman from being hired to a job for which she is perfectly suited.

Many people see little significance in these consequences; they share the widespread belief that women work for noneconomic reasons: to get out of the house, to keep from getting bored, or because it might be fun. For the vast majority of working women, these explanations are clearly wrong. Like their male counterparts in the work place, women work because they need the money.

Two-thirds of all working women are single, separated, divorced, widowed, or married to husbands with annual incomes of less than $10,000. These women and their families depend heavily upon the income they produce.

The working woman who is fired or quits her job suffers more than loss of wages until she obtains a new position. She also loses all seniority, health and life insurance benefits, sick days, and vacation time that had accrued during the tenure of her job. In addition, she will be unable to take advantage of the temporary assistance of unemployment benefits unless she can prove that she left her job for "good cause." Many states do not consider sexual harassment an adequate or important reason for leaving a job, so women who are forced to quit because of sexual harassment cannot qualify for unemployment benefits.

Physical Impact

The woman whose economic situation requires that she produce an income may feel trapped by sexual harassment. She may believe she has no alternative but to acquiesce or to endure.

Many women who experience sexual harassment on the job attempt to ignore it. They believe that confronting the aggressor or reporting his behavior would only result in increased harassment; ridicule from co-workers; or being branded a troublemaker, a label that would compound their problems in finding future work. Trying to endure these conditions in silence and, at the same time, be a productive worker can lead to a variety of physical problems, including tension and anxiety, nervous stomach, loss of appetite, loss of sleep, and extreme exhaustion. These problems can cause excessive absences from work and diminished productivity which can lead to poor job evaluations from supervisors.

Emotional Impact

The need to constantly tolerate demeaning treatment or fend off unwanted sexual advances can take its emotional toll on the working woman. She may feel anxious because so much of her energy is diverted from her purpose on the job. Her anxieties may follow her home and interfere with her familial relationships.

Many women and men still believe that sexual harassment is nothing more than the male response to female sensuality. Therefore, the woman must have done something to bring this treatment upon herself. If she did something to cause it, these people reason, she should be able to stop or control it. Accordingly, some women dress more conservatively on the job, keep more to themselves, stop smiling, and avert their faces and cast their eyes downward when speaking to a male boss or co-worker. Then, when none of these preventive measures stops the harassment (they invariably have *no* effect on the harassment), the woman is engulfed by guilt. She blames herself for something that is beyond her control. Because her guilt shames her, she is silent. For this reason, countless incidents of sexual harassment go unreported.

In addition to fighting guilt, the victim of sexual harassment is beset by confusion. She came into the work place to earn a living by being a productive worker. She expected to earn the respect of her co-workers and boss by doing her job proficiently. Instead she is subjected to crude, sexual language; she is manhandled; or she is told that intimacy with a supervisor is a condition of her employment. When she reacts negatively to being pinched, called "hon," or worse, she is accused of being unable to handle herself; she is told she should be flattered to receive such attention. But she knows, at some level, that the work place is an inappropriate setting for such behavior, that she is being treated as a sex object in a place where she expected to be treated as a worker. If she realized how prevalent sexual harassment is, in her work place and in most others, she would perhaps understand that what underlies this inappropriate and offensive behavior is not sexual attention or her own conduct, but an assertion of male power and dominance, a denigration of her right as a woman to be taken seriously on the job.

Various surveys have shown the shocking extent of this problem. A 1976 *Redbook* questionnaire revealed that 90 percent of the 9,100 respondents had experienced sexual harassment. Eighty-one percent of the women on a California naval base who answered the questionnaire reported experiences of sexual harassment. And a 1980 survey, based on the *Redbook* questionnaire and sponsored by the Kentucky Commission on Women, found that 56 percent of those responding (women workers in Kentucky state government) had experienced sexual harassment and 95 percent felt sexual harassment to be a problem. (See Appendix for full results of the Kentucky survey and References 1–3 for further information on existing surveys.)

WHY DOES SEXUAL HARASSMENT EXIST IN THE WORK PLACE TODAY?

Male Outlook

The advent of the Industrial Revolution drew increasing numbers of women from their homes and farms into the factories. The jobs available to women in these factories were primarily menial, monotonous tasks.

The bosses were men, and though they would have preferred to keep women at home and economically dependent, their factories required laborers. Perhaps because they felt that the influx of large numbers of women into the work force was in some way an encroachment upon their exclusive domain, male workers and bosses developed systematic and pervasive means of dealing with female workers. Women were relegated to low-paying, no-status positions; limited in the number of hours and the time of day which they could work; and subjected to a constant barrage of sexual harassment. Men acted as if they could approach their work relationships with women the same way they approached their personal relationships. Men were, according to the "natural law," the dominant and powerful persons in society. By taking jobs outside the home and producing their own income, however meager, women were stepping out of "their place," and men could not let them forget it. Where the superiority of one group over another is imagined rather than real, the supposedly superior group must assert itself more aggressively over the submissive group if it is to maintain its power and control of them. Men asserted themselves so over the women who went to work.

The Female Job Ghetto

An honest appraisal of the situation of working women today shows that very little has changed since the nineteenth century. Despite the attention the women's movement has gained in the mass media, the actual economic gains realized by all women—including both those who work outside the home and those who work within it—prove that the attention, the promises made, and the bargains struck have been little more than lip service.

There exists in the work place a "female job ghetto." There are 41 million women in the work force; they represent 42 percent of *all* American workers: almost one-half.[4] Although more women are entering occupations that are traditionally male preserves, the vast majority of the 41 million women who work are clustered in jobs that are characterized as secondary, helping, subservient, and unimportant to the economic sector. Over 75 percent of all women workers are employed in traditionally female clerical, sales, and service (including teaching and nursing) positions.[5] These are among the lowest-paying jobs in America.

The existence of the "female job ghetto" helps to explain another fact which says much about the esteem society holds for productive working women. In 1955, the median income for women was 64 cents for every dollar earned by men. Twenty-two years later, after a decade of feminist activism and breakthroughs for women in nontraditional occupations, the median income for women had *dropped* to 59 cents for each dollar earned by men.[6]

The average amount of formal education for both female and male workers is 12.5 years, yet the comparative average earnings of equally educated women and men is $8,618 per year for the average women compared to $14,626 per year for the average man.[6] Nor does this discrepancy decrease when men and women who have earned advanced degrees are compared. The median income for women with five or more years of college is $14,338 per year, while her male counterparts earn $21,941 per year.[7] The difference is $7,603, a notable increase in buying power. In fact, the excess earned by men over women is only $1,015 less than the amount the average female worker earns in a year. Put another way, a man with an eighth grade education earns, on the average, $350 more per year than a woman with a college degree. And a male who has graduated from high school earns $800 more in a year than a woman who has an advanced degree.[4] These discrepancies vividly illustrate the plight of working women.

The Traditional Inferior Position of Women

If women earn far less than men and hold jobs that are generally regarded as inconsequential, the system of patriarchy or male dominance, which has always been the political and economic reality in the United States, is perpetuated. The traditional "inferior" position of women is emphasized by male behavior that is totally inappropriate in the work place. When men create an atmosphere in which women are subjected to lewd comments, leers, inappropriate touching, pinching, or standing too close, it is clear to the women that men perceive them as sex objects and not as productive workers. When men demand that women employees accept dates or submit to unwanted sexual intimacy, with the clear understanding that the women's promotions, raises, or jobs themselves depend upon compliance, women are left with very little choice. If a woman is forced to choose between losing an economically essential job and succumbing to sex against her will, how can she value herself and her role in the economic structure in society? More basically, how can she function in such a situation on a daily basis and still retain even a shred of self-esteem?

RECOGNIZING THE VICTIM

Victims of sexual harassment display a variety of stress signals. When health professionals are counseling a patient or taking a medical history, they should be attuned to these signals and pursue them.

The strain accompanying sexual harassment will most certainly manifest itself in the work situation. A change in work schedule or duties, a demotion (or a denied promotion), being fired or laid off, calling in sick often, or quitting a job can indicate an underlying problem and should be explored. A health professional should be alerted also by complaints from the patient that she feels out of place or disrespected at work, that she can not concentrate on normal duties, that she does not understand the office "rules," that she wants to find a new job, or that something she cannot articulate is bothering her about her job.

Perhaps less obvious symptoms of sexual harassment are those not directly related to the work place. Physical symptoms such as tension, headaches, loss of sleep, irritability, depression, or increased use of drugs or alcohol *can* be signs of sexual harassment. Likewise, a woman who suddenly and inexplicably exhibits a lowered self-esteem may be a woman who, because she does not understand the basic meaning of sexual harassment, has begun to accept the perceived assessment of herself as valueless.

These signals apply to a number of other situations and syndromes, of course. They are mentioned here to show how crucial an awareness of the problem of sexual harassment is. Without an understanding of what sexual harassment entails, the patient's symptoms may be attributed to some other, unrelated cause. Nor can the health professional rely upon the patient to recognize and clearly understand that her symptoms may be caused by the boss's repeated insinuations that her promotion depends on her "loyalty" and "cooperation," or her boss's attitude that she is his possession and he is, therefore, at liberty to touch, pinch, squeeze, or stand too close. The notion that such incidents are an inevitable consequence of mingling men and women in the work place is firmly ingrained. Consequently, many women do not even consciously consider they are being sexually harassed. Other women do realize that they are being sexually harassed, but they remain silent because they consider it a personal problem. They do not understand sexual harassment in its broader sense, as a widespread social issue.

Making women, and the general public, aware of the problem would facilitate the diagnostic process in cases of sexual harassment. Some effective methods of making the issue "visible" include relating the problem to other issues of safety and rights of women on the job or to the issue of violence against women. Literature made available to patients should mention counseling or information on sexual harassment among the services. Comparing sexual harassment to other types of violence against women puts the problem into a context that most people understand to some extent. A basic awareness of the issue is thus established.

HELPING THE VICTIM

Counseling Services

Basic requirements for success in counseling, especially in an area as complex as sexual harassment, are a historical view of the issue and a clear understanding of one's own reactions to it. Effective counseling of victims of sexual harassment is impossible without a resolution of the counselor's position on the issue.

Although different health professionals may use different counseling techniques, there are certain things that counselors should impress upon the victim. They should attempt to make the woman understand that sexual harassment is a widespread social problem, that it happens to many women in many situations, and that it is by no means a problem that is uniquely hers. The counselor should encourage the patient to consider dealing with the problem immediately by confronting the harasser. The usual reaction to sexual harassment is to laugh nervously, look away, or pretend that it did not happen and that it will go away if ignored. The woman must understand that ignoring the problem will not alleviate it. The counselor should suggest specific methods of letting the harasser know his behavior is unwelcome, such as moving away when he is too close or asking about his wife and family when he touches or requests a date. After all, the woman must realize that she should not feel guilty when she refuses to acquiesce to sexual harassment; everyone has the right to a work atmosphere that is conducive to job performance.

The counselor should emphasize the importance of complete documentation of every occurrence of sexual harassment. Should the situation worsen, and the woman decide to take legal action, written accounts of a series of incidents will greatly facilitate the case.

Sexual harassment is not an isolated experience, and the victim can learn a great deal about other incidents of harassment at her work place by talking to other women about the problem. This kind of communication should be encouraged since it can not only provide emotional reassurance but also lead to corroborating testimony or to group pressure to compel the employer to take some action about the problem.

Referral Services

A victim of sexual harassment who wants peer counseling or help and understanding from other women who have dealt with the same problem can contact local women's organizations or feminist counselors. The National Organization for Women, the YWCA, and the State Commission on Women are among several organizations that take active interest in the issue of sexual harassment.

If the woman decides to seek legal assistance for her situation, the health professional must be prepared to refer her to appropriate persons or agencies. Local or state human rights commissions will investigate her situation and inform her about her legal options. These agencies make certain that a victim of sexual harassment knows enough about the legal procedures, the problems involved in pursuing a sexual harassment claim against an employer, and the probability of success in her particular claim so that she can make an informed decision about initiating legal proceedings. The victim of sexual harassment should contact the Equal Employment Opportunity Commission, the federal agency charged with enforcement of federal laws prohibiting discrimination in employment, as well as the state agency to ensure that she can pursue her claim in either state or federal court. A claim must be filed with the appropriate agency within 180 days of the occurrence of the harassment.

If the woman asks for a referral to an individual attorney, the health professional should be certain that any attorney recommended understands the emotional ramifications of sexual harassment and is familiar with the legal aspects of the issue.

CONCLUSION

This chapter provides some fundamental background on the complex social issue of sexual harassment. If health professionals understand the historical context of sexual harassment and the social and economic conditions that foster it, they can be effective counselors to the victim of sexual harassment. Without this general understanding, and without an acknowledgement of personal feelings about the issue, the health professional's service to the sexually harassed woman cannot be complete.

APPENDIX

SEXUAL HARASSMENT ON THE JOB IN KENTUCKY: THE QUESTIONNAIRE

(Modified from the *Redbook* Questionnaire on Sexual Harassment)

Sexual harassment is one-sided, unwelcome attention that comes from male supervisors, bosses, co-workers, or clients. Such actions are coercive because they contain the threat or insinuation that a woman's failure to go along will negatively affect her employment. Sexual harassment does not include mutual flirtation or genuinely consenting relationships.

The following questionnaire helped determine the scope of sexual harassment in Kentucky. All replies were anonymous and completely confidential. Thoughtful and honest answers to these questions made it possible to bring this serious problem to public attention. The results were as follows:

1. Which of the following, if any, have you experienced with male co-workers or supervisors? (Circle all that apply.)

    22.0% A. Leering or ogling.

    48.8% B. Sexual remarks, teasing, or sexual jokes.

    13.6% C. Sexually suggestive objects or pictures in the work place.

    23.2% D. Touching, brushing against, grabbing, pinching.

    4.4% E. Invitations to a date, with the implication that refusal may count against you.

    4.4% F. Sexual propositions, with the implication that refusal may count against you.

    0.7% G. Sexual relations against your will because you were afraid refusing would count against you.

    4.4% H. Other forms of sexual harassment. (Please specify.)

    43.6% I. No sexual harassment at all.

2. How often have these things happened?

    11.4% A. Regularly.

    34.0% B. Several times.

    13.5% C. Once or twice.

    41.1% D. Never.

3. Which one of the following statements best reflects the way you feel?

    11.4% A. Sexual tensions between men and women who work together are natural.

    18.1% B. An attractive woman has to expect sexual advances and learn how to handle them.

    2.5% C. Encouraging the boss's sexual interest is often a way of getting ahead.

    12.0% D. Women who are bothered by male co-workers are usually asking for it.

    57.2% E. Unwelcome male attentions on the job are offensive.

4. In general, how would you feel if a male supervisor or co-worker made sexual advances to you? (Circle all that apply.)

    77.5% { A. It would be embarrassing.

    B. It would be demeaning.

    C. It would be intimidating.

    4.6% D. It would be flattering.

    5.2% E. It would be a way of keeping me, a woman, "in my place."

    12.7% F. It would be of no consequence.

5. At work have you ever used your sexual attractiveness for any of the following purposes?

    4.3% A. To improve relations with a male supervisor.

    3.7% B. To catch the attention of higher-ups.

    0.0% C. To get out of chores you dislike.

    6.6% D. To obtain special help from men.

0.0% E. To maneuver into a better job situation.

2.7% F. To obtain other advantages.

82.7% G. Not applicable.

6. What do you think of a woman using her sexual attractiveness to gain job advantage?

   2.9% A. It's only natural—sexual attractiveness is a basic asset meant to be used.

   5.3% B. It's a woman's answer to the way men gain job advantages—in locker rooms, on the golf course.

55.9% C. It tends to perpetuate a system of sexism.

35.8% D. It's her own business and has nothing to do with me.

7. In getting your job how important do you think your physical attractiveness was?

   1.4% A. More important than my other qualifications.

   6.8% B. Equally important.

39.6% C. Less important, but it was a factor.

52.1% D. Unimportant.

8. At work how important is a man's physical attractiveness?

28.3% A. As important as a woman's.

20.0% B. Less important.

   0.7% C. More important.

51.0% D. Unimportant.

9. If a male co-worker or supervisor has made sexual advances to you, how did you react? (Circle all that apply.)

   1.2% A. I enjoyed it.

26.6% B. I ignored it, hoping it would stop.

   3.4% C. I worried that if I objected, it would somehow go against me.

   0.3% D. I played along with it, hoping it would lead to a promotion.

12.5% E. I asked the man to stop.

   4.7% F. I reported it to a supervisor or union representative.

51.2% G. Not applicable.

10. If you were to report a man's unwelcome attentions to a supervisor or union representative, what do you think would happen? (Circle all that apply.)

22.8% A. Nothing at all.

33.9% B. I would be told not to take it so seriously.

23.3% C. The man would be asked to stop—or else.

13.6% D. I would be labeled a troublemaker.

   4.3% E. I would be offered a job in another department to help me avoid the man.

   1.4% F. I would be moved to another department in retaliation.

   0.8% G. I would be fired.

11. How would you feel if you saw sexual advances being made to another woman at work?

65.9% A. I would sympathize with her.

   8.9% B. I would blame her.

   3.0% C. I would envy her ability to make sexual attractiveness work for her.

22.2% D. I would think nothing of it.

12. How do you feel about sexual harassment?

55.5% A. It is a serious problem.

39.7% B. It is a minor problem.

   4.8% C. It is of no importance at all.

13. Have you or any woman you know ever: (Circle all that apply.)

25.5% A. Quit a job because of sexual harassment.

   7.7% B. Been fired because of sexual harassment.

66.8% C. Not applicable.

14. Who was the harasser?

13.1% A. A supervisor.

18.4% B. Boss.

   9.8% C. Co-worker.

2.0% D. Client.

65.2% E. Not applicable.

15. If you quit or were fired because of sexual harassment:

A. Did you apply for unemployment benefits?
34.8% Yes   65.2% No

B. Did you receive them?
26.7% Yes   73.3% No

C. Did you pursue any discrimination proceedings?
4.5% Yes   95.4% No

D. Did you have difficulty getting another job?
0.0% Yes   100.0% No

16. How do you shield yourself from sexual harassment?

24.0% A. I pretend not to notice it.

3.2% B. I act silly and childish.

34.4% C. I adopt a cool, guarded manner.

9.6% D. I dress with extreme modesty.

2.9% E. I flaunt my wedding ring.

25.9% F. I've never had to cope with it.

17. What is your occupation?

18. What is your approximate salary?

31.5% A. Less than $5,000.

47.2% B. $5,000 to $10,000.

30.8% C. $10,000 to $15,000.

13.3% D. $15,000 to $25,000.

2.1% E. More than $25,000.

19. What is your total family income?

2.2% A. Less than $5,000.

17.6% B. $5,000 to $10,000.

17.6% C. $10,000 to $15,000.

31.7% D. $15,000 to $25,000.

31.7% E. More than $25,000.

20. What is your age?

3.5% A. Under 21.

45.1% B. 21 to 30.

28.3% C. 31 to 40.

12.6% D. 41 to 50.

10.5% E. 50 plus.

21. What is your marital status?

22.6% A. Single.

3.0% B. Living with a man.

56.6% C. Married.

12.8% D. Separated or divorced.

5.1% E. Widowed.

22. What is the highest level of education you have completed?

1.0% A. Grade school.

22.2% B. High school.

28.8% C. Some college.

20.1% D. College graduate.

12.5% E. Some graduate work.

14.6% F. Advanced degree.

REFERENCES

1. Bulzarik M: *Sexual Harassment at the Workplace: Historical Notes.* Somerville, Mass, New England Free Press, 1978.

2. Farley L: *Sexual Shakedown.* New York, McGraw-Hill Inc, 1978.

3. MacKinnon C: *Sexual Harassment of Working Women: A Case of Sex Discrimination.* New Haven, Conn, Yale University Press, 1979.

4. Rivers C: Sexual harassment: the executive's alternative to rape, *Mother Jones,* June 1978, p 21.

5. Silverman D: Sexual harassment: working woman's dilemma, *Quest,* Winter 1976–1977, pp 15–24.

SUGGESTED READING

Lindsey K: Sexual harassment on the job: how to spot it and how to stop it, *Ms,* November 1977, p 47.

Safron C: What men do to women on the job: a shocking look at sexual harassment, *Redbook,* November 1976, p 149.

RESOURCES

Alliance Against Sexual Coercion (AACS)
P.O. Box 1
Cambridge, Massachusetts 02139
617/482-0329
(Reading material, counseling groups, referrals)

Kentucky Commission on Women
614-A Shelby Street
Frankfort, Kentucky 40601
502/564-6643
("Sexual Harassment: A Report on Working Women in Kentucky")

Program on Women and Work
Institute of Labor and Industrial Relations
University of Michigan
108 Museums Annex
Ann Arbor, Michigan 48109
(Conference Report: "Sexual Harassment in the Workplace")

Working Women's Institute
593 Park Avenue
New York, New York 10021
212/838-4420
(Reading material, bibliography, attorney referral service)

Unit V

Children and Abuse

20

THE BATTERED CHILD SYNDROME

Cyril H. Wecht, M.D., J.D.
Glenn M. Larkin, M.D.

The puzzling association of chronic sub-dural hematoma and multiple limb fractures of different ages in young children was first described by Caffey in 1946.[1] He was unable to correlate these findings with any known disease and was looking for some heretofore undiagnosed, exotic new disease.

The medical profession was psychologically unprepared to accept the concept that parents could seriously maim their own children, and it took nine years before Woolley and Evans[2] suggested that parental violence was responsible for Caffey's observations. It remained for Kempe[3] to coin the phrase "the battered child syndrome" in 1962. Since then, multiple studies the world over have more clearly defined the "battered child syndrome" so that it is now well known to the medical profession, social service and law enforcement agencies, and the lay public alike.

In Anglo-American law, the King or state has always protected the young child more than the adult under the principle of *parens patriae*. An opinion dated 1722 states that "every loyal subject is taken to be within the King's protection, for reason it is, that idiots and lunatics, who are uncapable to take care of themselves, are provided for by the King and *pater patriae*, and there is same reason to extend this care to infants."[4]

In practice, this protection was not extended to all the children in the realm but only to the children of the landed gentry. By the nineteenth century, application of this principle was used to limit child labor and to enforce school attendance. The state claimed that it was able to rule and enforce regulations concerning the welfare of a child without consulting the child and even if the regulations were contrary to the parents' wishes. The state did not interfere in family discipline, which was often physical, brutal, and maiming. Despite the concept of *parens patriae*, a father had absolute control over his children, who lacked the means to protest his treatment of them.[5]

By the late nineteenth century, laws such as the Pennsylvania statute of June 11, 1879, P.L. 142: "An act to protect children from neglect and cruelty. . ."[6] still embraced the *parens patriae* concept but, again, did not enter a "man's castle" to evaluate acts of cruelty. Only after World War II, with medical awareness of the battered child, did the state legislatures start to act. Then they did so with unequaled haste: between 1962 and 1965, 47 states passed so-called "child-protection laws"[7] with either compulsory or voluntary reporting of suspected child abuse. Current Pennsylvania law, amended in 1975, is the "Child Protection Services Law," which particularly defines the abused child as "a child under 18 years of age who exhibits evidence of serious physical or mental injury not explained by the available medical history as being accidental. . . ."[8]

CLASSIFICATION

It is convenient, although somewhat artificial, to classify the child abuser into several categories.

The Intermittent Child Abuser

Parents who are intermittent abusers will periodically batter a child, with periods of proper care between batterings. These parents do not intend to hurt their children; they are driven by panic or compulsion into this behavior and are sincerely remorseful afterward. Often these parents are well motivated to "reform" and will be successful in time, if their children survive long enough. The child is usually grabbed by a convenient "handle," an arm or leg, and shaken forcefully. The broken bones are usually found to be at different stages of healing.

The One-Time Child Abuser

It is tempting to separate people who are one-time abusers from the previous group; however, it is more likely that the one-timer is a potential repeater and was only stopped from repeating the act either by killing the child or by a sudden surge of self-restraint.

For example, a 23-year-old mother of two young children, under the care of a psychiatrist for postpartum depression, appears to be in good control of herself and is taking proper care of her two young boys. One sunny June morning, she kisses her husband goodbye when he goes to work as if nothing is wrong. She then shoots her older boy in the chest with a rifle and places his two-and-one-half-month-old brother in the refrigerator freezer, neatly wrapped in a blanket. This grisly task completed, she shoots herself in the mouth with the rifle, and the whole family is discovered by the husband when he returns home from work that evening. What happened to this woman, after her husband left for work that morning, to make her behave with such an excess of violence is still a mystery.[9]

The Constant Child Abuser

Parents who constantly abuse their children actually hate them and callously and deliberately beat and miscare for them. The intent is to hurt the child—rationalized into "making it mind"—and the parent is indifferent to the child's suffering. These people often have personality disorders and are coolly indifferent to the destructive nature of their actions.

Consider the following: a 20-year-old father regularly beats his 14-month-old son with a leather belt, for the slightest infractions. The mother, either too weak or too frightened to protest, reluctantly cooperates with this parental savagery and cares for the frequently moribund toddler until the next infraction and beating. After one particularly harsh beating, the child lapses into a coma and this time does not survive.

Then, in an effort to dispose of the body, the parents concoct an elaborate kidnapping plot (complete with a ransom note demanding $500 in two weeks), bundle the other two children into their car, and bury the remains of their son. The ransom note is discovered, and because of its nature, the local police suspect a hoax. On interrogation, the mother changes her story and states that the child is with her sister. She then breaks down and, between tears, tells of the child's death and their subsequent attempt to hide the remains in a wooded area not far from their home. When arrested, the father seemingly shows no remorse.[10]

The Child is the Center of a Triangle

In this age of alternative life-styles and broken families, more and more young mothers look for and find live-in boyfriends. Often these men are affectionate to their girl-friend's children and contribute to their growth and well-being; more often, the child becomes the middle of an emotional triangle.

When resentment builds up in these circumstances, either the intermittent or habitual pattern of abuse can be present, and the woman's children are the common target of the man's hostility.

For example, a young divorcée, working and going to school, develops a relationship with a nonworking male. He moves into her small apartment and makes friends with her two-year-old daughter who plays with him joyfully while mama is out either working or at school. The man cooks and cleans when the spirit moves him and generally takes good care of the child, including toilet training her. At this stage of development, the child is able to use the commode with some help and is able to request the help. One morning, while the mother is buying food, the girl has an accident and wets herself, causing a violent reaction in the baby-sitter. He chases the child to the bathroom, picks her up, and shakes and starts to punch her violently. Finally, she frees herself from his grip and, allegedly, bangs her head against the bath-

room sink and dies of craniocerebral injuries. The young man surrenders to the police.[11]

The Ignorant Abuser

Ignorant abusers are perhaps the most tragic because the parents "mean well," but their attempts at child rearing result in permanent injury or death to their children, and they are "truly sorry" when a child dies.

Consider this example: a young mother on an intracity bus hears how a second mother corrects her children's behavior. The second mother tells the first that if a child "cries" too much, an easy solution is to pour pepper down the child's mouth; the child will stop crying immediately. The first mother gets home to her whining four-year-old and tells the child to stop whining. When the child continues, she pours about two teaspoons of pepper down her throat, and the child stops whining. On several other occasions, the child misbehaves, and the mother is quick to apply the pepper treatment. Late one afternoon, the child is cranky and the mother irritable. She pours about "one-half a dixie cup" of pepper into her daughter's mouth. This time the daughter becomes agitated, runs around the house making grunting noises, starts to convulse, and dies in agony. The frantic mother tries to resuscitate her but is unsuccessful.

At the coroner's inquest, the mother is genuinely remorseful but apparently does not understand the lethal potential of pepper.[12]

DISCUSSION

Between 1969 and 1979, 35 deaths that were possibly related to child abuse were handled by the Allegheny County Coroner's Office. Five of these cases were ruled "not child abuse," and four cases are now *sub judice.* One of the older cases was appealed. Only one case involved the murder of more than one child at the same time, and one of the abusers had been involved with a death in a previous documented case of child abuse.

Of the 28 children studied by the coroner's office, 15 (54 percent) were male and 13 (46 percent) were female; 14 were black and 14 were white. Over one-half, 18 children (64 percent), were "beaten"; of these, two were beaten by a baby-sitter, three by their mother, five by their father, and seven by the mother's "boyfriend." One child was beaten by "persons unknown."[13]

The next most common cause of death was drowning; four children were drowned by their mother and one by her grandmother. One of these drownings was "accidental"; the mother put the child in a bathtub while she had sexual relations with her boyfriend.

The two children who were shot, a six-month-old black male and a two-year-old white male, were both victims of a multiple homicide-suicide attempt. The young mother succeeded in her suicide. The father killed his child and wife but survived his own gunshot wound to the head and subsequently developed traumatic epilepsy. He refused treatment while awaiting trial and died in status epilepticus while incarcerated.

The remaining four children died as a result of diversified causes: one was frozen in a refrigerator, two were left outside in inclement weather, and one four-year-old aspirated pepper.

Forensic pathologists enter the drama in the epilogue and usually do so with much anxiety. They must be able to recognize the pattern of trauma and differentiate if from a "true accident." They must satisfy themselves that the injuries they document so meticulously are the result of a specific type of action by another person, and they must be able to exclude less sinister explanations offered. Since they do not work in a vacuum, forensic pathologists must accumulate a tremendous amount of data from a variety of sources, evaluate the data's authenticity, and reach a determination about the mode of death after sifting fact from speculation and fantasy. Finally, they must try not to lose their objectivity, a task which may be difficult in an emotionally charged situation involving a battered baby.

The insoluble conflict between medical and legal causality hampers communication between the pathologist and the lawyer. The physician sees an effect, such as a lacerated liver, that may result from several similar but not identical causes; it may not be possible to determine, "beyond a reasonable doubt," that the laceration was caused by one particular mechanism, for example, a "punch in the belly," to the exclusion of all other mechanisms, such as falling out of a tree or being "squeezed too hard."[13]

Since one is legally, ethically, and morally prohibited from doing controlled experiments on children to determine the mechanisms, patterns, and forces involved in the creation of fatal injuries, one can only infer from animal experiments or from retrospective studies of the victims how and with what force a specific injury is produced. Therefore, the *certainty* of causality aimed at in the law is far from realized, and the pathologist's *certainty* is much diluted.

The following exchange occurred at the end of a coroner's inquest between a defense attorney and the coroner's solicitor. The defendant had "hugged" his daughter so hard that her liver was torn, and the defense tried to mitigate the action.[13]

ATTORNEY: . . . I think the testimony would not, even on a prima facie basis, support a charge of murder. . . He hugged her too hard, not to injure, not to kill. And, I think perhaps it wouldn't be inappropriate to mention that Steinbeck novel, *Of Mice and Men,* where Lennie, larger than other people, just as Mr. W. is larger than his children, just hugged them too much. They were too soft and he loved them too much.

THE COURT: (paraphrased) If a normally sane man in front of us stated that he picked up his children and he squeezed them so hard that they died, but that he did not intend to kill them, I think that the question of intent should be determined by a court.

If a grown man bear-hugs a seven-week-old child, the amount of force has to be considered with respect to the child's fragility.

For the man to admit applying that force and then to say that because he did not apply it maliciously, the Coroner should dismiss murder charges is not a proper request at this stage (of the investigation). At this stage of the proceedings, it is like pointing a gun at someone, pulling the trigger and then saying, "I did not mean it."

ATTORNEY: I submit there is a world of difference.

THE COURT: We always know massive squeezing force can kill a child.

ATTORNEY: You have to use the facts that you have here on the record, Your Honor. This child didn't die when it was squeezed. It was hugged more than once.

THE COURT: Apparently over a period of time.

ATTORNEY: And therefore, there was no reason for this boy to think that what he's doing is harming someone. You heard the wife testify, and yet, the pathologist's objective testimony shows those other rib fractures existed. Therefore, this boy didn't think that he was harming the child, because the child went on living. The child was fine. This is not a question of just squeezing the baby and killing it in your arms, and then putting it down.

THE COURT: You are asking for me to read his mind, what he was thinking. I can't do that.

THE ATTORNEY: I'm asking Your Honor, if you examine this record, there is not testimony here that would support that one person took the life of another *with malice.*

THE COURT: I say there is enough on the record to raise a question which a trial jury might have to decide . . . .

Without the clinical background, the investigator may be unable to specifically determine the "mechanism" that caused the trauma. Investigators are further hampered by child abuse laws such as the Pennsylvania "Child Abuse Act,"[8] which provides privilege to any information given by an abusing parent to a social agency. In particular, anything said to a social worker in a "stress center" will not be revealed to the police and cannot be used, for the purpose of grand jury action, to establish prior abuse. The abusing parent may choose not to talk to the coroner or medical examiner's investigator or police, and this refusal cannot, in light of the Miranda decision, be used to infer guilt or complicity in a child abuse case. This problem, the inability to divulge certain information to the homicide detectives, can severely curtail an investigation.

MECHANISMS OF TRAUMA

The trauma associated with the battered child syndrome is primarily mechanical, as contrasted with thermal or radiological; the two most commonly encountered lesions are contusions and lacerations. The basic mechanism is the same, whether the lesion is a contusion or a laceration (Fig. 20-1).

A *wound* is a disruption of the anatomical integrity of a tissue. The magnitude of force applied, plus other factors, will determine the type of wound produced. The following equation treats these factors in a semiquantitative fashion: WOUND = Energy $\times$ 1/time $\times$ 1/area $\times$ "other factors."[14]

Other factors include modifying conditions, mostly unmeasurable, such as the elasticity and plasticity of the tissue, the medium of the surrounding tissue, the inertia of any "moving" tissue, and the hydrostatic pressure involved.

Energy

The physicist defines energy (E) as mass (m) times the square of velocity (v), divided by 2: $E = \frac{1}{2} mv^2$. Here the velocity is the important factor. This is why an M-16 bullet, a small mass, that travels at a high velocity (3200 feet per second), will do more damage than a .38 caliber bullet, a much larger mass but one that travels at a much slower velocity.

Time

The shorter the period of time needed for the transfer of energy, the greater the likelihood of producing damage. For example, the

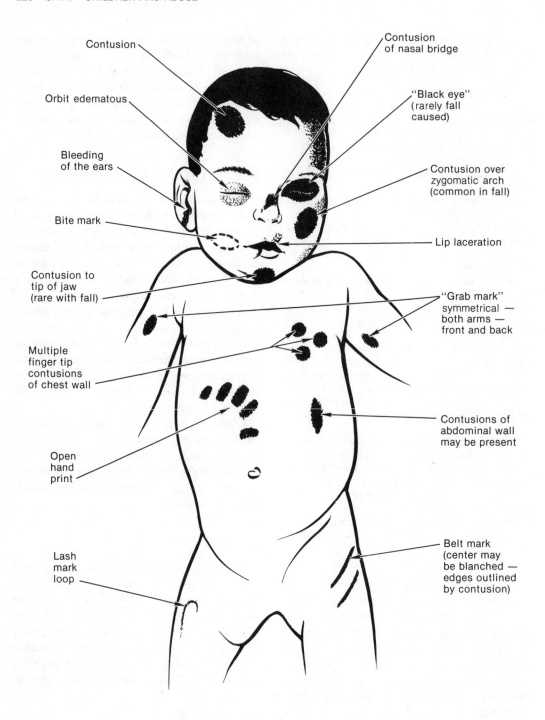

Fig. 20-1 Physical signs of child abuse.

bare-handed baseball player moves his hand in the direction the ball is moving to prolong the time of transfer of the ball's energy, to avoid soft tissue damage or broken bones. Likewise, a punch with a fist that is immediately withdrawn is more painful than one where the fist stays in place.

Area of Transfer

Since pressure is measured over a given area, a blow with a two-by-six-inch plank with a nail at its tip will have all the force concentrated at the nail point and will more greatly damage a small area than a blow with the same plank swung with the same strength without the nail. A stab wound is produced by a tremendous amount of force in a tiny area of contact.

Modifying Factors

In baseball, a full swing with a bat with the arms extended will drive a ball deeper than a full swing with the arms half-flexed and the bat choked up. The lever action is used to multiply the mechanical effect. The elasticity and plasticity of a tissue is the ability to return to its "normal" size and shape after being deformed by pressure. The less elastic and plastic the tissue, the greater is the likelihood that a laceration will result.

The inertia of a tissue means the tendency of a tissue struck by a force to move and its ability to stop moving without causing disruption of the tissue. The movement of parts of the body as a result of force being applied to them and the local stretching of tissue during acceleration and deceleration cause most of the internal injuries seen in trauma.

Hydrostatic pressure applies primarily to blood vessels in the body, although a hollow organ, such as the bladder or stomach, is also affected by this mechanism. A force transmitted through a fluid-containing tissue will force the fluid away from the area of contact

equally in all directions and frequently will cause the tissue to tear.

Common Types of Wounds

CONTUSIONS

A contusion is the rupture of small blood vessels and the spread of blood into the surrounding tissue. The force transmitted, for example, a fist, momentarily compresses the blood vessels at the point of contact, temporarily forces the blood out of the area, and sets up a fluid wave under pressure.[14] When this pressure exceeds the cohesive force of the cells forming the wall of a capillary, arteriole, or venule, the vessel ruptures. The result is the familiar "bruise," which may not be at the site of the force, but adjacent to it (Figs. 20-2, 20-3).

Contusions may be visible on the skin surface, in fat, in muscles, or on internal organs such as the lungs, liver, or kidneys (Fig. 20-4). When it is sufficiently large, a contusion is called a hematoma; the dividing line between the two terms sometimes varies with the pathologist's subjective interpretation. With the passage of time, the usual "black and blue" bruise will change to purple, green, and yellow as it is absorbed; the pathologist may be able to determine how old a bruise is by its color. Under usual circumstances, a contusion will heal with no visible formation of scar tissue.

LACERATIONS

If the force applied to a tissue is greater than its cohesive force and elasticity, the tissue tears, and a laceration is produced. This wound is often seen in a boxer whose eye is "cut." Again, the stretching of the tissue and its movement and change of direction cause a momentary strain at one point and rupture the tissue. Because the skin is composed of multiple types of tissues—epidermis, connective tissue, fat, blood vessels, nerves, glandular cells, and the like, and because each tis-

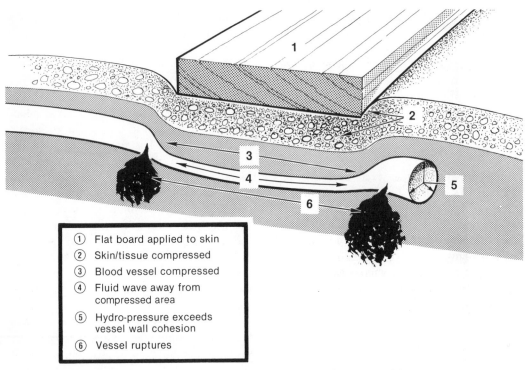

1. Flat board applied to skin
2. Skin/tissue compressed
3. Blood vessel compressed
4. Fluid wave away from compressed area
5. Hydro-pressure exceeds vessel wall cohesion
6. Vessel ruptures

Fig. 20-2 Mechanism of damage when a flat object strikes the skin.

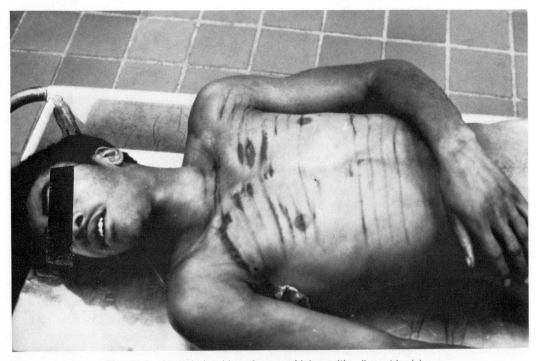

Fig. 20-3 Central blanching of areas of injury with adjacent bruising.

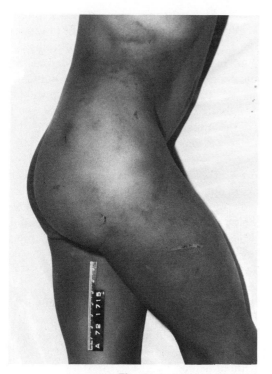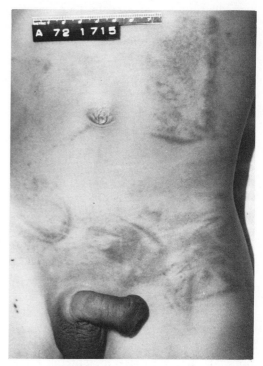

Fig. 20-4   Multiple contusions of the flank and abdominal wall.

sue has its own breaking point, often a laceration will be irregular and have strands of tissue bridging it. Sometimes the rupture of continuity may only extend deeper to a stronger layer such as the galea aponeurotica beneath the skin of the scalp.

Because the skin may be totally relaxed and may "give" when struck, the transfer of force may be prolonged. A force transmitted through the abdominal wall to the internal organs may not leave any visible contusions on the skin, but it can still lacerate or contuse the liver, spleen, or stomach and produce sufficient trauma to cause death quickly. Applied with the same energy, a kick by a boot will cause more damage than a blow with a railroad cross tie which has a greater area of contact. If the force is massive, it is irrelevant which area of the body it strikes.

ABRASIONS

An abrasion is a scrape with the top layers of the skin rubbed off. The cause may be movement of the body, such as a man falling down a rope he has just climbed and scraping his skin off, or movement of an object, such as a rope sliding quickly through a man's hands. The abraded area is a fertile field for infection.

FRACTURES

A fracture is a break in the continuity of a bone caused either by stretching the bone or by twisting and stretching the bone. For purposes of this discussion, there are three kinds of fractures:

1. Simple—no break in the skin
2. Open—a break in the skin (a laceration caused by either the tip of a broken bone being forced outward or the initial force applied on the outside)
3. Multiple—many fragments

While the mechanisms mentioned here apply, in general, to all ages, a young child presents certain characteristic anatomic differences that may diminish or accentuate the trauma. In the following discussion of trauma, these differences will be mentioned along with the adult counterpart.

HEAD

In contrast with the adult's, the young child's head is not a rigid, closed box. The fontanelles, two areas (anterior and posterior) where the bones have not yet met, allow the head to mold or change its shape at birth and usually remain open until the sixteenth and sixth months, respectively. The suture lines between the bones are coated with fibrous tissue, and the inner layer of the skull does not become bone until the age of two to three years.[15]

These factors allow the infant's head to absorb more energy than the adult's without causing trauma. The fluid wave in the cerebrospinal fluid can cause the anterior fontanelle to bulge momentarily and allow some of the energy from a blow to the head to dissipate. However, like the adult's, the child's brain is fixed in the skull only at the base, where the brain becomes the spinal cord, and by delicate bridging through the membranes around the brain, which contain the emissary veins.

When a hard enough blow is struck on the head, the force is transmitted to the brain. At the start of the acceleration, the brain will tend to move in a direction away from the blow and will stretch the small emissary veins.[16] The opposite side of the brain will be eventually stopped in its motion by the skull on the opposite side of the head, and the brain will change its direction before coming to rest.[16] At the point of maximum stretching, these bridging veins are under linear stress and, perhaps also, angular stress. They may rupture and cause subdural hemorrhage which can be fatal in a short time. Here, as in other examples, the critical moment is at the point of maximal stretching. If the brain strikes the skull with sufficient force, contusions may also result.

If a child's skull is struck with a hammer, a depression like a ping-pong ball may occur. The depression may return to its original shape, with or without fracture and with or without hemorrhage (Fig. 20-5).

Also common is a subarachnoid hemorrhage which is usually caused by rupture of the major arteries or veins on the surface of the brain. The rupture may be traumatic, with an accompanying contusion or laceration, or it may be spontaneous, secondary to a ruptured berry aneurysm (more rare in the pediatric age group) or some other vascular

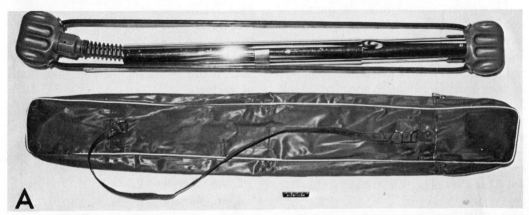

Fig. 20-5 Exercise device (A) used to strike the child in the head. Note relatively little damage on the skin (B) with extensive bleeding in the subperiostial area (C). A skull fracture can be seen (D) and there was extensive hemorrhage in and around the brain (E).

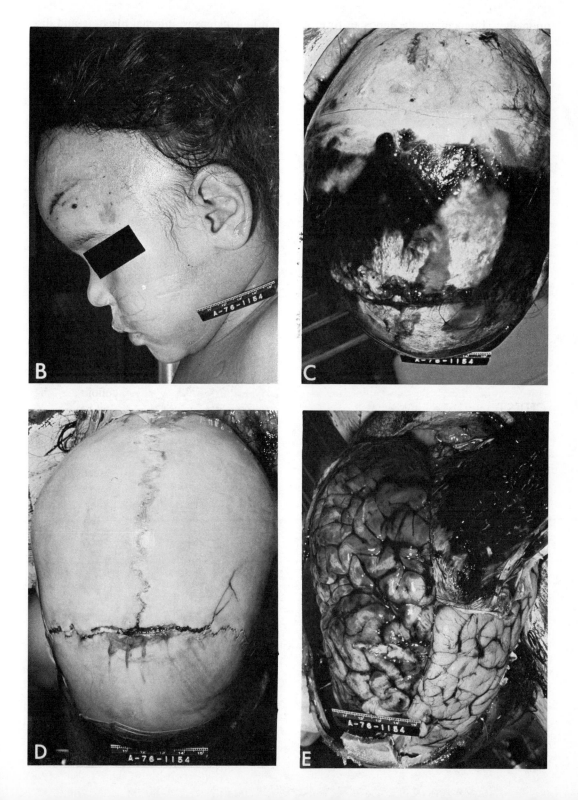

anomaly. This hemorrhage tends to form a thin film of blood which molds to the external outline of the brain and can diffuse through the ventricular system.

For the pathologist, the problem with hemorrhage is deciding if the trauma found was the result of more than one application of force. If head trauma is the only injury, it may be difficult to argue that a unilateral subdural hemorrhage is not due to a "fall." If the hemorrhage is multicentric and associated with several external lesions, particularly contusions or lacerations, or more than one abrasion, the implication is that the child either "fell" more than once after receiving an initial severe craniocerebral injury or was hit several times or "bounced" several times, down a flight of stairs or over a hillside.

Note that the same mechanism, acceleration-deceleration injury of the brain, can be caused by shaking a child hard by the body and can produce the same head lesions without any direct head trauma.

CHEST

Typically, the damage in chest trauma is the result of a combination of blows and squeezes. Many ribs may be fractured, either posteriorly where the ribs attach to the vertebrae or anteriorly where the cartilages attach to the breastbone (sternum). The ends of the broken ribs may be displaced and can perforate the lungs, the heart (rarely), or the liver. These internal injuries can cause excessive hemorrhage into the chest cavity and, if air is sucked into the chest cavity, respiratory difficulty from pneumothorax. With the exception of a pure squeeze, the chest wall will contuse more easily than the abdominal wall because the skin is closer to the semirigid ribs.

ABDOMEN

The internal organs can be traumatized from any direction, and an unmarked skin can hide extensive internal bleeding and disruption of internal organs. The areas most vulnerable are the points of attachment of an internal organ, especially at its sources of blood supply, and the points where blood vessels change direction (Fig. 20-6).

One of these areas is the middle of the superior half of the abdomen, a triangle bounded by the ribs on two sides and a line drawn through the umbilicus as the base. This triangle has several blood vessels that change direction, in particular, the branches of the celiac trunk, which terminate in the hepatic, splenic, and gastric arteries, and their branches, as well as the accompanying veins. The loop of duodenum, the ligament of Treitz, and the pancreas are in the retroperitoneal space, while the stomach and transverse colon are in the triangle in the perito-

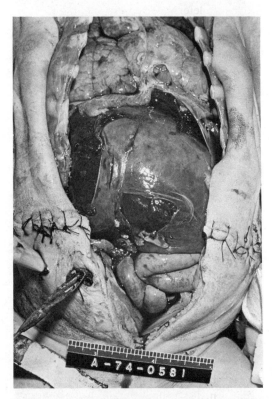

Fig. 20-6 Extensive internal bleeding and disruption of the internal organs in a case of child abuse.

neal cavity. Compression, whether prolonged, as in a hug or squeeze, or momentary, as from a blow, is the mechanism. A stretching stress of sufficient acceleration-deceleration will detach the jejunum from the ligament of Treitz, lacerate the liver, contuse the intestines or stomach, and may rupture any one of a number of blood vessels criss-crossing the area. With extensive blood loss, shock may get progressively worse, or the bleeding become so severe that collapse and death may occur within minutes. A child is more sensitive to acute blood loss than an adult.

Other direct blows, for example, a "kidney punch," may lacerate the kidney from behind and cause extensive bleeding into the surrounding space. In this case, a contusion is almost always present.

Again, it is more important for the pathologist to determine whether one blow or many caused all the damage than to find a mechanism that could explain all the lesions. A child dying of multiple internal injuries who has bruises over the entire body, especially if they are of different ages, is more likely to have been beaten than a child who has one contusion in an exposed portion of the body and internal injuries in the same area. The big problem comes when the parents allege that the child fell down a flight of steps. In this case, a careful cataloguing of *all* lesions and onsite study of the steps may resolve the issue.

Parents who battered their children have shown tremendous ingenuity in their choice of weapons. These include the open hand, fist, foot, boot (worn or used as a club), belt, baking dish, board, brick, electric cord, rope, or just about any nearby object. The lesions produced by these weapons are just as varied. Recognizing the pattern of the resultant injuries is sometimes quite easy; at other times, it is difficult or impossible. If a pattern is recognizable, the diagnosis of actual child abuse is easier.

AUTOPSY PROCEDURES

The pathologist who performs an autopsy on a child suspected of being abused must pay attention to many fine details. The autopsy must be carefully planned, and both negative and positive findings must be documented in a manner that nonmedical people can understand.

Before the autopsy is started, the pathologist should collect whatever pertinent information is available from the treating physician, the coroner's investigator, the police report, and any other medical records, especially prior x-ray films.

The child should be brought to the morgue as unchanged from the original state as possible, with the original clothing intact, unwashed, and uncleaned. In examining the clothing, the pathologist should look for contradictions. A clean nightshirt in the presence of vomiting or a clean, dry diaper in the presence of diarrhea may suggest that the body has been tampered with. Often the parents of a dead child will wash and clean the body before taking it to the hospital. The clothing should be checked carefully for possible correlation with any marks on the skin, and the presence or absence of stains on all articles of clothing should be noted.

In every suspected case of child abuse, complete postmortem x-ray films of the body should be taken. These films should be read by a competent pediatric radiologist. Often, the signature of child battering is clearly seen on x-ray films.

Because children are vulnerable to a rapidly developing microbial growth, appropriate specimens should be taken for culturing, even if the interval between death and autopsy is long. As a minimum, the examiner should take samples of blood, lung, tonsil, and spleen. Other specimens such as ear contents, cerebrospinal fluid, urine, or skin should be taken if indicated by the clinical history or gross anatomical findings.

The external examination must be meticulous; each scratch, scrape, and bruise must be measured, positioned, and sketched. Although color slides and black-and-white pictures should be taken at every stage of the autopsy, a diagrammatic sketch is useful for defining any pattern of injury. The pathologist must be careful not to miss bite marks, increasingly found in these cases,[17] and, in particular, should look for bruises on the inner surfaces of the lip and the neck and for parallel bruises, which suggest pinch marks, on the front and back of the chest, arms, and legs.

The internal examination should be designed to demonstrate any injury seen and to exclude any congenital, degenerative, or infectious cause of death. Therefore, statements of negative findings are as significant as positive findings.

If head trauma is suspected, the head and brain should be examined last, after all the congestion is drained. The pathologist should note any bruising and look for bleeding into the skin and muscles of the scalp. If any fractures are present, they should be photographed before the skull is removed. The decision to cut the brain immediately or to fix it first depends on the pathologist's ease with one method or the other.

In the case of chest trauma, one of the accepted methods should be used to check carefully for pneumothorax. Any rib fractures, lung and heart bruises, any anomalies, signs of infection, and other trauma should be noted. The negative observations may be just as important as positive findings for making an accurate diagnosis.

The abdominal organs are best dissected en bloc, except when the trauma is obvious. All bruises, cuts, and scrapes should be viewed with an eye towards an estimation of age and with special emphasis on determining whether the bruises are of different ages. This applies to the skin, musculoskeletal structures, and any internal organs.

The gastric contents should be retained and an estimate made of the time interval between the last meal and death. While this approach has severe limitations, it may be used to estimate the time of death, especially in conjunction with other factors.

A bone marrow sample should be taken and carefully evaluated to be certain that the child does not have any signs of leukemia or any other blood dyscrasia that causes "easy bruising."

With all the data collected, with the radiological, histological, and gross findings reviewed and compared with the history given by the parents, stark inconsistencies may become apparent. When confronted with these inconsistencies, many parents will volunteer the "true" facts. In any case, the pathologist should be able to confidently make the following statements:

- The child did not "bruise easily."

- No natural disease process could cause the injuries seen.

- The anatomical and/or pathological findings are not consistent with the history given by the parents.

- There are other possible explanations for the injuries.

- Certain patterns of injuries can be explained with greater certainty, especially if a weapon is found that physically matches the traumatic lesions.

PREPARATION FOR COURT

Once the cause and mode of death are certified by the coroner, a preliminary hearing and an indictment usually follow, and the implicated adult or adults are charged with homicide. At this point, pathologists must understand the legal procedures to know what is expected of them.

Obtaining a Conviction

In order to convict a person of any crime, the state must prove the following:

- The *actus reus*—that a crime was committed by the suspect
- The *mens rea*—that the defendant committing the crime did so knowing that what he did was "wrong"
- The *corpus delecti*—the body of evidence to prove *actus reus*

Assuming that the pathologist can state without reservation that the child did, in fact, die from the actions of another person and not from an accident or some strange and exotic disease, the major portion of the *corpus delecti* in a case of child abuse is the victim's body. Other witnesses will give testimony about the circumstances of the death, and the totality of the evidence will influence the trier of fact in reaching a verdict. The medical testimony bridges the gap between the medical and legal approaches to child abuse.

Legal Response

The legal approach to the battered child syndrome has been to write legislation. Current legislation not only seeks to curb child abuse but also attempts to reach this goal with the best interests of the child in mind. Unfortunately, this concern has not always been the case. At common law the child's interests were hardly acknowledged. Parental rights dominated all other concerns. Even during the twentieth century, the court held that the parents' right over their children would "transcend property rights."[5] Only if the parents grossly abused their rights would the state intervene under the principle of *parens patriae*. Unfortunately, in a Dickensian atmosphere where child labor was commonplace, it was highly unlikely that the state would regard abuse as severe enough to warrant intervention. Not until 1972 did the court decide that the parents' right to care, custody, and control over their children was no longer absolute.[18,19]

In 1875 the New York Society for the Prevention of Cruelty to Children was formed. Although this was a milestone for the advancement of child welfare, child abuse persisted with few deterrents until 1962 when Kempe and his colleagues aroused public concern with the phrase "battered child syndrome." At that time, the stage was being set for a youth-oriented decade. Abuse of many kinds fostered violent rebellion. Not surprisingly, the public demanded aid for this defenseless minority.

Reporting Statutes

Help came in the form of reporting statutes. In 1963 the United States Children's Bureau proposed a model reporting law.[20] By 1967 all 50 states had laws that mandated the reporting of child abuse. It was believed that these laws would direct the attention of social service agencies to families who needed help. In an effort to encourage reporting, immunity from criminal or civil liability was provided for those whose reports were filed in good faith. Penalties were set forth for those who "knowingly and willfully" failed to report.

Despite good intentions, the reporting statutes failed to promote much of anything. Many hesitated to report what they regarded as evidence of child abuse because they feared they would be initiating criminal proceedings on the basis of little more than intuition. In fact, child protection hearings are civil in nature. In addition, it is not very difficult to suspect child abuse when the child's story and the parent's story do not match or the parent's story is not supported by physical evidence. Nevertheless, physicians had been trained to treat physical injuries. Few were interested in the family environment of the patients. There was already enough paperwork from Medicare, Blue Cross, and Blue Shield. Why look for more?

Thus, not many physicians took these statutes seriously. However, in 1976, as a result of the decision in *Londeros* v. *Flood*,[21] their attitudes shifted. The court decided that a physician who failed to report a suspected case of child abuse could be held civilly liable for subsequent damages to the same child.

This ruling might have been more significant if the reporting statutes had set forth explicit guidelines. However, it is difficult to find someone guilty of failing to report a nebulous disease. Originally, reports were required of children who suffered from "nonaccidental injury." Later the court recognized that child abuse may be a series of unexplained injuries.[22] The Federal Child Abuse Prevention and Treatment Act[23] includes neglect, sexual molestation, and mental injury in its definition of these injuries. It is well and good to set forth these definitions, but realistically, there are no true guidelines to apply. In the case *In re Stacey*,[24] the court declared that there is "no fixed standard for neglect, so each case must be judged on its own particular facts . . . ." If a child came in with nonaccidental bruises sufficient to form blood clots, it might be argued that this child suffered from intentional physical abuse. However, the United States Supreme Court held that physical beatings by public teachers, resulting in similar injury, were not constitutionally prohibited.[25] It is apparent that without more specific guidelines, reporting is an unenforceable mandate.

Procedures for Recognition and Prevention

Despite the loose terminology, procedures were set forth to recognize and curb child abuse. Once a suspected case of abuse had been filed, a specific agency became responsible for determining the validity of the report. Many states now have central registries of reported cases so that abusing families who move will not be lost in the shuffle. Examinations are made of each injury, and photographs and x-ray films are taken. Any police reports or relevant psychiatric reports on the family should be included in the file. If the child's life is in danger, the court will issue a protective custody order to remove the child from the home.

Most importantly, Congress provided that a guardian *ad litem* represent the interests of abused and neglected children in judicial proceedings. Although the concept of a guardian *ad litem* is not new, the role has changed. Originally appointed by the court to represent that child as a defendant, the guardian now preserves and protects the child's interest in suits where the child's parent might be a defendant. Although the Model Child Protection Act[26] suggests the need for an attorney in this position, the federal regulations do not.[27] In Pennsylvania, the court has required that counsel be provided at all stages of any proceeding under the state's Juvenile Act.[28-30]

Many states have gone so far as to require counsel for indigent parents in child protective proceedings, despite the civil nature of these hearings. It has been argued that the mere intrusion of agency supervision and the proceedings themselves are sufficient infringements of the parent's liberty to warrant counsel.

Role of Attorneys and Trauma Teams

As lawyers enter the scene, the process becomes more complex. Whereas social service agencies once argued their own cases, now everyone walks in with an attorney. This does not even the scale. It merely complicates an already troubled system. Unfortunately, attorneys appointed by the courts are often fresh out of law school. They have little or no training in child abuse legislation and much less awareness of the psychological and physiological overtones that the abuse and possible removal from the home will have on the child and the family. Unbeknownst to the attorney, most abusing parents lack any criminal intent.[31] Therefore, rehabilitative services rather than punishment are preferable to protect the child. Most probably, however, the attorney will be unable to accurately assess the situation and unable to present the best interests of the child. Just proving that child abuse exists will force the attorney to assume the role of a prosecutor and, therefore, present a narrow interpretation of the situation.

The child, meanwhile, remains a pawn. Children who are too young to speak for themselves have no one who will speak for them. The attorneys, social workers, physicians, and hospitals have opposing approaches to the problem. In order to remove the child from the home, there must be friends to support the child, available housing, and a suitable guardian able to assume parental responsibilities. Too often, the foster home is worse than the child's original environment. Then, of course, there is the problem of how long to remove the child. Permanent psychological injury may result from bouncing children in and out of their original homes.

In an effort to alleviate some of these problems, trauma teams have been organized which include members from the medical, legal, social work, and institutional communities. Perhaps common discussions will lead to balanced solutions.

The attorney's role in these teams is to determine whether sufficient evidence exists to meet the burden of proof. This is the attorney's most difficult task. While a petition may be brought on the basis of a *res ipsa* standard, a higher standard must be met to prove the case at the hearing. At this time, the attorney must establish by "clear and

convincing" evidence that harm to the child occurred as a direct result of parental unfitness.

Available Evidence

Evidence is almost nonexistent in cases of child abuse. Other than the injury itself, most evidence is circumstantial. It is not easy to prove a case on the basis of circumstantial evidence, especially if the child is too fearful or physically injured to speak. Rarely are there witnesses. And those who do exist are reluctant to tell their story. In addition, evidentiary rules tend to favor the suspect and hamper thorough investigation.

As stated earlier, a protective custody hearing occurs in civil court. Homicide, however, is a criminal matter. Consequently, cases of child abuse that result in the death of the child must be brought in criminal court. As homicide is a more serious offense, the burden of proof increases accordingly. To convict someone of beating a child to death, the inexperienced, busy young attorney, who has little more than circumstantial evidence, must prove guilt beyond a reasonable doubt. It is apparent that much reliance must be placed on the pathologist's report, which may or may not be as unequivocal as the prosecutor would wish.

Establishing a Defense

The defense, however, is on much firmer ground. The main thrust, as in any criminal case, is to create doubt—any small amount of doubt—as to the guilt of the defendant. This may be done in several ways. First, the defense may argue that the child did not die as a result of being beaten: "Those bruises all over the body are an external manifestation of leukemia." The boy was not placed in a pot of boiling water but "accidentally spilled it on himself while the defendant mother was chasing the younger brother." The girl was not beaten by a wooden plank, instead she "fell down a flight of stairs." Whatever the explanation, if the cause of death can be attributed to an accident, there is no child abuse and, therefore, no conviction.

An alternative position is to argue lack of intent. A client who is declared insane or who acted under the influence of drugs or alcohol may receive a reduced sentence.

In a more sophisticated manner, the defense attorney may try to prevent the prosecution from introducing any of the gruesome details as evidence. Since few juries or judges can hear a tale of torture and horror and not recoil from it, the less the jury hears, the better. Evidentiary principles may enable the defense to prevent all photographs and color slides from being introduced into evidence. The success of this maneuver will vary from one jurisdiction to another and from judge to judge. If the case is really gruesome, the defense attorney should keep the pathologist on the stand for as short a time as possible.

Pathologists will be most helpful to a case if they can give a strong opinion backed by scientific conclusions. This is where a painstakingly detailed autopsy protocol will be of value. Information drawn from the autopsy notes can refresh the memory so that an opinion can be delivered in an objective, concise fashion. Often, the strength of the testimony will be enhanced if pathologists admit, when they lack sufficient evidence, that they cannot answer a specific question. Above all, the pathologists' testimony will be most helpful if they can articulate their findings in a manner that is understandable to the layman jury.

Conclusion

As can be seen, the pathologist and attorney are the final actors in a case of child abuse. Only after the incident is reported, the investigation is undertaken, the trauma team reaches a decision, and the system fails will the attorney and pathologist meet for the final reckoning. Unfortunately, they must realize, along with their colleagues involved in the "battered child" story, that the physician, psychiatrist, social worker, investigators, and others will take greater pleasure in preventing the tragic deed than in punishing someone after the fact.

REFERENCES

1. Caffey J: Multiple fractures in long bones of infants suffering from chronic subdural hematoma. *Am J Roentogenol Radium Ther* **56**:163–173, 1946.

2. Woolley PV Jr, Evans WA Jr: Significance of skeletal lesions in infants resembling those of traumatic origin. *JAMA* **158**:539–543, 1955.

3. Kempe CH, et al: The battered child syndrome. *JAMA* **181**:17–24, 1962.

4. *Eyre vs Shaftsbury,* 24 Eng Rep 659 (Ch 1722).

5. *Danton vs James,* 107 Kansas 729, 735, 193, p 307, 310, 1920.

6. Pennsylvania PL 142, June 11, 1879.

7. Paulson M, et al: Child abuse reporting laws: some legislative history. *Georgetown Law Rev* **34**: 179, 1966.

8. Child Protective Services Law, Chapter 17 §2201–2224 PL 1975, November 26.

9. Allegheny County Coroner's Office, Coroner's Inquest Docket 13, June 1969.

10. Allegheny County Coroner's Office, Coroner's Inquest Docket 689–171, September 1971.

11. Allegheny County Coroner's Office, Coroner's Inquest Docket 94, January 1976.

12. Allegheny County Coroner's Office, Coroner's Inquest Docket 152, October 1969.

13. Allegheny County Coroner's Office, Coroner's Inquest Docket 278, July 1970.

14. Francisco J: *The Pathology of Trauma.* Handout, University of Tennessee, Memphis, 1971, p 8.

15. Adelson L: *Pathology of Homicide.* Springfield, Ill, Charles C Thomas Publisher, 1974, p 425.

16. Lindenburg R: Mechanical injuries of brain and meninges, in Fisher R, Spitz W (eds): *The Medical-Legal Investigation of Death,* ed 2. Springfield, Ill, Charles C Thomas, Publisher, 1980, pp 420–469.

17. Sims M, et al, quoted by Cameron, JM: The battered child syndrome. *Leg Med Ann,* 1974, pp 123–134.

18. *Wisconsin vs Yoder,* 406 US 205, 1972.

19. *Poe vs Gerstein,* 417 US 218, 1972.

20. *The Abused Child: Principles and Suggested Language for Legislation on Reporting of the Physically Abused Child,* bulletin. US Children's Bureau, 1963.

21. *Londeros vs Flood,* 17 Cal 3d 399, 131 Cal Rept 69, 551, P2d 398, 1976.

22. *In re K D E,* 210 N W 2d 907, 910, S D 1973.

23. 42 USC § 5103 (2), 1976.

24. *In re Stacey,* 16 IL App 3d 179, 183, 365 N E 2d 634, 1973.

25. *Ingraham vs Wright,* 430 US 651, 1977.

26. Model Child Protection Act § 25 (a), August 1977 draft.

27. 45 C F R 1340.3-3 (d) (7), 1976.

28. *In re LaRue,* 244 Pa Super Ct 218, 366 A 2d 1271, 1976.

29. *In re Clouse,* 244 Pa Super Ct, 396, 368 A 2d 780, 1976.

30. *Stapleton vs Dauphin County Child Care Service,* 288 Pa Super Ct 371, 324 A 2d 562, 1974.

31. Steele BF, Pollock CB: A psychiatric study of parents who abuse infants and small children, in Helfer RE, Kempe CH (eds): *The Battered Child,* ed 2. Chicago, University of Chicago Press, 1968.

21

MANAGEMENT OF CHILD ABUSE

Norman S. Ellerstein, M.D.

Child maltreatment is one of the major problems affecting the physical, psychological, and emotional well-being of children in the United States. It is estimated that between one and three percent of the children in this country are, in some way, abused or neglected, including up to 4,000 deaths annually.[1] There is no other single health or environmental factor that exacts such a devastating toll on this country's youth.

Child maltreatment, a term that encompasses both abuse and neglect, has occurred since recorded time and has been present in most Eastern and Western societies. Maltreatment has ranged from infanticide to mutilation to child labor and prostitution to the intrafamilial physical and emotional abuse of children that is prevalent in this country.[2] The medical profession did not become active in the recognition and treatment of abuse and neglect until the second half of the twentieth century. Prior to 1960, only a few articles describing abused children appeared in the medical literature.[3-5] The 1962 article by Kemp and associates[6] drew national attention to the problem. Since that time, the involvement of health professionals,

as well as many other professionals, has steadily grown.

Historically, a variety of injustices has been done to children. Religious, political, economic, and psychopathological reasons have caused enormous suffering through the ages. The discussion in this chapter will be limited to the intrafamilial types of abuse and neglect that are most common in modern society. These include physical abuse and a variety of types of neglect. Emotional or psychological abuse always accompanies the physically demonstrable forms of maltreatment, but frequently they occur without physical signs. Sexual abuse of children is discussed in another chapter.

The cause of child maltreatment has been attributed to many different factors. Certain characteristics of an individual child may make that child more "abuseable" than another child.[7] If an infant was born prematurely, has physical handicaps, is hyperactive, has a personality or temperament different than the parent, or in some way does not meet the parent's expectations, that infant appears to be at an increased risk of being maltreated.[7-9] Individual psychological factors in the parents have traditionally been implicated as causative elements.[10] A parent who was reared in an abusive environment or has been surrounded by a life of violence might have lacked an appropriate role model for developing nonviolent parenting skills. Abuse of drugs or alcohol, absence of strong family bonds, individual mental illness, and lack of education in "mothercrafting" have all been mentioned as parental factors in etiology. The environment in which the family lives is frequently pointed to as the underlying cause for child abuse. It is believed that the greater the stress upon the family, the more likely it is that abuse will occur.[11] Stresses such as poverty, unemployment, poor housing, exposure to violence, and adolescent pregnancy are social issues that many feel must be addressed before the incidence of child abuse will be reduced. Still other issues such as the tolerance of corporal punishment and the controversy of the parent's rights versus the child's rights are perceived as problems that must be eliminated before a significant decrease in maltreatment can be expected. Some maltreating families exhibit many of the individual and social characteristics seen in abusive families. Others have none of the typical traits, and the etiology remains obscure. There does not seem to be a single causational theory which is operational for all, or even most, cases of child maltreatment.

The purpose of this chapter is not to explore the many etiological theories of abuse or to present a discussion of the very important issue of prevention. The chapter is designed to teach the medical practitioner how to recognize the child who might be abused or neglected. Recognition, of course, is only the first step in the helping process. Therefore, a discussion of the initial management of the maltreated child will follow. This includes the reporting process, presentation of the facts to the parents, and initial decision making about the child's disposition. It is assumed that the reader is a health professional who may come in contact with suspected cases of abuse in an emergency department or other similar setting.

RECOGNITION

The first step in recognizing that a child is maltreated is to acknowledge that the problem of maltreatment exists. To some individuals, the thought of parents injuring their own children is so abhorent that they may prevent themselves from even considering abuse as a diagnosis. The examiner who does not maintain a high index of suspicion will never recognize a case of abuse or neglect. Abuse is not the kind of diagnosis that the parent accompanying the child will suggest as a possibility. Therefore, the examiner is the one who must keep this diagnosis on a potential list of differential diagnoses. Some investigators feel that abuse may be present in up to 10 percent of children in certain age groups who come to emergency departments.[12] Therefore, maltreatment should not be a diagnosis of exclusion, but rather a common pediatric disorder that can be recognized in the hospital emergency department, the private practitioner's office, and the school.

Physical Indicators

Physical indicators of abuse are among the most easily recognizable signs that allow the examiner to make a diagnosis of maltreatment. Physical abuse tends to cause the largest variety of injuries.

ACCIDENT OR ABUSE

When evaluating a case of childhood trauma, the examiner must ask whether the trauma was caused by accident or intention. To determine if the injury was other than accidental, several additional questions must be answered. Is the injury an isolated one, or does it appear along with other traumatic lesions? If there are other injuries present, is it likely that all the injuries were caused by a single traumatic incident? For example, in an automobile accident, multiple trauma may occur, but it is usually obvious to the examiner what mechanisms caused the injuries. In a case of abuse a child may have an isolated lesion on the face and another one on the buttocks or arms. It would be unlikely that these geographically separated injuries occured by an easily explainable accidental mechanism.

A second issue is the different ages or stages of healing of the injuries. If a child has injuries at different stages of healing, a situation that indicates that they occurred at different chronological times, then a single episode, which was explained historically by the parents, would not adequately account for the various lesions. Therefore, fractures, bruises, or burns at different stages of healing are cardinal signs of abuse. Another major criterion used to test the accident-versus-abuse hypothesis is the developmental ability of the child. The question must be asked, "Is the child developmentally mature enough to have self-initiated the injury"? That is, could the unaided child have become involved in a situation that could have resulted in an accidental injury? The two-month-old cannot "crawl" to the stairs to fall down them. The 18-month-old could not have pedalled a tricycle into the street because 18-month-old children cannot pedal tricycles. Nonambulatory infants cannot get themselves into situations where they can climb to precarious heights or run fast enough to collide with objects so severely that they are seriously injured. In these types of situations, adults must be present to be instrumental, or at least neglectful, in producing the injury.

There is still another major principle that the physician must apply when evaluating trauma. It is the physician's decision, not the social worker's or policemen's or lawyer's, as to the mechanical likelihood that the accident happened the way the parent described it. The physician is the one who must decide

whether a fall from a certain height could produce a force powerful enough to cause the injury the child has. For example, it is uncommon for an infant or child who falls off a couch less than 63 centimeters (25 inches) high to sustain a head injury severe enough to cause serious brain contusion.[13] There are certain patterns of burns and bruises that cannot happen accidentally. The following present some common injuries of physically abused children.

SKIN INJURIES

Skin injuries are among the most common and easily recognized manifestations of maltreatment of children.[14] *Bruises* are by far the most common physical signs of intentional trauma (Fig. 21-1). Abusive bruises can be recognized by applying the principles discussed earlier: that is, bruises in different phases of healing, bruises that are hard to

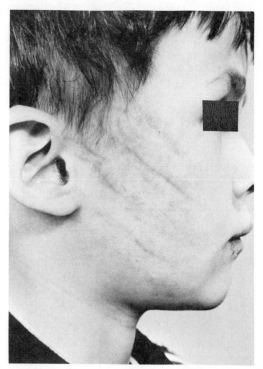

Fig. 21-1 The *ecchymoses* on this boy's face are representative of the fingers of the hand that struck him.

explain mechanically or by the developmental age of the child, and bruises that are geographically separated and, therefore, unlikely to have occurred by accident. One type of bruise in particular, *loop marks,* is pathognomonic of intentional injury (Fig. 21-2). It occurs frequently in children who receive excessive corporal punishment and is one of the only injuries that, by its configuration alone, is definitely diagnostic of intentional trauma.

Burns are commonly caused intentionally.[15] Feldman et al. reported that 28.6 percent of tap-water burns in children were the result of abuse.[16] These were commonly immersion injuries in which a part of the body, such as the buttocks, legs, or hands, was forcibly immersed into hot water. The pattern of the burn, showing a typical "stocking" or "glove" distribution without associated splash or satellite burns, is indicative of intentional scalding[17,18] (Figs. 21-3, 21-4). Other burns caused by implements may brand the child

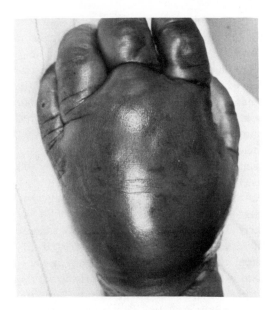

Fig. 21-3 Forcible immersion of the boy's left hand into hot tap-water caused the massive enlargement representative of a second degree *burn.*

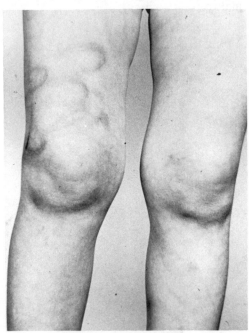

Fig. 21-2 The *loop marks* on this child's right leg are caused by blows from a folded flexible object, such as an electric cord or clothesline.

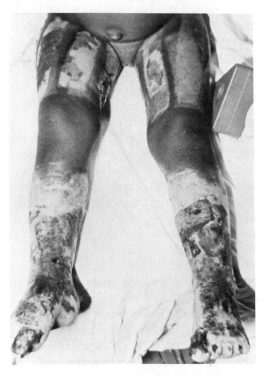

Fig. 21-4 The *burns* on this girl's lower legs are in a "stocking" distribution. She was forcibly immersed in hot water. Graft donor sites are seen on her thighs.

with the characteristic shape of the hot instrument.

Another dermatological finding pathognomonic of intentional trauma is the human *bite mark*. When bite marks are found on the skin of a child, they cannot be assumed to be accidental. Forensic dentists and pathologists may be able to identify the attacker by analyzing the bite mark. The size of the arch, tooth size, and other data can frequently be used to identify the specific assailant.[19,20] Because the skin is so easily examined, the clinician should always perform a thorough external examination of the child. The etiology of other injuries that the child has may remain obscure until they are viewed in the context of cutaneous signs that are suggestive or pathognomonic of child maltreatment.

HEAD TRAUMA

Head trauma accounts for the majority of disability and death associated with physical abuse of children. Much of the long-term sequelae of mental and developmental retardation of abused children can be attributed to brain injury. Serious brain injury is frequently the result of a single violent act; often it occurs in a child who has been battered before.[21-23] Any serious head trauma in a child less than one year of age should be evaluated for the possibility of abuse. In general, infants in this age group are unable to self-initiate accidents that would cause brain injury. They cannot run fast enough, climb high enough, and create enough force to seriously injure themselves without an adult being instrumental in the trauma. In addition to a single violent act, some children are injured by shaking. This causes the head to experience the forces of rapid acceleration and deceleration that cause stress injuries to the vessels within the brain and subsequent bleeding. This injury is referred to as "the whiplash shaken infant syndrome."[24] Any head injury in an infant should immediately arouse suspicion and prompt further studies such as a skeletal survey for other fractures

and an exploration of family dynamics. Special anatomical features in infants, such as poor muscular development of the neck and pliable cranial bone, make them particularly susceptible to serious brain injury. They are also completely dependent on adults and are, therefore, vulnerable to injury from the action of those adults.

EYE INJURIES

Frequently accompanying head trauma, but also occurring independently, are eye injuries. Since the head is a common site of the attack,[21] the eyes are frequently injured. There may be isolated eye trauma;[25] but more commonly the eyes are affected when there is intracranial bleeding, skull fracture, or a direct blow to the face. The presence of retinal hemorrhages in an infant should prompt evaluation of the infant's central nervous system.[26,27] Any traumatic eye or periorbital lesion in a nonambulatory child should arouse suspicion of possible maltreatment.

BONY FRACTURES

Bony fractures have long been associated with physical child abuse.[3,4,6] Since traditional radiological technique can graphically demonstrate the majority of fractures, this type of injury has been very useful in establishing tangible evidence of abuse in children. X-ray films can serve to date the fracture and, thereby, document that injuries in a particular child may have occurred at different chronological times (Fig. 21-5). Since this feature is one of the cardinal signs of physical abuse of children, radiological examination is extremely important in the evaluation of a child who is suspected of being abused. Any infant or young child suspected of being physically abused should have a radiological survey of the long bones, ribs, spine, skull, pelvis, and hands and feet. In addition to multiple fractures at different states of healing, another pathognomonic finding is epiphyseal-metaphyseal fractures in infants

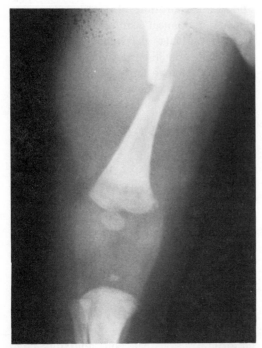

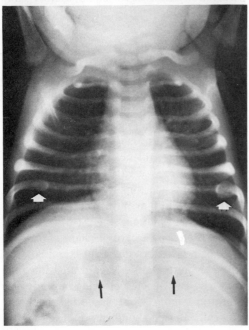

Fig. 21-5 A. A *fractured femur* in this young infant led the examiner to order a complete skeletal survey. B. These four healing *rib fractures* were then identified. The fresh femur fracture and old rib fractures in infancy are virtually diagnostic of abuse.

(Fig. 21-6). This type of injury is seldom seen other than in battered children. Even though other injuries, such as those to brain or eyes, may cause more permanent damage than fractures, bony fractures and their radiological representation are one of the most accepted and best documented pieces of evidence in cases of abuse. Therefore, they should be diligently searched for in all suspected cases.

INJURIES TO THE ORAL STRUCTURES

Other injuries may be seen less frequently. These include injuries to the oral structures. Torn frenula, fractured teeth and jaws, and lacerations of the tongue and other oral structures are usually caused by blows to the mouth and face.[28,29] Tears of the frenula, specifically the labial frenula, are sometimes caused when spoons or bottles are forcibly shoved into the infant's mouth in an attempt to facilitate feeding.[28] A parent may be frustrated with the infant's crying or slowness of the feeding process, and, in an attempt to quiet the infant and speed up the feeding, the bottle or utensil is forced into the mouth tearing the frenulum. This injury does not occur accidentally in the nonambulatory infant.

ABDOMINAL INJURIES

Injuries to the abdominal structures are caused by blows to the abdomen or back or by sudden acceleration and deceleration of the body which cause shearing forces that affect the abdominal organs and vessels.[30-32]

Injuries to any abdominal organ may occur, but especially characteristic of child abuse is the duodenal hematoma.[33] This injury is caused when the duodenum is compressed against the spine, and a hematoma develops in the wall of the intestine, causing the classic signs of upper gastrointestinal obstruction. In a child who is suspected of being abused and who is vomiting, traumatic duodenal hematoma must be considered as a diagnosis. Injuries to the kidneys, liver, spleen, pancreas, and other parts of the

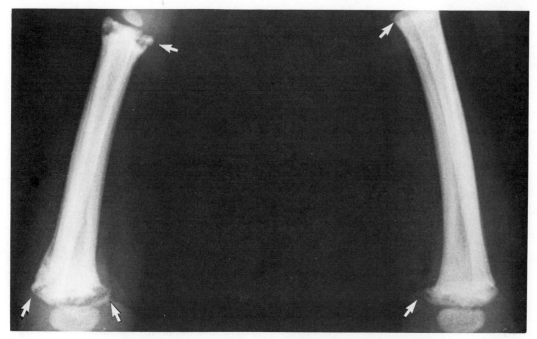

Fig. 21-6   The x-rays of the lower legs of this 20- month-old child demonstrate classic *epiphyseal- metaphyseal injuries*, also called traumatic metaphysitis or metaphyseal chip fractures. Most commonly, these are caused by shaking and twisting.

gastrointestinal tract, including the stomach, have also been reported in physically abused children.[21,32,34-36] Thoracic injuries also occur in maltreated children but at a much lower incidence than abdominal injury. Thoracic injuries may range from trauma to the external chest to fractured ribs with underlying pulmonary contusion.[37]

PATTERN OF INJURIES

In addition to the single injury, which may or may not be characteristic of abuse, the pattern of multiple injuries may be helpful in making a diagnosis. If the child has multiple visits to the emergency department for serious trauma, one must question why this child is vulnerable to repeated trauma. It is important not only to examine the child and take a careful history but also to review any available medical records. If the child has been to the same emergency facility or clinic before, it is important to note if there were previous suspicious injuries, evidence of

growth failure, or complaints relating to behavioral or psychological problems. Then the child's current injury can be seen in the context of a pattern of repeated trauma or other medical visits that may be manifestations of child maltreatment.

Indicators of Neglect

Physical abuse is not the only form of maltreatment that may be recognized in the emergency department. Child neglect may also precipitate visits for emergency medical care.

POISONING

One of the most common manifestations of neglect is accidental poisoning. Multiple visits to an emergency department for repeated ingestions of medication or dangerous chemicals may indicate a neglect of supervision or safety.[11] The improper storage of medicines and household chemicals (furni-

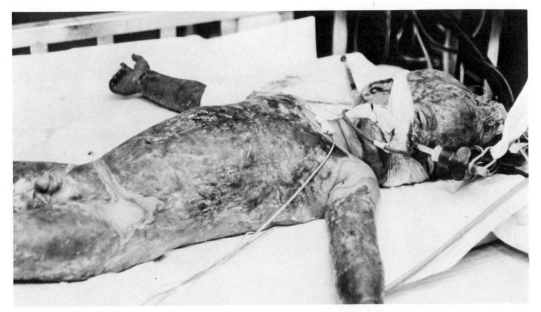

Fig. 21-7   This 2-year-old boy has third degree *burns* over 90 percent of his body. This was a "preventable" accident which happened because of *supervisional neglect.* It should not be assumed that neglect is a less serious problem than abuse.

ture polish, lubricants, lighter fluids, paint, and so forth) represents safety neglect in the home. Factors that exist in families who abuse their children also exist in home situations in which multiple ingestions occur. Most of these factors are related to environmental and family stresses.[38] "Accidental" ingestions may also be manifestations of supervisional neglect. That is, the caretaker is not adequately supervising the child, and, therefore, the child can "get into" household substances that may be dangerous. These facts do not mean that every child who experiences an accidental ingestion is neglected. However, children who have had multiple accidental poisonings should prompt the examiner to question the adequacy of the parents in supervising the children's behavior and providing a safe environment for them.

PREVENTABLE ACCIDENTS

Another manifestation of supervisional neglect may be "preventable" accidents (Fig. 21-7). These are accidents that could have

been avoided if the child were in a more controlled situation. Obviously, not all accidents are predictable or preventable. However, leaving a five-month-old infant unattended where the infant may roll off the furniture and become injured is an example of an injury caused by a preventable accident. Multiple preventable accidents usually occur in infants and young children who require the closest supervision by their parents. Occasionally, children are reported to be "accident-prone." There are children who are more active than others and who do tend to suffer more "accidents" than others. However, parents must be able to appreciate the level of mobility and the explorative nature of their child and take measures to prevent injury. The child who comes to the emergency department repeatedly for burns, fractures, head trauma, and so on must be suspected of having parents who are less than attentive to their child's potential for accidents. However, one must be cautious and not falsely accuse parents of neglectful behavior. "True" accidents do occur in children of all ages. It is the pattern and number of accidents that may indicate the possibility of neglect.

OTHER SIGNS

Other signs of neglect may be evident. A child's clothes may smell of urine or feces. A child may be grossly underweight. Skin infections, numerous insect bites, animal bites, or other signs of poor hygiene may be present on the patient or the patient's siblings. If any of these are found, one should not immediately assume that the child is being physically neglected; one should ask why the child is in this condition. If the answer is not satisfactory, the family and home situation should be explored, and a report for possible neglect might be indicated. The examiner should not confuse poverty or inability to meet middle-class standards with gross physical neglect. However, every child is entitled to a minimum of cleanliness and freedom from infection.

Behavioral Indicators

THE CHILD'S BEHAVIOR

There are other indications of child maltreatment that may be evident in the emergency department. These are not specific injuries or accidents but certain behaviors that may subtly indicate that the child has been maltreated. That is, the child may be in the emergency department for any reason, abuse related or not, and the child's behavior may be characteristic of an abused child. If an injured child does not turn to the accompanying parent for comfort for pain, and if the child appears to be more comfortable in the presence of the health personnel than in the presence of the parent, these behaviors should be recognized by the emergency department personnel as abnormal. A child who has not received comfort and support at home may not turn to the parents for this support while being treated for an injury in the emergency department. Another classic

behavior is the pseudocatatonic state: children will remain, without complaint, in almost any position in which they are placed. If, upon discharge from the emergency department, children appear fearful of returning home with their parents or indicate that they would prefer to stay at the hospital, these communications are obviously abnormal and must be viewed with suspicion.

THE PARENT'S BEHAVIOR

It is not only the child's behavior that should be observed; the parent's behavior is also important. The interactions between the parent and the child and between the parent and the health care provider can offer helpful clues to maltreatment. If the parent does not offer comfort and support to the child or leaves a young child alone on a precarious examining table, suspicion should be aroused. Furthermore, if the parent is not willing to provide very much information to the examiner or is defensive when questioned about particular injuries or past medical problems, the examiner must question why this is so. Why would a parent whose child is suffering be unwilling to offer needed medical information? Other behavior may be more blatant. The parent may leave the hospital before the child's treatment is completed. Certainly this abandonment of the child in the emergency department requires referral to the child protection authorities. If, in the course of seeking medical care for the injured child, the parent left other young children at home unattended, emergency department personnel should suggest that the mother immediately obtain care for the children at home. If the mother indicates that these young children "will be okay by themselves," one must question their usual level of parental supervision.

REPORTING

Once it is recognized that a child may be abused or neglected, what should the examiner do? What are the examiner's responsibilities? To whom does the examiner turn for help?

Why Report?

One of the most important things to remember is that the examiner does not have to prove that the child has been maltreated. All that is necessary is a suspicion that the child is at some risk for abuse or neglect. The suspicion, and not the proof, should be the stimulus to report the case. Many would ask, Why should I report? Many would prefer to remain uninvolved with social and legal agencies. Many clinicians have difficulty interacting with possibly abusive parents because the clinicians are unable to deal with their personal feelings of hostility, contempt, and abhorrence. However, health personnel must remember that if they do not initiate a report about the welfare of the child, perhaps no one will step forward to report, and the child may continue to suffer. The health care provider who is truly interested in helping the child, and not just in treating the superficial problems of bruises and burns, must initiate the report of possible child maltreatment.

In addition to the moral and professional obligation of reporting, there is a legal mandate to report suspected child abuse or neglect. All states have mandatory reporting laws for certain individuals. In all states, physicians are required to report suspected cases, and in most states other individuals, such as nurses, policemen, teachers, and others who have contact with children in a professional capacity, are also obligated to report suspected child maltreatment. Accompanying the legal mandate to report are penalties for failure to report. Failure to report is usually a misdemeanor. However, since child maltreatment is now an accepted medical diagnosis, those individuals who fail to recognize and take appropriate measures to report and treat abuse are professionally negligent and, therefore, subject to litigation for mal-

practice. Consequently, once there is reasonable suspicion of maltreatment, reporting the case to the appropriate local authorities is mandatory.

How To Report

To whom do nurses or physicians report the fact that they suspect a patient to be abused or neglected? The laws that govern child abuse and neglect and mandate certain people to report their suspicions of maltreatment are state laws. Therefore, each state has established a mechanism for reporting suspected cases and for investigating those cases. Many states have a statewide, centralized toll free telephone number for reporters to call. The central registry accepts the information about a suspected case and calls the local mandated investigator of child maltreatment who then must investigate the case. In most instances, the local mandated investigator is the county department of social services which usually has a child protection unit to investigate reports. Some communities do not have statewide telephone numbers; these communities have a local telephone number which should be called. Health care professionals who may come in contact with maltreated children should learn the specific reporting process in their community. Occasionally, it may be necessary to report a case anonymously; however, this is not the preferred manner. If local caseworkers do not have the name of the reporting individual, they may be hampered in their investigation by the unavailability of supporting evidence which the reporter may possess. Therefore, it is important to give the intake caseworker as much information as possible about the family, the child, the alleged maltreatment, and how to contact the reporter.

Some mandated reporters are reluctant to report a case of suspected maltreatment because they fear legal retaliation by parents. They are fearful of being sued for reporting a case that may later prove to be unfounded. This fear is unwarranted because mandated reporters are protected by the same law that requires them to report. Each state social service law that addresses child abuse and neglect specifically states that mandated reporters are immune from liability for reports, whether or not the report is valid. That is, if health care professionals, as mandated reporters, report a case that proves to be unfounded, they cannot be sued.

If the physician is caring for a child who dies, or if the physician is on duty in the emergency department when the child arrives dead, and the cause of death is either undetermined or abuse or neglect is suspected, the medical examiner or coroner must be informed. If abuse and neglect are initially suspected, the child protection agency should also be informed.

Informing the Parents

The next step that the physician must take is to discuss with the parents the fact that child maltreatment is a possible diagnosis of their child's problem. This is probably one of the most difficult duties. This is the time when physicians must be aware of their own feelings so that they can deal with those feelings, and, thereby, effectively communicate with the parents. As mentioned earlier, physicans may feel hostility toward the parents because they think that the parents have injured the child. They fear confronting the parents because the parents may become angry. Physicians must maintain their objectivity, control their hostility, and be honest so that they do not alienate the parents at this pivotal point in initiating diagnostic and therapeutic modalities. Physicians cannot be accusatory or judgmental in their interaction with the parents. Frequently, it is helpful to explain to the parents the facts as they appear to the physician. The physician can say that the injuries cannot be explained by the parents' history, and, therefore, another mechanism must be present. Instead of saying, "One of you must have injured the child," it is less alienating to say, "The child could not have caused this injury; this was not accidental, and, therefore, some other person must have been instrumental in causing the injury." It is when confronted with the possible diagnosis that many parents are alienated from the physician and the medical profession in general. If the physician tries to cover up the diagnosis or report the suspected case to the child protection agency without telling the parents, the parents may generalize their distrust and avoid contact with medical professionals in the future. If handled properly, the parents can be informed of the suspected diagnosis, will cooperate with the recommendations of the physician, and probably cooperate with the initial investigation by the appropriate child protection agency. If parents offer an argument or accuse physicians of falsely persecuting them, the physicians can defend themselves by stating that the diagnosis was based on the medical facts, the report to the child protection authorities is mandated by law, and it would be breaking the law or risking a charge of professional negligence if the case were not reported.

In summary, any health professionals who come in contact with children should know the policies about reporting suspected abuse and neglect in their community. A health professional who suspects that a patient may be maltreated is legally mandated to report this suspicion to the appropriate authorities. In addition, while it is not mandated by law, it is advisable to discuss the findings and the diagnosis of possible maltreatment with the parents. This discussion is frequently a difficult and anxiety-producing obligation. It is a responsibility that physicians should become more comfortable with as they gain experience in dealing with suspected maltreatment cases.

INITIAL DISPOSITION OF THE CHILD

Once a child has been recognized as being possibly abused or neglected, it is implicit that the child is at risk for further maltreatment. Therefore, some decisions must be made about the child's immediate disposition.

Hospitalization Versus Returning Home

In a medical setting, the first decision to be made is whether or not to hospitalize the child. There are several criteria for hospitalization.

MEDICAL REASONS

Obviously, if the child is severely injured and needs medical attention that can only be offered in an inpatient setting, then hospitalization is indicated. A child may also need to be hospitalized if the injuries cannot be fully evaluated on an outpatient basis. Further observation or additional tests may be necessary to fully evaluate the extent of the injuries. If the emergency department physician is unclear about the family environment, short-term admission to the hospital may give the medical and social service staff the extra time needed to evaluate the social situation. If the patient exhibits growth failure, hospitalization may be necessary to determine the etiology of the failure-to-thrive. In families with interactional problems, nonorganic failure-to-thrive secondary to maternal deprivation is the most likely diagnosis. Usually hospitalization is necessary to confirm that diagnosis.

NEED FOR IMMEDIATE PROTECTION

A second major consideration that may indicate the need for hospitalization is the immediate protection of the child. If the caseworker from the child protection agency is not able to immediately respond to the situa-

tion, if an emergency foster home is not readily available, or if it is decided that the child would be in jeopardy immediately upon returning to the child's natural home, hospitalization for the protection of the child may be indicated. It is not optimal to use hospital beds to protect children from their natural environment. Hospitalization is costly, beds are usually in short supply, and the hospital is not an appropriate environment for a healthy child. However, the hospital may be the most readily accessible haven in which to protect the child from a dangerous home environment for a brief period of time. Certainly, if the child is admitted to the hospital for protective reasons only, a better environment, such as an emergency foster home or a relative's home, should be found as soon as possible.

RETURN HOME

Not all children who are suspected of being abused and neglected will need to be removed from their homes even for a short period of time. When a case is reported, and a caseworker comes to the hospital to begin an investigation, the physician and the caseworker or the physcian and the hospital social worker may decide that the situation is not imminently dangerous. In these instances it may be perfectly acceptable to allow the child to return to the natural home. Obviously, it is necessary to have some idea of the adequacy of the home situation before such a decision is made. In these cases, a specific follow-up appointment should be made for further evaluation of the current illness or injury and for initiation or continuation of preventive health maintenance. If the examining physician or the caseworker discovers that the parent is not compliant with the physician's recommendations or fails to keep the follow-up medical appointments, then it is important to report these facts to the child protection agency. It is important not only to see that the injury that brought the child to the emergency department is properly treated and is healing but also to see that the child is receiving preventive health care, including appropriate immunizations and measurements of growth. Medical neglect is a frequent finding in abusive homes, and continued medical supervision should be part of the treatment plan.

Admission to the Hospital

Once the decision is made to hospitalize the child, it is best to have the parents voluntarily admit the child. If there are medical reasons for inpatient evaluation or treatment, the parents are usually willing to accept the physician's recommendations and voluntarily admit the child. If the physician has been honest with the parents and handled the physician-parent interaction with tact, the parents will usually agree with the physician's recommendations. However, if the parents were alienated by hostile or accusatory behavior by the health care personnel, they will usually react defensively and hostilely and not agree with the recommendations. In these instances it may be necessary to admit the child to the hospital over the parents' objections. In some states the hospital administrator, medical director, or director of emergency services has the power to hospitalize the child for up to 24 hours without the parents' consent. It is understood that, within the 24 hours, the physician must contact the mandated child protection agency. At the same time, the caseworker must obtain and place in the medical record a letter indicating that the custody of the child has temporarily been assigned to the county department of social services and that the county has agreed that the child may remain in the hospital as long as medically necessary. A hearing is usually held within a few days so that the juvenile or family court can issue an order officially granting custody to the state or county social services department. It is, of course, desirable to obtain the parents' consent and have them be cooperative in the ensuing evaluation and treatment of the child. In this way they are more likely to visit and be supportive to the child during this stressful time. If the child is hospitalized against their wishes, they will likely remain alienated from the medical personnel, not visit the child, and not offer the support and comfort the child needs.

Treatment and Evaluation

The time the child is in the hospital should be used efficiently for treatment and evaluation. Obviously, any acute injuries should be treated appropriately. Since abused children may have multiple injuries, other trauma besides the already-discovered injury should be diligently sought. If physical abuse is the precipitating event, the child should have a radiological skeletal survey to search for other new or healing bony injuries. The child's height and weight should be recorded and plotted on a growth chart to see if growth failure is present. If it is, the etiology should be determined. In most children who are maltreated and fail to thrive, the reason for growth failure is maternal deprivation and nutritional neglect. This condition should be documented during the hospitalization by giving the child an adequate diet and having the child show an accelerated gain in weight during the hospitalization.

If injuries are visible on the outside of the child's body, photographs should be taken. Photographs serve several purposes: they document the injury better than the physician's narrative description; they can later be used in court to show the judge or jury the nature of the injuries; and they frequently can describe the injury much more graphically and dramatically than the medical record or testifying physician. Most states allow, and some states require, that photographs be taken of any visible injuries. It is recommended that a professional medical photographer or other qualified individual take the photographs so that they best represent the injuries. However, when these services are unavailable, physicians themselves might have to take the photographs.

If the child is not overwhelmingly ill while in the hospital, a screening developmental assessment should be made. Since most children who fail to thrive and many other maltreated children are understimulated, they are particularly susceptible to developmental and language delays. Therefore, the initial hospitalization is an appropriate time to begin assessment of this potential problem.

Most hospitals that care for children have a social service or behavioral science department. In addition to the caseworker from the child protection agency, the hospital-based social workers should be involved with the family to maintain a liaison between the hospital and the child protection agency. This liaison does not absolve the physician from maintaining communication with the caseworker, but it is helpful to have a social worker involved who is familiar with hospital routine and medical procedures. In addition, the hospital-based social worker may help the parents find transportation or lodging or, in a general way, make the hospital a less hostile environment. Parents who are involved in investigations by a child protection agency tend to become alienated from the hospital personnel and need support and encouragement to maintain their visits with the child and their communication with the health care providers.

When the treatment of the child's acute medical problems and evaluation of any other health-related issues are completed during the initial hospitalization, the various people dealing with the child should have a discharge meeting to arrange for continued care after the hospitalization. This meeting should include, at least, the physician, the hospital-based social worker, and the child protection agency caseworker. It must be realized that the hospitalization has only allowed for the initial evaluation of the child and the family; the posthospitalization period must be used to continue consideration of the medical, psychological, and environmental stresses on the child.

SUMMARY

Health care professionals have a unique opportunity and obligation to be directly involved in the recognition and reporting of children who are suspected of being abused or neglected. There are many physical and behavioral indicators which should be familiar to these professionals. Physicians and nurses should learn how to report suspected cases in their community and how to discuss their suspicions with the child's parents. Once a case is suspected and reported, provision should be made for the immediate protection of the child and for initiation of any medical evaluation and treatment that is necessary. These procedures may or may not require hospitalization.

REFERENCES

1. Sturner WQ: Pediatric deaths, in Curran WJ, et al (eds): *Modern Legal Medicine Psychiatry and Forensic Science.* Philadelphia, FA Davis Co, 1980, p 236.

2. Radbill SX: A history of child abuse and infanticide, in Helfer RE, Kempe CH (eds): *The Battered Child,* ed 2. Chicago, University of Chicago Press, 1968, pp 3–21.

3. Caffey J: Multiple fractures in the long bones of infants suffering from chronic subdural hematoma. *Am J Roentgenol Radium Ther* **56**:163–173, 1946.

4. Silverman FN: The roentgen manifestations of unrecognized skeletal trauma in infants. *Am J Roentgenol Radium Ther Nucl Med* **69**:413–427, 1953.

5. Woolley PV, Evans WA: Significance of skeletal lesions in infants resembling those of traumatic origin. *JAMA* **158**:539-543, 1955.

6. Kempe CH, et al: The battered child syndrome. *JAMA* **181**:105-112, 1962.

7. Friedrich WN, Boriskin JA: The role of the child in abuse: a review of the literature. *Am J Orthopsychiatry* **46**:580-590, 1976.

8. Klaus MH, Kennell JH: *Maternal Infant Bonding.* St Louis, The CV Mosby Co, 1976.

9. Klein M, Stern L: Low birth weight and the battered child syndrome. *Am J Dis Child* **72**:15-18, 1971.

10. Steele BF, Pollock CB: A psychiatric study of parents who abuse infants and small children, in Helfer RE, Kempe CH (eds): *The Battered Child,* ed 2. Chicago, University of Chicago Press, 1968, pp 89-133.

11. Newberger EH, et al: Pediatric social illness: toward an etiologic classification. *Pediatrics* **60**: 178-185, 1977.

12. Holter JC, Friedman SB: Child abuse: early case finding in the emergency department. *Pediatrics* **42**:128-138, 1968.

13. Helfer RE, et al: Injuries resulting when small children fall out of bed. *Pediatrics* **60**:533-535, 1977.

14. Ellerstein NS: The cutaneous manifestations of child abuse and neglect. *Am J Dis Child* **133**: 906-909, 1979.

15. Stone NH, et al: Child abuse by burning. *Surg Clin North Am* **50**:1419-1424, 1970.

16. Feldman KW, et al: Tap water scald burns in children. *Pediatrics* **62**:1-7, 1978.

17. Gillespie RW: The battered child syndrome: thermal and caustic manifestations. *J Trauma* **5**: 523-534, 1965.

18. Lenoski EF, Hunter KA: Specific patterns of inflicted burn injuries. *J Trauma* **17**:842-846, 1977.

19. Levine LJ: The solution of a battered-child

homicide by dental evidence: report of a case. *J Am Dent Assoc* **87**:1234-1236, 1973.

20. Levine LJ: Bite mark evidence. *Dent Clin North Am* **21**:145-158, 1977.

21. O'Neill JA, et al: Patterns of injury in the battered child syndrome. *J Trauma* **13**:332-339, 1973.

22. Ryan MG, et al: One hundred eighty-seven cases of child abuse and neglect. *Med J Aust* **2**: 623-628, 1977.

23. Smith SM, Hanson R: 134 battered children: a medical and psychological study. *Br Med J* **3**: 666-670, 1974.

24. Caffey J: The whiplash shaken infant syndrome: manual shaking by the extremities with whiplash-induced intracranial and intraoccular bleeding, linked with residual permanent brain damage and mental retardation. *Pediatrics* **54**: 396-403, 1974.

25. Taylor D, Bentovim A: Recurrent nonaccidentally inflicted chemical eye injuries to siblings. *J Pediatr Ophthalmol* **13**:238-242, 1976.

26. Friendly DS: Occular manifestations of physical child abuse. *Trans Am Acad Ophthalmol Otolaryngol* **75**:318-332, 1971.

27. Harcourt B, Hopkins D: Ophthalmic manifestations of the battered baby syndrome. *Br Med J* **3**: 398-401, 1971.

28. Sims BG, et al: Bite marks in the battered baby syndrome. *Med Sci Law* **13**:207-210, 1973.

29. Sopher IM: The dentist and the battered child syndrome. *Dent Clin North Am* **21**:113-122, 1977.

30. Grosfeld JL: Surgical aspects of child abuse (trauma X). *Pediatr Ann* **45**:113-120, 1976.

31. Haller JA Jr: Injuries of the gastrointestinal tract in children: notes on recognition and management. *Clin Pediatr* **5**:476-480, 1966.

32. Touloukian RJ: Abdominal visceral injuries in battered children. *Pediatrics* **42**:642-646, 1968.

33. Woolley MM, et al: Duodenal hematoma in infancy and childhood: changing etiology and changing treatment. *Am J Surg* **136**:8-14, 1978.

34. Hartley RC: Pancreatitis under the age of five years: a report of three cases. *J Pediatr Surg* 2:419–423, 1967.

35. Morse TS: Renal injuries. *Pediatr Clin North Am* 22:379–391, 1975.

36. Siemens RA, Fulton RL: Gastric rupture as a result of blunt trauma. *Am Surg* 43:229–233, 1977.

37. Thomas PS: Rib fractures in infancy. *Ann Radiol* 20:115–122, 1977.

38. Sibert R: Stress in families of children who have ingested poisons. *Br Med J* 3:87–89, 1975.

22

CONTINUING CARE OF ABUSED CHILDREN AND THEIR FAMILIES

Norman S. Ellerstein, M.D.

The role of the health care professional does not end with the reporting of a suspected case of child abuse to the appropriate authorities. The physician who is truly interested in benefiting the patient, and not just expediting the situation, will continue to be involved in the care of abused and neglected children. All children who are maltreated, or who are at high risk, need evaluation of any existing medical, neurodevelopmental, language, or psychological problems. Some of these children may be able to remain in the care of the primary physician; others will need to be referred to consultants or specialized evaluation and treatment centers.

The physician not only has the responsibility to take care of the injuries that are the manifestations of abuse but also must help reduce the factors that may precipitate an abusive situation. Children who are physically handicapped, mentally retarded, hyperactive, or, in some other way, different from normal children are at higher risk for abuse than the average child. Therefore, these continuing problems must be addressed to reduce the potential for further abuse in the family.

In the long-term management of cases of maltreatment, the physician plays an important role in assessing the physical, developmental, and psychological needs of the child and in referring the child for appropriate further evaluation or treatment. Physicians cannot act alone in the management of abuse cases; they must act in concert with nurses, social workers, attorneys, psychologists, and other professionals. Both parents and children need continuing services to effectively treat the family and prevent further abuse. Treating just the adults or just the children is not optimally effective in helping the family interrupt the ongoing cycle of maltreatment. To this end, the physician must not only remain active in the care of the child but also be aware of the various treatment modalities available to the parents.

PHYSICIAN ROLES

Primary Care

The physician may assume many different roles in the continuing care of maltreated children.[1-4] A health care provider who is a

251

primary care physician should continue to provide all the primary medical services to the patient, including medical, developmental, and psychoemotional screening. If there is a problem area beyond the primary physician's range of competence, the physician must serve as the referral source so that the patient may receive additional help.

Member of a Multidisciplinary Team

A physician may choose to become part of a multidisciplinary child protection team.[5] A team is usually hospital-based or community-based and has many professionals; each of them has something to contribute to the diagnosis and treatment of abuse. Most frequently, these teams are made up of nurses, social workers, attorneys, physicians, child development specialists, and others who may aid in the management of abuse and neglect. Even though the individual composition of the team may vary from community to community, a physician is almost always a key person on the team. The team needs a clear understanding of the medical issues involved in the case such as failure-to-thrive, fractures, or other injuries. In addition to treating specific injuries, the physician can aid in assessing the child's development and interpret medical records from other sources. The team physician is commonly a pediatrician or family physician, but physicians with a variety of training may serve in this capacity. The willingness to serve on the team and an interest in child advocacy are more important than the physician's specific training.

Child Abuse Specialist

A highly specialized role that a physician may choose is that of the child abuse specialist.[3] This person is commonly a pediatrician who practices in a hospital-based setting. The specialist serves as a consultant to other physicians and nurses for children hospitalized with trauma or failure-to-thrive and may

see patients with suspected abuse on an outpatient basis. These physicians should become familiar with the court process since they are frequently called upon to testify in family or juvenile court about suspected cases of abuse. Generally, this type of physician is asked by primary physicians or surgeons to determine the likelihood of maltreatment in their patients. In addition, the specialist usually performs the administrative and legal functions for the referring physician. Sometimes performing these functions serves to preserve a nearly normal relationship between the primary physician and the parent of the possibly maltreated child. The child abuse specialist may have greater success in communicating with difficult parents and probably alienates fewer social workers, parents, attorneys, and other nonhealth professionals because of the specialist's experience in dealing with these highly charged situations.

Medical Specialist

Another way that many physicians can provide care to maltreated children is in the capacity of a medical specialist. That is, ophthalmologists, neurologists, orthopedists, neurosurgeons, or other specialists may have the opportunity to provide ongoing care for a child with injuries or sequelae dealt with by their particular medical or surgical subspecialty. Since the incidence of long-term sequelae of abusive and neglectful injuries is reasonably high, the specialist may see many maltreated children for follow-up care for an injury that required hospitalization or as a referral from a primary care physician.

Whenever health care providers come in contact with a child who is known to be maltreated, they should never assume that the child is receiving health care. Because of the possible family disorganization, economic problems, and other environmental stresses, it is likely that the family has not obtained adequate health care for the child. Even though the family and child may have been referred to a specific physician or clinic upon hospital discharge, there is a high probability that they never kept the appointments. Therefore, any physician who comes in contact with the family should either deliver the medical services that are needed or refer the patient to someone who can deliver these services and have a public health nurse, caseworker, or parent aide see to it that the appointments are kept and the needed services are obtained.

TREATMENT FOR THE PARENTS

Evaluation of the Family

Once the diagnosis of abuse has been made, delineation of the family problems that precipitated the maltreatment is necessary. Much of the evaluation of the family is done by the caseworker from the child protection service. In addition, the caseworker may seek help from mental health professionals for understanding individual psychological problems as well as abnormal family dynamics. The decisions about what would be the best therapeutic modalities for the family are made by the child protection service agency or by the multidisciplinary child protection team. Obviously, not all treatment modalities are available in each community.[6] The parents may voluntarily accept the recommendations of the caseworker. However, in some cases the parents will not cooperate, and the court will be asked to mandate certain services and treatments. There may be a large variety of treatment modalities available to the parents in a maltreating family. The child protection team or caseworker will decide which types of treatments would be appropriate for each family. In a family that acknowledges there is a problem and is highly motivated to correct the situation, many treatment modes are potentially effective. There are other families that are so chaotic, disorganized, or deeply rooted in aberrant par-

enting that few, if any, of the standard treatments would be effective.

Types of Treatment Available

CASEWORK

The most widely used treatment is traditional casework. Most commonly, this is delivered by a social worker from the local child protection service. The social worker is an individual who works for the agency that is mandated by state law to deal with child protection issues in the local community. The child protection caseworker is the central individual who monitors the parents' performance of their child-care responsibilities once the case has been reported. The caseworker may also be responsible for coordinating any other helping strategies that may be appropriate for the individual family. Many times the caseworkers are assigned too many families and are unable to perform optimally for each of the cases. Since the caseworker who is responsible for providing the family with long-term care may also be the same individual who investigated the case and brought it to court, the family may have a very distrustful and adversary relationship with the assigned worker. Therefore, even though traditional casework is the most commonly used method of helping an abusive family, there are many drawbacks which frequently limit its effectiveness.

PSYCHOTHERAPY

Psychotherapy, on an individual or group basis, may be appropriate for some abusive individuals. This mode of treatment focuses on the parents' individual psychological problems. It may be effective in a minority of cases. Psychotherapy requires that the parent voluntarily see a mental health professional, usually on a regular basis, for an extended period of time. Because of this aspect of treatment and its usually significant financial burden, it is not one of the most common or most effective therapies.

LAY THERAPY

Lay therapy is becoming an increasingly popular treatment modality for abusive families. These individuals, sometimes called parent aides, are nonprofessionals who receive some training so that they can be useful to the maltreating family. These individuals are usually parents themselves; they befriend the abusive parent, usually the mother, and offer support as would a relative or friend. The parent aide may visit the home several times a week and be available to the mother by telephone. The parent aide may informally show the mother how to deal with certain child-rearing and home environment situations. The parent aide may also provide transportation to the mother for medical visits, shopping, or other family needs. The advantages of lay therapists are their volunteer and, therefore, minimal-cost status and the many hours per week they are available to the mother. Ideally, the lay therapist interacts with only one to three families at a time. Therefore, the aide is usually available to the family when needed. A caseworker or psychotherapist has a much larger patient or client population and can devote only a minimal amount of time to each family. The increasing popularity of lay therapy programs is because of their low cost and high degree of effectiveness.[7]

SELF-HELP GROUPS

Self-help groups such as Parents Anonymous (PA) are analogous to other self-help groups like Alcoholics Anonymous. This type of therapy seems to be most effective for the highly motivated individual who is willing to communicate with other families with similar problems at group meetings or via the telephone. Some Parents Anonymous groups, as part of their commitment to help other abusing parents, operate a crisis hotline. The crisis telephone line is usually available to any parent who feels the need to reach out and talk to someone about a problem. In some communities, the hotline may be operated by

agencies other than Parents Anonymous. The hotline provides someone to turn to in time of acute need. The advantages of the hotline are that callers can maintain their anonymity, if they wish; the call does not cost the needy parent; and the service is usually available 24 hours a day.

RESIDENTIAL TREATMENT CENTER

A relatively uncommon form of treatment is the residential treatment center which provides living quarters and treatment for the entire family, parents and children. The use of these centers is not widespread and appears to be costly.

MARITAL COUNSELING

For some families, marital counseling may be useful. If the primary problem is between the parents, then treatment should be directed at this dyad. The child becomes the victim when the anger between the parents is displaced to the child. Marital counseling requires that both parents attend counseling sessions; they must understand that the problem and, therefore, the solution is shared by both of them.

PUBLIC HEALTH NURSING SERVICES

Another mode of therapy, which is not derived from social welfare or psychological disciplines, is public health nursing services.[8] The public health nurse is usually recommended by a physician or health agency. The public health nurse, sometimes known as the visiting nurse, can go to the family's home and help the parents by offering advice on child care. The public health nurse may advise on the child's development, hygiene, acute illnesses, immunizations, and the prevention of accidents and poisonings. One advantage of public health nursing services is the nurses' ability to go to the family home and offer help based on the parent's environmental situation; the mother does not have to travel to a clinic or public agency to receive this instruction or advice. The public health nurse can assess the hygiene, safety, and appropriateness of the home environment. Another advantage is the rapidity with which a nurse may be dispatched to a family in need. Often the nurse can make an initial visit to the home within days of the referral. Other treatment modalities may have lengthy waiting lists which decrease the likelihood of their effectiveness. A sympathetic, nonaccusatory, nonjudgmental, and compassionate nurse may be able to establish a truly supporting and helping relationship with the family and eventually be viewed as a trusted ally. In some communities, there are designated units within the public health nursing service that specialize in helping families that are at high risk for maltreatment.

PARENTING CLASSES

Parenting classes, also known as discipline counseling, are another treatment mode. Very frequently parents use corporal punishment and violence to control their children's behavior because they have not learned any other way to discipline the children or to modify behavior. It is very common for the abusing parent to have been treated violently as a child. The only role model for parenting skills was the abusing parent's own mother or father who probably used corporal punishment. Therefore, it may be useful to take an educational approach and try to teach the parent that there are other ways to manage or discipline children. This approach can be useful for high-risk and low-risk parents as well as for those who have already physically abused their children. If the parent can be taught that other methods, instead of violence, are useful in disciplining children, then preventing the use of corporal punishment or reducing the use of violence in an abusive family may be successful. Integral to parenting classes is the concept of age-appropriate expectations. That is, parents must be taught when it is appropriate to expect children to perform in certain ways and when children can gain control over certain behav-

iors. For example, parents must be taught that it is not appropriate to expect a one-year-old child to be toilet trained, nor is it appropriate to think that an infant should know that its crying is upsetting or provoking the parent.

STRESS-REDUCING SERVICES

Stresses, from various sources, are major contributing factors to abusive situations. They can also be specific precipitating factors in individual episodes of violence. Therefore, it is important, as part of the treatment of maltreating families, to reduce the number of stresses upon the family.[2] Economic assistance is one of the basic stress-reducing services that a public agency caseworker can provide to a family in need. The caseworker can assist the family in acquiring public assistance, food stamps, unemployment compensation, and entry into other programs that may help the family with money problems. The caseworker can also help locate adequate housing and may refer employable members of the family to employment counseling or vocational training.

Sometimes the number of children in the family is so large that the parents are unable to adequately care for each child. In these instances, helping the parents enroll some of the children in day-care programs may reduce the likelihood of physical neglect or abuse in the home. At times there may be exacerbations of especially stressful situations and additional short-term services may be needed. Crisis nurseries are sometimes available to care for an infant or young child until the urgent stress-producing situation is relieved. The crisis nursery not only provides a place for the child to stay and a respite for the parents but also may provide crisis counseling services for the parents. In a preventive mode, family planning clinics can prevent the stress of additional, and possibly unwanted, new family members. The abusive family may have been stressed in the past by children whose births were too closely spaced or who were unwanted at time of conception or birth. The caseworker, parent aide, or other individual helping the family can recommend the use of family planning services. Certainly an alcoholic or drug-abusing parent poses a major threat to the normal functioning of a family. Therefore, programs that treat alcoholics and drug abusers should be offered to the parent who needs such services as an attempt to eliminate these problems.[9]

In summary, there is a wide variety of treatment modalities that directly or indirectly assist the parents in an abusing family. The availability of each of the services varies from community to community; some have many different types of treatments; others have few. Professionals who deal with maltreating families should become familiar with locally available treatment services. By combining proper diagnostic evaluation of the family with a knowledge of the available treatments, the child protection agency or multidisciplinary team should be able to choose the course of action that is potentially most effective. Depending on the dynamics of the individual family, providing a treatment plan that benefits the family may range from relatively easy to impossible. Some families will be helped by a modicum of intervention, while others will remain unresponsive to a wide variety of treatment modalities. Perhaps knowing the variety of services that could be effective will stimulate professionals to establish those services they think will be appropriate in their community.

TREATMENT FOR THE CHILDREN

In the 1960s and early 1970s, when recognition of the problem of child abuse and neglect was rapidly increasing, virtually all treatment services were directed toward the parents. It was felt that since the parents were the perpetrators of the abuse or neglect, efforts to change their behaviors would cause a decrease in maltreatment. However, as more was learned about maltreatment and its effects, it became clear that the children were being adversely affected in ways that would leave them permanently damaged physically or psychologically. It also became known that individuals who abuse their children were frequently abused in their own childhood; therefore, some intervention should be directed toward the maltreated child in an effort to break the cycle of multigenerational abuse.

Treatment of Physical Problems

In the long-term care of the maltreated child, one of the most obvious areas to address is that of physical problems. The abuse may have come to light because of a traumatic injury to the child, but once the case is reported to the child protection agency, and many nonhealth professionals became active in its management, the health care providers tend to withdraw as active participants in the care of the child. However, the need for medical attention is higher in the maltreated child than in the normal child.[4] The injuries that required medical attention should be followed until they are totally healed. In general, cutaneous injuries, such as ecchymoses and most burns, heal within weeks of their occurrence. But other injuries, such as third-degree burns that require grafting, skeletal fractures, and abdominal trauma, may need active medical attention for several months. Head trauma, with damage to the central nervous system, causes the most morbidity and mortality. Injury to the central nervous system requires the longest follow-up of any of the sequelae of physical abuse. There may be significant neurological damage with paralysis, deafness, mental and motor retardation, visual loss, or other specific organic sequelae. The patient must be monitored over a long period of time for possible hydrocephalus, onset of seizures, progressive neurological loss, or improvement in the patient's abilities. For children with functional losses secondary to neurological damage, it is frequently useful to refer the child to a center for pediatric physical medicine and rehabilitation. The professionals at these centers can assess the child's physical status and, through occupational and physical therapy, develop the child's existing abilities to the fullest potential. They can also recommend the best educational facilities for children with specific handicaps.

General Pediatric Medical Care

Another important part of the long-term physical care of the child is the provision of general pediatric medical care. In the maltreated child, this serves several purposes. First, frequent pediatric examinations provide surveillance for any new manifestations of child maltreatment. The physician may see new trauma, onset of growth failure, or physical neglect. Second, the pediatrician can provide counseling to the parents on discipline, accident prevention, and appropriate treatment of acute medical problems. The pediatrician has the opportunity to provide this kind of counseling because the parent may not view this physician as negatively as a caseworker or other agency-associated professional. Since maltreated children are not the only children who are treated by a physician, there is no stigma attached to a visit to the pediatrician. Third, the physician can take care of any immunizations that the child may have missed in the past because of family disorganization or stresses. Another very important service the physician can provide is the surveillance of growth failure. Since failure-to-thrive secondary to maternal deprivation is a common manifestation of problems of family bonding, the longitudinal surveillance of growth is especially important in high-risk families.[4]

Reduction of Stress

The physician has an important role to play in reducing stress in the family. If it is known that a particular family has a predisposition to maltreatment, it is important that medical problems do not add to the family stress. The physician should be a conscientious counselor during episodes of acute illness so that minor infections do not become major stress-producing issues. A sick child, with increased crying and irritability, may be especially annoying to a parent; the illness may provoke an abusive event. The same situation is probably true for children with chronic diseases or handicaps. The stress the "abnormal" child brings to the family unit adds to the other pressures affecting family dynamics.[10] Furthermore, families who tend to be somewhat disorganized or neglectful have a higher incidence of accidental ingestions and accidental trauma because they neglect the supervision and safety of the child.[11] These families need supplementary counseling in poisoning control and accident prevention. In high-risk families, these measures are as important as immunizations in the long-term prevention of debilitating conditions. A child who is permanently brain damaged from a preventable fall may be just as handicapped as the child who was thrown down the stairs. The physician may become one of the few individuals whom the family trusts. Therefore, the physician's ability to provide compassionate and sensitive counseling to the family, even if it concerns only medical matters, may be significant in the overall treatment of that family.

Developmental Issues

A major area that must be addressed in the long-term management of the maltreated child is development. Much has been written about developmental issues in abused and neglected children.[12-15] There are many causes for the neurodevelopmental delays. In children who exhibit growth failure, undernutrition may be a major cause of developmental problems.[16] Traumatic injury to the central nervous system can produce dramatic changes in a child's intellectual and motor functions. However, the most pervasive cause of developmental abnormalities in maltreated children is the emotional or psychological environment in which the child lives. Maltreated children, whether they are subjected to physical trauma or not, have suffered the psychological abuses of abnormal family interaction. Understimulation by the parents, inconsistent parental responses, and an environment steeped in violence provide sufficient cause for the psychodevelopmental pathology seen in most maltreated children.[14]

Discovery of any existing psychodevelopmental abnormalities is essential. Initial evaluation of intellectual, motor, language, and social abilities is necessary. If the primary practitioner is unable to perform these tasks, or if abnormalities are discovered during the screening procedure, referral to a specialist or developmental center is mandatory. Depending on the resources in the community, the child may be referred to a pediatrician who specializes in developmental disabilities, a rehabilitation center, or an institution familiar with the problems of developmentally delayed children. In the older child, the school system may evaluate and address any educational handicaps.

Once the specific deficits are determined, a treatment plan must be formulated. Frequently, it is difficult to differentiate neurodevelopmental from psychological problems. However, since some of the manifestations are similar, the treatment modalities are frequently the same.

Enrichment Programs

Enrichment programs may compensate for environments that do not provide enough social and psychological stimulation for the child. Probably the most common of these programs are the preschool day-care center and the nursery school. Preschool programs may be specialized to address the needs of psychologically scarred and emotionally dis-

turbed individuals such as abused children, or they may be regular nursery schools where normal and developmentally immature children mix. The basic idea in preschool programs is to provide the child with an environment that is more stimulating than the child's home environment and to provide individuals, in the form of teachers and counselors, who can specifically address the psychological needs of the children. In specialized programs, most of the teachers have advanced training in dealing with children who have problems. Usually professional consultations are available from psychologists and developmental specialists who advise the teachers how to more appropriately address the needs of specific children.

Psychotherapy

Treatment may also be offered in the form of psychotherapy. Short-term therapy may be needed at times of special stress to the child such as hospitalization, separation from the parent, or illness. At other times, more long-term forms of psychotherapy may be indicated. Group therapy may be effective with some children; play therapy may work for those who are younger or less verbal. In treatment modalities such as psychotherapy or preschool programs, it is important that a variety of individuals address the problems of abused children. That is, teachers, psychologists, psychiatrists, occupational therapists, lay persons, medical personnel, and others must work together to help the child. No one discipline has all the answers.

Speech and Language Development

Speech and language development appears to be particularly sensitive to the negative environmental forces that exist in maltreating families.[17] In stimulation programs, in preschool or other settings, language is one area that can be objectively measured to evaluate a child's progress. Sometimes specific language development programs are indicated. If language seems to be the child's area of greatest difficulty, it may be advisable to enroll the child in a program in which language is the primary area of stimulation.

FOSTER CARE

Foster care is one of the most discussed topics in the area of child protection. There are several reasons why it is used.

Protection of the Child

The most obvious reason for foster care is to provide for the protection of the child. The cost of foster care is far less than that of hospitalization, and certainly a family's home is less offensive for the child than the hospital environment. Schmitt and Beezley[8] have offered some criteria for using foster care to protect the child:

- Severe or repeated physical abuse, incest, or severe malnutrition
- Repeated abuse after initial reporting of and intervention in the case
- Any physical abuse in a child less than one year old
- If the child is unwanted or rejected
- If the child's behavior is unduly provocative or obnoxious to the parents
- If an adolescent is beyond the control of the parent and refuses to return home
- If the parent is psychotic, suicidal, or homocidal
- If the parent does not want the child to return home, even after appropriate counseling
- If the parents refuse to be involved in treatment services

Diagnostic Tool

The second reason for foster care is its use as a diagnostic tool. If a child is exhibiting growth failure thought to be secondary to

maternal deprivation, and a trial in another environment is necessary, a foster home might be an appropriate location. Usually, admission to the hospital for one to two weeks will establish if nonorganic failure-to-thrive is the likely diagnosis. But, sometimes a longer period of observation outside the natural home is required to see if the child can re-establish a normal pattern of growth. Another diagnostic use of the foster home is to watch the child's development. This usually requires a somewhat longer period of foster care than observation for growth. When a child is developmentally delayed in the natural home, and understimulation is the suspected cause, living in a different environment may allow the child's development to advance. A similar situation is true for children who exhibit bizzare behavior. Parents may complain that their child is acting very strange, and this situation may even be confirmed by psychiatric consultation. A trial period in a foster home may allow professionals to observe the child in a setting away from the natural parents. If the bizzare behavior is reduced or disappears, it may confirm the suspicion that the parent-child interaction was the main cause of the child's aberrant behavior.

Therapy

The third reason for foster care is its use as a therapy in correcting the child's problems. The foster home acts as a therapeutic milieu for children with developmental delays, language problems, or manifestations of emotional disturbance induced by their environment. Even without the help of professional treatment in psychotherapy or preschool programs, the normal environment of the foster home is directly therapeutic to the child. A home without physical violence or psychological abuses, with the warmth of adults and children who are concerned with the growth, safety, and nurturing of a child, should have a positive impact on the child's personality and development. Foster care may also be beneficial to the abusive parents. With the maltreated child out of the home, the natural parents may have greater opportunity to work on the problems that predisposed their family to maltreatment.

Improvement of the System

Increasing the number of effective foster care homes requires improvement in the foster care system. The screening process for choosing foster parents could be improved. There are many excellent foster parents, but there are also many who do not provide an optimally nurturing environment for maltreated children. With improved screening, a generally higher-quality group of foster parents can be found. Parents who open their homes to children with special needs should have supplemental training to address the specific problems of the children. Foster parents should have help available from psychologists, child development specialists, and others when problems arise in dealing with the children. Frequently, antagonism develops between the foster and natural parents and causes the child's loyalties to be torn between the two sets of parents. If eventual reunion of the natural family is planned, foster parents should be aided in maintaining relationships between the natural parents and the child. In summary, foster care is an integral part of the child protection system, and it is frequently employed as a protective, diagnostic, or therapeutic modality in the management of cases of child abuse and neglect. A larger number of foster homes could achieve maximum effectiveness if there were better screening, training, and support of foster parents.

SUMMARY

This chapter has shown that the care of the maltreated child extends far beyond the recognition of an abusive injury in the emergency department. The physician must remain responsive to the needs of these children long after the initial recognition of abuse or neglect. Physicians can take care of specific medical problems of the child and act as referral sources for developmental, psychological, and other problems frequently seen in abused children. In addition, the physician may serve on a multidisciplinary child protection team and continue to be involved in the counseling of parents and children from abusive families.

Successful long-term treatment of abuse and neglect must address issues that affect both children and parents. There are a variety of treatment modalities for parents. Some parents may be responsive to a modicum of intervention while others may need many different services before their family situation will improve. There are also different types of services for children in abusive situations. Children who are raised in an abusive milieu may have physical, behavioral, or intellectual handicaps that are secondary to injury, environmental understimulation, or psychological abuse. No single discipline can adequately address the long-term needs of maltreated children and their families. Therefore, physicians, nurses, social workers, psychologists, child development specialists, attorneys, judges, and others must work together to bring about effective child rearing, reduce suffering, and interrupt the multigenerational propagation of abuse and neglect.

REFERENCES

1. Bell CJ: Medical consultations: appropriate selection and utilization in child welfare. *Child Welfare* **55**:445–458, 1976.

2. Kerns DL: Child abuse and neglect: the pediatrician's role. *J Contin Educ Pediatr* **21**:11–27, 1979.

3. Schmitt BD: Current pediatric roles in child abuse and neglect. *Am J Dis Child* **133**:691–696, 1979.

4. Schmitt BD, Kempe CH: The pediatrician's role in child abuse and neglect. *Curr Probl Pediatr* **5**:3–47, 1975.

5. Schmitt BD (ed): *The Child Protection Team Handbook.* New York, Garland Publishing Inc, 1978.

6. Kempe CH, Helfer RE: Innovative therapeutic approaches, in Kempe CH, Helfer RE (eds): *Helping the Battered Child and His Family.* Philadelphia, JB Lippincott Co, 1972, pp 41–54.

7. Cohn AH: Effective treatment of child abuse and neglect. *Social Work* **24**:513–519, 1979.

8. Schmitt BD, Beezley P: The long-term management of the child and family in child abuse and neglect. *Pediatr Ann* **5**:165–176, 1976.

9. Behling DW: Alcohol abuse as encountered in 51 instances of reported child abuse. *Clin Pediatr* **18**:87–91, 1979.

10. Friedrich WN, Boriskin JA: The role of the child in abuse: a review of the literature. *Am J Orthopsychiatry* **46**:580–590, 1976.

11. Sibert R: Stress in families of children who have ingested poisons. *Br Med J* **3**:87–89, 1975.

12. Applebaum AS: Developmental retardation in infants as a concomitant of physical child abuse. *J Abnorm Child Psychol* **5**:417–423, 1977.

13. Elmer E, Gregg GS: Developmental characteristics of abused children. *Pediatrics* **10**:596–602, 1967.

14. Martin HP (ed): *The Abused Child: A Multidisciplinary Approach to Developmental Issues and Treatment.* Cambridge, Mass, Ballinger Publishing Co, 1976.

15. Martin HP, et al: The development of abused children. *Adv Pediatr* **21**:25–73, 1974.

16. Chase HP, Martin HP: Undernutrition and child development. *N Engl J Med* **282**:933–939, 1970.

17. Blager F, Martin HP: Speech and language of abused children, in Martin HP (ed): *The Abused Child: A Multidisciplinary Approach to Developmental Issues and Treatment.* Cambridge, Mass, Ballinger Publishing Co, 1976, pp 83–92.

23

MANAGEMENT OF THE SEXUALLY ABUSED CHILD

Suzanne M. Sgroi, M.D.

Sexual abuse of children is rarely a true medical emergency. Persons who sexually abuse children usually do not use force or violence to engage the victims in sexual activity. As a result, most children who have been sexually abused do not show signs of physical injury. Medical examination of child victims does not often elicit physical evidence of sexual abuse—a fact largely unrecognized by medical professionals, police, the courts, and the general public. Accordingly, children are brought to hospital emergency departments at all hours with the expectation that an immediate medical examination will validate a complaint of sexual abuse. This is unfortunate, unrealistic, and inappropriate. Although medical examination is an important step, it is only one component of the validation process.

Health professionals who work in hospital emergency departments or in settings that deal with troubled children and their families need a conceptual framework for sexual abuse of children[1] in order to evaluate cases successfully. Knowledge of the usual dynamics and mechanics of sexually abusive behavior toward children is essential.

DYNAMICS AND MECHANICS OF CHILD SEXUAL ABUSE

Known Perpetrator

The person who sexually abused the child is nearly always someone who is known to the victim and has easy access to the child—either a relative or else a neighbor, friend of the family, school professional, baby-sitter, recreational leader, or the like. Perpetrators are rarely complete strangers to their victims.

Lack of Force

Few perpetrators use force or violence to engage their victims in sexual activity. Instead, they use a variety of techniques first described by Burgess and Holmstrom[2] to entice the child: misrepresenting moral standards, presenting the activity as a game, offering rewards or bribes, and so forth. Sometimes the child is entrapped by the perpetrator, that is, pressured to participate in sexual behavior to fulfill an obligation or in return for some favor. These nonviolent techniques rarely result in physical trauma to the victims. When children *are* physically injured, the perpetrators are more likely to be adolescents or strangers to the victims or both. Physical trauma notwithstanding, all of the children suffer some degree of emotional trauma as a result of their sexual victimization.

Abuse of Power

Cases of sexual victimization of children always involve abuse of power, even when force or violence are not involved. An adult or adolescent, someone who is older, larger, and more powerful, misuses and exploits a position of relative power and authority over the child victim. Often the perpetrators occupy positions of power and authority legitimately accorded by society (parents, guardians, school personnel, and the like). Other perpetrators (baby-sitters, older siblings) are accorded authority over the child by the parents. Sexual abuse of children is commonly viewed as a sexual aberration; however, the dynamics are easier to understand when it is viewed as a power disorder. Persons who sexually abuse children often do so in the service of nonsexual needs: the need to dominate, to feel powerful, to be in control.[3] The child victim always occupies a subordinate position with respect to the perpetrator. The youngster's relative powerlessness, ignorance, and naivete constitute an absolute barrier to the child's *consent* to the sexual activity; it is more accurate to describe the child's sexual behavior as *cooperation* within the context of abuse of power by the perpetrator.

Sex of Participants

Perpetrators can be either male or female. Most of the recognized perpetrators are males. Female perpetrators may go unrecognized, for the most part, because of cultural bias. Females are considered to be "natural" protectors and nurturers of children, and there are relatively few societal limits placed on interactions between women and children. Thus, only women whose sexual behavior with children blatantly violates broad societal limits are likely to be recognized.

Female victims outnumber male victims by a factor of 9 or 10 to 1 in most series. Again, a cultural bias that only females are likely to be victimized sexually is probably responsible. However, male children are probably victims of sexual abuse nearly as often as female children, and a recent study indicates that male children are equally at risk.[4]

Patterns of Victimization

Sexual abuse of children tends to be a family affair; multiple children within families, kinships, or groups may be victimized by a single perpetrator. The most important factors are the perpetrator's access to the child or children and the opportunity for sexual abuse to take place when the perpetrator and the victim are alone together. It is impossible to generalize about the probable number, age, sex, or familial relationships of child victims. Some perpetrators victimize only boys; others focus on girls; still others victimize children of both sexes. Sometimes perpetrators concentrate on one child victim at a time; other times, perpetrators have sexual relationships with multiple victims during the same time period. Some perpetrators seem to select victims who are all the same age; other perpetrators are less discriminating and sexually abuse children whose ages range from infancy to adolescence. Lastly, some perpetrators focus exclusively on children within their own families; others sexually victimize only children who are not related to them; still others do not discriminate between child victims inside or outside their own families.

Family Contribution

In most cases, there is a significant family contribution to child sexual abuse. In incest cases, perpetrators are family members, and often other family members are aware that the sexual abuse is taking place. Extrafamily cases are also likely to be characterized by various degrees of family contribution. Frequently, in extrafamily cases, the child may be sexually abused because of poor supervision, poor choice of surrogate caretakers, or inappropriate sleeping arrangements by parents or guardians.

Child's Contribution

Despite a widespread belief that children contribute to their own victimization by being seductive, the author has not encountered such cases. Although they frequently attempt to shift blame to the child, the perpetrators' own power positions place the responsibility for the sexual behavior squarely upon *them.* It is true that young children often engage in a variety of exploratory and acting-out behaviors that have sexual connotations. The appropriate response of adults is to limit and redirect such behaviors, not to regard them as an invitation. However, in most cases, those aspects of the victims' behavior most likely to be viewed as attractive by the perpetrator are, in fact, childlike characteristics: affectionate, trusting, naive behavior; absence of body hair and secondary sex characteristics; and the like.[3]

False Allegations

It is also widely believed that children frequently come forward with false allegations of sexual abuse. In the author's experience, children who disclose that they are being sexually abused are nearly always telling the truth. When children later recant their stories, it is usually in response to intense pressure placed upon them by the perpetrators and the children's families. In the very few real cases of false allegations by children, the youngsters and their families tend to be seriously disturbed.

Frequency and Progression of Victimization

Few children are sexually victimized only once by a known perpetrator who had continuous access to them over time. Instead, the children are usually abused in multiple sexual encounters that occur repeatedly over months and years. In most cases, there is also a progression of the sexually abusive activity over time. The multiple encounters usually progress from less intimate to more intimate types of activity, that is, from exposure and fondling to various types of sexual penetration.

Phases of Sexual Abuse

The dynamics of most cases predictably fall into five separate and distinct phases.

ENGAGEMENT PHASE

During the engagement phase, the perpetrators engage the child in some type of sexual activity. They take full advantage of their position of power over the child and, whenever applicable, their previous relationship. Since children commonly look to adults or to older children for direction, guidance, and cues as to appropriate behavior, it is not surprising that they are unlikely to question or resist being engaged in sexual activity. Usually there is little or no force or even threat of force in the engagement phase. Instead, the perpetrator persuades or gently pressures the child by presenting the activity as a game or by offering a reward. Directly or indirectly the perpetrator conveys to the child that the sexual behavior is "okay" or appropriate.

Occasionally, the child is threatened by the perpetrator; still less often, physical force is employed to induce compliance. Most of the time, however, the children cooperate and do not resist or attempt to evade the perpetrators.

SEXUAL INTERACTION PHASE

At the stage of sexual interaction, some type of sexual activity takes place. The following types of sexual behavior have been encountered.

Exposure

The perpetrators expose their genitals and/or persuade the child to expose the child's genitals (wholly or in part). Sometimes the perpetrator and the child do no more than look at each other.

Masturbation

Predictably, perpetrators may masturbate and encourage the children to mimic the masturbatory behavior. Sometimes the perpetrator and the child simply masturbate in each other's presence without attempting to touch each other. Male perpetrators often masturbate to ejaculation, sometimes ejaculating upon the child's body.

Fondling

If the participants touch each other, it usually begins with fondling—gentle, stroking, external contact ultimately focused on breasts, buttocks, genitorectal area, and inner aspects of the thighs. If masturbation precedes fondling the child, the perpetrator's hands may be covered with genital secretions. If the perpetrator has a genital gonococcal infection, it may be possible for a victim to acquire genital or rectal gonorrhea in this way.

Oral Penetration

If any sexual penetration of the child occurs, it usually begins with oral penetration. A male perpetrator may persuade the child to fellate him (the perpetrator's penis is taken into the child's mouth). This is commonly presented to the child as, "I want you to lick me," or "I want you to suck me." A female perpetrator may persuade the child to perform cunnilingus upon her (the child's mouth, lips, and tongue penetrate the perpetrator's vulvovaginal region). If perpetrators of either sex have genital gonococcal infections, the child victim is at risk for acquiring gonorrheal infection of the pharynx.

Rectal Penetration

Rectal penetration usually begins with finger exploration of the child's anus. Perpetrators who are gentle and adept can easily insert a finger, thumb, or foreign object through the anal sphincter. A male perpetrator sometimes then progresses to penile penetration of the child's rectum. Depending upon the age, size, and previous experience of the child, an adept male perpetrator can achieve full penile penetration without causing rectal trauma.

Vulvovaginal Penetration

Perpetrators predictably begin with finger exploration of the vulvovaginal area. The condition of the hymenal ring depends upon the age, size, and previous experience of the child; the perpetrator may gradually dilate the hymenal opening over time. The diameter of the hymenal opening in five-year-old girls ranges from 0.5 to 1.5 centimeters. In some girls, the hymenal ring is entirely absent. In others, there may be marked dilation of the vaginal opening. Unless forcible penetration is attempted, little or no trauma may be seen on examination.

"Dry" Intercourse

The term, "dry" intercourse, describes a frequently encountered behavior. A male perpetrator rubs his penis against the child's body, either anteriorly (interfemoral intercourse) or posteriorly (intercrural intercourse) between the buttocks. "Dry" intercourse sometimes takes place with the child's clothing in place. Since little or no vaginal lubrication is involved, "dry" intercourse is usually described by the female victim as uncomfortable or even painful. This behavior is not necessarily accompanied by penetration or attempts at penetration.

SECRECY PHASE

Initially described by Burgess and Holmstrom,[2] the secrecy phase predictably follows sexual interaction. The perpetrator conveys directly or indirectly to the child that their sexual activity must be kept secret. The perpetrator usually employs the same techniques used in the engagement phase. Sometimes the secrecy is reinforced by threats. Children are usually threatened with harm to themselves or, perhaps, to a third person. Sometimes the threats involve separation as well. A child might be told, "If you tell Mommy about us, she will go away." Sometimes the perpetrator tells the child, "If you tell anybody, I will get put in jail," or "You will be put away if you tell anyone about what you did." All threats are potent enforcers of the secrecy, especially for a young child.

Children keep the secret of sexual abuse for various lengths of time—weeks, months, years—sometimes forever. They tend to keep the secret for the same reasons that they engaged in the sexual activity to begin with: naivete, desire to please the perpetrator, enjoyment of the secrecy (most children enjoy keeping secrets), material rewards, and because the behavior itself is self-reinforcing and meets nonsexual needs for them. If they are threatened by the perpetrator, they keep the secret because they fear retribution. Often children keep the secret because they feel guilty about their own participation in the sexual activity. Also, they fear that they will not be believed if they tell someone else about the sexual activity.

DISCLOSURE PHASE

When cases become known to others, the dynamics enters the disclosure phase.[2] There are two types of disclosure: accidental and purposeful. Cases that initially come to light in medical settings are usually accidentally disclosed. By contrast, cases of purposeful disclosure (the child or perpetrator decides to tell someone) more commonly occur in the school or in the community.

Accidental Disclosure

Any or all of the following types of accidental disclosure have taken place.

Physical Trauma. Sometimes the child is injured (usually by accident) as a result of the sexual activity, and genital or rectal trauma draws attention to the sexual abuse. Occasionally, signs of abnormal dilation of the vulvovaginal or anal openings are found on routine physical examination and lead the examiner to suspect abuse.

Sexually Transmitted Disease. Some children acquire sexually transmitted diseases as a result of the sexual abuse. Gonorrheal infections in children beyond infancy should always be regarded as indicators of sexual abuse.[5] A child may acquire a syphilis infection congenitally, via sexual or nonsexual contact with an infected person. Vaginal infections caused by candida, trichomonas, or mixed populations of microorganisms, although widely regarded as sexually transmitted diseases in adults, can also occur under certain other circumstances: antibiotic therapy, swimming in heavily chlorinated water, and so forth. Genital herpes infections and venereal warts (condylomata acuminata), both viral infections, are probably indicators of sexual abuse; there are no systematic studies to substantiate this speculation.

Pregnancy. Some cases are accidentally disclosed when a girl's unsuspected pregnancy is detected. This occurs more often in younger girls (ages 11 to 13 years); sometimes the male perpetrator believes that the child is too young to be impregnated and does not take proper precautions to prevent pregnancy.

Genital or Rectal Foreign Objects. These cases usually involve only young children. It is unfortunate that the presence of genital or rectal foreign objects in a young child does not immediately arouse suspicion that a child has been sexually abused. In one such case, a father regularly inserted a bullet into the vagina of his two-year-old daughter as part of the sexual interaction.[6]

Observation By a Third Party. Some cases are accidentally disclosed because the sexual activity is inadvertently observed by a third party. Although observers do not always report the abuse, some do so. Often the observer is a family member who chooses to ignore or to deny the significance of the observed sexual activity.

Age-inappropriate Sexual Behavior. Some young victims draw attention to the sexual abuse by acting out sexual behavior with other children and adults. Although a certain level of sexual exploration (usually limited to exposure and observation) is considered to be normative behavior among age-mates, it is not usual to see sexually agressive behavior displayed by young children, especially when genital fondling and various types of sexual penetration (fellatio; cunnilingus; urethral, rectal, and vulvovaginal penetration) are involved. Sometimes these types of age-inappropriate sexual behavior immediately alert others to the probability that the children are victims of sexual abuse. Too often, however, even young children who display such behavior are simply regarded as obnoxious and delinquent. Likewise, children who masturbate excessively and openly should be considered probable victims of sexual abuse.

Purposeful Disclosure

Many cases are disclosed purposefully by one of the participants—most often the child victim. Sometimes the child tells someone else (usually a family member) about the sexual activity very soon after it begins. These disclosures are usually motivated by the child's desire for protection from further sexual abuse. Unfortunately, the people who receive these early disclosures of sexual abuse usually respond inappropriately with anger, disbelief, or denial or by promising to protect the child and then failing to keep that promise. It is not at all unusual to discover these prior disclosures if interviewers are aware of their frequency and ask, "Did you ever tell anyone about this before?" Children are then likely to tell about the first disclosure and to relate that they had concluded, "Nobody cares," or "Nobody will believe me." Accordingly, the youngsters are likely to keep the secret for months or years before disclosing it again—this time often to an outsider.

The immediate task of professionals who work with cases characterized by a child's purposeful disclosure is to determine *why* the child is disclosing the secret now. Very few of the victims tell someone outside the family about the sexual abuse simply because they want the victimization to stop. Usually, these disclosures to outsiders occur for some other reason: wanting more freedom or independence, to protect another child from being victimized, fear of becoming pregnant, and so forth. People who interview these children need to determine why the children decided to tell about the sexual abuse, to learn what they expected or hoped would occur as a result of the disclosure, and to help them formulate more realistic expectations. In contrast, professionals who work with cases of accidental disclosure need first to help the children decide to admit the secret and then to support them in this decision.

SUPPRESSiON PHASE

The final phase, suppression, begins as soon as the family members who occupy power positions learn of the disclosure. In this phase, everyone who has something to lose by the disclosure usually tries to deny that sexual abuse actually took place, to undermine the credibility of the allegation, to minimize the seriousness of the behavior, and to ward off outside attempts at intervention. It is not surprising that perpetrators try to suppress the allegation. However, most professionals are unprepared for the intensity of suppressive behavior by family members and, sometimes, by the child victim as well. Since all perceive the degree of disruption that would probably result from disclosing that the child was sexually victimized, any or all family members, including the victim, may try to restore the status quo, to turn back the clock, and to behave as if the sexual abuse never happened. Sometimes professionals join in the suppression phase, usually because they are personally threatened by the issue or unsure of their competence or, sometimes, because they are unwilling to make the commitment of time and energy that an appropriate response would require.

RESPONSIBILITIES OF HEALTH PROFESSIONALS

Although physical injury is infrequent in sexually abused children, the public's expectation that a medical examination will prove or disprove the allegation virtually always leads to an early involvement of health professionals. In addition, the disclosure of sexual abuse tends to precipitate a psychosocial crisis not only for victims, offenders, and their families but also for professionals in the community who must become involved. Professionals usually respond to the disclosure with three questions:

1. Is this a valid complaint?
2. Is the child damaged physically or emotionally?
3. What will this mean to me? (What do I have to do about it? Will my own life be changed?)

Medical examination can contribute information for responses to all three questions but cannot provide complete answers. Input from health professionals will be required for investigation, case management, and treatment. However, no physician, physician's assistant, nurse practitioner, or registered nurse, working alone, can effectively perform all of the essential case management tasks.[7] In addition to knowledge of the mechanics and dynamics of the sexual abuse of children, health professionals who work in hospital settings need to understand their special responsibilities toward child victims. These include the following:

- Reporting cases to child protection services and to the police
- Assisting with investigative interviewing
- Collecting physical evidence
- Determining physical and emotional trauma
- Treating physical trauma; assisting in treatment of emotional trauma

In-service Training

None of these responsibilities can be consistently addressed without in-service training of staff, development of a comprehensive policy and protocols, and commitment to providing high-quality care for the sexually abused child. For example, most health professionals who work in hospital emergency departments are well aware of their responsibility to report cases of child sexual abuse either to child protection services or to the police. However, the need to report cases to both child protection services *and* to the police is less well appreciated. In most states authorities must be notified by the hospital when sexual abuse of a child is alleged or suspected. Who reports to whom is generally determined by hospital policy, but sometimes by circumstances (if the victim is brought to the hospital by someone from child protection services or by a police officer, the issue may be academic). Nevertheless, a clear definition of reporting responsibilities and the reporting process is an essential part of the emergency department's protocol for sexually abused children. Other hospital departments (pediatrics, gynecology, outpatient) should participate in formulating that protocol, and their staff should use it as well.

Investigative Interview

Few health professionals are aware of the body of knowledge about investigative interviewing of sexually abused children.[8] An experienced professional can usually use investigative interviewing to determine if the child's history is consistent with the usual dynamics and mechanics of sexual abuse. The interview may be done by a health professional, worker from the child protection services, police officer, counselor, or therapist. In general, interviewing is best accomplished when members of the three essential professional groups who will be involved, health, child protection services, and law enforcement, have agreed in advance who will be responsible for what components. Regardless of who performs what task, the child should always be interviewed alone in a neutral setting (perhaps in a quiet office or playroom away from the hustle and bustle of the emergency department if the interviewing takes place in the hospital). Interviewers should try to talk to the child's parents first but should not question them in the presence of the child victim. If someone else must be present during the interview with the child, it

should be a sympathetic professional rather than a family member. The latter may try to suppress the allegation; in any event, the child is not likely to feel free to fully discuss the sexual interaction phase if a parent, guardian, or caretaking adult is present.

A full discussion of the "how to" of investigative interviewing would occupy many pages and is not possible here. Briefly, one must take the time to establish a relationship with the child and try to determine *why* he or she disclosed the secret. With a young child, the interviewer may need to use arts or play media to help the youngster relax and feel safe. The child's terminology should be used. Interviewers should avoid asking leading questions but should try instead to persuade the youngster to tell the story in his or her own words. It helps to begin with the first incident, "Can you tell me about the first time it ever happned?" It is never appropriate to pressure a child who is not yet ready to talk about the sexual activity. Often, the hospital setting is not conducive to establishing the required relationship of trust between the interviewer and the child. In some hospitals, however, members of the nursing or social work staff who have developed their interviewing skills perform the bulk of the investigative interviewing.

Medical Examination

Collecting physical evidence and determining and treating physical trauma are undisputed responsibilities of medical professionals. However, it is not unusual for physicians to profess ignorance or discomfort in performing medical examinations of sexually abused children. A full medical history should be obtained, and a complete physical examination should be performed. It is never acceptable to "zero in" on a genital examination since this may frighten or embarrass the child as well as misplace the emphasis of the entire examination process. In addition, failing to do a complete examination risks overlooking important signs that may be present.

The ideal person to perform the medical examination is a physician who is trained in the care of children—a pediatrician, family practitioner, or a specialist in emergency medicine. Although nurse practitioners or physician assistants may be perfectly competent to perform the examination, it is preferable, for medicolegal reasons, that the examiner be a physician. An outline for examination is presented in the last portion of this chapter.

Treatment

Most sexually abused children will not have a physical injury. A small number will have physical trauma, foreign bodies, or perhaps, a sexually transmitted disease. Treatment for these youngsters should be instituted as soon as the problem is apparent. Measures to prevent pregnancy are not indicated except in postpubertal girls who give a clear history of unprotected vaginal intercourse. Likewise, prophylaxis for gonorrhea is not indicated unless there is a history of exposure to a person who is known to be infected. It is preferable to arrange for a follow-up examination and repeat cultures in two to four weeks if the initial studies were negative. The follow-up examination provides a valuable opportunity to see the child and family again and to determine how they are doing.

Psychological Assessment

It is important for the person who performs the medical examination to assess the child's emotional status. This assessment cannot and should not substitute for a more comprehensive psychological assessment, but it is often possible to learn a great deal about the youngster's feelings during the medical examination. Most victims feel guilty about their participation in sexual activity; they are aware of their own degree of cooperation with the perpetrator and frequently accept society's misperception that cooperation equals consent. It is not unusual for people to insist that a very young child bear responsibility for "seducing" an adult perpetrator. Also, the sexually experienced child may be profoundly disturbing to other family members and persons in the community. Society's investment in sexual interaction as a "rite of passage" into adulthood makes the sexually experienced child—even a very young child—both a paradox and an anomaly. The tendency is for others to view the child victim as damaged, defiled, oversexed, and mysteriously changed by the experience.

At the time of the medical examination, some youngsters may display behavior consistent with emotional trauma; they are withdrawn, depressed, hostile, extremely fearful, or guilty. Others may appear entirely unaffected by their experiences, but it is important not to misinterpret a bland or unconcerned exterior. In any event, the person who examines the child should reassure the youngster, the parents, and all others who will be involved in the case that the child is *not* damaged. If treatment for injury or infection is required, the message should be that the youngster will be "cured." Both the child and his or her parents need to hear these messages; initial reassurance and affirmation by the physician are important first steps in treating the emotional consequences of sexual abuse.

MEDICAL EXAMINATIONS OF SEXUALLY ABUSED CHILDREN

It has been difficult to persuade physicians from various medical specialties to take full responsibility to perform complete examinations of child victims of sexual abuse. For example, gynecologists usually limited themselves to genital examination of female children; urologists tended to focus exclusively on the urinary system of male children; and pediatricians were often reluctant to perform genital examinations at all.

This section describes my personal approach to medical examination of sexually abused children. It draws on all different types of clinical experiences—evaluations in the emergency department, outpatient department, venereal disease clinic, and private practice—and attempts to cover all aspects of the problem.

Preliminary Considerations

PERMISSION TO EXAMINE THE CHILD

Before examining a child for sexual abuse, I require a signed permission slip from the child's parent or guardian that authorizes me to perform a complete examination, including a genital examination. If the youngster is in the custody of child protection services, I ask a departmental representative who can authorize medical examinations to sign the permission slip. The sole exception I make to this rule is the case of a child who requests to be examined for a venereal disease; in most states this is the only condition for which a minor can authorize his or her own examination. This procedure not only protects the examining physician from a possible charge of assault and battery for performing an unauthorized examination but also insures that information obtained during the examination can be used in court, if necessary. In some jurisdictions, evidence obtained from unauthorized medical examinations cannot be introduced in court.

REPORTS TO CHILD PROTECTION SERVICES AND THE POLICE

As a general rule, I inform the child's parent or guardian that, as a mandated reporter of suspected child abuse, I must report the case to child protection services, regardless of the findings. In a case referred by child protection services, this issue is academic. However, when a child is brought to any medical facility by a parent or guardian who wishes to have the child evaluated for sexual abuse (to see "if someone has been messing" with him or her, health professionals must remember that a medical examination alone cannot exclude the possibility of sexual abuse. Regardless of medical findings, a case that comes in with a request to "rule out" child sexual abuse *must* be reported to child protection services for additional assessment.

I believe that all validated cases of child sexual abuse should be reported to the police, not only because criminal acts are involved but also because the authority of the criminal justice system is needed to stop the perpetrator and to protect the child. Thus, at the outset, I routinely inform the child's parent or guardian that it is my policy to insist that the police be informed whenever the findings support the allegation of sexual abuse. If the parent or guardian refuses to report, I inform them that I myself will notify the police about the case if it appears to be a valid complaint.

RELEASE OF INFORMATION

Whenever I am asked by child protection services or the police to evaluate a child for sexual abuse, I first ask the parent or guardian to sign a release authorizing me to report my findings to the referral source. Obtaining this release permits me to file a complete report and eliminates the necessity for a civil or criminal court to issue a subpoena to learn my impression of the case situation.

Investigative Interviewing

PRIVATE INTERVIEW WITH THE REFERRING PROFESSIONAL

Whenever other professionals refer a child for evaluation, I make it a practice to first discuss the situation with them privately. This approach enables me to learn whatever information has been elicited already by others and to determine the referring person's level of understanding of the dynamics and mechanics of child sexual abuse. The more information I have before discussing the case with the child and/or family members, the more effective my assessment will be. It is not unusual for referring professionals to withhold information from consultants in a misguided effort to avoid bias. In general, I refuse point-blank to provide consultation under such conditions; the secrecy, guilt, and suppression common in the sexual abuse of children make blind "fishing expeditions" both risky and potentially harmful to the child.

PRIVATE INTERVIEW WITH PARENT OR GUARDIAN

Next, I prefer to talk privately to the child's parent or guardian. This order of interviewing makes it possible to elicit more information about the facts of the case before talking to the child. Parents or guardians are likely to be anxious about the impending examination of the child, and I find that it allays their anxiety if they have an opportunity to talk to be me before I attempt to obtain information from the child. When the parent is initially reluctant to speak about the sexual abuse, it may be easier to begin by asking routine questions about the child's past medical history. Usually some anxiety is allayed while discussing these less threatening details. I always ask the parent why he or she decided to bring the child for a medical examination. Often parents must make a major effort to articulate the complaint. If necessary, I gently urge the parent to describe the sexual activity directly. It helps them to confront reality more effectively by "saying the words." One mother reacted first with anger when I encouraged her to tell me what happened to her daughter. She kept replying, "He sexually molested her." I kept repeating,

"Yes, but what did they actually do?" When she could finally utter, "He put his finger into her rectum and her vagina," she broke down and cried with relief. Later she said, "I didn't think I could ever live with it until after I could finally say the words."

After I have spent some private time with the parent, there is usually little difficulty in getting him or her to consent to allow me to talk to the child alone. Sometimes parents express concern that the child will be intimidated and refuse to talk to me. This is usually a projection of their own fears and is rarely a problem in reality. I respond by promising to terminate the interview whenever the child makes a request to stop talking. In fact, a child rarely, if ever, asks to terminate an interview. I also tell the parent that I prefer to examine the child with only a nurse in attendance. Most parents also agree willingly to this arrangement.

As a matter of policy, I never interview a parent or guardian in the presence of the child victim. Such circumstances are inhibiting for both the child and the parent and encourage the parent to convey an "official" version of the story. It is implicit to the child that he or she must then adhere to the parental version of the story thereafter. This places an unfair burden on the child and severe constraints on the reliability of information obtained from either party. It also becomes very difficult to establish a relationship with either the parent or the child. Hence the private interviews as outlined.

PRIVATE INTERVIEW WITH THE CHILD

Whenever possible, I try to arrange for another professional person to be with the child while I am talking to the people who brought the child in. An ideal scenario in my office would proceed as follows: After appropriate introductions, I begin to interview the accompanying child protection services worker while my secretary obtains basic information from the parent, explains policies, and obtains signatures on permission slips and release forms. Meanwhile, my nurse brings the child to another room, measures height, weight, and blood pressure, and performs a Snellen test for vision. If further time is available, the nurse engages the youngster in casual conversation or offers toys or coloring materials. We try to insure that each party is fully occupied while waiting to be interviewed.

Although slightly more time-consuming, I defer having the child undress and don an examination gown until after the interview. Youngsters tend to be intimidated by medical settings anyway, but they seem to feel less vulnerable during an interview if fully clothed. With very young children, I do not attempt a full investigative interview on the same visit as the medical examination. Constraints of time do not usually permit the multiple and leisurely play interviews required for children up to ages seven or eight years. With older children, it is usually possible to discuss the sexual activity and to perform a medical examination during the same visit.

In general, I refuse to interview children about sexual abuse in the presence of a parent or guardian. If the parent insists on being present, I respond by saying that no one can elicit reliable information under such circumstances and refuse to try.

There is usually little difficulty, under the circumstances just described, in establishing a relationship with most children eight years old or older; most are willing to discuss the sexual activity with little apparent hesitation. A good opener is, "Tell me the first time it ever happened." I ask what room the sexual activity occurred in, where the participants were standing or sitting or lying, what clothes the child was wearing, what the perpetrator had on, and where other family members were at the time. It helps to use "event time" to establish dates: How old were you on your last birthday? What grade were you in? What

was your teacher's name? How old was your brother? Where did your family live then?

Whenever possible, I try to have the child tell me what occurred in his or her own words, and I try to establish the exact meaning of the child's terminology: "pookie" may mean vagina; "butt-hole" may mean rectal opening; "blow job" may mean fellatio; and so forth. If the youngster finds it difficult to articulate names of body parts, I suggest that we point at body parts on our own bodies. Some interviewers like to use drawings or anatomically correct dolls for this process.

Although I avoid leading the child whenever possible, it is sometimes necessary to ask specific questions about sexual interaction. It is always useful to establish credibility at the outset by telling the child, "I have talked to many kids about these things." In addition to conveying that the child is not unique regarding the sexual experience (a new concept for many victims), it helps to lay groundwork for eliciting specific details later. For example, if the child seems to be blocking about details of sexual activity, the interviewer can say, "Some kids I have talked to had somebody touch them here," (indicating a body part). Or the interviewer might say, "One girl I talked to had a big brother who tried to get her to lick him." Sometimes children will respond with their own stories if given these general leads. One little boy blurted in response, "How did you know that's what happened to me? Did Jimmy (the uncle who had pressured the child to fellate him) tell you?"

Before completing the interview, it is necessary to question the child about all forms of sexual interaction that might have taken place. It is especially important for interviewers to be sure that they understand the child's terminology. One 13-year-old girl told me emphatically that she had had vaginal intercourse with her father's best friend. I did not, however, elicit specifics from her: Did he put his penis into your vagina? How far inside? What happened then? and so forth. Physical examination revealed that the hymenal opening was less than two centimeters, and the introitus was obviously too small for penile penetration to take place. When I questioned her again, it was clear that she was not lying but had mistaken "dry intercourse" for penile penetration of her vagina. It is never desirable for the interviewer's naivete to exceed that of the child!

If interviewing a child who has been in continuous access to a known perpetrator elicits a history of multiple sexual encounters, a progression of sexual activity over time, and elements of secrecy, I usually regard the story to be validated. If I believe the child, I tell him or her that I believe the story. To be believed may be the single most helpful experience for a child victim.

I like to end the interview by asking the child's permission to perform a medical examination. Most agree readily; a few want to know, "Will it hurt?" I always promise that I will explain everything I do before I do it, that nothing is going to hurt, and that the child can ask me to stop the examination whenever the child wishes. In this way, I try to convey to the child that he or she has control over his or her body and that the medical examination is not another violation. It helps to say, "Let us check you over from top to bottom so we can be sure that everything is okay." The idea is to convey a shared process, not something that is being "done to" him or her.

General Medical Examination

MEDICAL HISTORY

Part of the medical history is obtained from the parent or guardian; with older children, I like to repeat all of these questions. This gives me an opportunity to test their memories, to examine congruence between the parent's history and the child's history,

and to elicit additional background information about family functioning: What time do you usually go to bed? Who usually wakes you up to go to school? Do you eat breakfast? Who fixes breakfast? Responses to questions about sleeping and eating may also yield valuable insights into the child's emotional status. Decreased appetite or sleep disturbance may signal depression. Sleep disturbance may also yield clues about sexual abuse, especially if the child reports that he or she is afraid to fall asleep. Review of systems can also elicit somatic complaints related to anxiety and depression: headaches, stomach pain, nausea, emesis, and so forth. Urinary complaints, dysmenorrhea, vaginal problems, rectal discomfort, or bowel complaints may all signal specific aspects of the sexual abuse.

GENERAL PHYSICAL EXAMINATION

It is important to perform a complete physical examination because it conveys to the child that the physician is interested in the child as a whole human being and deemphasizes the genital examination by placing it in a larger context. The complete physical assessment establishes the child's general health and nutritional status, provides information about growth and development, rules out physical illness, and discovers signs of abuse and neglect. Also, it allows the examiner to touch the child gently in a caring and nonthreatening fashion. I like to tell the child what I am doing and why and encourage him or her to ask me questions during the process. These examinations are conducted with the door closed and with the child attired in an examining gown. A sheet is used as a drape whenever appropriate.

PHYSICAL EXAMINATION FOR SEXUAL ABUSE

Genital examinations should always be performed with an assistant present. It helps to have everything ready and set aside for collecting specimens.

EXAMINATION OF THE MALE CHILD

First, I inspect the genitals for swelling, excoriations, abrasions, bite marks, ecchymoses, or other evidence of trauma. In uncircumcised boys, I retract the foreskin to inspect the glans penis. I then inspect the urethral meatus for trauma, abnormal dilation, foreign bodies, and urethral discharge. If discharge is present, I collect a specimen with a swab and plate it immediately on Thayer-Martin media (to be incubated under CO_2 for 24 hours before it is sent to an outside laboratory) to test for *Neisseria gonorrhoeae*. Next, I palpate the scrotum and testicles and check for hernia, and then I apply gentle traction to the buttocks to inspect the anorectal opening for trauma, abnormal dilation, and foreign bodies. Next, I insert a moistened cotton swab approximately 1.5 centimeters into the anus and gently move it from side to side for 15 seconds to swab the anal crypts. I then plate the specimen directly onto Thayer-Martin media. If the boy did not have a urethral discharge, I ask him to obtain a small urine specimen (he should void a few drops only into a container to obtain urethral washings) which may then be plated directly onto Thayer-Martin media.[9] A throat culture for gonorrhea is usually the last part of the examination as it is usually also the most uncomfortable specimen to be obtained. This specimen should also be plated directly onto Thayer-Martin media.

EXAMINATION OF THE FEMALE CHILD

Little girls can usually be checked most comfortably when they are lying supine on a examining table with their thighs abducted. (It is not often necessary to use stirrups with prepubertal females.) After the girl is lying down with her thighs widely spread, gentle traction to the labia nearly always spreads the labia majora and minora completely so that genital and perineal inspection is easily done.

I look for perineal abrasions, excoriations, and ecchymoses and check the urethral meatus for trauma and abnormal dilation. I note the condition of the hymenal ring and the diameter of the hymenal opening. If the hymenal ring is absent or not readily visible, I gently touch the introitus with one gloved finger. Sometimes the tissues fall to obscure the introitus; gentle anterior palpation usually makes it possible to visualize the introitus readily in such circumstances.

If no trauma is present, and the hymenal ring is intact and less than two centimeters in diameter with no evidence of a foreign body, I do not attempt to insert a speculum. If the hymenal ring is absent, and the diameter of the introitus will admit a narrow speculum, I perform a speculum examination, visualize the cervix, do a Papanicolaou smear, obtain cervical specimens to test for gonococci, and finish with a bimanual examination. Otherwise, I obtain a swab of vulvovaginal secretions to be plated immediately on Thayer-Martin media for gonococci. Regardless of the condition of the vagina, I routinely obtain urethral and rectal swab specimens for gonococcal culture (technique described for male children). If the history suggests sexual interaction in the past 72 hours, I also obtain swabs of vulvovaginal secretions to be checked for sperm and acid phosphatase. Lastly, a throat culture for gonococci is obtained.

I do not routinely do serological tests for syphilis on children unless there is a history of contact with syphilis or the perpetrator is unknown. If there is another sexually transmitted disease present, for example, gonorrhea or herpes progenitalis, a test for syphilis should be done also.

Treatment

GONORRHEA

I do not routinely advocate initial prophylactic treatment for gonorrhea unless the child is a contact of someone who is known to be infected. If a culture reveals that the child does have gonorrhea, I prefer to use oral rather than parenteral treatment. Amoxicillin, 50 milligram per kilogram of body weight, with probenecid, 25 milligram per kilogram, both given orally, is an effective one-dose regimen for uncomplicated gonococcal infection.[10] When infected children are treated with oral medication, they are not traumatized by the treatment process, and follow-up examination is far easier. Specimens, from all sites, should be obtained and tested, one month after treatment to be sure that the infection has been eliminated. Repeat cultures should be done again in six months to rule out reinfection.

PREGNANCY

Postpubertal girls with a history of vaginal intercourse should be checked for pregnancy at the time of the medical examination. I do not advocate routine treatment with diethylstilbestrol to prevent pregnancy; this issue must be examined carefully for each patient, and the approach should be individualized. Girls should be counseled to keep a menstrual calendar and to ask for a repeat pregnancy test if menses are missed after a sexual exposure.

EMOTIONAL TRAUMA

As previously stated, I believe that every child who is examined for sexual abuse should be told that he or she is normal and not damaged. Both the child and parents should receive anticipatory guidance for this issue. For example, I might say, "Lots of kids your age think there has to be something wrong with them after they have had things like this happen to them. You may think about this quite a bit, later on. Keep remembering that you are okay. Do not keep your feelings bottled up inside you. Talk to your mom or dad. Come back and talk to me. Ask all the questions you want to ask. Even though you are all right, it is normal to have

questions about all this later on." I also inform both the child and the parents that I believe conseling is indicated for all child victims, regardless of any initially apparent lack of emotional trauma.

PHYSICAL TRAUMA

Whenever physical injury of the genital or rectal area is present, the appropriate surgical subspecialist (gynecologist, urologist, proctologist) should be consulted. Although serious injuries are rare, the presence of superficial genital or rectal injury may require internal examination of the injured area. These children may require hospital admission and examination under anesthesia.

Closing Considerations and Follow-up

CONVEY FINDINGS

Each party involved should be told something about the findings at the end of the examination. It is not appropriate to send people away wondering, "What did the doctor find?" I believe telling the child, the parent, and the accompanying professional what I found before they leave. Again, all need reassurance that the child will be all right. If I believe that the allegation of sexual abuse is validated, I convey this to all parties.

FOLLOW-UP

Often an additional visit will be rquired to complete the evaluation or to monitor treatment. All parties should be informed of this fact, and arrangements should be made for follow-up before they leave.

REPORT WRITING

I find that writing a report is always a helpful way to organize my findings. The report will be invaluable to the referring professional, and a comprehensive and well-documented report by a physician frequently obviates the need to testify in court.

COMPREHENSIVE MEDICAL EXAMINATION FOR SEXUALLY ABUSED CHILDREN

Summary of Components

PRIMARY CONSIDERATIONS

- Obtain permission to examine the child
- Report all cases to child protection services
- Report validated cases to police
- Obtain a release authorizing a report to the referral source

INVESTIGATIVE INTERVIEWING

- First, interview accompanying professional in private
- Next, interview parent or guardian in private
- Last, interview child in private

GENERAL MEDICAL EXAMINATION

- Obtain careful medical history
- Perform general physical examination

PHYSICAL EXAMINATION FOR SEXUAL ABUSE

- Examination of male child
  - Genital and rectal inspection for trauma, abnormal dilation of urethra or anus, and foreign bodies
  - Urine or urethral specimens to be cultured for gonococci
  - Anorectal specimens to be cultured for gonococci
  - Pharyngeal specimens to be cultured for gonococci
- Examination of the female child
  - Genital, rectal, and perineal inspection for trauma, abnormal dilation of urethral, vulvovaginal, and anorectal openings, and foreign bodies

- Urethral, vulvovaginal, anorectal, and pharyngeal specimens to be cultured for gonococci
- Vulvovaginal specimens for sperm and acid phosphatase

TREATMENT FOR

- Gonorrhea
- Pregnancy
- Emotional trauma
- Physical trauma

FOLLOW-UP

- Convey findings
- Arrange follow-up examination
- Write a report

REFERENCES

1. Sgroi SM, et al: A conceptual framework for child sexual abuse, in Sgroi SM (ed): *A Handbook of Clinical Intervention in Child Sexual Abuse.* Lexington, Mass, Lexington Books, 1982.

2. Burgess A, Holmstrom L: Sexual assault of children and adolescents: pressure, sex and secrecy. *Nurs Clin North Am* **10**:551–563, 1975.

3. Groth AN, Burgess A: Motivational intent in the sexual assault of children. *Crim Justice Behav* **4**:253–264, 1977.

4. Groth AN, Birnbaum H: *Men Who Rape.* New York, Plenum Press, Plenum Publishing Corp, 1978, p 149.

5. Sgroi SM: Pediatric gonorrhea beyond infancy. *Pediatr Ann* **8**:326–336, 1979.

6. Groth AN: The incest offender, in Sgroi SM (ed): *A Handbook of Clinical Intervention in Child Sexual Abuse.* Lexington, Mass, Lexington Books, 1982.

7. Sgroi SM: Case management in child sexual abuse, in Sgroi SM (ed): *A Handbook of Clinical Intervention in Child Sexual Abuse.* Lexington, Mass, Lexington Books, 1982.

8. Blick L, et al: Validation of child sexual abuse, in Sgroi SM (ed): *A Handbook of Clinical Intervention in Child Sexual Abuse.* Lexington, Mass, Lexington Books, 1982.

9. Feng W, et al: Diagnosis of gonorrhea in male patients by culture of uncentrifuged first-voided urine. *JAMA* **237**:896–897, 1977.

10. Nelson J, et al: Gonorrhea in preschool and school-aged children. *JAMA* **236**:1359–1364, 1976.

24

COUNSELING AND FOLLOW-UP INTERACTION FOR THE SEXUALLY ABUSED CHILD

Lucy Berliner, M.S.W.

Counseling the sexually abused child presents the challenge of treating a child whose disturbance is the result of an externally imposed event. The main goal of intervention is to restore the child to normal developmental functioning whenever possible. Many children face barriers to achieving this goal because of societal attitudes reflected in the institutions encountered by the child who reports sexual abuse. Many are not believed or are blamed, or the seriousness of the abuse is minimized. The child must not only be treated for the trauma associated with the sexual abuse but also be helped to deal with the societal institutions that act on the child's behalf, the child protection services and the criminal justice system. The advocate-therapist approach to treatment combines counseling and advocacy. Counseling focuses on alleviating any sense of responsibility or guilt that the child may feel and on assisting the child to integrate the sexual abuse into the normal developmental process. Advocacy focuses on protecting the child and identifying a supportive environment for the child's continued growth and development. Advocacy usually involves intervention, on behalf of the child, with various community agencies. Both aspects of treatment are necessary for adequate intervention.

INITIAL INTERVENTION

Unless the child can be assured of a safe and caring environment, counseling will accomplish little. Counselors may not actually become involved in providing for the protection of the child, but they must be sure that the proper authorities are. If the abuser is a member of the household or a caretaker, a report must be made to the child protection service as mandated by state laws in all 50 states.[1] Although the specific conditions that require a report vary, any case where the parent does not believe the child, is not willing or able to protect the child from the offender, or where the parent fails to provide proper medical or psychological care to the child should be reported.

THE PROBLEM

Retrospective studies indicate that at least one-fifth of all children experience sexual molestation.[2] Those cases coming to the attention of official agencies or authorities represent only a small portion of the incidence of child sexual abuse.[3] Among reported cases, about one-fourth of the victims are boys. Children are usually sexually abused by someone known to them or by a family member. The abuse can range from a single incident of fondling to repeated acts of intercourse over many years. Most cases of ongoing abuse involve a family member as the offender, and the largest category of offender is a parent, almost always a father, stepfather or the mother's live-in partner.[4] (See Appendix for complete statistics on sexual assault of children.)

There are many levels of coercion that may be used to involve the child: exploiting the child's lack of knowledge or the adult's natural authority over the child, misrepresentation of moral standards, withdrawal of affection, trading privileges for sexual favors, and the threat or use of violence.

The child who is sexually abused by a parent is most likely to be severely disturbed. This child experiences not only the trauma associated with forced premature sexual activity but also the distortion of the parent-child relationship. Parents who sexually abuse their child permanently alter the child's perceptions of adults. A child is completely dependent on the parents for meeting basic needs. When a parent violates the basic responsibilities to protect and nurture the child and commits a criminal act of abuse, the child's belief in the adult is compromised. Children are often without the knowledge or resources to stop the abuse or seek outside help. Children who live with the fear that their father may have sexual contact if they are ever left alone with him cannot experience normal growth. All aspects of the child's functioning are affected by this fundamental distortion of parental roles.

Child victims are almost always persuaded to maintain silence about the sexual abuse by threats or instructions not to tell. Many children are told they will be responsible for the consequences of disclosure such as father going to jail or the family breaking up. The child internalizes a sense of guilt and responsibility for both the abuse and the disruption that usually follows revelation.

Most children fear reporting sexual abuse because, from their perspective, their involvement in the abuse somehow carries responsibility. Fequently, children report that they feared they would get in trouble or that they would be blamed.

If the abuse is discovered or reported after a single incident or several incidents, the child is less likely to have developed adaptive behavior that allows the child to survive in a sexually abusive situation. Many of the coping mechanisms that are effective within the pathological framework of intrafamily sexual abuse are inappropriate or self-destructive in a normal environment. The symptoms that bring a child to the attention of the authorities may be learned responses, such as stylized sexual behavior, that may require professional intervention.

INTERVENTION

When the abuse is a single incident and is not extremely violent, it can often be handled in a relatively matter-of-fact fashion. The child may exhibit a transient situational reaction which is a natural response to an unusual, frightening, or uncomfortable experience. Clarification of correct behavior between adults and children, placement of the responsibility for the behavior on the adult offender, assurance that the child will be protected from further abuse, and support for revealing the abuse are the basic elements of treatment. The child should be encouraged to express any concerns or fears, and all questions should be answered simply and honestly. With a very young child, the parents can often be enlisted to convey these messages and to monitor changes in the child's behavior and functioning. Most parents are able to handle the situation with sensitivity and support if they are included in the process and are provided with adequate information.

The closer the relationship of the offender to the family, the more complex the reaction because both the child and the family have ambivalent feelings toward the offender. Virtually all child victims dislike being sexually abused; a few are physiologically stimulated by the contact. Some children, although they dislike the actual molestation, continue to like the offender or like other parts of the relationship. The family may be less likely to believe the accusation if it is a friend or relative or baby-sitter whom they trust. Sometimes, even when they believe the child, they may blame the child for causing the problem or for provoking the abuse. Often the parents are simply torn between two people and have mixed feelings which tend to be communicated to the child as blame or anger.

When the offender is a parent and the abuse is repeated, as it is in four-fifths of incest cases, the child often will have an extensive psychosocial reaction. The child becomes resigned to the sexual abuse and adapts certain coping behaviors. Even when there is an opportunity to leave the situation, the child may no longer seek help. Treatment must then focus on dealing not only with sexual abuse and its consequences but also with behavior patterns the child may have adopted. Most of these children are not operating at the appropriate developmental level and need reorientation toward normal behaviors and activities.

When the parent is unable or unwilling to take an active role in supporting the child, treatment is much more important because the child has no other source of support. The therapist may become the only adult who is completely committed to supporting the child victim. The counselor faces the task of trying to convince the parents to adopt a supportive attitude or to overcome their resistance to a proper response to the child.

CHILD REACTIONS

The preadolescent child who is sexually abused will often be precociously mature, confused about appropriate adult-child roles and responsibilities, overly compliant and anxious to please, constricted in emotional responses, and guarded in sharing feelings or thoughts. The child may exhibit certain situational symptoms such as sleeping problems, eating problems, irritability, crankiness, withdrawal, somatic complaints, inappropriate or unusual sexual language or behavior, and regression. Depending on the age of the child, treatment usually consists of play therapy or modified play therapy.

Treatment for the sexual abuse itself focuses on making it clear to the child victim that the adult is responsible for the behavior, regardless of the extent of the child's involvement, and that it was wrong for the adult to do it. It is important to distinguish forced sexual activity between an adult and a child from sexual activity between consenting peers so that the child does not associate the two. The child also needs reinforcement that reporting the abuse is the only way of stopping it. If the child is told that this way makes it possible for the offender to receive treatment, guilt for reporting may be alleviated.

ADOLESCENT REACTIONS

The adolescent victim of incest is most likely to display severe psychosocial dysfunction because most adolescents have been involved in the sexual abuse over a period of years and have developed self-destructive, denying patterns of behavior. There are two general modes of coping: internalizing or externalizing the effects of the sexual abuse.

The victim who internalizes the sexual abuse may be apparently normal in many ways. In most cases, however, the victim is depressed and has suicidal ideations; shows somatization, with headaches and stomachaches the most prevalent; and is overly compliant or precociously adult in style. Many are self-destructive in thoughts and behaviors. The adolescent who externalizes the consequences may appear to be acting out by running away, skipping school, being rebellious at home, being promiscuous, or abusing drugs or alcohol or may become involved in criminal activity. Regardless of the style of coping, almost all of the victims report common symptoms of distress such as sleep disturbance and nightmares, flashbacks, or an association that triggers a reminder of the abusive situation. One of the coping methods for handling the sexual abuse itself is to disassociate during the sexual activity. Many of these children have the ability to remove themselves mentally from the situation they are in.

Virtually all the adolescents are self-denigrating and self-blaming. They continue to accept responsibility for the sexual abuse and for the consequences of revealing the abuse; they are confused and sometimes fear they are going crazy because they are unable to make some sense out of the world around them. They will often regret telling because of the disruption that follows and the lack of support they feel. Most have some concerns about their sexuality; they may become too casual about sexual involvement or be frightened of any sexual contact at all.

In addition, all of the teenage victims are experiencing normal adolescent turmoil which includes confronting the issues of sexuality, increased desires for independence, separation from the family, increasing reliance on peers, and planning for their future. They have not had the normal developmental foundation for entering adolescence, and they often feel as though they have

had no childhood, a period that should be characterized by a sense of security and freedom to play, experience, and grow. For most, home life and the family has represented fear, uncertainty, and confusion. These victims are alienated from the experiences of peers and usually feel isolated and different from other teenagers. In many cases, the normal struggles of adolescence precipitate the disclosure of the sexual abuse.

When a victim of incest discloses the abuse, by telling a parent or a friend or an outside agency, there is an inevitable disruption to the family. Often the victim is pressured to either recant the history of the abuse or not pursue criminal charges or any other kind of official intervention. The offender may pressure the child because the offender fears incarceration or criminal penalties. The mother may pressure the child if she is dependent upon the offender and fears that the financial and psychological stability of the home will be disrupted. Siblings may be resentful and angry at the victim for the disruption. Other relatives may also put pressure on the child. Whether the victim is removed from the home or the offender is removed from the home certainly has an effect on how the victim feels about the results of disclosure.

Treatment strategy should view the victim as a normal person to whom something bad has happened. It is important to remove the sense of guilt and blame that the child inevitably feels. The child also needs information about the meaning of the adult's sexual behavior, the placement of the responsibility on the adult who committed the abuse, information about proper expectations of children and adults within a family, and information about normal sexual functioning and attitudes. In addition, it is important to reintegrate the child into normal adolescent functioning whenever possible. The therapist often acts as an adult advisor for the victim by providing an opportunity for the child to express concerns without the possibility of repercussions.

Individual and group treatment are both important methods of intervening with the incest victim. Group treatment lessens the sense of isolation and provides peer support. Individual treatment is usually necessary also to deal with the specific concerns of each adolescent. Traditional therapy in the office may not be as effective with teenagers as a combination of home visits, telephone contacts, and shared activities.

FAMILY INTERVENTION

Obviously, treatment for the sexually abused child must be accompanied by counseling for the parents. The parents need education and guidance in the proper parental response to the trauma caused by sexual abuse and its impact on normal developmental growth. It is often difficult to distinguish between normal behavior and sequelae of traumatic events. Parents can learn to respond to the child in a responsible, supportive, adult manner which will lead to recovery and growth in the child.

If the abuse is committed by someone outside the family, the parents generally need short-term assistance with their own reactions as well as advice and support in the appropriate response to the child victim. When there is no ongoing contact or relationship with the offender, the family is usually able to focus exclusively on supporting and helping the child. If there will be a continuing relationship with the offender, the child's parents must be helped to clearly communicate to the child that the primary concern and commitment is the protection of and support for the victim. When the offender is a parent, when there is already a divorce or separation, or when the mother chooses not to continue the relationship, the child may still wish to maintain a relationship with the offender. When the nonoffending parent and the of-

fender wish to be reunited, child victims may feel that they are the obstacle to everyone's happiness unless they agree to the offender's return to the family. Ideally, the extent of the relationship should be determined by the child's true wishes in the context of safety for the child. Since children often feel that they are supposed to love a parent regardless of the parent's behavior, it is necessary to sort out what the child truly wants from what are social or parental assumptions and expectations.

INCEST INTERVENTION

When the nonoffending parent and the offender wish to be reunited, it is much more difficult to ascertain the child's wishes. Both parents may deny or fail to recognize the child's needs if those needs conflict with the desire to reunite. Many children would prefer that the mother choose to separate from the offender so long as the child is not responsible for the decision. Since some mothers wish to continue the relationship with the offender regardless of the child's desires, child victims often feel that they are faced with the choice of no membership in the family or living with the offender. Children are usually so attached to the mother that they will prefer living with the offender again to not living with any parent. In this case it is most important to correctly assess and reassess the child's feelings and provide an outlet for the confusion. The focus should be on structuring the family environment to be as supportive and protective as possible and providing stringent supervision to insure the physical and psychological safety of the child.

PROTECTION

Contact between the child and the offender should always be carefully monitored. Only when the offender has admitted guilt, accepted responsibility for the behavior, and entered into an approved treatment program should contact be allowed at all. There should be no unsupervised contact for young children who are unable to assert themselves with an adult or parent. Even with an adolescent, direct contact should be supervised until the victim has demonstrated adequate strength and resources to cope with a sexual advance or pressure. The child who is returned to a living situation with an offender should be in contact with outside professionals on a regular basis for an indefinite time; these professionals provide structure and access to assistance when necessary. The victim can be encouraged to establish ongoing relationships with responsible adults, teachers, medical personnel, counselors, or employers.

SUMMARY

The sexually abused child has experienced the imposition of adult sexual behavior without regard for the impact on the child. Factors that determine the child's response include the nature of the abuse itself, the degree of violence, the relationship to the offender, the response to the child victim at disclosure, ensuing decisions about placement, and the child's individual personality.

The intervener must address the individual treatment needs of both the child victim and the victim's family, protection of the child from further abuse, and placement in a supportive environment. This form of intervention requires a therapist-advocate approach that encompasses both individual and structural change and improvement.

APPENDIX

CHILD SEXUAL ASSAULT — SEXUAL ASSAULT CENTER

Harborview Medical Center
Seattle, Washington

A group of 593 different children (and their families or caretakers) received medical and counseling services from October 1977 to August 1979. This population includes all cases of incest reported to the Sexual Assault Center as well as children and adolescents who were raped or molested by someone known to them. (Cases in which adolescents were forcibly raped by strangers are excluded.)

VICTIM CHARACTERISTICS		%
Sex: Female		85
Male		15
Age: 1–6 years		22
7–12 years		40
13–16 years		38

OFFENDER CHARACTERISTICS		
Sex: Male		96
Female		4
Relationship to Victim:		
Relatives		53
Natural parent	16	
Stepparent	16	
Other parental figure	6	
Other relative	15	
Child or family acquaintance		36
Stranger		8
Other		2

ABUSE CHARACTERISTICS

Nature of Offense (in addition to fondling):*

Forced masturbation	13
Digital penetration	11
Anal intercourse	6
Vaginal intercourse	25
Oral intercourse	25

	Intra-family Abuse (%)	Non-family Abuse (%)	Both Groups (%)
Type of Force:			
Physical force or weapon	16	29	22
Threatened force	16	16	16
Coercion by adult authority	63	40	52
Tangible enticement	3	10	6
Other	2	5	4
Duration of Offense:			
Single incident	17	73	45
Ongoing, less than 6 months	22	21	22
Ongoing, 6–12 months	23	3	12
Ongoing, 1–5 years	29	3	17
Ongoing, more than 5 years	9	0	4

	Intra-family Abuse (%)	Non-family Abuse (%)	Both Groups (%)
DISCLOSURE			
Reported to			
Parent	49	49	49
Other relative	13	8	11
Peer	10	5	8
Nonrelated adult	7	12	9
Medical or social agency	7	4	5
Legal agency	2	8	5
Discovered	11	14	13

Lapse between Last Incident of Abuse and Report:			
Less than 48 hours	16	57	36
2 days to 2 weeks	30	21	25
2 weeks to 6 months	31	17	24
More than 6 months	23	5	15
Action Taken by Parents:			
Immediate	61	86	72
Delayed	22	6.5	15
None	17	7.5	13

INTRAFAMILY ABUSE* additional information	%
Siblings of primary client also abused	34
Offenders known to have committed prior offenses	20
Other problems reported in family:	
Alcohol or drug abuse	20
Spouse abuse	10
Physical abuse of child	14
Mental illness	7
Other (e.g., severe marital discord)	19
None reported	50

*Multiple responses or no response are possible. Therefore, totals may be less than or greater than 100%.

REFERENCES

1. National Center on Child Abuse and Neglect Children's Bureau, Administration for Children, Youth, and Families, US Dept of Health, Education, and Welfare, 1979.

2. Finkelhor D: *Sexually Victimized Children.* New York, The Free Press, 1979.

3. Sarafino EP: An estimate of nationwide incidence of sexual offenses against children. *Child Welfare* **58**:127–134, 1979.

4. Sexual Assault Center Statistics: Child Sexual Assault. Sexual Assault Center, Seattle, 1979.

Unit VI

Evaluation and Planning

25

EVALUATION OF THE SERVICE NETWORK: IMPLICATIONS FOR CHANGE

Lana K. Willingham, M.S.W.

The need for funds to address the problems of social and domestic violence and the need to demonstrate the relative effectiveness of various intervention strategies are especially important. Consequently, the evaluation of a program becomes a key concern. An evaluation serves two major functions: it accounts for the program's use of public funds, and it provides objective data to be used in making decisions about the planning or redirection of the program. Evaluation is often defined as an effort to determine what changes occurred as the result of a planned program. It does so by comparing actual changes with desired changes (stated goals) and determining the degree to which the program is responsible for the changes.[1]

RATIONALE FOR EVALUATION

Accountability

Since the 1960s, there has been heavy emphasis on the need to account for the use and expenditure of public funds. Evaluations not only ensure that funds are appropriately spent but also ensure that programs are planned to derive the maximum benefit from those funds. Decisions must be made about the relative benefits of various programs. For instance, is a program aimed at training emergency care personnel in techniques of detection and crisis intervention for victims of violence of greater benefit than a program aimed at educating the general public about the myths and prevalence of domestic violence in order to decrease the stigma that often prevents a victim from obtaining necessary treatment? Similar questions must be answered about the relative benefit of a crisis hotline for rape victims or a training course in self-defense. Evaluations also objectively demonstrate that services are provided without stigmatizing, labeling, or degrading the consumer and that the rights of victims and alleged perpetrators are handled in a manner that respects their human dignity while adequately protecting society.

Need for Objective Data

The second major reason for evaluation is the need for objective data. The need for information on the background, history, and current functioning of the client has long been recognized by professionals who treat the individual. Without information, identifying problems, defining intervention strategies, and setting realistic goals is impossible. The process of obtaining information from individual clients in the initial assessment is similar to the research process used by evaluators. Effective practitioners follow the same research steps as effective evaluators.

The historical separation of practitioners and researchers has not benefited the development of good programs or good intervention models. Decisions on program development should be based on objective information about existing problems and successes in implementation. Too often evaluation to demonstrate accountability takes precedence over evaluation to provide information.

Summative and Formative Evaluations

Evaluation models that focus on accountability are called summative evaluation. Models that focus on program planning and reformulation are called formative evaluation. There are important distinctions between these two models.[2,3]

Summative evaluation is used after a program is well established. The intent is to show that the program has accomplished its stated purpose. Formative evaluation is used while a program is developing or changing. The intent is to provide a data base for making decisions. The purpose is not to document the total worth of the program but to demonstrate its strengths and weaknesses so that restructuring or planning can improve the present intervention strategies.[4] Assessment occurs periodically, and feedback is used to improve performance.[5]

Tripodi defines summative evaluation as providing information that can be used to compare a program to other similar programs.[4] Rossi suggests that two considerations are important: the impact of the program and the coverage of the program (its applicability to a large number of cases or situations). Rossi believes that too much attention has been paid to impact without any regard for coverage.[6]

In the previous example of a program to increase the skills of emergency medical staff versus a program to educate the public at large, one program may have greater impact on victims themselves while the other program may compensate with broader coverage. Determining the comparative worth of these two programs must consider both coverage and impact.

Since few funds are available for direct provision and evaluation of service strategies, evaluations must be designed to provide both formative and summative information. Formative evaluation is extremely important when a program involves relatively new intervention strategies and dispells historical myths. New strategies and old myths are very prevalent in the area of social and domestic violence.

Designs for formative and summative evaluation should influence and augment each other. If program design is improved through decision making based on information from formative evaluation, then the final summative evaluation will show an enhanced, more effective program. Similarly, well-designed summative evaluations can enhance the design of other programs aimed at similar social problems.

EVALUATION MODELS

An understanding of the different types of evaluation used for gathering information is important. To obtain maximum benefits, the design of the evaluation must be specific for the program under review.

All evaluative information should provide data that management can use to make decisions. Therefore, even simple, descriptive data that increases the managers' knowledge of the program can be valuable.

The following briefly describe the different models commonly used in social programs:

Descriptive Evaluation

In descriptive evaluations a review is made of program goals, objectives, intervention strategies, implementation, and desired outcome. Phenomenological information or reports from participants are often included. No measurement of efficiency or outcome is attempted. Detailed descriptive statements often provide the basis for further refinement of evaluation strategies.

Effort Evaluation

Effort evaluations assess the amount of energy, units of service, or inputs in a program. No attempt is made to ascertain inputs in relation to outputs achieved. Counting the number of counseling visits or presentations for community education would be an example of this type of evaluation. No outcome or results of such contacts is ascertained. Information from this type of evaluation is often used to budget or allocate staff. The major drawback is that one must assume that the effort put forth affects the defined problem. No results of the effort expended are defined.

Efficiency Evaluation

Efficiency evaluation establishes the number of outputs (benefits of the program) resulting from the number of inputs (efforts and material put into the program). Project performance is divided by project effort. Some decisions are possible, such as whether the project could improve results by changing the types of inputs. The effectiveness of the outputs is not determined.

Effectiveness (Outcome) Evaluation

Effectiveness evaluation assesses the results of the inputs and outputs. It asks, Are maximum results or benefits being obtained? or What is the outcome of the efforts being expended? An assessment of the quality of the result is often included.

Impact Evaluation

Impact evaluation assesses the amount of change in the client group or community that is a direct result of the planned intervention techniques of the program. It determines how much of the change would not have occurred if the program did not exist. What differences did the intervention make?

Impact evaluations are the most difficult and the most productive evaluations to conduct. They are both formative and summative and should provide the data required to answer five questions:

1. Should the program be continued?
2. Which programs achieve the greatest benefits for a given cost?
3. Which program strategies or combinations of strategies achieve the greatest effect in relation to the costs (what effect is achieved at what cost)?
4. Which programs best serve certain types of people?
5. What modifications would maximize a program's impact?

The major purpose of impact evaluation is to demonstrate that an intervention strategy has caused a particular outcome, one that would not have occurred otherwise. An attempt is made to control extraneous or conflicting variables which might obscure the results. For example, if the incidence of rape drops in a metropolitan area, is the drop because of a community watch program or because of changes in the reporting system? Impact evaluation accounts for a program's use of funds and provides information necessary for making decisions about program planning or reformulation.

EVALUATION DESIGN SHOULD BE DEFINED DURING INITIAL PROGRAM DESIGN

A well-designed program is an easily evaluated program. Clearly defining program goals and objectives in the initial stage will not only aid in obtaining funds but also result in a program that can be easily evaluated. This point cannot be overemphasized. It is too late to define a program when a summative evaluation is needed. Too often evaluators are consulted when a program is in trouble or needs additional funding. They are asked to evaluate a program that has never clearly stated its purpose and intended results. Evaluations of such programs cannot provide information about a program's impact or make recommendations for improvements. Clearly defined goals or objectives are a necessary base for judgment.

When a program is not defined in measurable terms until the time of evaluation (after the program has been in operation), the data necessary for determining its success or impact has not been accumulated, and evaluation cannot assess the actual benefits derived from the program. Another important concern is that the staff and community work together to achieve a program's goals and purposes. When goals are unclear or nonexistent, individuals may actually be working toward different ends, a situation that causes friction and discord. It is essential to define a program's goals and objectives during the initial design so that its worth or benefit can be determined later.

GOALS AND OBJECTIVES

A program or project goal is a general statement that defines the intended purpose of a program. It should include the following information:

- The general purpose of the program
- A description, in general terms, of the population area to be served
- The anticipated results

The program goal should answer the question: What is the project trying to accomplish?

A program or project objective is a clear, specific, time-limited statement of the major measurable changes that will result from the program. Each objective must be clearly linked to the stated goal. If any objective is not a necessary step for realizing the goal, the objective should not be linked to that goal.

For instance, in the case of spousal assault, the goal may be to maximize the physical health of husbands and wives. One objective might be that no couples will file for divorce during their six-month counseling period or for two years after. The objective may be worthwhile, but it is in no way related to the goal. Sometimes divorce may be the best way of maximizing a couple's physical health.

Objectives must contain four essential elements:

1. Clear, understandable terms
2. Realistic change
3. Measurability
4. Time limits

Clearly stated goals and objectives have additional benefits. Funding agencies can clearly understand the purpose and intent of the program, and there is less chance that staff will work at cross-purposes. A clear goal statement provides the basis for ascertaining the worth or relevancy of each program activity. If the activity is not related to accomplishing an objective, it may be a questionable use of staff time.

Since statements of goals and objectives are essential for measuring change, the following example, for a program to decrease social and domestic violence, is provided for review:

- Goal—The program will enhance the safety and health of young couples in the metropolitan area.

- Objective—Twenty-five percent of all couples with a history of spousal assault will not be involved in violent acts between the marital partners for one year after counseling.

COOKBOOK FOR MEASURING CHANGE

The best, clearest, and most decisive measurement of change is the impact a program has on a client or community in resolving the identified problem. For example, consider a program to decrease social and domestic violence. A measurement of the extent of violence before the program's inception compared to its occurrence afterwards would be an excellent indicator of the program's impact. However, the cost of this type of measurement might be prohibitive, or measurement itself might be impossible because of problems in reporting cases of social and domestic violence. Consequently, other measures might be implemented. The cost of evaluation should be carefully assessed since these expenses reduce the amount of funds available for direct service. Care should be taken in determining the evaluation strategy; good evaluation results can lead to allocation of additional funds for direct service.

The following is a cookbook for measuring change. As with any cookbook, it presents a list of alternatives ranging from gourmet measurement with expensive ingredients to basic recipes that can be prepared at little cost. Each recipe is only an example of possible measures. The reader is encouraged to review the recipes and then jot down additional measures that come to mind; the number of possible measurements is unlimited. Creative thought usually produces the most valuable measure with the greatest cost-benefit ratio.

Scaling of Goal Attainment

Measuring how completely goals or objectives are accomplished within stated time frames. Scaling can be used in relationship to program goals or client goals.

INGREDIENTS

- Clear, measurable, realistic, time-limited goals set at the program or client level
- Planned intervention to accomplish goals
- Assessment of goal attainment at the end of the intervention
- Scale of goal attainment (goal achieved, goal partially achieved, goal not achieved)
- Assignment of individual cases or program elements to the appropriate step on the scale

Feedback Information

Questionnaires soliciting clients' comments on services provided, their reactions to the services, and suggestions for improvements.

INGREDIENTS

- Feedback questionnaire mailed to clients after services are delivered
- Telephone interview with a sample of clients
- In-depth interview with a few clients
- Content analysis for pervasive thoughts or trends

Follow-up Information

Questionnaires soliciting client information or collateral information on status changes or behavioral changes in the client as a result of the service intervention.

INGREDIENTS

- Follow-up questionnaire mailed to clients or collateral contacts or both after services are rendered
- Telephone interview with a sample of clients
- In-depth interview with a few clients
- Aggregation of data to determine
  - Percentage of clients needing additional services
  - Percentage of clients with reductions or absence of the targeted behavior
  - Percentage of clients continuing with planned changes in their status

Preintervention and Postintervention Questionnaires

Measuring the status of the individual or client prior to implementation and after termination of the intervention strategy.

INGREDIENTS

- Preintervention questionnaire
- Intervention strategy
- Postintervention questionnaire

There are three variations of this recipe: (1) attitudinal testing instruments may be used for intervention strategies aimed at changing attitudes; (2) fund-of-information questionnaires may be used for programs aimed at increasing knowledge and awareness of alternatives and resources for problematic situations; and (3) behavior measurement questionnaires may be used for programs aimed at changing the behaviors of individuals.

Community Surveys

Using questions or interviews to assess community needs or the impact of a project on the specific target area.

INGREDIENTS

- A survey to assess initial needs prior to or concurrent with starting the program
- Periodic surveys of the community to assess the project's impact on the targeted area

Phenomenological Evaluation

Having a participant-observer present an objective report of how the program functions. Phenomenological evaluation assists in determining the process or factors used to bring about change.

INGREDIENTS

- Selection of an outside observer to work within the program to be served by the program
- Presentation by the observer of objective reports of the processes of the program from an unbiased viewpoint

Observation

Objective viewing of program activities by a nonparticipating outsider in order to determine problems or improvements in processes or procedures.

INGREDIENTS

- Periodic visits to observe program operations
- Periodic, detailed reporting of program strengths and weaknesses

Progress Reports

Ongoing reports of the number and types of services provided or clients served to demonstrate that the program is meeting agreed-upon levels of service. Progress reports are used to demonstrate that the project is performing at an appropriate level.

INGREDIENTS

- Periodic reports of the identified, relevant variables
- Plotting the variables on a graph to demonstrate variances in services provided
- Different variables can be used as appropriate: number of days of care, number of different clients served, number of activities provided, etc.

Content Analysis

Review of documents resulting from the program or changes in documents related to the targeted area after the program intervention.

INGREDIENTS

- Identification of the potential variables to be tracked through documents
- Reading of all documents to identify changes in these variables over time
- Analysis of the relationship between any changes noted and the program strategies

Testing

Giving tests before and after intervention to demonstrate changes in knowledge, behavior, or conditions that result from the program interventions. Many different tests can be employed ranging from I.Q. tests to physical examinations to reflex or agility tests.

INGREDIENTS

- Test administered before the intervention
- Test administered after the intervention
- Analysis of differences and changes noted

Social Indicator Information

Analysis of various social indicators related to the targeted area of the program to determine if any changes are the result of the program.

INGREDIENTS

- Review of social indicators at various intervals before, during, and after the program to ascertain any significant changes
- Analysis to determine if any changes are the result of the program

Controlled Experiments

Determining the impact of the program strategies on the targeted area. A controlled experiment is the only truly scientific way to ascertain the results of the program.

INGREDIENTS

- Random assignment of targeted clients to either the experimental or the control group
- Using the intervention strategy on all experimental group members
- Using a placebo with the control group if the situation warrants
- Analysis of subsequent changes or lack of changes in the control and experimental groups
- Determination and analysis of any extraneous or conflicting variables
- Presentation of the results

SUMMARY

The preceding cookbook does not include all possible measurements of changes. The ideas presented are a starting point for determining the most appropriate method of measuring change for a particular program.

Administrators should decide what information they need for making relevant program decisions and demonstrating account-ability to actual or potential funding agencies. Then the most cost-effective strategy for obtaining the required information should be employed.

Some of the previously mentioned "recipes" are more expensive than others. Several involve ethical concerns such as confidentiality and the withholding of needed or requested services. All these aspects must be weighed to determine the most cost-effective type of evaluation. Administrators and evaluators must work together to select the optimal design.

REFERENCES

1. Anderson WF: *Managing Human Services.* Washington, DC, International City Management Association, 1977, pp 284–285.

2. Scriven M: The methodology of evaluation, in *Perspective of Curriculum Evaluation, AERA.* Chicago, Rand McNally & Co, 1967.

3. Washington RO: *Program Evaluation in the Human Services.* Ohio State University, College of Social Work, April 1979, p 86.

4. Tripodi T: *Research Techniques for Program Planning, Monitoring and Evaluation.* New York, Columbia University Press, 1977, p 112.

5. Anderson WF: *Managing Human Services.* Washington, DC, International City Management Association, 1977.

6. Rossi PH: *Evaluating Social Programs: Theory, Practice and Politics.* New York, Seminar Press Inc, Academic Press Inc, 1972, p 131.

26

COMMUNITY PLANNING

John H. Robbins, B.A., M.S.W.

Central to any definition of planning is the notion of establishing a program for reaching certain goals; this is no less true for emergency care personnel than for city planners.[1] Because it is a specialized field, emergency care is generally treated as an entity unto itself. This chapter proposes that emergency care is an integral part of any service network and should be considered in that context.

Traditionally, community planning in the United States has focused primarily on acquiring and allocating land and physical resources. This circumstance was, in large part, a logical result of the historical pattern of growth experienced by a young nation; early concerns of this country were the development of commerce and industry. The Industrial Revolution and the rapid industrialization of urban centers caused an accompanying shift in population. These urban centers held out the hope for a better way of life, and for many they provided just that: better wages, more opportunity for career development, culture, and the excitement of the city. The price for that better life is being

exacted, however, by overcrowding, pollution, the increasing drain on natural resources, and the lack of adequate resources to effectively solve the problems of urban living. None of these problems is more threatening than the rapidly increasing phenomenon of social and domestic violence. This violence is becoming a way of life.

Spurred on by increased mobility, this nation has witnessed what appears to be the gradual eradication of individual values grounded in the concepts of community, family, and ancestral "roots." Traditional support systems have given way to increased isolation and alienation. Deteriorating and crowded cities have been fertile ground for breeding and nurturing an apparently tacit public acceptance of ever-increasing levels of social and domestic violence.

The unfortunate reality of twentieth-century America is that violence is increasing geometrically compared to the ability to generate combative resources. The author believes there will never be sufficient resources to effectively arrest this escalation. Society must use every tool at its disposal to rekindle community awareness, involvement, and intervention in an attempt to maximize the impact of available resources. The challenge is two-fold: first, to develop and maintain a capability for responding to the emergency needs of victims and second, to initiate the development of a planned approach for delivering service and allocating resources.

GOVERNMENT, PLANNING, AND EMERGENCY CARE

Two systems of emergency care exist in contemporary society. One is powered by the principles of the market place: quality health care belongs to those who can pay for it. The alternative structure, supported primarily by federal or state funds or both, is intended for those incapable of purchasing services at market rates.

Government is by definition a political process and by nature a reactive organism. The response of government agencies to the deterioration of urban centers has clearly demonstrated this reactive tendency. Reaction to the problem of social and domestic violence has been painfully slow and woefully inadequate.

Development of urban centers in this country has followed a predictable pattern: growth and development of industry and commerce, which become the heart of the city, are accompanied by an initial residential development. As the city becomes more populated, it spreads outward from this center—thus, the creation of the suburban community, with housing in the center city relegated to lower socioeconomic groups. The pattern continues until the distance to the suburbs becomes prohibitive. This flight to the suburbs poses a critical dilemma for the city: an increasingly poor population, declining property values, a diminished tax base, a need for expanded services, and the inevitable crowding which further strains social and domestic relationships. The increasing magnitude of

the problems and the lack of adequate resources to cope with them make it imperative that cities create a planned approach for allocating of resources.

Traditional governmental response to this situation has been categorical grants to address various aspects of the problems faced by local communities. This approach has, in some ways, prevented local communities from effectively addressing their own problems. The categorical approach has seemingly been dictated by the structure of federal bureaucracy rather than by any notion of intent. This practice violates a basic tenet of planning logic: that form should follow function. Consequently, various departments and agencies of the federal government develop their categorical grant packages in total isolation from one another. In addition, the rigid regulations and narrow focus of federal and state grants make it virtually impossible for a local community to develop a comprehensive approach to its peculiar concerns. Federal emphasis on the creation of block grants for health and social services does not assure the more thoughtful allocation of resources but does remove some of the previous constraints.

In addition to the barriers imposed by granting agencies, the very structure of political jurisdictions has impeded community planning. The ability of political leaders to respond to the needs of the constituency is often a measure of their success and the predictor of their political future. Staying in office may be directly linked to positions or actions on the issue of human services and health care. Decisions to provide or deny financial support to a particular organization or medical facility or to purchase a particular service can and do occur without regard or relationship to a planned approach. This political reality cannot and will not tolerate a complete planned approach for providing services and allocating resources. Such an approach is antithetical to the political process. Consequently, many attempts toward planning have failed.

ANALYSIS OF THE PROBLEM

An initial step in the development of any planning effort is a clear understanding of the scope and nature of the problems. The nature and interrelationships of medical and social problems are still not clear. For example, consider the issues of social and domestic violence. Are these really problems, or are they symptoms of problems? Are there circumstances that are central or pivotal for both social and domestic violence? Is there a direct relationship between these two phenomena? If social and domestic violence are, in fact, symptoms rather than problems, what are the problems? And if these phenomena are problems, what is their relationship to other problems which have served as a catalyst?

An initial pitfall to be avoided is the historical tendency to characterize symptoms as problems.[2] This tendency frequently leads to the assumption that eradication of a symptom is *de facto* proof of eradication of the problem. For the most part, program efforts do not affect problems but only address the symptoms. Consequently, the problems continue to escalate, and the symptoms change, creating the illusion that efforts are productive. In reality, society has invested considerable resources tilting at windmills. The situation today is no better than yesterday; it is only different.

The problems of social and domestic violence do not respect political jurisdiction or arbitrary limitations prescribed by categorical grant programs. Continuing to seek resolution through this narrow and parochial approach appears doomed to failure. The primary agencies responsible for addressing these problems are in the criminal justice system (police, courts, and so on). They inter-vene after a violation has occurred, and their charge is to restore order and to exact the prescribed penalty. Their role is clearly defined, and the system is structured to discharge that responsibility. The limitation on resources does not permit activity other than that necessary to maintain the system, and the criminal justice system struggles under the weight of the ongoing failure of other social institutions. The fragmented approach of allocating resources provides no avenue for coordinating or integrating efforts.

Ideally, communities could have agreements among various political, law enforcement, and medical jurisdictions that would allow for the development of a single, comprehensive data source. A single data source would reduce costs, make more effective use of available computer time and capacity, avoid unnecessary duplication of data systems, permit development of common data items and regions, develop the capacity for more refined data analysis, and be capable of projecting future problems and needs. The effective development of a planned approach for solving problems demands recognition of the fact that planning is a political process. Success in creating viable planning strategies parallels the existence of a viable political atmosphere. Textbook formulas for the planning process become obsolete when political considerations are not dealt with initially and built into the process. This is a particularly critical factor when the demands for services are increasing and the resources are shrinking.

THE CONCEPT OF AN INTEGRATED AND COORDINATED SYSTEM

The optimal goal of an integrated and co-ordinated system would be political support for a cooperative venture between major political jurisdictions and privately controlled organizations in allocating resources.[3] The purpose of the cooperative effort would be the creation of a single system for accomplishing the goals and objectives of a planning process. The primary value of this approach is that it allows for

- Development of a single assessment process for determining the scope and nature of community needs
- Establishment of common goals and objectives
- Development of common priorities
- Joint determination of funding responsibility
- Development of a true comprehensive plan
- A greater measure of resource control and strategic planning
- A unified effort to address community problems.

Suggesting this approach by no means implies that it is easy to accomplish. On the contrary, territoriality has historically developed boundaries that are sometimes difficult to transcend. There is also the prevailing notion that funds from the private sector are inherently incompatible with public funds. In spite of the difficulties, current circumstances require that fresh and different approaches be sought. Social problems and the attendant needs already far surpass available resources, and the specter of inflation promises that the already limited resources will shrink, while problems and demands continue to increase.

BARRIERS TO SUCCESS

A critical factor frequently overlooked concerns barriers to success. These barriers may be administrative regulations, legislative restrictions, political jurisdictions, or peculiarities of community life-style. The importance of barriers is linked directly to the issue of goal attainment. Failing to recognize barriers minimizes the importance of reaching goals and ultimately diminishes the potential impact of planned objectives.

Since medical and social services are frequently tied to legislation, involvement of local communities in the law-making process becomes important. If a community is confronted with existing legislation that constitutes a barrier to service objectives, there are a variety of mechanisms for seeking waivers. Local communities and governmental jurisdictions should seek out these avenues for waivers; they represent the potential for increased latitude in planning and implementation.

In the case of community barriers, it is critical that planning incorporate, as an integral element, the analysis of social and political conditions that dictate feasibility for planned activities. An idea or planned objective may be a sound program; however, it may be politically unfeasible because of timing or an adverse political climate. Awareness of this fact must be built into the planning process as a part of the analytical groundwork. The potential for modifying planning or altering the political climate will differ from community to community, and it may be necessary to omit certain elements until the atmosphere is more receptive. The critical point is the determination, as a part of the planning process, of essential elements for goal achievement. This process will permit the phased implementation of planned activities, and even though the planned phases may not follow a logical or desired pattern, each phase or part will have a known and direct relationship to the whole.

There may be some barriers that cannot be changed. These circumstances may require planning around a barrier to accommodate what would be an otherwise counterproductive force.

It has been said that politics is the art of compromise. If planning is a political activity, then realistic planning must be sufficiently flexible to accommodate compromise without losing sight of purpose. A substantial portion of realistic planning is thoroughly understanding existent barriers.

CONCEPTUAL MODEL

Ideally, the development of a plan for action should be based on a conceptual model that serves as a guide for the various activities. The model constitutes an action plan or blueprint.

Resources necessary for addressing a particular problem occur on three basic levels: primary, secondary, and tertiary. Labeling resources according to these levels permits maximum use of available information and avoids the unnecessary creation of gaps in service or duplication of effort.

Graphically, this conceptual model could be displayed in three tiers, with the broad base representing the tertiary services, the midsection representing secondary services, and the small peak representing primary services (Fig. 26-1). These designations provide

a framework for developing strategy. Labeling parts of a program as primary, secondary, and tertiary allows for their natural separation into a logical planning strategy. Consider, for example, victims of domestic violence: spouse, children, siblings, and grandparents. The structure for service response within this conceptual framework might appear as follows:

PRIMARY (CENTRALIZED)

- Crisis intervention hotlines
- Law enforcement agencies

The common feature of these agencies is their probability of being the initial contact or source of assistance in cases of domestic violence. Both should have the capacity for immediate response and, if properly orchestrated, will have standard procedural linkages with each other as the entry point into the service network. Their centralized character reduces the chance of people getting lost in the cracks, provides for immediate

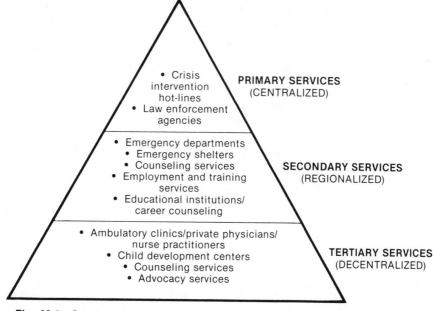

Fig. 26-1   Conceptual model for planning and allocating resources.

intervention by law enforcement in the event of physical danger, and affords access to the vast resources of services, such as information and referrals and crisis intervention counseling, that are available 24 hours a day. Toll free, well-advertised telephone numbers can also ease the problem of selection in times of crisis. Primary or centralized services are frequently expensive, but they are essential to the proper functioning of a system or network for delivering services. Primary services are unique because they do not require duplication, a process that would be neither cost-effective nor efficient.

SECONDARY (REGIONALIZED)

- Hospitals (emergency departments)
- Emergency shelters
- Counseling services
- Employment and training services
- Educational institutions, career counseling

The primary characteristic that distinguishes the secondary or regionalized category of services from the primary or centralized category is the requirement for greater access (secondary services are used more frequently) and more immediate proximity (as in the case of hospital emergency departments). Secondary services address the needs of a relatively small percentage of the consumer population and, for the most part, already exist as an integral part of government and private enterprise. Secondary services are an essential element in the development of a comprehensive system since they provide a significant portion of the necessary ancillary services.

TERTIARY (DECENTRALIZED)

- Ambulatory clinics, private physicians, nurse practitioners
- Child development centers
- Counseling services
- Advocacy services

Tertiary or decentralized services are a broad spectrum of services located throughout the community. These services may be single-purpose and highly specialized or an integral part of a multiservice facility. The distinguishing characteristic of tertiary services is their high degree of accessibility. Services within this category may be age, sex, or culture specific. Their primary objective is to provide effective outreach and a recognizable point of entry into the service network.

Any conceptual model is a valuable frame of reference for planning and developing timetables and specifically determined steps for action. These models must be tailored to the needs of individual communities, and they must be broad enough to encompass all the considerations necessary for effectively determining and addressing the problems they hope to solve.

ALLOCATION OF RESOURCES

The allocation of resources is too often an expedient act in response to the "squeaky wheel syndrome." This is particularly true in the cases of social and domestic violence because of their immediacy and severity. This tendency, however, does not diminish the need for a planned approach; the persistent escalation of crimes of violence in the United States makes the need more critical than ever.[4]

Deciding how to allocate resources includes the following phases:

- Determination of goals and objectives
- Determination of the most effective strategy for solving or mitigating problems
- Assessment of feasibility
- Determination of the resources necessary for carrying out strategy
- Implementation
- Evaluation

Table 26-1 Explanation of Matrix

SUBPROBLEM	SERVICE	OTHER RESOURCES	SOCIOECONOMIC/ POLITICAL FEASIBILITY
In order to address the complexities and distinctions of major categories, each problem is broken into a smaller subproblem.	The services listed in this column are those deemed the most appropriate in addressing the subproblem (services shown by research to have the most impact on alleviating the problem).	The organizations named here are those that have mandated responsibility or have been selected to provide the designated service(s).	This column states the socioeconomic and/or political feasibility of a proposed strategy.

A frequent problem in planning and in making decisions based on planning is the tendency to mix problems and services in the determination of needs. The usual result is that needs (both perceived and real), problems, target populations, and services are incorporated into statements of need. Table 26-1 shows one method for examining the question of problems and the allocation of resources.

One possible addition to this matrix is a measurement of the severity of various problems. There are three basic gradations which provide the basis for establishing a priority for problems and service strategy:

1. Problems that pose a danger to health or life
2. Problems that, if untreated, may prevent adequate functioning
3. Problems that are related to personal enrichment or fulfillment

When resources are limited, a format of this type makes it possible to determine the most pressing problems, the appropriate services, and other resources; consider the political or socioeconomic feasibility; and establish a priority of problems by determining the severity of each problem (Table 26-2).

CONCLUSION

Community planning for medical and social services seeks to eradicate the barriers that prevent the most efficient use of existing resources.

The human service and health care industry has been plagued by uncoordinated efforts in planning and in allocating resources. The inevitable consequence has been duplication of efforts and an exaggeration of the gaps in resources and services. A variety of factors has contributed to this dysfunction:

- Issues related to political jurisdiction
- Funding policies and practices of federal and state governments
- The political nature of planning
- The state of the art of planning

An additional aspect of planning is the need for a common data base. Developing a planned approach for addressing community problems requires data. Since the possession of data makes it possible to understand available options and to exercise wisdom in making decisions, it is imperative to develop the most effective and complete data system possible.

Table 26-2 Problem Category: Social and Domestic Violence

INTENSITY OF NEED	SUBPROBLEM	SERVICE	OTHER RESOURCES	FEASIBILITY SOCIOECONOMIC	POLITICAL
Grade 1 — Essential Life Support Subproblems designated as essential life support are considered to have the most severe impact (i.e., life-threatening).	Child neglect/ abuse	Protective placement Counseling Residential treatment Foster care	Department of Public Welfare Community Mental Health (CMH) State and private facilities Private organizations		
	Spouse assault	Shelter Counseling Legal assistance Hotline	State and private facilities Private organizations		
Grade 2 — Basic Quality of Life Subproblems designated as basic quality of life are severe in their impact on the individual or society but are not life-threatening. If not addressed, problems in this category may result in the inability to sustain adequate function.	Marital conflict Parent-child conflict Dislocation (family disruption)	Advocacy Counseling Hotline Emergency housing Foster care Family education Home management	Court system/private CMH Probation Department		
Grade 3 — Personal Enrichment Subproblems designated as personal enrichment are those problems that preclude access to enrichment experiences but do not pose a threat to life or family stability.	Inadequate social, recreational, or cultural opportunities	Social Cultural Recreational	City and county recreation departments Private, nonprofit organizations		

The ability to create an effective and responsive system for the delivery of human services and health care depends on

- A reliable data system

- An accurate analysis of the problem

- An accurate analysis of the most effective service or intervention strategy

- An efficient and effective mechanism for allocating resources that eliminates duplication of effort

- An effective design for evaluation.

The degree to which communities are successful in planning will be borne out in the quality of life available to their children. The extent to which they fail will be painfully evident.

REFERENCES

1. Warner CG: Dimensions in planning: A blueprint for action, in Warner CG (ed): *Rape and Sexual Assault: Management and Intervention.* Rockville, Md, Aspen Systems Corp, 1980, pp 331–344.

2. Haber S, Seidenberg B: Society's recognition and control of violence, in Kutash IL, et al (eds): *Violence Perspectives on Murder and Aggression.* San Francisco, Jossey-Bass Inc Publishers, 1978, pp 462–479.

3. Zweig FM, Morris R: The social planning design guide: process and proposal. *J Soc Work* 11:11–20, 1966.

4. Warner CG: Innovations in systems planning, in Warner CG (ed): *Conflict Intervention in Social and Domestic Violence.* Bowie, Md, Robert J Brady Co, 1981, pp 271–281.

27

HOLISTIC ASSESSMENT: EVALUATION OF BEHAVIORAL AND PHYSICAL NEEDS

Carmen Germaine Warner, R.N., M.S.N., F.A.A.N.

Professionals who work with victims of violence and their families are just beginning to address the process of assessment from a holistic point of view. The unseen factors that influence the process of regrowth and recovery are especially critical as they are easily overlooked by many, including the victim. Unless the process of assessment focuses on the victim as a total person and uncovers these unseen factors, intervention will be ineffective.

CONSIDERATIONS IN ASSESSMENT

Before implementing specific medical intervention and counseling or concepts for teaching victims and their families, the individual and personalized needs of each victim must be determined. It is essential that assessment begin with the initial contact in order to

- Analyze the impact of the trauma holistically
- Establish priorities about the order of intervention

- Plan and assign the staffing functions of medical and social services
- Determine the strategy for teaching the victim and the victim's family
- Determine the appropriate referral sources essential for each victim
- Outline the mechanism for follow-up intervention.

Assessment techniques are essential as they survey the total characteristics of wellness within the victim.

The continuing education of emergency professionals should inform them of the importance of this ongoing process of assessment and intervention and teach them proficiency in the specific techniques incorporated. The information acquired during assessment serves as a blueprint that clinicians can use in their individual settings.

The Interview

One of the initial functions of emergency or social service professionals is to plan and

Table 27-1 Important Factors in the Interview Process

POSITIVE	NEGATIVE
Take the victim to a quiet, private place, free of distractions and interruptions.	Do not attempt to question the victim in the presence of other patients.
Use the victim as the most reliable source of information.	Do not consider that information from others is more reliable.
Before the interview, secure information about other episodes of trauma from law enforcement personnel, community service professionals, or medical personnel.	Do not question the victim about previous documented incidents of trauma.
Explain the purpose and intent of the interview beforehand.	Do not assume the victim understands the purpose of the interview.
Write brief comments about the interview.	Do not rely on your memory or record data in full sentences.
Accept and acknowledge everything the victim says.	Do not question the authenticity of the victim's comments.
Refer to the victim by name and express gentleness, warmth, and concern.	Do not force your professional standards and beliefs on the victim.
Speak clearly, slowly, and loud enough to avoid repeating yourself.	Do not act hurried or busy.
Practice active listening.	Do not place words in the victim's mouth.
Be calm, concerned, and unhurried.	Do not become irritated if the victim cannot remember certain facts.
Use good eye contact and respect body language.	Do not stare at the victim.
Incorporate the use of open-ended questions.	Do not make assumptions or hasty decisions.
Use language the victim can understand.	Do not use technical phrases or speak too fast.
Encourage discussion of the victim's concerns first.	Do not probe into personal aspects of the trauma.
Allow the victim to complete a particular thought.	Do not interrupt or attempt to talk for the victim.

implement a nonthreatening, thorough, pertinent interview. The primary purpose of this interview is to determine relevant data:

- Medical history
- Personal history
- Family history
- Social history
- Record of the incident
- Predisposing factors
- Existing family conditions
- Physical level of wellness
- Emotional level of wellness
- Systems of support
- Ability to cope

Collecting these data may require considerable time and be frustrating and overwhelming for the victim. It is essential that the professional who interviews the victim initially explain the intent and value of each section of the interview. The victim should also receive ample opportunity to initiate specific questions and to ventilate such feelings as fear, anger, hostility, guilt, or embarrassment. Allowing this open interchange of information will facilitate the development of trust and cooperation, valuable conditions to maintain throughout the continuing process of assessment and intervention.

The interview is only as valuable as the overall effectiveness of the interviewing techniques. These techniques require knowledge and practice in areas such as

- Establishing initial contact
- Communication (see Chapter 6)
- Questioning procedures

- Appropriate use of silence
- Good listening
- Collecting valuable data.

There is an art to designing and conducting an effective interview.[1] The methods used to assess the levels of physical and emotional wellness can greatly influence a victim's openness, feelings of trust, and cooperation with ongoing intervention. Some tools for effective interviewing are outlined in Table 27-1.

PROCESS OF AN ASSESSMENT

A realistic application of the process of assessment depends on understanding the importance of each contributing factor (Fig. 27-1). Five factors that make up the total assessment network include the physical, emotional, social or community, spiritual,

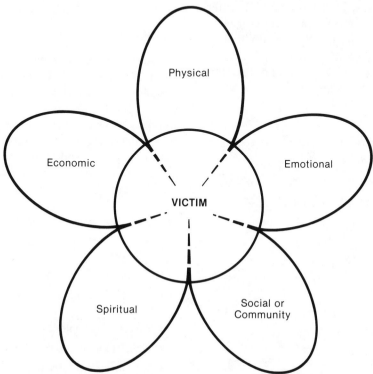

Fig. 27-1   Components of holistic assessment

and economic. All professionals in the assessment network must realize that even though all five factors may not be assessed concomitantly, they must be interlinked to facilitate the holistic approach.

Physical

The physical assessment is an extremely important part of the general sequence of assessment. When a victim enters the emergency department, clinic, or physician's or nurse's office, it is essential to determine the extent of both external and internal injuries. Because of the nature of the trauma, victims are frequently reluctant to discuss the incident and frequently deny or conceal any physical injury.

Each facility should design a specific format for acquiring a uniform physical assessment of all victims.

The victim, except for any specific trauma-related injuries, is a well person and the interviewer usually describes the victim's general health and summarizes the health maintenance needs and activities.[2]

Some of the following components may help professionals establish a form for assessing the present injury:

- INTRODUCTION
  A. Victim's summary of incident
  B. Victim's general level of wellness
- ASSESSMENT OF CONTRIBUTING FACTORS
  A. Onset of incident
  B. Date and time
  C. Occurrence (gradual or sudden episode); force used
  D. Duration
  E. Precipitating factors
  F. Degree of injury
  G. Type of injury
  H. Location of incident

  I. Related circumstances
  J. Aggravating factors
- ASSESSMENT OF EVIDENCE
  A. Explanation of need for law enforcement reporting
  B. Identification of victim's rights
  C. Obtaining appropriate signatures for consent, photography, collection of evidence, and release of information
  D. Gathering of relevant evidence[3]
  E. Record of all findings[3]
  F. Establishing a chain of evidence[3]
- RELEVANT FAMILY INFORMATION
  A. Association with traumatic incident
  B. Possible related injuries
  C. Awareness of incident
- DISABILITY ASSESSMENT
  A. Physical impairment
  B. Emotional trauma

Emotional

Assessment of the emotional factors that occur after an act of violence is very important. Victims harbor considerable feelings of guilt, blame, hostility, denial, and fear. Repressions of these feelings may compound the problems. There are several indicators that emergency and social service professionals may notice while assessing the emotional factors:[4]

- Victim's response to stress
- Interpersonal relationships between the victim and others
- Victim's personal drive and motivation
- Victim's thoughts and verbal response about the incident
- Nonverbal communication
- Victim's self-awareness
- Existing systems of support
- Victim's natural resources for recovery

RESPONSE TO STRESS

Victims of violence react in various ways. For example, one victim might attempt to cope with the stress by sharing feelings with a family member or a supportive listener. Another might use a defense mechanism and avoid the reality of the incident by denying it.

Professionals must remember that the victim may manifest various responses to the incident. These feelings are likely to be quite realistic and should be respected. If professionals recognize that certain responses may be quite appropriate for the situation, the victim's method of adaptation may be easier to understand and may serve as a foundation for ongoing intervention and counseling.

INTERPERSONAL RELATIONSHIPS

Maintenance of interpersonal security is a goal of life.[5] When low self-esteem develops as a result of trauma, victims experience a loss of interpersonal security. This loss evolves into social isolation, even from those who wish to help.

PERSONAL DRIVE AND MOTIVATION

Human beings strive to meet basic human needs as well as individual needs for personal growth. Concomitant with this drive is the concept of motivation which includes one's hope of pursuing a particular goal.[6] Attempting to achieve that specific goal requires hope. In dealing with victims of violence, a professional should assess existing levels of both hope and motivation, understand their relationship to the victim's ultimate state of wellness, and attempt to elevate them.

THOUGHTS AND VERBAL RESPONSE

Rational thought is reflected in language, while thought disorder is evident in a disturbance of word association. Emergency and social service professionals should assess the thought processes of victims in an attempt to determine if the victim is experiencing any psychotic or other disturbances.

NONVERBAL COMMUNICATION

Professionals aware of clues provided by nonverbal communication can detect any presence of discomfort, fear, guilt, and anxiety. Careful observation of gestures allows professionals to focus more directly on the real problem and develop lines of communication which will aid in appropriate medical intervention and counseling.

SELF-AWARENESS

Victims frequently block attempts to deal with their true feelings. Professionals need to support the victim and provide assistance in dealing with these feelings. Once this process has begun, the victim can develop a self-awareness and feelings as a person of self-worth and pride.

EXISTING SYSTEMS OF SUPPORT

Professionals should assess the existence of supporting family members. In addition to family, other factors of support might include the victim's job or profession, religious background, value system, educational plans, future goals, and friends. Victims frequently are unaware of the strength that lies in their existing support systems and should be directed toward the use of these systems.

NATURAL RESOURCES

If professionals focus on determining available strengths, talents, and assets, a healthier, more optimistic approach can be pursued. This approach can be a beginning for establishing specific, meaningful, achievable goals.

Social or Community

Social health or well-being refers to one's ability to fulfill societal roles and tasks.[7] Both a victim's physical and emotional well-being greatly influence the potential for and the ultimate outcome of a high degree of social health. If physical and emotional levels of wellness are low, a victim will not be as inclined to care for immediate needs or personal commitments. The victim's potential for accomplishing routine functions will be diminished.

A yardstick for measuring a victim's social potential should be developed during the assessment process. Professionals who attempt a holistic examination of the victim must appreciate the victim's ability to

- Remain employable
- Continue educational pursuits
- Sustain a managing role in the home
- Continue functioning at a standard of self-preservation and safety.

It is also essential to determine and assess the quality and number of community agencies. Once the medical assessment has been completed, these agencies must provide the support and expertise for short-term and long-term recovery. This process of intervention not only includes the acute phase of readjustment but also promotes a level of prevention and protection.

Unless the social or community segment of assessment remains intact, the victim will be void of the supportive recovery phase that is responsible for most of an individual's personal growth and adjustment.

Spiritual

Victims who experience the trauma of violence frequently undergo a spiritual crisis. This crisis forces them to reappraise feelings about

- What they really want from life
- What has personal value
- What constitutes happiness for the future
- What are the real possibilities for life.

These representative questions, which are part of a victim's spiritual dimension, indicate the basis for one's total satisfaction or dissatisfaction with life. Trauma resulting from acts of violence may disrupt an individual's thoughts and belief in self and gravely affect the process of recovery and regrowth.

The impact of a spiritual crisis differs from emotional concerns because the victim needs assistance in expanding emotional and intellectual horizons to make a place for spiritual needs. Professionals should be aware of this need and of the community resources available for this type of guidance. A renewed spiritual belief will help victims restore faith and belief in themselves. This restoral is most critical in cases of violent abuse that destroy the victim's concept of self, self-respect, and confidence.

Professionals must help the victim learn to take full responsibility for important decisions about the future.[8] If someone else attempts to make decisions for the victim, the conflict will not be resolved.

Economic

The improved economic well-being of a victim is related to the contribution of health and wellness to the victim's economic growth and development.[7]

There are two methods a victim may use to build such a relationship: establishment of human potential, which indicates the individual's ability to be a productive asset to society, and development of a relationship between society's need for productivity and resourcefulness and the individual's potential for contributing to that relationship.

Victims and family members involved in violent trauma may be so affected that the entire family structure and routine levels of daily existence may be disrupted. Factors indicative of this disruption include

- Absenteeism or ineffective functioning at one's place of employment
- Lack of interest in personal gain and economic security

- Diminished financial resources, both income and outgoing cash flow.

The impact of economic security and feelings of personal contribution significantly affect one's holistic realization of self-worth and self-growth. This part of the assessment is as important as the other components and should be dealt with in concert with the other elements of wellness.

SUMMARY

Professionals who work with victims of violence must deal with specific techniques for holistic assessment. A practical framework has been presented for consideration and application at an individual level of performance. Since the needs of each victim are unique, this framework should function solely as a blueprint for designing an individualistic approach to the concept of regrowth and recovery.

REFERENCES

1. Eggland ET: How to take a meaningful nursing history. *Nursing 77* **7**:22–30, 1977.

2. Malasanos L, et al: *Health Assessment.* St Louis, The CV Mosby Co, 1977, p 21.

3. Braen GR: Assessment and management of adult victims, in Warner CG (ed): *Rape and Sexual Assault: Management and Intervention.* Rockville, Md, Aspen Systems Corp, 1980, p 65.

4. Snyder JC, et al: Elements of a psychological assessment. *Am J Nurs* **4**:235–239, 1977.

5. Sullivan HS: *Clinical Studies in Psychiatry.* New York, WW Norton & Co Inc, 1956, pp 7–11.

6. Stotland E: *The Psychology of Hope.* San Francisco, Jossey-Bass Inc Publishers, 1969, p 14.

7. Cordes SM: Assessing health care needs: elements and processes. *Fam Community Health* **1**:5, 1978.

8. Bloomfield HH, Kory RK: *The Holistic Way to Health and Happiness.* New York, Simon & Schuster Inc, 1978, p 256.

Index